MODERN LEADERS:

BEING A SERIES OF

BIOGRAPHICAL SKETCHES.

BY JUSTIN McCARTHY,
Author of "Lady Judith: A Tale of Two Continents," etc.

NEW YORK:
SHELDON & COMPANY,
677 BROADWAY and 214 and 216 MERCER STREET.
1872.

CONTENTS.

INTRODUCTION.

THE sketches which make up this volume are neither purely critical nor merely biographical. They endeavor to give the American reader a clear and just idea of each individual in his intellect, his character, his place in politics, letters, and society. In some instances I have written of friends whom I know personally and well; in others of men with whom I have but slight acquaintance; in others still of persons whom I have only seen. But in every instance those whom I describe are persons whom I have been able to study on the spot, whose character and doings I have heard commonly discussed by those who actually knew them. In no case whatever are the opinions I have given drawn merely from books and newspapers. This value, therefore, these essays may have to an American, that they are not such descriptions as any of us might be enabled to put into print by the mere help of study and reading; descriptions for example such as one might make of Henry VIII. or Voltaire. They are in every instance, even when intimate and direct personal acquaintance least assist them, the result of close observation and that appreciation of the originals which comes from habitual intercourse with those who know them and submit them to constant criticism.

I have not made any alteration in the essays which were written some years ago. Let them stand as portraits bearing that date. If 1872 has in any instance changed the features and the fortunes of 1869 and 1870, it cannot make untrue what then was true. What I wrote in 1869 of the Prince of Wales, for example, will probably not wholly apply to the Prince of Wales to-day. We all believe that he has lately changed for the better. But what I wrote then I still believe was true then; and it is a fair contribution to history, which does not consent to rub out yesterday because of to-day. I wrote of a "Liberal Triumvirate" of England when the phrase was an accurate expression. It would hardly be accurate now. To-day Mr. Mill does not appear in political life and Mr. Bright has been an exile, owing to his health, for nearly two years from the scenes of parliamentary debate and triumph. But the portraits of the men do not on that account need any change. Even where some reason has been shown me for a modification of my own judgment I have still preferred to leave the written letter as it is. A distinguished Italian friend has impressed on me that King Victor Emanuel is personally a much more ambitious man than I have painted him. My friend has had far better opportunities of judging than I ever could have had; but I gave the best opinion I could, and still holding to it prefer to let it stand, to be taken for what it is worth.

I think I may fairly claim to have anticipated in some of the political sketches, that of Louis Napoleon, for instance, the judgment of events and history, and the real strength of certain characters and institutions.

These sketches had a gratifying welcome from the American public as they appeared in the "Galaxy." I hope they may be thought worth reading over again and keeping in their collected form.

JUSTIN McCARTHY.

48 GOWER STREET, BEDFORD SQUARE, LONDON, July 31, 1872.

QUEEN VICTORIA AND HER SUBJECTS.

"AND when you hear historians tell of thrones, and those who sat upon them, let it be as men now gaze upon the mammoth's bones, and wonder what old world such things could see."

So sang Byron half a century ago, and great critics condemned his verse, and called him a "surly Democrat" because he ventured to put such sentiments and hopes into rhyme. The thrones of Europe have not diminished in number since Byron's day, although they have changed and rechanged their occupants; and the one only grand effort at the establishment of a new Republic—that of France in 1848—went down into dust and ashes. Naturally, therefore, the tendency in Europe is to regard the monarchical principle as having received a new lease and charter of life, and to talk of the republican principle as an exotic forced for a moment into a premature and morbid blossom upon European soil, but as completely unsuited to the climate and the people as the banyan or the cocoa tree.

I do not, for myself, quite agree in this view of the aspect of affairs. Of course, if one were inclined to discuss the question fairly, he must begin by asking what people mean when they talk of the republican principle. What is the republican principle? When you talk of a Republic, do you mean an aggressive, conquering, domineering State, ruled by faction and living on war, like the Commonwealth of Rome? or a Republic like that planned by Washington, which should repudiate all concern in foreign politics or foreign conquest? Do you mean a Federal Republic, like that of the United States, or one with a centralized power, like the French Republic of 1848? Do you mean a Republic like that of Florence, in which the people were omnipotent, or a Republic like that of Venice, in which the people had no power at all? Do you mean a Republic like that of Switzerland, in which the President is next to nobody, or a Republic like that of Poland, which was ornamented by a King? In truth, the phrase "republican principle" has no set meaning. It means just what the man who uses it wishes to express. If, however, we understand it to mean, in this instance, the principle of popular self-government, then it is obvious that Europe has made immense progress in that direction since Byron raged against the crimes of Kings. If it means the opposite to the principle of Divine Right or Legitimacy, or even personal loyalty—loyalty of the old-time, chivalric, enthusiastic fashion—then it must be owned that it shows all over Europe the mark of equal progress. The ancient, romantic, sentimental loyalty; the loyalty which reverenced the Sovereign and was proud to abase itself before him; the loyalty of the Cavaliers; the loyalty which went wild over "Oh, Richard! Oh, mon Roi!" is dead and gone—its relics a thing to be stared at, and wondered over, and preserved for a landmark in the progress of the world—just like the mammoth's bones.

The model Monarchy of Europe is, beyond dispute, that of Great Britain. In England there is an almost absolute self-government; the English people can have anything whatever which they may want by insisting on it and agitating a little for it. The Sovereign has long ceased to interfere in the progress of national affairs. I can only recollect one instance, during my observation, in which Queen Victoria put her veto on a bill passed by Parliament, and that was on an occasion when it was discovered, at the last moment, that the Lords and

Commons had passed a bill which had a dreadful technical blunder in it, and the only way out of the difficulty was to beg of the Queen to refuse it her sanction, which her Majesty did accordingly, and the blunder was set right in the following session. If a Prime Minister were to announce to the House of Commons, to-morrow, that the Queen had boxed his ears, it would not create a whit more amazement than if he were to say, no matter in what graceful and diplomatic periphrasis, that her Majesty was unwilling to agree to some measure which her faithful Commons desired to see passed into law.

Nothing did Mr. Disraeli more harm, nothing brought greater contempt on him than his silly attempts last session to induce the Commons to believe, by vague insinuations and covert allusions, that the Queen had a personal leaning toward his policy and himself. So long ago as the time of the free trade struggle, the Tories, for all their hereditary loyalty, complained of and protested against the silent presence of Prince Albert in the Peers' gallery of the House of Commons, on the ground that it was an attempt to influence the Parliament improperly, and to interfere with the freedom of debate. No one has anything to say against the Queen which carries any weight or is worth listening to. She is undoubtedly a woman of virtue and good sense. So good a woman, I venture to think, never before reigned over any people, and that she is not a great woman, an Elizabeth, a Catherine of Russia, or even an Isabella of Castile, is surely rather to the advantage than otherwise of the monarchical institution in its present stage of existence. Here, then, one might think, if anywhere and ever, the principle of personal loyalty has a fair chance and a full justification. A man might vindicate his loyalty to Queen Victoria in the name of liberty itself; nay, he might justify it by an appeal to the very principle of democracy. Yet one must be blind, who, living in England and willing to observe, does not see that the old, devoted spirit of personal loyalty is dead and buried. It is gone! it is a memory! You may sing a poetic lament for it if you will, as Schiller did for the gods of Hellas; you may break into passionate rhetoric, if you can, over its extinction, as Burke did for the death of the age of Chivalry. It is gone, and I firmly believe it can never be revived or restored.

I do not mean to say that there are many persons in England who feel any strong objection to the Monarchy, or warmly desire to see a Republic substituted for it. I know in England several theoretical republicans—they are to be met with in almost any company. I have never met with any one Englishman living in England, who showed any anxious, active interest in the abolition of the Monarchy. I do not know any one who objects to drink the usual loyal toasts at a public dinner, or betrays any conscientious reluctance to listen to the unmeaning eulogy which it is the stereotyped fashion for the chairman of every such banquet to heap on "Her Majesty and the rest of the Royal Family." But this sort of thing, if it ever had any practical meaning, has now none. It has reached that stage at which profession and practice are always understood to be quite different things. Every one says at church that he is a miserable sinner; no one is supposed really to believe anything of the sort. Every one has some time or other likened women to angels, but we are not therefore supposed seriously to ignore the fact that women wear flannel petticoats, and have their faults, and are mortal. So of loyal professions in England now. They are understood to be phrases, like "Your obedient servant," at the bottom of a letter. They do not suggest hypocrisy or pretence of any kind. There is apparently no more inconsistency now in a man's loyally drinking the health of the Queen, and proceeding immediately after (in private conversation) to abuse or ridicule

.ier and her family, than there would be in the same man beginning with "Dear Sir," a missive to one whom he notoriously dislikes. Every one who has been lately in London must have heard an immense amount of scandal, or at all events of flippant joking at the expense of the Queen herself; and of more serious complaint and distrust as regards the Prince of Wales. Yet the virtues of the Queen, and the noble qualities of the Prince of Wales are panegyrized and toasted, and hurrah'd at every public dinner where Englishmen gather together.

The very virtues of Queen Victoria have contributed materially toward the extinction of the old-fashioned sentiment of living, active loyalty. The English people had from the time at least of Anne to our own day a succession of bad princes. Only a race patient as Issachar could have endured such a line of sovereigns as George II., George III., and George IV. Then came William IV., who being a little less stupidly obstinate than George III., and not so grossly corrupt as George IV., was hailed for a while as the Patriot King by a people who were only too anxious not to lose all their hereditary and traditional veneration. Do what they would, however, the English nation could not get into any sincere transports of admiration about the Patriot King; and they soon found that any popular reform worth having was to be got rather in spite of the Patriot King, than by virtue of any wisdom or patriotism in the monarch. Great popular demonstrations and tumults, and threats of marching on London; and O'Connell meetings at Charing Cross, with significant allusion by the great demagogue to the King who lost his head at Whitehall hard by; the hanging out of the black flag at Manchester, and a general movement of brickbats everywhere—these seem to have been justly regarded as the persuasive influences which converted a Sovereign into the Patriot King and a Reformer. Loyalty did not gain much by the reforms of that reign. Then followed the young Victoria; and enthusiasm for a while wakened up fresh and genuine over the ascension of the comely and simple-hearted girl, who was so frank and winning; who ran down stairs in her night-dress, rather than keep her venerable councillors waiting when they sought her out at midnight; who openly acknowledged her true love for her cousin, and offered him her hand; who was at once queenly and maidenly, innocent and fearless.

But this sort of thing did not last very long. Prince Albert was never popular. He was cold; people said he was stingy; his very virtues, and they were genuine, were not such as anybody, except his wife and family, warmly admires in a man; he was indeed misunderstood, or at all events misprized in England, up to the close of his life. Then the gates of the convent, so to speak, closed over the Queen, and royalty ceased to be an animating presence in England.

The young men and women of to-day—persons who have not passed the age of twenty-one—can hardly remember to have ever seen the Sovereign. She is to them what the Mikado is to his people. Seven years of absolute seclusion on the part of a monarch must in any case be a sad trial to personal loyalty, at least in the royal capital. A considerable and an influential section of Queen Victoria's subjects in the metropolis have long been very angry with their Sovereign. The tailors, the milliners, the dressmakers, the jewellers, the perfumers, all the shopkeepers of the West End who make profit out of court dinners and balls and presentations, are furious at the royal seclusion which they believe has injured their business. So, too, are the aristocratic residents of the West End, who do not care much about a court which no longer contributes to their season's gayety. So, too, are all the flunkey class generally. Now, I am sure there are no three sections of the population of London more influential in the spreading of scandal and the nursing of this discontent than the shopkeepers, the aristocrats, and the flunkeys of the West End. These are actively and demonstratively dissatisfied with the Queen. These it is who spread dirty scandals about her, and laugh over vile lampoons and caricatures of which she is the object.

Every one knows that there is a low, mean scandal afloat about the Queen—and it is spread by the clubs, the drawing-rooms, the shops, and the servants'-halls of the West End. I am convinced that not one of those who spread the scandal really believes it; but they like to spread it because they dislike the Queen. There can be no doubt, however, that much dissatisfaction at the Queen's long seclusion is felt by persons who are incapable of harboring any motives so mean or spreading any calumnies so unworthy. Most of the London papers have always found fault rather sharply and not over decently with the royal retirement. Mr. Ayrton, representative of the Tower Hamlets—the largest constituency in England—openly expressed this sentiment at a public meeting; and though his remarks were at once replied to and condemned by Mr. Bright, they met with a more or less cordial response from most of his audience.

There is or was in the House of Commons (the general election has got happily rid of him), a foolish person named Reardon, a Piccadilly auctioneer, who became, by what we call in England "a fluke," a member of the House of Commons. This person moved last session a resolution, or something of the kind, calling on the Queen to abdicate. The thing was laughed down—poor Mr. Reardon's previous career had been so absurd that anything coming from him would have been hooted; and the House of Commons is fiercely intolerant of "bores" and men with crotchets. But I have reason to believe that Mr. Reardon's luckless project was concocted by a delegation of London tradesmen, and had the sympathy of the whole class; and I know that many members of the House which hooted and laughed him down had in private over and over again grumbled at the Queen's retirement, and declared that she ought to abdicate.

"What on earth does it matter," I asked of a member of Parliament—one of the most accomplished scholars and sharp logicians in the House—"What on earth does it matter whether or not the Queen gives a few balls to a few thousand West End people in the season? How can rational people care, one way or the other?" "My dear fellow," was the answer, "*I* don't care; but all that sort of thing is her business, and she is paid to do it, and she ought to do it. If she were a washerwoman with a family, she would have to do her work, no matter what her grief." Now this gentleman—who is utterly above any sympathy with scandal or with the lackey-like grumblings of the West End—did, undoubtedly, express fairly enough a growing mood of the public dissatisfaction.

Beyond all this, however, is the fact that people—the working-class especially—are beginning to ask whether we really want a Sovereign at all, seeing that we get on just as well during the eclipse of royalty as in its brightest meridian splendor. This question is being very often put; and it is probably more often thought over than put into words. Now I think nothing worse could possibly happen to royalty in England than that people should begin quietly to ask whether there really is any use in it. If there is a bad King or Queen, people can get or look for, or hope and pray for a good one; and the abuse of the throne will not be accounted a sufficient argument against the use of it. But how will it be when the subjects begin to find that during the reign of one of the best sovereigns possible to have, they can get on perfectly well although the monarch is in absolute seclusion ?

George IV. was an argument against bad kings only—Queen Victoria may come to be accepted as an illustration of the uselessness of the very best kind of Sovereign. I think King Log was much better calculated to do harm to the institution of royalty than King Stork, although the frogs might have regretted the placid reign of the former when the latter was gobbling up their best and fattest.

Decidedly the people of England are learning of the Queen how to do with out royalty. A small section of her subjects are angry with her and bitter of heart against her ; a much larger number find they can do perfectly well without her ; a larger number still have forgotten her. On a memorable occasion Prince Albert declared that constitutional government was on its trial in England. The phrase, like many that came from the same well-meaning lips, was unlucky. Constitutional government was not upon its trial then ; but Monarchy is upon its trial now.

Do I mean to say that Great Britain is on the verge of a revolution ; that the dynasty is about to be overthrown ; that a new Cromwell is to make his appearance ? By no means. It does not follow that even if the English people weie to be convinced to-morrow of the absolute uselessness of a throne, and a sovereignty, they would therefore proceed to establish a republic. No people under the sun are more strongly governed by tradition and "the majesty of custom" than the English. Cobden used to say that they had a Chinese objection to change of any kind. The Lord Mayor's show, long threatened, and for a while partially obscured, has come out again in full gingerbread. There is a functionary who appears every night at the door of the House of Commons just at the moment when the sitting is formally declared to be over, and bawls out to the emptying benches the resonant question, "Who's for home?" I believe the practice originated at a time when Westminster was unpeopled, and midnight roads were dangerous, and members were glad to make up parties to travel home together ; and, so a functionary was appointed to issue stentorian appeal to all who were thus willing to combine their strength and journey safely in company. The need of such an arrangement has, I need hardly say, passed away these many generations ; but the usage exists. It oppresses no one to have the formal call thundered out ; the thing has got to be a regular performance ; it is part of the whole business and system ; nobody wants it, but nobody heeds it or objects to it, and the functionary appears every night of every session and shouts his invitation to companionship as regularly as if the Mohocks were in possession of Charing Cross, and Claude Duval were coming full trot along Piccadilly.

Now, this may be taken as a sort of illustration of the manner in which the English people are naturally inclined to deal with any institutions which are merely useless, and have the recommendation of old age and long descent. The ordinary Englishman to-day would find it hard to bring up before his mind's eye a picture of an England without a Sovereign. If it were made fully plain to him, and thoroughly impressed upon his mind that he could do just as well without a Sovereign as with, and even that Monarchy never could possibly be of use to him any more, I think he would endure it and pay its cost, and drink its health loyally for all time, providing Monarchy did nothing outrageously wrong ; or provided—which is more to my present purpose—that no other changes of a remarkable nature occurred in the meantime to remove ancient landmarks, tc disturb the basis of his old institutions and to prepare him for a new order of things. This is indeed the point I wish to discuss just now. I have explained what I believe to be the depth and strength and meaning of the average Englishman's loyal feelings to his Sovereign at the present moment. I should like to consider next how that feeling will, in all probability, be affected by the changes in the English political system, which seem inevitable, and by the accession, or expected accession, of a new Sovereign to the throne.

England has, just now, something very nearly approaching to manhood suffrage; and to manhood suffrage it will probably come before long. The ballot will, doubtless, be introduced. The Irish Church is as good as dead. I cannot doubt that the English State Church will, ultimately, and before very long, succumb to the same fate. Not that this logically or politically follows as a matter of necessity; and nothing could be more unwise in the interest of their own cause than the persistency with which the Tories keep insisting that the doom of the one is involved in the doom of the other. The Irish Church is the foreign church of a miserably small minority; the English Establishment is the Church of the majority, and is an institution belonging to the soil. The very principle which maintains the English Church ought of right to condemn the Irish Church. But it is the fact that an agitation more influential than it seemed to the careless spectator, has long been going on in England for the abolition of the State Church system altogether; and there can be no doubt that the fate of the Irish Establishment will lend immense courage and force to that agitation. Revolutionary movements are always contagious in their nature, and the movement against the Irish Church is in the strictest sense revolutionary. The Dutch or the Scotch would have carried such a movement to triumph across rivers of blood if it were needful; and no man of spirit could say that the end would not be worth the cost. I assume, then, that the overthrow of the Irish Church will inflame to iconoclastic fervor the movement of the English Dissenters against all Church establishments. I do not stop just now to inquire whether the movement is likely to be successful or how long it may take to accomplish the object. To me, it seems beyond doubt that it must succeed; but I do not care to assume even that for the purpose of my present argument. I only ask my readers to consider the condition of things which will exist in England when a movement resting on a suffrage which is almost universal, a movement which will have already overthrown one State Church within Great Britain, proceeds openly and exultingly to attack the English Church itself, within its own dominions. I ask whether it is likely that the institution which is supposed to be bound up inseparably with that Church, the Monarchy which is based upon, and exists by virtue of religious ascendency, is likely to escape all question during such a struggle, and after it? The State Church and the Aristocracy, if they cannot always be called bulwarks of the throne, are yet so completely associated with it in the public mind that it is hard even to think of the one without the others, and yet harder to think of the one as existing serene and uninjured after the decay or demolition of the others.

Now, the Aristocracy have, as Mr. Bright put it so truly and so effectively the other day, already capitulated. They have given up all notion of any longer making the laws of the country in the interest of their own class. One of the first things the Reformed Parliament will do, when it has breathing-time to think about such matters, will be to abolish the purchase system in the army, and throw open promotion to merit, without reference to class. The diplomatic service, that other great stronghold of the Aristocracy, will be thoroughly reorganized and made a real, useful department, doing solid work, and open to talent of whatever caste ; or it will be abolished altogether. Something will have to be done with the House of Lords. It, too, must be made a reality, or dismissed into the land of shadows and the past. Efforts at reforming it, while it stands on its present basis, are futile. Its existence is, in its present form, the one great objection to it.

The good-natured, officious Lord Shaftesbury went to work, a few months ago, to prepare a scheme of reform for the House of Lords, in order to anticipate and conciliate the popular movement which he expected. He could think of nothing better than a recommendation that the House should meet an hour earlier every evening, in order, by throwing more time on their hands, to induce the younger Peers to get up debates and take part in them. This, however, is not precisely the kind of reform the country will ask for when it has leisure to turn its attention to the subject. It will ask for some reorganization which shall either abolish or reduce to a comparative nothing the hereditary legislating principle on which the House of Lords now rests. A set of law-makers or law-marrers intrusted with power only because they are born to titles, is an absurd anomaly, which never could exist in company with popular suffrage. "Hereditary law-makers!" exclaimed Franklin. "You might as well talk of hereditary mathematicians!" Franklin expressed exactly what the feeling of the common sense of England is likely to be when the question comes to be raised. I expect then, not that the House of Lords will be abolished, but that the rule of the hereditary principle will be brought to an end—that the Aristocracy there, too, will have to capitulate.

Now, I doubt whether an American reader can have any accurate idea, unless he has specially studied the matter and watched its practical operation in England, of the manner in which the influence of the Peers makes itself felt through the political life of Great Britain. Americans often have some kind of notion that the Aristocracy govern the country directly and despotically, with the high hand of imperious feudalism. There is nothing of the kind in reality. The House of Lords is, as a piece of political machinery, almost inoperative—as nearly as possible harmless. No English Peer, Lord Derby alone excepted, has anything like the political authority and direct influence of Mr. Gladstone, Mr. Disraeli, or Mr. Bright. There are very few Peers, indeed, about whose political utterances anybody in the country cares three straws. But, on the other hand, the traditional *prestige* of the Peers, the tacit, time-honored, generally-conceded doctrine that a Peer has first right to everything—the mediæval superstition tolerated largely in our own time, which allows a sort of divinity to hedge a Peer—all this has an indirect, immense, pervading, almost universal influence in the practical working of English politics. The Peers have, in fact, a political *droit du seigneur* in England. They have first taste of every privilege, first choice of every appointment. Political office is their pasture, where they are privileged to feed at will. There does not now exist a man in England likely to receive high office, who would be bold enough to suggest the forming of a Cabinet without Peers in it, even though there were no Peers to be had who possessed the slightest qualification for any ministerial position. The Peers must have a certain number of places, because they are Peers. The House of Commons swarms with the sons and nephews of Peers. The household appointments, the ministerial offices, the good places in the army and the church are theirs when they choose—and they generally do choose—to have them. The son of a Peer, if in the House of Commons, may be raised at one step from his place in the back benches to a seat in the Cabinet, simply because of his rank. When Earl Russell, two or three years ago, raised Mr. Goschen, one of the representatives of the city of London and a partner in a great London banking-house, to a place in the Cabinet, the whole country wondered: a very few, who were not frightened out of their propriety, admired; some thought the world must be coming to an end. But when the Marquis of Hartington was suddenly picked out of West End dissipation and made War Secretary, nobody expressed the least wonder, for he was the heir of the House of Devonshire. Indeed, it was perfectly notorious that the young Marquis was presented to office, in the first instance, because it was hoped by his friends hat official duties might wean him from the follies and frivolities of a more than ordinarily heedless youth. Sir Robert Peel the present, the *magni nominis umbra*, is not, of course, in the strict sense, an aristocrat; but he is mixed up with aristocrats, and is the son of a Peer-maker, and may be regarded as claiming and having the privileges of the class. Sir Robert Peel was presented with the First Secretaryship as something to play with, because his aristocratic friends, the ladies especially, thought he would be more likely to sow his wild oats if he were beguiled by the semblance of official business. A commoner must, in fact, be supposed to have some qualification for office before he is invited to fill a ministerial place. No qualification is believed necessary for the near relative or connection of a Peer. Even in the most favorable examples of Peers who are regular occupants of office, no special fitness is assumed or pretended. No one supposes or says that Lord Clarendon, or Lord Granville, or Lord Malmesbury has any particular qualification which entitles him, above all other men, to this or that ministerial place. Yet it must be a man of bold imagination indeed, who could now conceive the possibility of a British Cabinet without one of these noblemen having a place in it.

All this comes, as I have said, out of a lingering superstition—the faith in the divine right of Peers. Now, a reform in the constitution of the Upper House, which should purge it of the hereditary principle, would be the first great blow to this superstition. Julius Cæsar, in one of his voyages of conquest, was much perplexed by the priests, who insisted that he had better go back because the sacred chickens would not eat. At last he thought the time had come to prove his independence of the sacred chickens, "If they will not eat," he said, "then let them drink"—and he flung the consecrated fowls into the sea; and the expedition went on triumphantly, and the Roman soldiers learned that they could do without the sacred chickens. I think a somewhat similar sensation will come over all classes of the English people when they find that the hereditary right to make laws is taken from the English Peerage. I do not doubt that the whole fabric of superstition will presently collapse, and that the privilege of the Peer will cease to be anything more than that degree of superior influence which wealth and social rank can generally command, even in the most democratic communities. The law which gives impulse and support to the custom of primogeniture is certain to go, and with it another prop of the mediæval superstition. The Peerage capitulates, in fact—no more expressive word can be found to describe the situation.

Now, in all this, I have been foreshadowing no scheme of wild, vague, far-distant reform. I appeal to any one, Liberal or Tory, who is practically acquainted with English politics, to say whether these are not changes he confidently or timidly looks to see accomplished before long in England. I have not spoken of any reform which is not part of the actual accepted programme of the

Radical party. To the reform of the House of Lords, of the military and diplomatic service; to abolition of the law of primogeniture, the whole body of the Liberals stands pledged; and Mr. Bright very recently renewed the pledges in a manner and with an emphasis which showed that change of circumstances has made no change in his opinions, brought no faltering in his resolution. The abolition of the English Church is not, indeed, thus openly sought by so powerful a party; but it is ostentatiously aimed at by that solid, compact, pertinacious body of Dissenters who, after so long a struggle, succeeded at last in getting rid of Church rates; and the movement will go on with a rush after the fall of the Irish establishment. Here then we have, in the not distant future, a prospect of an England without a privileged Aristocracy, and with the State Church principle called into final question. I return to my first consideration—the consideration which is the subject of this paper—how will this affect the great aristocratic, feudal and hierarchical institution of England, the Throne of the Monarch?

The Throne then will stand naked and alone, stripped of its old-time and traditional surroundings and associations. It cannot be like that of France, the throne of a Cæsar, a despotic institution claiming to exercise its despotism over the people by virtue of the will and delegated power of the people. The English Crown never can be an active governing power. It will be the last idol in the invaded sanctuary. It will stand alone, among the pedestals from which popular reform has swept the embodied superstitions which were its long companions. It must live, if at all, on the old affection or the toleration which springs out of custom and habit. This affection, or at least this toleration, may always be looked upon as a powerful influence in England. One can hardly imagine, for instance, anything occurring in our day to dethrone the Queen. However one class may grumble and another class may gibe, the force of habit and old affection would, in this instance, prove omnipotent. But, suppose the Prince of Wales should turn out an unpopular and ill-conditioned ruler? Suppose he should prove to be a man of low tastes, of vulgar and spendthrift habits, a maladroit and intermeddling king? He is not very popular in England, even now, and he is either one of the most unjustly entreated men living, or he has defects which even the excuse of youth can scarcely gloss over.

An illustrated weekly paper in London forced itself lately into a sudden notoriety by publishing a finely-drawn cartoon, in which the Prince of Wales, dressed as Hamlet, was represented as breaking away from the restraining arms of John Bull as Horatio, and public opinion as Marcellus, and rushing after a ghost which bore the form and features of George IV., while underneath were inscribed the words, "Lead on; I'll follow thee!" This was a bold and bitter lampoon; I am far from saying that it was not unjust, but I believe it can hardly be doubted that the Prince of Wales has, as yet, shown little inclination to imitate the example or cultivate the tastes of his pure-minded and intellectual father. Now suppose, for the sake of argument, that the Prince of Wales should turn out a George IV., or suppose, and which would be far worse from a national point of view, he or his son should turn out a George III. And suppose further that, about the same time any great crisis should arise in England —suppose the country entangled in a great foreign war, or disturbed by some momentous domestic agitation—can any one doubt that the Crown, in its then isolated condition, would be really in danger?

We must remember, when the strength of English institutions is boasted, that they have not, since 1815, stood any strain which could fairly be called critical. England has never had her national strength, her political position, or even her *prestige* seriously imperilled since that time. Even the Indian war could not be called a great supreme trial, such as other nations have lately had to bear. No one, even for a moment, could have doubted how that struggle would end. It was bitter, it was bloody; but the life of the nation was not staked upon it, even had its issue been uncertain; and its issue never was uncertain. It would be superfluous to say that England has passed through no ordeal like that to which the United States were lately subjected. She has not even had to confront anything like the crisis which Prussia voluntarily invited, which Austria had to meet, in 1866. It will be time to consider English feudal institutions, or what may remain of them, safe and firmly-rooted, when they have stood the worst result of such a crisis as that, and not been shaken down.

What I contend is that there is nothing in the present condition of the English public mind, and nothing in the prospect of the immediate future to warrant the almost universal assumption that the throne of England is founded on a rock. The stupidity of loyalty, the devotion as of the spaniel to his master, of the idolator to his god, is gone. I doubt if there exists one man in England who feels the sentiment of loyalty as his grandfather would have felt it. The mass of the people have learned satisfactorily that a sovereign is not a part of the necessary machinery of the government. The great problem which the Duke of Wellington used to present for solution—"How is the Queen's Government to be carried on?" has been solved in one and an unexpected sense. It can be carried on without a queen. Here then we have the institution proving itself superfluous, and falling into public indifference at the very same moment that some other institutions which seemed always involved with it as its natural and necessary companions, are about to be broken to pieces and thrown away. He must, indeed, be full of a verily transcendental faith in the destinies and divinity of royalty who does not admit that at least there is a time of ordeal awaiting it in England, such as it has not encountered before during this century.

To me it seems that the royal principle in England is threatened, not with sudden and violent extinction, but with death by decay. I do not expect any change of any kind to-morrow or the day after, or even the week after next. I do not care to dogmatize, or predict, or make guesses of any kind. I quite agree with my friend Professor Thorold Rogers, that an uninspired prophet is a fool. But I contend that as the evident signs of the times now show themselves, the monarchical principle in England does seem to be decaying; that the national faith which bore it up is sorely shaken and almost gone, and that some of the political props which most nearly supported it are already being cut away. There may, indeed, be some hidden virtue in the principle, which shall develope itself unexpectedly in the hour of danger, and give to the institution that seemed moribund a new and splendid vitality. Such a phenomenon has been manifested in the case of more than one institution that seemed on the verge of ruin—it may be the fortunate destiny of British royalty. But unless in the sudden and timely development of some such occult and unlooked-for virtue, I do not see what is to preserve the monarchical principle in England through the trials of the future.

Let it be remembered, too, that the one great plea hitherto always made in England for monarchy, is that it alone will work on a large scale. "We admit," it was said, "that your republican theory looks better and admits of more logical argument in its favor. But we are practical men, and we find that our system, with all its theoretical disadvantages, will work and stand a strain ; and your republican theory, with all its apparent advantages in logic, is not suited for this rough world. Our machinery will stand the hardest trial; yours never did and never will. Don't tell us about Switzerland. Switzerland is a little country. Kept out of the stress and danger of European commotions, and protected by a guarantee of the great powers, any constitution ought to work under such advantages. But a great independent republic never did last; never did stand a sudden strain, and never will." So people thought and argued in England—even very intelligent people, until at last it became one of the British Philistine's articles of faith, that the republican principle never will work on a large scale. When Sir John Ramsden declared in the House of Commons at the beginning of the American civil war, that the republican bubble had burst, and all Philistinism in Britain applauded the declaration, the plaudits were given not so much because of any settled dislike Philistinism had to the United States, as because Philistinism beheld what it believed to be a providential testimony to its own wisdom and foresight. Since then Philistinism has found that after all republicanism is able to bear a strain as great as monarchy has ever yet borne, and can come out of the trial unharmed and victorious.

The lesson has sunk deeply. The mind of something better than Philistinism has learned that republics can be made to work on a large scale. I believe Mr. Gladstone is one of the eminent Englishmen who now openly admit that they have learned from the American war something which they did not know before, of the cohesiveness and durability of the republican system. Up to the time of that war in fact, most Englishmen, when they talked of republican principles, thought only of French republicanism, and honestly regarded such a system as a brilliant empty bubble, doomed to soar a little, and float, and dazzle, and then to burst.

That idea, it is quite safe to say, no longer exists in the English mind. The fundamental, radical objection to republicanism—the objection which, partly out of mere reaction and partly for more substantial reasons, followed the brief and romantic enthusiasm of the days of Fox—is gone. The practical Englishman admits that a republic is practicable. Only those who know England can know what a change in public opinion this is. It is, in fact, something like a revolution. I think the most devoted monarchist will hardly deny that if some extraordinary combination of chances (after all, even the British Throne is but a human institution) were to disturb the succession of the house of Brunswick, Englishmen would be more likely to try the republican system than to hunt about for a new royal family, or endeavor to invent a new scheme of monarchy. Here, then, I leave the subject. Take all this into account, in considering the probabilities of the future, and then say whether, even in the case of England, it is quite certain that Byron's prediction is only the dream of a cynical poet, destined never to be fulfilled among human realities.

THE REAL LOUIS NAPOLEON.

"HOW will it be with him," said Richard Cobden to a friend, one night, as they spoke of a great and successful adventurer whom the friend was striving to defend—"how will it be with him when life becomes all retrospect?" The adventurer they spoke of was not Louis Napoleon; but the inquiry might well apply just now to the Emperor of the French. Life has reached that point with him when little more than retrospect can be left. In the natural course of events, there can be no great triumphs for Louis Napoleon still to achieve. Great blunders are possible, though hardly probable; but the greatest of blunders would scarcely efface the memory of the substantial triumphs. "Not heaven itself," exclaimed an ambitious and profane statesman, "can undo the fact that I have been three times Prime Minister." Well, the Fates—let them do their best—can hardly undo the fact that the despised outcast of Constance, and Augsburg, and London, and New York, whom Lord Palmerston excused himself to Guizot for tolerating, on the ground that really nobody minded the dull, harmless poor fellow; the Fates cannot undo the fact that this man has elected himself Emperor of the French, has defeated the Russians and the Austrians, and made a friend and ally of England.

So much of the past, then, is secure; but there are hardly any triumphs to be won in the future. If one may venture to predict anything, he may venture to predict that the Emperor of the French will not live to be a very old man. He has already led many lives—fast, hard, exhausting lives, "that murder the youth in a man ere ever his heart has its will." Exile, conspiracy, imprisonment, hard thinking, hard working, wild and reckless dissipation, prolonged to the very outer verge of middle life, the brain, the nerves, the muscles, the whole physical and mental constitution always strained to the utmost—these are not the ways that secure a long life. Louis Napoleon is already an "*abgelebter mann*"—an outworn, used-up, played-out man. The friends and familiars with whom he started in life are nearly all gone. Long since laid in earth is the stout form of the wild Marquis of Waterford, who was a wonder to our fathers (his successor to the title ran away with somebody's wife the other day; and I thought Time had turned back by thirty years when I read of the *escapade*, with the name, once so famous, of the principal performer), and who rode by Louis Napoleon's side at the celebrated, forgotten Eglintoun Tournament, and was, like Louis Napoleon, one of the Knights Challengers in that piece of splendid foolery. Dead, lang syne, is Eglintoun himself, the chivalrous Earl of the generous instincts and the florid, rotund eloquence, reminding one of Bulwer Lytton diluted. I do not know whether the Queen of Beauty of that grand joust is yet living and looking on the earth; but if she be, she must be an embodied sermon on the perishableness of earthly charms. De Morny is dead, the devoted half-brother, son of Louis Napoleon's mother, the chaste Hortense, and the Count de Flahault—De Morny, the brilliant, genial, witty, reckless gambler in politics and finance, the man than whom nobody ever, perhaps, was more faithful to friendship and false to morality, more good-natured and unprincipled. I have seen tears in men's eyes when De Morny died—in the eyes of men who owned all the time, smiling through their tears like Andromache, that the lost patron and friend was the most consummate of *roués* and blacklegs. Walewski is dead—Walewski of romantic origin, born of the sudden episode of love between the great Napoleon and the Polish lady—Walewski, who, like Prince Napoleon-Jerome, carried his pedigree stamped upon his face—Walewski, the lover of Rachel, and, to do him justice, the steady friend of Poland. Old Mocquard is gone, the faithful scribe and confidant: he is dead, and the dramas he would persist in writing are dead with him, nay, died even before him. I do not know whether the faithful, devoted woman who worked for Louis Napoleon, and believed in him when nobody else did; the woman to whose inspirings, exertions, and ready money he owes, in great measure, the fact that he is now Emperor of the French—I do not know whether this woman is alive or dead. I think she is dead. Anyhow, I suppose the dignity of history, as the phrase is, can hardly take account of her. She helped to make an Emperor, and the Emperor, in return, made her a Countess; but then he had to marry—and so we take leave of the woman who made the Emperor, and do our homage to the woman who married him. All those are gone; and St. Arnaud, of the stormy youth, and Pelissier, the bland, sweet-tempered chevalier, who, getting into a dispute (on his way to be governor of Algeria) with the principal official of a Spanish port, invited that dignitary to salute a portion of the Pelissier person which assuredly the foes of France were never allowed to see—all these are gone, and many more, and only a very few, fast fading, of the old friends and followers remain. Life to Louis Napoleon must now, indeed, be nearly all retrospect. His career, his Imperial reign may be judged even now as fairly and securely as as if his body had just been laid beside that of his uncle, under the dome of the Invalides.

Recent events seem specially to invite and authorize that judgment. Within the past twelve months, the genuine character of Louis Napoleon has displayed itself, strikingly, nakedly, in his policy. He has tried, in succession, mild liberalism, severe despotism, reactionary conservatism, antique Cæsarism, and then, in an apologetic, contrite sort of way, a liberalism of a rather pronounced character. Every time that he tried any new policy he was secretly intriguing with some other, and making ready for the possible necessity of having to abandon the former and take up with the latter. He was like the lady in "Le Diable Boiteux," who, while openly coquetting with the young lover, slily gives her hand behind her back to the old admirer. So far as the public could judge, Louis Napoleon has, for many months back, been absolutely without any settled policy whatever. He has been waiting for a wind. Such a course is probably the safest a man in his position can take; but one who, at a great crisis, cannot originate and initiate a policy, will not be remembered among the grand rulers of the world. I do not remember any greater evidence given in our time of absolute incapacity to seize a plan of action and decide upon it, than was shown by the Emperor of the French during the crisis of June and July. So feeble, so vague, halting, vacillating was the whole course of the government, that many who detest Louis Napoleon, but make it an article of faith that he is a sort of all-seeing, omnipotent spirit of darkness, were forced to adopt a theory that the riots in Paris and the provinces were deliberately got up by the police agents of the Empire, for the purpose of frightening the *bourgeois* class out of any possible hankering after democracy. No doubt this idea was widely spread and eagerly accepted in Paris; and there were many circumstances which seemed to justify it. But I do not believe in any such Imperial stage-play. I fancy the riots surprised the Government, first, by their sudden outburst, and next, by their sudden collapse. Probably the Imperial authorities were very glad when the disturbances began. They gave an excuse for harsh conduct, and they seemed, for the time, to put the Government in the right. They restored Louis Napoleon at that moment, in the eyes of timid people, to that position, as a supreme maintainer of order, which for some years he had not had an opportunity effectively to occupy. But the obvious want of stamina in the disturbing force soon took away from the Imperial authorities this opportune *prestige*, and very little political capital was secured for Imperialism out of the abortive barricades, and incoherent brickbats, and effusive chantings of the "Marseillaise." In truth, no one had anything else to offer just then in place of the Empire. The little crisis was no test whatever of the Emperor's hold over his people, or of his power to deal with a popular revolution. To me it seems doubtful whether the elections brought out for certain any fact with which the world might not already have been well acquainted, except the bare fact that Orleanism has hardly any more of vitality in it than Legitimacy. Rochefort, and not Prevost Paradol, is the typical figure of the situation.

The popularity and the success of Rochefort and his paper are remarkable phenomena, but only remarkable in the old-fashioned manner of the straws which show how the wind blows. Rochefort's success is due to the fact that he had the good-fortune to begin ridiculing the Empire just at the time when a general notion was spreading over France that the Empire of late had been making itself ridiculous. Louis Napoleon had reached the turning-point of his career—had reached and passed it. The country saw now all that he could do. The bag of tricks was played out. The anticlimax was reached at last.

The culmen, the crisis, the turning-point of Louis Napoleon's career seems to me to have been attained when, just before the outbreak of the Schleswig-Holstein war—so small a war in itself, so fateful and gigantic in its results—he appealed to the Emperors and Kings of Europe, and proposed that the nations should hold a Congress, to settle, once and forever, all pending disputes. I think the attitude of Louis Napoleon at that moment was dignified, commanding, imperial. His peculiar style, forcible, weighty, measured—I have heard it well described as a "monumental" style—came out with great effect in the language of the appeal. There was dignity, and grace, there was what Edmund Burke so appropriately terms "a proud humility," in Louis Napoleon's allusion to his own personal experience in the school of exile and adversity as an excuse for his presuming to offer advice to the sovereigns of Europe. One was reminded of Henry of Navarre's allusion to the wind of adversity which, blowing so long upon his face, had prematurely blanched his hair. I do not wonder that the proposed Congress never met. I do not wonder that the European governments put it aside—some with courteous phrase and feigned willingness to accept the scheme, like Russia and Austria; some with cold and brusque rejection, like England. Nothing worth trying for could have come of the Congress. Events were brooding of which France and England knew nothing, and which could not have been exorcised away by any resolutions of a conclave of diplomatists. But that was, I think, the last occasion when Louis Napoleon held anything like a commanding, overruling position in European affairs, and even then it was but a semblance. After that, came only humiliations and reverses. In a diplomatic sense, nothing could be more complete than the checkmate which the Emperor of the French drew upon himself by the sheer blundering of his conduct with regard to Prussia. He succeeded in placing himself before the world in the distinct attitude of an enemy to Prussia; and no sooner had he, by assuming this attitude, forced Prussia to take a defiant tone, than he suddenly sank down into quietude. He had bullied to no purpose; he had to undergo the humiliation of seeing Prussia rise in public estimation, by means of the triumph which his unnecessary and uncalled-for hostility had enabled her to win. In fact, he was outgeneralled by his pupil, Bismarck, even more signally than he had previously been outgeneralled by his former pupil, Cavour. More disastrous and ghastly, by far, was the failure of his Mexican policy. That policy began in falsehood and treachery, and ended as it deserved. Poetic and dramatic justice was fearfully rendered. Never did Philip II., of Spain, never did his father, never did Napoleon I., never did Mendez Pinto, or any other celebrated liar, exceed the deliberate monstrosity of the falsehoods which were told by Louis Napoleon or Louis Napoleon's Ministers at his order, to conceal, during the earlier stages of the Mexican intervention, the fact that the French Emperor had a *protégé* in the background, who was to be seated on a Mexican throne. The world is not much affected by perfidy in sovereigns. It laughs at the perjuries of princes as Jove does at those of lovers. But it could not overlook the appalling significance of Louis Napoleon's defeat in that disastrous chapter of his history. Wisdom after the event is easy work; but many, many voices had told Louis Napoleon beforehand what would come of his Mexican policy. Not to speak of the hints and advice he received from the United States, he was again and again assured by the late Marshal O'Donnell, then Prime Minister of Spain; by General Prim, who commanded the allied forces during the earlier part of the Mexican expedition; by Prince Napoleon, by many others—that neither the character of the Mexican people nor the proximity of the United States would allow a French proconsulate to be established in Mexico under the name of an Empire. It is a certain fact that Louis Napoleon frequently declared that the foundation of that Empire would be the great event of his reign. This extraordinary delusion maintained a hold over his mind long after it had become apparent to all the world that the wretched bubble was actually bursting. The catastrophe was very near when Louis Napoleon, in conversation with an English political adventurer, who then was a Member of Parliament, assured him that, however the situation might then look dark, history would yet have to record that he, Louis Napoleon, had established a Mexican Empire. The English member of Parliament, although ordinarily a very shrewd and sceptical sort of person, was actually so impressed with the earnestness of his Imperial interlocutor that he returned to London and wrote a pamphlet, in which, to the utter amazement of his acquaintances, he backed the Empire of Mexico for a secure existence, and said to it *esto perpetua.* The pamphlet was hardly in circulation when the collapse came. If Louis Napoleon ever believed in anything, he believed in the Mexican Empire. He believed, too, in the certain success of the Southern Confederation. No Belgravian Dundreary, no *exaltée* Georgian girl, could have been more completely taken by surprise when the collapse of that enterprise came than was the Emperor Napoleon III., whose boundless foresight and profound sagacity we had all for years been applauding to the echo. "That which is called firmness in a King," said Erskine, "is called obstinacy in a donkey." That which is called foresight and sagacity in an Emperor, is often what we call blindness and blundering in a newspaper correspondent. The question is whether we can point to any great event, any political enterprise, subsequent to his successful assumption of the Imperial crown, in regard to which Napoleon III., if called upon to act or to judge, did not show the same aptitude for rash judgments and unwise actions? Certainly no great thing with which he has had to do came out in the result with anything like the shape he meant it to have. The Italian Confederation, with the Pope at the head of it; the Germany irrevocably divided by the line of the Main; the Mexican Empire; the "rectification" of frontier on the Rhine; the acquisition of Luxembourg; these are some of the great Napoleonic ideas, by the success or failure of which we may fairly judge of the wisdom of their author. At home he has simply had a new plan of government every year. How many different ways of dealing with the press, how many different schemes for adjusting the powers of the several branches of legislation, have been magniloquently announced and floated during the last few years, each in turn to fail rather more dismally than its predecessor? Now, it seems, we are to have at last something like that ministerial responsibility which the Imperial lips themselves have so often described as utterly opposed to the genius of France. Assuredly it shows great mental flexibility to be able thus quickly to change one's policy in obedience to a warning from without. It is a far better quality than the persistent treachery of a Charles I., or the stupid doggedness of a George III. But unless it be a characteristic of great statesmanship to be almost always out in one's calculations, wrong in one's predictions, and mistaken in one's men, the Emperor has for years been in the habit of doing things which are directly incompatible with the character of a great statesman.

Contrasting the Louis Napoleon of action and reality with the Louis Napoleon of the journals, I am reminded of a declaration once made by a brilliant, audacious, eccentric Italian journalist and politician, Petruccelli della Gattina. Petruccelli was, and perhaps still is, a member of the Italian Parliament, and he had occasion to find fault with some office or dignity, or something of the kind, conferred by Count Cavour on the Neapolitan, Baron Poerio, whose imprisonment and chains, during the reign of the beloved Bomba, aroused the eloquent anger of Mr. Gladstone, and through Gladstone's efforts and appeals became the wonder and the horror of the world. Petruccelli insisted that Poerio's undeserved sufferings were his only political claim. "You know perfectly well," he said, in effect, to Cavour, "that there is no such man as the Poerio of the journals. It suited us to invest the poor victim with the attributes of greatness, and therefore, we, the journalists, created a Poerio of our own. This imposed upon the world, but it did not impose upon you, and you have no right to take our Poerio *au serieux*." I do not know whether the journals created an imaginary Poerio, but I am convinced that they have created an imaginary Louis Napoleon. The world in general now so much prefers the imaginary to the real Louis, that it would for the present be as difficult to dethrone the unreal and set up the real, as it would be to induce the average reader to accept Lane's genuine translation of the "Arabian Nights" instead of the familiar translation from a sprightly, flippant, flashy French version, which hardly bears the slightest resemblance to the original. English journalism has certainly created a Disraeli of its own—a dark, subtle, impenetrable, sphinx-like being, who never smiles, or betrays outward emotion, or is taken by surprise, or makes a mistake. This Disraeli is an immense success with the public, and is not in the least like the real Disraeli, who is as good-natured and genial in manner as he is bold and blundering in speech and policy. So, on a wider scale, of Louis Napoleon. We are all more or less responsible for the fraud on the public; and, indeed, are to be excused on the ground that, enamored of our own creation, we have often got the length of believing in it. We have thus created a mysterious being, a sphinx of far greater than even Disraelian proportions, an embodiment of silence and sagacity, a dark creature endowed with super-human self-control and patience and foresight; one who can bend all things, and all men, and destiny itself to his own calm, inexorable will.

I do not believe there is anything of the sphinx about Louis Napoleon. I do not believe in his profound sagacity, or his foresight, or his stupendous self-control. I have grown so heretical that I do not even believe him to be a particularly taciturn man. I am well satisfied that Louis Napoleon is personally a good-natured, good-tempered, undignified, awkward sort of man, ungainly of gesture, not impressive in speech, a man quite as remarkable for occasional outbursts of unexpected and misplaced confidence as for a silence that often is, if I may use such an expression, purely mechanical and unmeaning. I calmly ask my *confrères* of the press, is it not a fact that Louis Napoleon is commonly made the dupe of shallow charlatans, that he has several times received and admitted to confidential counsel and conference, and treated as influential statesmen and unaccredited ambassadors. utterly obscure American or English busybodies who could hardly get to speech of the Mayor of a town at home ; that he has entered into signed and sealed engagements with impudent adventurers from divers countries, under the impression that they could render him vast political service ; that he has paid down considerable sums of money to subsidize the most obscure and contemptible foreign journals, and never seemed able for a moment to comprehend that in England and the United States no journal that can be bought for any price, however high, is worth buying at any price, however low ; that his personal inclinations are much more toward quacks and pretenders than toward men of real genius and influence ; that Cobden was one of the very few great men Louis Napoleon ever appreciated, while impostors, and knaves, and blockheads, of all kinds, could readily find access to his confidence ? Of course, a man might possibly be a great sovereign although he had these weaknesses ; but the Louis Napoleon of journalism is not endowed with these, or indeed with any other weaknesses.

Those who know Paris well, know that there is yet another Louis Napoleon there, equally I trust a fiction with him of the journals. I speak of the Louis Napoleon of private gossip, the hero of unnumbered *amours* such as De Grammont or Casanova might wonder at. I have heard stories poured into my patient but sceptical ears which ascribed to Louis Napoleon of to-day, adventures illustrating a happy and brilliant combination of Haroun Al Raschid and Lauzun—the disguises of the Caliph employed for the purposes of Don Juan. Now, Louis Napoleon certainly had, and perhaps even still has, his frailties of this class, but I reject the Lauzun or Don Juan theory quite as resolutely as the sphinx theory.

What we all do really know of Louis Napoleon is, that having the advantage of a name of surpassing prestige, and at a moment of unexampled chances not created by him, he succeeded in raising himself to the throne made by his uncle ; that when there, he held his place firmly, and by maintaining severe order in a country already weary of disturbance and barren revolution, he favored and stimulated the development of the material resources of France ; that he entered on several enterprises in foreign politics, not one of which brought about the end for which it was undertaken, and some of which were ludicrous, disastrous failures ; that he strove to compensate France for the loss of her civil liberty, by audaciously attempting to make her the dictator of Europe, and that he utterly failed in both objects ; for here toward the close of his rule, France seems far more eager for domestic freedom than ever she was since the *coup d'état*, while her influence over the nations of Europe is considerably less than it was at any period since the fall of Sebastopol. Now, if this be success, I want to know what is failure ? If these results argue the existence of profound sagacity, I want to know what would show a lack of sagacity ? Was Louis Napoleon sagacious when he entered Lombardy, to set Italy free from the Alps to the sea, and sagacious also when, after a campaign of a few weeks, he suddenly abandoned the enterprise never to resume it ? Was he wise when he told Cavour he would never permit the annexation of Naples, and wise also when, immediately after, he permitted it? Was he a great statesman when he entered on the Mexican expedition, and also a great statesman when he abandoned it and his unfortunate pupil, puppet, and victim together? Did it show a statesmanlike judgment to bully Prussia until he had gone near to making her an irreconcilable enemy, and also a statesmanlike judgment then to "cave in," and declare that he never meant anything offensive? Was it judicious to demand a rectification of frontier on the Rhine, and judicious also to abandon the demand in a hurry, when it was received as anybody might have known that a proud, brave nation, flushed with a splendid success, would surely have received it? Did it display great foresight to count with certainty that the Southern Confederation would succeed, and that Austria would win an easy victory over Prussia? Was it judicious to instruct an official spokesman to declare that France had taken steps to assure herself against any spread of Prussian influence beyond the Main, and to have to stand next day, amazed and confounded, before an amazed and amused Europe, when Bismarck made practical answer by contemptuously unrolling the treaties of alliance actually concluded between France and the principal States of South Germany? Was it a proof of a great ruling mind to declare that France could never endure a system of ministerial responsibility, and also a proof of a great ruling mind to declare that this is the one thing needful to her contentment? All this bundle of paradoxes one will have to sustain, if he is content to accept as a genuine being that monstrous paradox, the Louis Napoleon of the press. Of course, I do not deny to Louis Napoleon certain qualities of greatness. But I believe the public was not a whit more gravely mistaken when it regarded the King street exile as a dreamy dunce, than it is now, when it regards Napoleon III. as a ruler of consummate wisdom.

There was much of sound sense as well as wit in the saying ascribed to Thiers, that the second Empire had developed two great statesmen—Cavour and Bismarck. I do not know of any one great idea, worthy of being called a contribution to the science of government, which Louis Napoleon has yet embodied, either in words or actions. The recent elections, and the events succeeding them, only demonstrate the failure of Imperialism or Cæsarism, after a trial and after opportunities such as it probably will never have again in Europe. I certainly do not expect any complete collapse during the present reign. Doubtless the machine will outlast the third Emperor's time. He has sense and dexterity enough to trim his sails to each breeze that passes, and he will, probably, hold the helm till his right hand loses its cunning with its vital power. But I see no evidence whatever which induces me to believe that he has founded a dynasty or created an enduring system of any kind. Some day France will shake off the whole thing like a nightmare. Meantime, however, I am anxious to help in dethroning the Louis Napoleon of the journals rather than him of the Tuileries. The latter has many good qualities which the former is never allowed to exhibit. I believe the true Louis Napoleon has a remarkably kind and generous heart; that he is very liberal and charitable; that he has much affection in him, and is very faithful to his old friends and old servants; that people who come near him love him much; that he is free and kindly of speech; that his personal defects are rather those of a warm and rash, than of a cold and stern nature. But I think it is high time that we were done with the melodramatic, dime-romance, darkly mysterious Louis Napoleon of the journals. He belongs to the race of William Tell, of the Wandering Jew, the Flying Dutchman, the Sphinx to whom he is so often compared, the mermaid, the sea-serpent, Byron's Corsair, and Thaddeus of Warsaw.

EUGENIE, EMPRESS OF THE FRENCH.

THERE are certain men and women in history who seem to have a peculiarity, independent of their merits or demerits, greatness or littleness, virtues or crimes—a peculiarity which distinguishes them from others as great or as little, as virtuous or as criminal. They are, first and above all things, interesting. It is not easy to describe what the elements are which make up this attribute. Certainly genius or goodness, wit or wisdom, splendid public services, great beauty, or even great suffering, will not always be enough to create it. The greatest English king since the First Edward was assuredly William the Third; the greatest military commanders England has ever had were Marlborough and Wellington; but these three will hardly be called by any one interesting personages in the sense in which I now use the word. Why Nelson should be interesting and Wellington not so, Byron interesting and Wordsworth not so, is perhaps easy enough to explain; but it is not quite easy to see why Rousseau should be so much more interesting than Voltaire, Goethe than Schiller, Mozart than Handel, and so on through a number of illustrations, the accuracy of which nearly all persons would probably acknowledge. Where history and public opinion and sentiment have to deal with the lives and characters of women, the peculiarity becomes still more deeply emphasized. What gifts, what graces, what rank, what misfortunes have ever surrounded any queens or princesses known to history with the interest which attaches to Mary Stuart and Marie Antoinette? Lady Jane Grey was an incomparably nobler woman than either, and suffered to the full as deeply as either; yet what place has she in men's feelings and interest compared with theirs? Who cares about Anna Boleyn, though she too shared a throne and mounted a scaffold?

Absit omen! I am about to speak of an illustrious living lady, who has in common with Mary Stuart and Marie Antoinette two things at least: she has a French sovereign for a husband, and she has the fame of beauty. But she has likewise that other peculiarity of which I spoke: she is interesting. It is only speaking by the card to say that by far the most interesting of all the imperial and royal ladies now living is Eugénie, Empress of the French. I think there are princesses in Europe more beautiful and even more graceful than she is, or than she ever could have been; I fancy there are some much more highly gifted with intellect; but there is no woman living in any European palace in whom the general world feels half so much interest. There is not the slightest reason to believe that she is a woman of really penetrating or commanding intellect, and should she be happy enough to live out her life in the Tuileries and die peacefully in her bed, history will find but little to say about her, good or bad. Yet so long as her memory remains in men's minds, it will be as that of a princess who had above all things the gift of being interesting—the power of attracting toward herself the eyes, the admiration, the curiosity, the wonder of all the civilized world

"We count time by heart-throbs, not by figures on a dial," says a poet who once nearly secured immortality, Philip James Bailey. There certainly are people whose age seems to defy counting by figures on a dial. Ask anybody what two pictures are called up in his mind when he hears the names of Queen Victoria and the Empress of the French, no matter whether he has ever seen the two illustrious ladies or not. In the case of the former I may safely venture to answer for him that he sees the face and figure of a motherly, homely body; a woman who has got quite beyond the age when people observe how she dresses; to whom personal appearance is no longer of any importance or interest. In the case of the latter he sees a dazzling court beauty; a woman who, though not indeed in her youth, is still in a glorious prime; a woman to captivate hearts, and inspire poets, and set scandal going, and adorn a ball-room or a throne. The first instinctive idea would be, I think, that the Empress of the French belonged positively to a later generation than the good, unattractive, dowdyish Queen of England. Yet I believe the difference in actual years is very slight. To be sure, you will find in any almanac that Queen Victoria was born on the 24th of May, 1819, and is consequently very near to fifty-one years of age; while the fair Eugénie is set down as having been born on May 5th, 1826, and consequently would now appear to be only in her forty-fourth year. But then Queen Victoria was born in the purple, and cannot, poor thing, make any attempt at reducing by one single year the full figure of her age. History has taken an inexorable, ineffaceable note of the day and hour of her birth; and even court flattery cannot affect to ignore the record. Now Eugénie was born in happy obscurity; even the place of her birth is not known by the public with that certainty which alone satisfies sceptics; and I have heard that the date recorded as that of her natal hour is only a graceful fiction, a pretty bit of polite biography. Certainly I have heard it stoutly maintained that if any historian or critic were now to be as ungallant in his researches as John Wilson Croker was in the case of Lady Morgan (was it not Lady Morgan ?), he would find that the birth of the brilliant Empress of the French would have to be dated back a few years, and that after all the difference between her and the elderly Queen Victoria is less an affair of time than of looks and of heart-throbs.

About a dozen years, I suppose, have passed away since I saw the Empress Eugénie and Queen Victoria sitting side by side. Assuredly the difference even then might well have been called a contrast, although the Queen was in her happiest time, and has worn out terribly fast since that period. But the quality which above all others Queen Victoria wanted was just that in which the Empress of the French is supreme—the quality of imperial, womanly grace. I have never been a rapturous admirer of the beauty of the Empress; a certain narrowness of contour in the face, the eyes too closely set together, and an appearance of artificiality in every movement of the features, seem to me to detract very much from the charms of her countenance. But her queenly grace of gesture, of attitude, of form, of motion, must be admitted to be beyond cavil, and superb. She looks just the woman on whom any sort of garment would hang with grace and attractiveness; a blanket would become like a regal mantle if it fell round her shoulders; I verily believe she would actually look graceful in Mary Walker's costume, which I consider decidedly the most detestable, in an artistic sense, ever yet indued by mortal woman. Poor Queen Victoria looked awkward and homely indeed by the side of this graceful, noble form; this figure that expressed so well the combination of suppleness and affluence, of imperial dignity and charming womanhood. Time has not of late spared the face of the Empress of the French. Lines and hollows are growing fast there; the bright eyes are sinking deeper into their places; the complexion is fading and clouding; malicious people now say that, like that of the lady in the "School for Scandal," it comes in the morning and goes in the night; and the hair is apparently fast growing thin. But the grace of form and movement is still there, unimpaired and unsurpassed. The whitest and finest shoulders still surmount a noble bust, which, but that its amplitude somewhat exceeds the severe proportions of antique

Grecian beauty, might be reproduced in marble to illustrate the contour of a Venus or a Juno. I have seldom looked at the Empress of the French or at any picture or bust of her without thinking how Mary Wortley Montagu would have gone into bold and eloquent raptures over the superb womanhood of that splendid form.

Well, the face always disappointed me at least. It seems to me cold, artificial, narrow, insincere. It wants nobleness. It does not impress me as being the face of a frivolous woman, a coquette, a court butterfly; but rather that of one who is always playing a part which sometimes wearies. If I were to form my own impressions of the Empress of the French merely from her face, I should set her down as a keen, politic woman, with brains enough to be crafty, not enough to be great. I should set her down as a woman who needs and loves the stimulus of incessant excitement, just as much as a certain class of actress does. Indeed, I think I have seen in the face of more than one actress just such an habitual expression, off the stage, as one may see in the countenance of the French Empress. I fear that sweet and gracious smile, which is said to be so captivating to those for whose immediate and special homage it is put on, changes into sudden blankness or weariness when its momentary business has been done. Sam Slick tells us of a lady whose smile dropped from her face the moment the gazer's eyes were withdrawn "like a petticoat when the strings break;" and if I might apply this irreverent comparison to the smile of an Empress, I would say that I think I have noted just such a change in the expression of the brilliant Eugénie. Indeed, it must be a tiresome part, that which she has had to play through all these resplendent years; a part thrilling with danger, made thorny by many sharp vexations. Were the Empress of the French the mere *belle* of a court, she might doubtless have joyfully swallowed all the bitternesses for the sake of the brightness and splendor of her lot; were she a woman of high, imperial genius, a Maria Theresa, an Anne of Austria, she might have found in the mere enjoyment of power, or in the nobler aspirings of patriotism, abundant compensation for her individual vexations. But being neither a mere coquette nor a woman of genius, being neither great enough to rise wholly above her personal troubles, nor small enough to creep under them untouched, she must have suffered enough to render her life very often a weary trial; and the traces of that weariness can be seen on her face when the court look is dropped for a moment.

The Empress seems to have passed through three phases of character, or at least to have made on the public opinion of France three successive and different impressions. For a long time she was set down as a mere coquette, a creature whose soul soared no higher than the aspiration after a bonnet or a bracelet, whose utmost genius exhausted itself in the invention of a crinoline. Indeed, it may be questioned whether any invention known to modern Europe had so sudden and wonderful a success or made the inventor so talked about as Eugénie's famous *jupon d'acier*. A sour and cynical Republican of my acquaintance once declared that anybody might have known the Empress to be a *parvenue* by the mere fact that she could and did invent a petticoat; for he maintained that no born emperor or empress ever was known to have done even so much in the way of invention. Decidedly, the Empress did a great deal of harm in those her earlier and more brilliant days. To her influence and example may be ascribed the passion for mere extravagance and variety of dress which has spread of late years among all the fashionable and would-be fashionable women of Europe and America. It is not too much to say that the Empress of the French demoralized, in this sense, the womanhood of two generations. How literally debauching her influence was to the women immediately under its control, the women of the fashionable world of Paris, I need not stop to tell. Graceful, gracious, and elegant as she is, she did undoubtedly succeed in branding with a stamp of vulgarity the brilliant court of the Second Empire. It is not wonderful if scandal said coarse and bitter things about the goddess of prodigality who presided over the revels of the Tuileries. The most absurd stories used to be told of the amusements which went on in the private gardens of the palace and in its inner circles; and the levity and occasional flightiness of a vivacious young woman thirsting for fresh gayeties and new excitements were perverted and magnified into reckless and wanton extravagances. Of course it was inevitable that there should be scandal over the birth of the Prince Imperial. Were the Empress Eugénie chaste as ice, pure as unsunned snow, she could not, under the circumstances, escape that calumny.

About the time of her sudden and mysterious escapade to London, the Empress began to emerge a little from the character of a mere woman of fashion, and to become known and felt as a politician. People say that some at least of the influence and control which she began to obtain over her husband was owing to her knowledge of his many infidelities and his reluctance to provoke her into open quarrel. Unless Eugénie was wholly free from the jealousy which is supposed to lie in the heart of every other woman, she must have suffered cruelly in this way for many years. In her own court circles, at her own side, were ladies whom universal report designated as successive *maîtresses en titre* of the Emperor Napoleon. Stories, too, of his indulgence in low and gross amours were told everywhere, and, true or false (charity itself could not well doubt that some of them were true), must have reached the Empress's ears. She suffered severely, and she took to politics—perhaps as a harassed man sometimes takes to drinking. Her political influence was, in its day, simply disastrous. She was always on the wrong side, and she was always impetuous, unreasoning, and pertinacious, as cynical people say is the way of women. She became a devotee of the narrowest kind; and just as Madame de Maintenon's religious bigotry did infinitely more harm to France than the vilest profligacy of a Pompadour or a Dubarry could have done, so the religious fervor of the Empress Eugénie threatened at one time to prove a worse thing for the State and for Europe than if she had really carried on during all her lifetime the palace orgies which her enemies ascribed to her. Reaction, Ultramontanism, illiberalism, superstition, found a patroness and leader in her. She fought for the continued occupation of Rome; she battled against the unity of Italy; she recommended and urged the Mexican expedition. Louis Napoleon is personally a good-natured, easy-going sort of man, averse to domestic disputes, fully conscious, no doubt, of his frequent liability to domestic censure. What wonder if European politics sometimes had to suffer heavily for the tolerated presence of this or that too notorious lady in the inner circles of the French court? "Who is the Countess de ——?" I once asked of a Parisian friend who was attached to the Imperial household—I was speaking of a lady whose beauty and whose audacities of dress were then much talked of in the French capital. "The latest favorite," was the reply. "I shouldn't wonder if her presence at court cost another ten years of the occupation of Rome."

With the Empress's introduction to politics and political intrigue, the era of scandal seems to have closed for her. She dressed as brilliantly and extravagantly as ever, and she would take as much pains about her toilet for the benefit of Persigny and Baroche and Billault at a Council of State as for a ball in the Tuileries. She received the same sort of company, was surrounded by the same ladies and the same cavaliers as ever. But she ceased to be herself a subject of scandal—a fact which is not a little remarkable when one remembers how many bitter enemies she made for herself at this period of her career. She seems to have seriously contemplated the assumption of a great political and religious part—the part of the patroness and protectress of the Papacy. I believe she studied hard to educate herself for this part, and indeed for the work in politics generally which devolved upon her. The position of Vicegerent, assigned to her by the Emperor during his absence in the Lombardy campaign, stirred up political ambition within her, and she seems to have shown a remarkable aptitude for political work. She certainly sustained the opinion expressed by John Stuart Mill in his "Subjection of Women," that the business of politics, from which laws in general shut women out, is just the one intellectual occupation in which, whenever they have had a chance, they have proved themselves the equals of men. When Eugénie was raised to the Imperial throne, she appears to have had no better education than any young Spanish woman of her class, and that certainly is not much. A lady once assured me that she was one of a group who were presented to the Empress at the Tuileries, and that there being in the group two beautiful girls from America, to whom Eugénie desired to be particularly gracious, her Imperial Majesty began to ask them several questions about their native land, and astonished them almost beyond the capacity to reply by kindly inquiring whether they had come from New York "over the sea, or over the land." But the Empress has read up a good deal, and mastered much other knowledge besides that of geography, since those salad days. Meanwhile, she became more and more the divinity of the Ultramontanes; and the French court presented the interesting spectacle of having two rival and extreme parties, one led by the Emperor's wife, and the other by his cousin, Prince Napoleon, between whom the Emperor himself maintained an attitude something like that of the central figure in a game of seesaw. I presume there can be little doubt that the Empress regarded her husband's portly cousin with a cordial detestation. She is not a woman endowed with a keen sense of humor, nor in any case would she be quite likely to enjoy anything which was humorous at her own expense; and Prince Napoleon is credited broadly with having said things concerning her which doubtless made his friends and followers and boon companions laugh, but which, reported to her, as they assuredly would be, must have made her cheek flame and her lips quiver. Moreover, the Red Prince was notoriously in the habit of turning into jest some things more sacred in the eyes of the Imperial devotee than even her own reputation. She feared his tongue, his reckless wit, his smouldering ambition. She feared him for her boy, whose rival and enemy he might come to be; and Prince Napoleon had more sons than one. Therefore the rivalry was keen and bitter. She was for the Pope; he was for Italy and the Revolution. She sympathized with the South in the American civil war; Prince Napoleon was true to his principles and stood by the North. She favored the Mexican enterprise; he opposed it. She was for all manner of repressive action as regarded political speaking and writing; he was for a free platform and free press. Her triumph came when, during the Emperor's visit to Algeria, Prince Napoleon delivered his famous Ajaccio speech—a speech terribly true and shockingly indiscreet—and was punished by an Imperial rebuke, whicn led him to resign all his political offices and withdraw absolutely from public life for several successive years.

But just when the Empress seemed to have the field all to herself, her political influence began somehow to wane. Perhaps she grew a little weary of the work of statecraft; perhaps she had not been so successful in some of her favorite projects as she had expected to be. The Mexican expedition turned out a dismal, ghastly failure, and that enterprise had always been regarded as the joint work of the two influences which cynical people say have usually been most disastrous in politics—the priest and the petticoat. Then the idea of working out the scheme of European politics from the central point of the Tuileries was suddenly exploded by the unexpected intrusion of Prussia, and the dazzling victory in which the Bonaparte as well as the Hapsburg was overthrown and humbled. The old framework of things was disjointed by this surprising event. A new political centre of gravity had to be sought for Europe. France was rudely pushed aside. The fair Empress, who had been training herself for quite a different condition of things, found herself now confronted by new, strange, and bewildering combinations. One thing is highly to her credit. I have been assured by people who claim to know something of the matter, that her earnest influence was used to induce the French Government to accept, without remonstrance, the new situation. While Louis Napoleon was committing the inexcusable blunder of feeling his way towards a war with Prussia, and thereby subjecting himself to the ignominy of having to draw hastily back, the voice of the Empress, I am assured, was always raised for peace. But I think the new situation was too much for her. She had made up for a game of politics between the Pope and Italy; when other players and other stakes appeared, the Empress was disinclined to undertake a new course of education. She thereupon passed into the third phase—that of philanthropic devotee, Lady Bountiful, and mother of her people; and since then, if she cannot be said to have grown universally popular, she may fairly be described as having got rid of nearly all her former unpopularity. Her good deeds began to be magnified everywhere, and even ancient enemies were content to sing her praises, or, at least, to hear them sung.

Undoubtedly she has a kindly, charitable heart, and can do heroic as well as graceful things. Her famous visitation of the cholera hospitals may doubtless have been done partly for effect, but even in this sense it showed a lofty appreciation of the duties of an Fmpress, and could not have been conceived or carried out by an ignoble nature. When the cholera appeared in Madrid, the fat, licentious woman who then cumbered and disgraced the throne of Spain, fled in dismay from her capital; and this act of peculiarly unwomanlike cowardice told heavily against her and hurried her deeply down into that public contempt which is so fatal to sovereigns. The Empress Eugénie, on the other hand, dignified and served herself and her husband by her fearless exposure of her own life in the cause of humanity and charity. Kindly and generous deeds of hers are constantly reported in Paris, and these things go far in keeping up the superstition of loyalty. Every one knows how gracious and winning the Empress can be in her personal relations with those who approach her. Sometimes her demeanor and actions come into sharp contrast with those of other sovereigns in matters less momentous than the visiting of death-charged hospital wards. I have heard of an American lady who once made some rich and complete collections of specimens of American foliage, collected them at immense labor, arranged them with exquisite taste in two large and beautiful volumes, and sent one as an offering to Queen Victoria, the other to the Empress of the French. From the British court came back the volume itself, with a formal reply from an official intimating that Her Majesty the Queen made it a rule not to accept such gifts. From Paris came a letter of genial, graceful acceptance, written by the Empress Eugénie herself, full of good taste, good feeling, and courteous, lady-like expression. These are small things, but womanly tact and grace seldom have much opportunity of expressing themselves save in just such small things.

The Empress then has of late years faded a little out of political life. I think it may be taken for granted that although she is a quick, clever woman, with talents far beyond the mere inventing of bonnets and petticoats, she is not gifted with any political genius, not qualified to see quickly into the heart of a difficult question, not endowed with the capacity to surmount a great crisis. I have never heard anything which induces me to think that Eugénie's intellect and power would count for much in the chances of the dynasty should Louis Napoleon die while his son is yet a boy. Like Louis Napoleon himself, she was twice misjudged: first when people set her down as an empty-headed coquette, and next when they cried her up as a woman with a genius for government. So far as one may venture to predict, I think she would not prove strong enough for the place, if evil fortune should throw upon her the task of preserving the throne for her boy.

Recent events seem to me to prove that the imperial system is less strong and more shaky than most of us would have supposed six months ago. I for one do fully believe that the recent disturbances are the genuine indications of a profound and bitter popular discontent. I beg the readers of THE GALAXY to be very cautious how they form an estimate of the situation from the correspondence and editorial articles of the London press. If the "Times" believes Bonapartism safe and strong in Paris, I have only to remark that the "Times" believed the same, almost up to the bitter end, of Bonapartism in Mexico. There are very few London journals which can be trusted where the politics of France are concerned. Not that the journals are bribed; everybody knowing anything of the London press knows how absurd the idea of such bribery is; but that all London Philistinism (and Philistinism does a good deal of the writing for the London papers) considers it genteel and respectable, and the right sort of thing generally, to go in for the Empire and sneer at revolution. I have read with no little wonder many of the comments of the London, and indeed some of the New York journals, on Henri Rochefort and his colleagues. One would think that in order to prove a certain revolutionary movement powerless and contemptible, you had only to show that its leaders were themselves contemptible and disreputable persons. Some of the journals here and in London write as if the Empire must be safe because the satire of the "Lanterne" and the "Marseillaise" seems to them coarse and witless, and because they have heard that Henri Rochefort is an insincere man, of doubtful courage and tainted moral character. One longs to ask whether the "Père Duchesne" and the "Vieux Cordelier" were publications fit to be read in the drawing-rooms of virtuous families; whether Mirabeau's private character was quite blameless; whether Marat and Hébert had led reputable lives; whether Camille Desmoulins was habitually received into the highest circles; whether Théroigne de Méricourt was the sort of young woman one's wife would like to invite to tea. The imbecility with which certain journalists go on day after day trying to assure themselves and the world that imperialism has nothing to fear at the hands of a movement led by scurrilous and disreputable men, has something in it at once amusing and provoking. The strength of a revolutionary movement is not exactly to be estimated by the claims of its leaders to carry off the *prix Monthyon* or the Holy Grail. Perhaps if it were to be so estimated, it would be hard to say where the victory should go in the present instance. For the worst of Rochefort's colleagues have never been accused of any profligacies and basenesses so bad as those which universal public opinion ascribes to the leading Bonapartes and some of their most influential supporters. Undoubtedly there is a great deal of scurrility and even worse in the papers conducted by Rochefort. It is not in good taste to go on asking who was the mother of De Morny, who was the father of Walewski; how the present Walewski, Walewski *fils*, comes to be called a count, and who was his mother, and so on; and the direct and libellous attacks on the Empress are utterly indefensible. If one were making up a memoir of Henri Rochefort, or engaged in a debating society's controversy on his character, one would have to admit that he is by no means a model demagogue, a pattern patriot. But one might at the same time hint that, judging by historical precedent, he is probably all the more formidable as a revolutionary leader for that very reason. His literary attacks on the Government are by no means all vulgar, or scurrilous, or contemptible. There was fresh and genuine humor as well as telling satire in the "Lanterne's" early declaration of allegiance to the Napoleons, the purport of which was that, feeling bound to express his devotion to a Napoleon, Rochefort had selected as the object of his loyal homage Napoleon the Second, the sovereign who never coerced the press, or corrupted the Senate, or robbed the nation of its liberty, or exiled its patriots, or carried on a Mexican expedition, or impoverished the country to maintain a gigantic army. But there is one thing certain—that whether Rochefort is witty or not, wise or not, he has waked an echo throughout France and Europe in general which even very wise and undeniably witty enemies of the Empire did not succeed in creating. Nothing he has written will compare in artistic strength of satire or invective with Victor Hugo's "Châtimens" or "Napoléon le Petit." Eugène Pelletan's "Nouvelle Babylone" was a prolonged outpouring of indignant eloquence by a gentleman, a scholar, and a thinker. Rogeard's "Propos de Labienus" was a piece of really fine sarcasm. But not the most celebrated of these attacks on the Empire created anything like the sensation which Rochefort has succeeded in creating by the constant "pegging away" of his bitter, envenomed, and unscrupulous pen. Indeed, the reason is obvious—at least to those who, like me, believe that the great mass of the Parisian population (the army, the officials, and the priests not counted) are heartily sick of Bonapartism, and would get rid of it if they could. Rochefort assails the Empire and the Emperor in a style which they can understand. He is a master of a certain kind of coarse, rasping ridicule, which delights the disaffected *ouvrier;* and he has no scruple about assailing any weak place he can find in his enemy, even though in doing so the heart of a woman has likewise to be wounded. An angry and disaffected populace delights in this kind of thing. The fact that Rochefort has created such a sensation is the best proof in the world that the Parisian populace is angry and disaffected. Rochefort has a happy gift of epithets, which goes a long way with admirers and followers such as his. I doubt whether a whole chapter could have described more accurately and vividly the person, character, and career of Prince Pierre Bonaparte than Rochefort did when he branded him as "a social bandit." Personally, Rochefort is not qualified to be a demagogue in the sense that Danton was a demagogue, and he can make no pretension to be a revolutionary leader of a high class. But he can incite a populace, madden the hearts of disaffected crowds, as the bitter tongue of a shrill woman might do, and as the tongue of a great orator might perhaps fail to do. Doubtless Rochefort and his literary sword-and-buckler men are not strong enough to create a serious disturbance of themselves alone. But if a moment of general uncertainty and unsettlement came, they might prove a dangerous disturbing force. If, for example, there should come a crisis which of itself rendered change of some kind necessary, when all the chances of the future might depend upon a single hour or perhaps a single decisive command, and when it was not certain who had the right, who would assume the responsibility to give the command, then indeed the bitter screams, and jeers, and invectives of these reckless literary bravos might have much to do with the ordering of the situation. If, for example, the Emperor were to die just now, who shall venture to say how much the chances of the Empress and her son might not be affected at that moment of terrible crisis by the pens and the tongues of Rochefort and his followers?

Some time, in the natural course of things, the Empress may expect to have to face such a crisis. It is highly probable that the time will come while yet her boy is young and dependent upon her guardianship and care. Has she won for herself the affection, confidence, and loyalty of France, to such an extent that she could count upon national support? I am convinced that she has not. She is much liked and even loved by those who know her. They have countless anecdotes to tell of her affectionate ways as a mother, of her generosity and kindness as a woman. But although she has outlived many of the early prejudices against her, she is still regarded with distrust and dislike by the older families of France; and I am confident that a large proportion of the working classes in Paris and the large towns delight to believe the worst things that malice.and slander can say to her detriment. The priests and the shopkeepers are probably her best friends; but I am not aware that priests and shopkeepers have ever proved themselves very powerful bulwarks against sudden popular revolution. The generals and the army might of course remain perfectly loyal to her; probably would if they had no time to consider the situation, and there were no favorite rival in the way (if Prince Napoleon, for example, were a brilliant soldier, she would not have a ghost of a chance against him); but it must be remembered that the loyalty of an army is something like the epigrammatic description of the honor of a woman: when there is any deliberation, it is likely to be lost; and the claims of the Empress are certainly not such as absolutely to forbid deliberation and render it impossible. Much of course would depend on the woman herself. There was a moment when Catharine of Russia's unfortunate husband might have carried all before him if he had only seized the chance; and he did not seize it, and so lost all. There was a moment when Catharine might have utterly failed if she had not risen to the height of the crisis, and seized the opportunity with both hands; and she did rise to the height of the crisis, did seize the opportunity, and so won all. Place Eugénie in such a position, and is she a woman to win? Is she in fact a woman of genius? I think not. Nothing that I have ever heard of her—and I have known many who were her intimate friends—has led me to believe her endowed with a quick, strong, commanding intellect. Mentally she seems to be narrow and shallow; in temper she is quick, capricious, full of warm personal affections and almost groundless personal dislikes. I have a strong idea that no matter what the urgency of the .crisis, she would stay to make herself picturesque before taking any public action; and I venture to think she would be guided by counsel only where she happened to have a personal liking for the counsellor. She cannot, I fancy, be trusted at a great crisis to make the fortune of her son. Enough if she do not mar it at such a time.

Political considerations apart, one can only wish her well. Her face is one which ought to smile sweetly and gracefully through history. If fate and France will endure the Bonapartes for another generation or so, there will be some consolation to gallant and romantic souls in the thought that thereby this gracious, queenly woman will be allowed to make a happy end of her brilliant, not untroubled life. Thus far we may, in summing up her career, describe her, first, as a bright, vivacious young coquette, with a dash of the adventuress about her, ranging the world in search of a husband; then a woman suddenly and surprisingly raised to the dazzling rank of an Empress, and a little bewildered by the change; then a splendid leader of the world's fashion, magnificently frivolous and heedless; then a political *intrigante*, the supreme patroness of Ultramontanism; and now a quiet, queenly mother, verging toward that kind of devoteeism in which some satirical person declares that coquetry in France is sure to end. She is not a woman to make any deep impression on history. She has neither gifts enough nor faults enough. As a politician she has been a failure, and perhaps worse than a failure; but she has been fortunate enough to escape from all public responsibility for her mistakes, and may get quietly into history as merely an intelligent, good-natured, and beautiful woman. Posterity will probably see her and appreciate her sufficiently in her portrait by Winterhalter: a name, a vague memory, and a smooth fair picture with bright complexion, shining hair, and noble shoulders, alone carrying down to other times the history of the Third Napoleon's wife. Only great misfortunes could redeem her from this destiny of half oblivion; and history has names enough that are burnt by misfortune into eternal memory, and may well spare hers. One great claim she has to a liberal construction of her character: her personal enemies are those who do not know her well; her intimates seem to be always her friends. She has one good quality, which her husband with all his faults likewise possesses: she has never in her imperial splendor forgotten or neglected or been ashamed of old acquaintances and friends. I have heard scores of anecdotes from people who know her well—I have heard one such anecdote since I began writing this article—which prove her to be entirely above the mean and vulgar weakness of the *parvenu*, who shrinks in her magnificence from any acquaintanceship or association likely to remind her of less brilliant days. Taken on the whole, the Empress Eugénie is better than her fortunes and her surroundings might have made her. She is, I think, a woman much more deserving of respect than Josephine Beauharnais, whose misfortunes, joined with the quiet pathetic dignity of her retirement and her later years, have made the world forget the levities, frivolities, and follies of her earlier life. She has shown a quicker and better appreciation of the duties and difficulties of her station, and the temper of the people among whom she had to live, than was at any time shown by Marie Antoinette. Whether she could ever under the most favorable conditions prove an Anne of Austria may well be doubted; and we must all hope for her own sake that she may never be put to the proof. She has at least made it clear that she is no mere Reine Crinoline; she has shown that she possesses some heart, some courage, and some brains; she has had sense enough to retrieve blunders, and merit enough to live down calumny. The best thing one can hope for her is that she may never again be placed in a position which would tempt and allow her to make political influence the instrument of religious bigotry. The greatest woman her native country ever produced, Isabella of Castile, became with all her virtues and genius a curse to Spain, because of her bigotry and her power; and there was a time when it seemed as if the Empress Eugénie was likely to make for herself an odious fame as the chief patroness of a conspiracy against the religious and political liberties of the south of Europe. Let us hope that in her future career she may be saved from any such temptation, and that she may be kept as much as possible out of all political complications where religion interferes; and if she be thus graced by fortune, it is all but certain that whatever her future years may bring, she will deserve and receive a genial record in the history of France.

THE PRINCE OF WALES.

"IT is now sixteen or seventeen years," says Edmund Burke, in that famous passage to which one is almost ashamed to allude any more, so hackneyed has it been, "since first I saw the Queen of France, then the Dauphiness, at Versailles; and surely never lighted on this orb, which she hardly seemed to touch, a more delightful vision." That glowing, impassioned apostrophe did more to make partisans and admirers for poor Marie Antoinette among all English-speaking peoples, probably for all time, than any charms, or virtues, or misfortunes of the Queen and the woman could have done. I can never of late read or recall to mind the burning words of Burke, without thinking of a certain day in March some seven years ago, when I stood on a platform in Trafalgar Square, London, and saw a bright, beautiful young face smiling and bending to a vast enthusiastic crowd on either side, and I, like everybody else, was literally stricken with admiration of the beauty, the sweetness, and the grace of the Princess Alexandra of Denmark. In truth, I am not in general an enthusiast about princes or princesses; I do not believe that the king's face usually gives grace. In this instance the beauty of the Princess Alexandra had been so noisily trumpeted by literary lacqueys already, that one's natural instinct was to feel disappointed, and to say so, when the Princess herself came in sight. But it was impossible to feel disappointment, or anything but admiration, at the sight of that bright, fair face, so transparent in the clearness of its complexion, so delicate and refined in its outlines, so sweet and gracious in its expression. I think something like the old-fashioned, chivalric, chimerical feeling of personal loyalty must have flamed up for the moment that day in the hearts of many men, who perhaps would have been ashamed to confess that their first experience of such an emotion was due to a passing glimpse of the face of a pretty, tremulous girl.

If ours were days of augury, men might have shuddered at the omens which accompanied the wedding ceremonies of the Prince and Princess of Wales. When Goethe, then a youth, surveyed the preparations for the reception of Marie Antoinette at Strasbourg, on her way to Paris, he observed significantly on the inauspicious fact that in the grand chamber adorned for her coming, the tapestry represented the wedding of Jason and Medea. The civil authorities of London certainly did not greet the fair stranger with any such grisly and ghastly emblazonings; but there were other and even more inauspicious omens offered by chance and the hour. The sky darkened, a dreary wind whistled; presently the rain came down in drenching streams that would not abate. There was a mourning-garb at the wedding—the black dress of the Queen, who would not lay aside her widow's-weeds even for that hour; and the night of the wedding, when the streets of London were illuminated, the crowd was so great that, as on a memorable occasion in the early married life of Marie Antoinette, people were crushed and trampled to death amid the universal jubilation.

Well, we defy augury, with Hamlet. But I think some at least in the crowd who welcomed Alexandra felt a kind of doubt and pity as to her future, which needed no inspiration from omens and superstition. No foreign princess has ever been so popular in England as Alexandra; and assuredly some at least of the affection felt for her springs from a pity which, whether called for or not, is genuine and universal. The last time I saw the Princess of Wales was within a very few days of my leaving England to visit the United States. It was in Drury Lane Theatre, then fitted up as an opera house in consequence of the recent burning of Her Majesty's Theatre. The Prince of Wales, his wife, and one of his sisters were in their box. I had not seen the Princess for some time, and I was painfully impressed with the change which had come over her. Remembering, as it was easy to do, the brightness of her beauty during the early days of her marriage, there was something almost shocking in the altered appearance of her face. It looked wasted and haggard; the complexion, which used to be so dazzlingly fair, had grown dull, and, if I may say so, discolored; and I must be ungracious enough to declare bluntly that, to my eyes at least, there seemed little trace indeed of the beauty of a few years before left in that dimmed and worn countenance. "Only the eyes remained—they would not go." Of course, it must be remembered that the Princess was then only just recovering from a long, painful, and exhausting illness; and she may have—I truly hope she has—since then regained all her brightness and beauty. In any case, it would be unjust indeed to assume that the wasted look of the Princess was to be attributed to domestic unhappiness. But even a very matter-of-fact and unsentimental person, looking at her then, and remembering what she so lately was, might be excused if he fancied that some of the unpropitious omens which surrounded the Princess's marriage had already begun to justify themselves in practical fulfilment.

For even at the time of the marriage of the Prince and Princess there were not wanting prophets of evil who predicted that this royal union would not prove much happier than state-made marriages commonly are. Even then there were stories and reports afloat which ascribed to the Prince habits and tendencies not likely to promote the domestic happiness of a delicate and refined young wife, hardly more than a mere child in years. Indeed, there was already considerable doubt in the public mind as to the personal character of the Prince of Wales. He certainly did not look a very intellectual or refined sort of person even then, and some at least were inclined to think him, as Steerforth says of little Em'ly's lover, "rather a chuckle-headed kind of fellow," to get such a girl. There was, certainly, a breath of serious distrust abroad. On the Prince's coming of age, and again, I think, on the announcement of his approaching marriage, the London daily papers had set themselves to preaching sermons at him; and a very foolish chorus of sermons that was which broke out from all those tongues together. The only marked effect of this outburst of lay-preaching was, I fancy, to impress the public mind with the idea that the Prince was really a very much more dreadful young man than there was any good reason to believe him. People naturally imagined that the writers who poured forth such eloquent, wise, and suggestive admonitions must know a great deal more than they felt disposed to hint at; whereas, I venture to think that, in truth, the majority of the writers were disposed to hint at a great deal more than they knew. For, indeed, almost all that is generally and substantially known of the Prince of Wales has been learned and observed since his marriage.

Still, even before, and long before the marriage, there were ominous rumors. Those that I mention I give simply as rumors—not, indeed, the mere babble of the streets, but as the kind of thing which people told you who professed to know—the talk of the House of Commons, and the clubs, and the fashionable drawing-rooms and smoking-rooms. People told you that the Prince and his father had had many quarrels arising out of the extravagance, dissipation, and wrong-headedness of the former; and there was even a painful and cruel report thus whispered about that the death of Prince Albert was the result of a cold he had taken from walking incautiously in a heavy rain during excitement caused by a quarrel with his son. Stories were told of this and that *amour* and *liaison* in Ireland when the Prince of Wales was with the camp on the Curragh of Kildare; of his excesses when he was a student at the University; of his escapades at many other times and places. Certain actresses of a low class, and other women of a still lower class, were pointed out in London as special favorites of the Prince of Wales. Of course every man of sense knew, first, that stories of this kind must be taken with a large amount of allowance for exaggeration; and, next, that the public must not expect all the virtues of a saint to belong to the early years of a prince of the family of Guelph. In England public opinion, although it has grown much more exacting of late years on the score of decorum than it used to be, is still disposed to look over without censure a good deal of extravagance and dissipation in young and unmarried men, especially if they be men of rank. Therefore, if the rumors which attended the early career of the Prince of Wales had not followed him into his married years, the world would soon have forgotten all about his youthful indiscretions. But it became a serious question for the whole nation when it began to be whispered everywhere that the Prince was growing worse instead of better during his married life, and when to the suspicion that he was wasting his own youth and his own credit came to be added the belief that he was neglecting and injuring the young and beautiful woman whom state reasons had assigned to him as a wife. In good truth, it is really a question of public and historical interest whether the Queen of England is likely to be succeeded by an Albert the Good or another George the Fourth; and I am not therefore inviting the readers of THE GALAXY to descend to the useless discussion of a mere piece of idle court scandal when I ask them to consider with me the probabilities of the future from such survey as we can take of the aspects of the present.

Those who saw the Prince of Wales when he visited this country, would surely fail to recognize the slender, fair-haired, rather graceful youth of that day in the heavy, fat, stolid, prematurely bald, elderly-young-man of this. It would not be easy to see in any assembly a more stupid-looking man than the Prince of Wales is now. On horseback he shows to best advantage. He rides well, and the pleasure he takes in riding lends something of animation to his usually inexpressive face. But when his eyes and features lapse into their habitual condition of indolent, good-natured, stolid repose, all light of intellect seems to have been banished. The outline of the head and face, and the general expression, seemed to me of late to be growing every day more and more like the head and face of George the Third. Anybody who may happen to have a shilling or half-crown of George the Third's time, can see on the coin a very fair presentment of the countenance of the present heir-apparent of the English throne. Whether the Prince of Wales resembles George the Fourth in character and tastes or not, he certainly does not resemble him in face. Even a court sycophant could not pretend to see beauty or grace in our present Prince.

I think that to the eye of the cynic or the satirist the Prince of Wales shows to greatest advantage when he sits in his box at an advanced hour of some rather heavy classic opera, or has to endure a long succession of speeches at a formal public dinner. The heavy head droops, the heavy jaws hang, the languid eyes close, the heir-apparent sinks into a doze. Loyalty itself can see nothing dignified or kingly in him then. I have watched him thus as he sat in his box during some high-class, and to him, doubtless, very heavy performance at the

Italian opera, and have thought that at times he might remind irreverent and disloyal observers of Pickwick's immortal fat boy. I have sometimes observed that his little dozes appeared to afford innocent amusement to his sisters, if any of them happened to be in the box; and occasionally one of the Princesses would playfully poke her slumbering brother in the princely ribs, and the Heir of all the Ages would open his eyes and smile languidly, and try to look at the stage and listen to the music; and then, after a while, the heavy head would sink once more on the vast expanse of shirt-front in which the Prince seems to delight, and the fat boy would go to sleep again. But this would only happen at certain performances. There were times when the Prince had eyes and ears open and attentive, even in the opera house. His tastes in general, however, are not for high art in music or the drama. He is very fond of the little theatres where the vivacious blondes display their unconcealed attractions. There are, as everybody knows, several minor theatres in London where the audience, or, I should say more properly, the spectators, will be found to consist chiefly of men, while, on the other hand, the performers are chiefly women. These are the temples of the leg drama. "*Pièce aux jambes? Pièce aux cuisses!*" indignantly exclaims Eugene Pelletan, denouncing such performances in his "Nouvelle Babylone"; and he goes on to add some cumulative illustrations which I omit. Well, the Prince of Wales loves the *pièce aux jambes*, and the theatres where it flourishes. He constantly visits theatres at which his wife and sisters are never seen, and in which it would be idle to deny that there are actresses who have made themselves conspicuous objects of popular scandal.

Now, I am far from saying that this necessarily implies anything worse than a low taste on the part of the Prince of Wales. But there are stations in life which render private bad taste a public sin. In London, of late, there has been a just outcry against a certain kind of theatrical performance. It is held to be demoralizing and degrading that the stage should be made simply a show-place for the exhibition of half-naked women, for the audacious display of legs and bosoms. Now, I beg to say for myself that I have entire faith in the dramatic as in every other art; that I believe it always when truthfully pursued vindicates itself, and that I think any costume which the true and legitimate needs of the drama require is fitting, proper, and modest. I regard the ballet, in its place, as a graceful and delightful entertainment; and I do not believe that any healthy and pure mind ought to be offended by the kind of costume which the dance requires. But artists and moralists in London alike objected, and justly objected, to performances the whole purpose, and business, and attraction of which was the exhibition of a crowd of girls as nearly naked as they could venture to show themselves in public.

Now this was undoubtedly the kind of exhibition which the Prince of Wales especially favored and patronized. Night after night, even during the long and lamentable illness of his young wife, he visited such theatres, and gazed upon "those prodigies of myriad nakednesses." Likewise did he much delight in the performances of Schneider—that high priestess of the obscene, rich with the spoils of princes. I say emphatically that there were actions, gestures, *bouffonneries* performed amid peals of laughter and thunders of applause by this fat Faustina in the St. James's Theatre, London, which were only fit to have gladdened the revels of Sodom and Gomorrah. And this woman was, artistically at least, the prime favorite of the Prince of Wales; and when his brother, the Duke of Edinburgh, reached England for the first time after his escape from the Fenian bullet in Sydney, the *par nobile fratrum* celebrated the auspicious event by hastening to the theatre where Schneider kicked and wriggled and helped out the point of lascivious songs by a running accompaniment of obscene gestures.

So much at least has to be said against the Prince of Wales, and cannot be gainsaid. All that he could do by countenance and patronage to encourage a debauching and degrading style of theatric entertainment, he has done. He is said to be fond of the singing of the vulgar and low buffoons of the music-halls, and to have had such persons brought specially to his residence, Marlborough House, to sing for him. I have been assured of this often by persons who professed to know; but I do not know anything of it myself, nor is it indeed a matter of any importance. The other facts are known to everybody who reads the London papers. The manager or manageress of a theatre takes good care to announce in the journals when a visit from the Prince of Wales has taken place, and we all thus come to know how many times a week the little theatric temples of nakedness have been honored by his presence.

Am I attaching too much importance to such matters as this? I think not. The social influence and moral example of a royal personage in England are now almost the only agencies by which the royal personage can affect us for good or evil. I hold that no man thoughtful or prudent enough, no matter what his morals, to be fit to occupy the position assigned to the Prince of Wales, would be guilty of lending his public and constant patronage to such exhibitions and amusements as those which he especially patronizes. Moreover, the Prince has often shown a disregard, either cynical or stupid—probably the latter—for public opinion, a heedlessness of public scandal, in other matters as well. He has made çompanionship for himself among young noblemen conspicuous for their debauchery. At a time, not very long ago, when the Divorce Court was occupied with the hearing of a scandalous cause, in which a certain young duke figured most prominently and disgracefully, this young duke was daily and nightly to be seen the close companion of the Prince of Wales.

Let me touch upon another subject, of a somewhat delicate nature. I have said that there were times when our Prince was always wide awake at the opera house. There is a certain brilliant and capricious little singer whom all England and Germany much admire, and who in certain operatic parts has, I think, no rival. Now, public scandal said that the Prince of Wales greatly admired this lady, and paid her the most marked attentions. Public scandal, indeed, said a great deal more. I hasten to record my conviction that, so far as the fair artiste was concerned, the scandal was wholly unfounded, and that she is a woman of pure character and honor. But the Prince was credited with a special admiration for her; and I am sure the Prince's father under such circumstances would have taken good care to lend no foundation, afford no excuse, for scandal to rest upon. Now, I speak of what I have myself observed when I say that the Prince of Wales, whenever he had an opportunity, always demeaned himself as if he really desired to give the public good reason for believing the scandal, or as if he was too far gone in infatuation to be able to govern his actions. For he was always at the opera when this lady sang; and he always conducted himself as if he wished to blazon to the world his ostentatious and demonstrative admiration. When the prima donna went off the stage, the Prince disappeared from his box; when she came on the stage again, he returned to his seat; he lingered behind all his party at the end, that he might give the last note of applause to the disappearing singer; he made a more pertinacious show of his enthusiasm than even the military admirer of Miss Snevellicci was accustomed to do. Now, all this may have been only stolidity or silliness, and may not have denoted anything like cynicism or coarse disdain of public opinion ; but whatever it indicated, it certainly did not, I think, testify to the existence of qualities likely to be found admirable or desirable in the heir to a throne.

Of the truth or falsehood of the private scandals in general circulation concerning the Prince of Wales I know nothing whatever. But everybody in England is aware that such stories are told, and can name and point out this or that titled lady as the heroine of each particular story. It need hardly be said that when a man acquires the sort of reputation which attaches to the Prince of Wales, nothing could be more unjust or unreasonable than to accept, without some very strong ground of belief, any story which couples his name with that of any woman belonging to the society in which he moves. Obviously, it would be enough, in the eyes of an English crowd, that the Prince should now pay any friendly attention to any handsome duchess or countess in order to convert her into an object of scandal. I am myself morally convinced that some of the titled ladies who are broadly and persistently set down by British gossip as mistresses of the Prince of Wales are as innocent of such a charge as if they had never been within a thousand miles of a court. But the Prince is a little unlucky wherever he goes, for scandal appears to pursue him as Horace's black care follows the horseman. When the Prince of Wales happens to be in Paris, he seems to be surrounded at once by the same atmosphere of suspicion and evil report. Some two years ago I chanced to be in Paris at the time the Prince was there, and I can answer for it that observers who had never heard or read of the common gossip of London formed the same impression of his general character that the public of London had already adopted. The Prince was then paying special attention to a brilliant and beautiful lady moving in the court circles of the French capital, a lady who had but very recently distinguished herself by appearing at one of the fancy balls of the Tuileries in the character of the Archangel Michael or Raphael—it does not much matter which—and attired in a costume which left the company no possibility of doubting the symmetry of her limbs and the general shapeliness of her person. Malicious satirists circulated thereupon an announcement that the lady was to appear at the next fancy ball as "La Source," the beautiful naked nymph so exquisitely painted by Ingres. This lady received the special attentions of the Prince of Wales. He followed her, people said, like her shadow ; and a smart pun was soon in circulation, which I refrain from giving because it contrives ingeniously to blend with his name the name of the lady in question, and I am not writing a scandalous chronicle. This was the time when the Prince made his royal mother so very angry by attending the Chantilly races on a Sunday. When he came back to London he had to take part in some public ceremonial—I forget now what it was—at which the Queen had consented to be present. Her Majesty was present, and I have been assured by a friend who stood quite near that a sort of little scene was enacted which much embarrassed those who had to take part in the official pageantry of the occasion. Up came the Prince, who had travelled in hot haste from Paris, and with a somewhat abashed and sheepish air approached his royal mother. She looked at him angrily, and turned away. The Duke of Cambridge, her cousin, made an awkward effort to mend matters by bringing up the Prince again, and with the action of a friendly and deprecating intercessor presenting the delinquent. This time, I am assured, the Queen, with determined and angry gestures, and some words spoken in a low tone, repelled intercessor and offender at once ; and the Prince of Wales retired before the threatened storm. The Duke of Edinburgh, who had been lingering a little in the background—he, too, had just come from Paris, and he had been to Chantilly—anxious to see what kind of reception would be accorded to his brother, thought, apparently, that he had seen enough to warrant him in keeping himself at a modest distance on that occasion, and not encountering the terrors of what Thackeray, in "The Rose and the Ring," describes as "the royal eye."

I have little doubt that Queen Victoria is a somewhat rigorous and exacting mother, and I should be far from accepting her frown as decisive with regard to the delinquencies of one of her sons. Cigar-smoking alone would probably be accounted by the Queen a sin hardly allowing of pardon. Her husband, Prince Albert, was a man so pure of life, so free from nearly all the positive errors of manhood, so remarkably endowed with at least all the negative virtues, that his companionship might easily have spoiled her for the toleration of natures less calm and orderly. I suspect that the Queen is one of that class of thoroughly good women who, from mere lack of wide sympathies and genial toleration, are not qualified to deal to the best advantage with children who show a little inclination for irregularity and self-indulgence. Nor do I believe that the Prince of Wales is the wicked and brutal profligate that common libel makes him out. The shocking story which one sees so often alluded to in the London correspondence of certain American papers, and which attributes the long illness of the Princess of Wales to the misconduct of her husband, I believe to be utterly unfounded and unjustifiable. One of the London medical journals, the "Lancet" I think it was, had the courage to refer directly to this monstrous statement, and to give it an emphatic and authoritative refutation. If the worst things said of the Prince of Wales with any appearance of foundation were true, it is certain that he would still not be any worse than many other European princes and sovereigns. I have never heard anything said of the Prince of Wales half so bad as the stories which are believed everywhere in Paris of the enormous profligacies of Prince Napoleon; and it would be hardly possible for charity itself to doubt that up to a very recent period the private life of the Emperor of the French himself was stained with frequent and reckless dissipation. Those who were in Vienna anywhere about the autumn of 1866, will remember the stories which were told about the fatal results of the exalted military command given by the imperial will to certain favored generals, and the kind of influence by which those generals had acquired imperial favor. Common report certainly describes the Empress of Austria as being no happier in her domestic relations than the Princess of Wales. Everybody knows what Victor Emanuel's private character is, and what sort of hopeful youth is his eldest son, Umberto. Therefore, the Prince of Wales could doubtless plead that he is no worse than his neighbors; and even in his own family he might point to other members no better than himself. The Duke of Cambridge, for instance, has often been accused of profligacy and profligate favoritism. I wish I could venture to repeat here, for the sake of the genuine wit and keen satire of it, a certain epigram in Latin, composed by an English military officer, to describe the influence which brought about the sudden and remarkable promotion of another officer who was not believed to be personally quite deserving of the rank conferred on him by the Duke of Cambridge, commander-in-chief of the British army. But the position of the Prince of Wales is very different from that of the Duke of Cambridge, and he has to face a public opinion quite unlike that which surrounds Prince Napoleon or the Emperor of the French. People in France are not inclined to make any very serious complaint about the amours of a prince, or even of an emperor. I do not venture to say that there is much more of actual immorality in Paris than in London; but, assuredly, a man may, without harm to his public and political influence, acknowledge an amount of immorality in Paris which would be utterly fatal to his credit and reputation in London. Moreover, some of the illustrious profligates I have mentioned are distinguished by other qualities as well as profligacy; but I cannot say that I have ever heard any positively good quality, either of heart or intellect, ascribed to the Prince of Wales.

Unless his face, his head, his manners in public, and the tastes he so conspicuously manifests wholly belie him, the heir to the British throne is a remarkably dull young man. He cannot even deliver with any decent imitation of intelligence the little speeches which Arthur Helps or somebody else usually gets up for him when the exigencies of the situation compel the Prince to make a speech in public. He is reputed to be parsimonious even in his pleasures, and has managed to get himself deeply into debt without being supposed to have wasted any of his substance in obedience to a generous impulse. The Prince inherited a splendid property. His prudent father had looked well after the revenues of the duchy of Cornwall, which is the appanage of the Prince of Wales (even in some very dingy parts of London you may if you hire a house find that you have the Prince of Wales for a landlord), and the property of the heir must have been raised to its very highest value. Yet it is notorions that a very few years after he had attained his majority, Albert Edward had contrived to get deeply immersed in debt. There was for some time a scheme in contemplation to apply to Parliament for an addition to the huge allowance made to the Prince of Wales; and the "Times" and other newspapers were always urging the fact that the Queen left the Prince to perform nearly all her social duties for her, as a reason why the nation ought to award him an augmented income. It puzzles people in London, who read the papers and who study, as most Britons do, the occupations and pastimes of royalty, to know where the lavish and regal hospitalities take place which the Prince of Wales is supposed to dispense on behalf of his mother. However, the project for appealing to the generosity of Parliament seems to have been put aside or to have fallen through—I have read somewhere that the Queen herself has agreed to increase her son's allowance out of her own ample and well-hoarded purse—and the English public are not likely to be treated to any Parliamentary debate on the subject just yet. But this much is certain, that the same almost universal rumor which attributes coarse and dissipated habits to the Prince of Wales attributes to him likewise a mean and stingy parsimony where aught save his own pleasure is concerned; and even there, if by any possibility the pleasure can be obtained without superfluous cost.

This then is the character which the son of the Queen of England bears, in the estimation of the vast majority of his mother's subjects. Almost any and every one you meet in London will tell you, as something beyond doubt, that the Prince of Wales is dull, stingy, coarse, and profligate. As for the anecdotes which are told of his habits and tastes by the artists and officials of the theatres which he frequents, I might fairly leave them out of the question, because most of them that I have heard seem to me obvious improbabilities and exaggerations. They have nevertheless a certain value in helping us to a sort of historical estimate of the Prince's character. Half the stories told of the humors and debaucheries of Sheridan and Fox are doubtless inventions or exaggerations; but we are quite safe in assuming that the persons of whom such stories abound were not frugal, temperate, and orderly men. If the Prince of Wales is not a young man of dissipated habits, then a phenomenon is exhibited in his case which is, I fancy, without any parallel in history—the phenomenon of a whole watchful nation, studying the character and habits of one whose position compels him to live as in a house of glass, and coming, after years of observation, to a conclusion at once unanimous and erroneous. But were it proved beyond the remotest possibility of doubt that the Prince is personally chaste as a Joseph, temperate as Father Mathew, tender to his wife as the elder Hamlet, attached to his mother as Hamlet the younger, it would still remain a fact indisputable to all of us in London, who have eyes to see and ears to hear, that the Prince is addicted to vulgar amusements; that he patronizes indecent exhibitions; that he is given to the companionship of profligate men, and lends his helping hand to the success and the popularity of immoral and lascivious women.

What is to be the effect upon England of the reign of the Prince of Wales? Will England and her statesmen endure the rule of a profligate sovereign? No country can have undergone in equal time a greater revolution in public taste and sentiment at least, if not in morals, than England has since the time of George the Fourth. No genius, no eloquence, no political wisdom or merits could now induce the English people to put up with the open and undisguised excesses of a Fox; nor could any English statesman of the rank of Fox be found now who would condescend to pander to the vices of a George the Fourth. Thirty years of decorum in the Court, the Parliament, and the press have created a public feeling in England which will not long bear to be too openly offended by any one. But, although I may seem at first to be enunciating a paradox, I must say that all this is rather in favor of the chances of the Prince of Wales than against them. It will take so small a sacrifice on his part to satisfy everybody, that only the very extravagance of folly could lead him long astray on any unsatisfactory course, when once he has become directly responsible to the nation. We are not exacting in England as regards the private conduct of our great people. We only ask them to be publicly decorous. Everywhere in English society there is a quite unconscious, naive sort of Pharisaism, the unavowed but actual principle of which is that it matters very little if a man does the wrong thing, provided he publicly acts and says the right thing. I am perfectly satisfied that the great bulk of respectable and Philistine society in England would regard Robert Dale Owen, with his pure life and his views on the question of divorce, as a far more objectionable person than the veriest profligate who did evil stealthily, and professed to maintain the theory of a rigid marriage bond. The Prince of Wales will therefore need very little actual improvement in his way of life, in order to be all that his future subjects will expect, or care to ask. No one wants the Prince to be a man of ability; no one wishes him to be a good speaker. If Albert Edward were to rise in the House of Lords some night, and deliver a powerful and eloquent speech, as Prince Napoleon has often done in the French Senate, the English public would be not only surprised but shocked. Such a feat performed by a Prince would seem almost as much out of place, as if he were to follow the example of Caligula or Nero and exhibit himself in the arena as a gladiator. Of course the idea of the Prince of Wales fulminating against the policy of the Crown and the Government, after the fashion of Prince Napoleon, would be simply intolerable to the British mind of to-day—a thing so outrageous as indeed to be practically inconceivable. The Prince of Wales's part during the coming years, whether as first subject or as ruler, is as easy as could well be assigned to man. It is the very reverse of Bottom's; it is to avoid all roaring. He must be decorous, and we will put up with any degree of dulness; he must be decent, and we will all agree to know nothing of any private compensations wherewith he may repay himself for public propriety. All the influences of English statesmanship, rank, religion, journalism, patriotism, Philistinism, and flunkeyism, will instinctively combine to screen the throne against scandal, if only the throne will consent to allow of the possibility of such a protection. I have hardly ever known an Englishman whose hostility to monarchical institutions went so far that he would not be ready to say, "We have got a monarchy; let us try to make the best we can of it." Therefore the Prince of Wales must be the very Marplot or L'Etourdi of princes, if he cannot contrive to make himself endurable to a people who will bear so much rather than be at the trouble of a change. Of course it is possible that his faults may become grosser and more unmanageable with years (indeed, he is quite old enough already to have sown his wild oats long since); and it would be a hard trial upon decorous English statesmen and the English public to endure an openly profligate King. Yet even that nuisance I think would be endured for one lifetime at all events, rather than encounter the danger and trouble of any organic change.

So long as the Prince of Wales keeps out of politics, he may hold his place well enough; the England of to-day could far better endure even a George the Fourth than a George the Third. I have little doubt that the Prince of Wales, when he comes to be King, will be discreet in this matter at least. He has never indeed shown any particular interest in political affairs, so far as I have heard. He seems to care little or nothing about the contests of parties. Some three or four years ago, at the time of the celebrated Adullamite secession from the Liberal party, there was some grumbling among Radicals because it was reported that the Prince of Wales had expressed a wish to make the acquaintance of Robert Lowe, the brilliant, eccentric chief of the secession, and had had Lowe brought to him and spent a long time talking with him; and it was urged that this was done by the Prince to mark his approval of the Adullamites and his dislike of radicalism. But just about the very same time the Prince took some trouble to make the acquaintance of John Bright, and paid what might have been considered very flattering attentions to the great popular tribune. The Prince has more than once visited the Pope, and he has likewise more than once visited Garibaldi. Indeed, he seems to have a harmless liking for knowing personally all people who are talked about; and I fancy he hunted up the Pope, and Garibaldi, and John Bright, and Robert Lowe, just as he sends for Mr. Toole the comic actor, or Blondin, or Chang the giant. Nothing can be safer and better for the Prince in the future than to keep to this wholesome indifference to politics. In England we could stand any length of the reign of King Log. I shall not venture to conjecture what might happen if the Prince of Wales were to develop a perverse inclination to "meddle and muddle" in politics, because I think such a thing highly improbable. My impression is, on the whole, that things will go on under the reign of the next sovereign in England very much as they have been going on under the present; that the Prince of Wales will be induced to pay a little more attention to decorum and public propriety than he has hitherto done; and that the people of England will laugh at him and cheer for him, talk scandal about him and sing God save him, and finally endure him, on somewhat the same principle as that which induces the New York public to endure overcrowded street-cars and miserable postal arrangements—just because it is less trouble to each individual to put up with his share of a defective institution, than to go out of his way for the purpose of endeavoring to organize any combination to get rid of it.

THE KING OF PRUSSIA.

RONSARD, in one of his songs addressed to his mistress, tells her that in her declining years she will be able to boast that "When I was young a poet sang of me." In a less romantic spirit the writer of this article may boast in old age, should he attain to such blest condition, that "When I was young a king spoke to me." That was the only king or sovereign of any kind with whom I ever exchanged a word, and therefore I may perhaps be allowed to be proud of the occasion and reluctant to let it sleep in oblivion. The king was William, King of Prussia, and the occasion of my being spoken to by a sovereign was when I, with some other journalists, was formally presented to King William after his coronation, and listened to a word or two of commonplace, good-humored courtesy.

The coronation of King William took place, as many readers of THE GALAXY are probably aware, in the old historic town of Königsberg, on the extreme northeastern frontier of Prussia, a town standing on one of the inlets of the Baltic Sea, where once the Teutonic Knights, mentioned by Chaucer, were powerful. Carlyle's "Frederick the Great" had brought Königsberg prominently before the eyes and minds of English-speaking readers, just previously to the ceremony in which King William was the most conspicuous performer. It is the city where Immanuel Kant passed his long and fruitful life, and which he never quitted. It is a picturesque city in its way, although not to be compared with its neighbor Dantzic. It is a city of canals and streams, and many bridges, and quaint, narrow, crooked streets, wherein are frequent long-bearded and gabardined Jews, and where Hebrew inscriptions are seen over many shop-windows and on various door-plates. In its centre the city is domineered over by a Schloss, or castle-palace, and it was in the chapel of this palace that the ceremony of coronation took place, which provoked at the time so many sharp criticisms and so much of popular ridicule.

The first time I saw the King was when he rode in procession through the ancient city, some two or three days before the performance of the coronation. He seemed a fine, dignified, handsome, somewhat bluff old man—he was then sixty-four or sixty-five years of age—with gray hair and gray moustache, and an expression which, if it did not denote intellectual power, had much of cheerful strength and the charm of a certain kind of frank manhood about it. He rode well—riding is one of the accomplishments in which kings almost always excel—and his military costume became him. Certainly no one was just then disposed to be very enthusiastic about him, but every one was inclined to make the best of the sovereign and the situation; to forget the past and look hopefully into the future. The manner in which the coronation ceremony was conducted, and the speech which the King delivered soon after it, produced a terrible shock of disappointment; for in each the King manifested that he understood the crown to be a gift not from his people, but from heaven. To me the ceremonies in the chapel, splendid and picturesque as was the *mise en scène*, appeared absurd and even ridiculous. The King, bedizened in a regal costume which suggested Drury Lane or Niblo's Garden, lifting a crown from off the altar (was it, by the way, an altar ?) and, without intervention of human aid other than his own hands, placing it upon his head, to signify that he had his crown from heaven, not from man; then putting another crown upon the head of his wife, to show that *she* derived her dignities from him; and then turning round and brandishing a gigantic sword, as symbolical of his readiness to defend his State and people—all this seemed to me too suggestive of the *opéra comique* to suit the simple dignity of the handsome old soldier. Far better and nobler did he look in his military uniform and with his spiked helmet, as he sat on his horse in the streets, than when, arrayed in crimson velvet cloak and other such stage paraphernalia of conventional royalty, he stood in the castle chapel, the central figure in a ceremonial of mediæval splendor and worse than mediæval tediousness.

But the King's face, bearing, and manner, as I saw him in Königsberg, and immediately afterwards in Berlin, agreeably disappointed me. It was one of the best faces to be seen among all the throng at banquet and ball and pageant during those days of gorgeous and heavy ceremonial. At the coronation performances there were two other personages who may be said to have divided public curiosity and interest with the King. One was the illustrious Meyerbeer, who composed and conducted the coronation ode, which thus became almost his swan-song, his latest notes before death. The other was a man whose name has lately again divided attention with that of the King of Prussia—Marshal MacMahon, Duke of Magenta. MacMahon was sent to represent the Emperor of the French at the coronation, and he was then almost fresh from the glory of his Lombardy battles. There was great curiosity among the Königsberg public to get a glimpse of this military hero; and although even Prussians could hardly be supposed to take delight in a fame acquired at the expense of other Germans, I remember being much struck by the quiet, candid good-humor with which people acknowledged that he had beaten their countrymen. There was, indeed, a little vexation and anger felt when some of the representatives of Posen, the Prussian Poland, cheered somewhat too significantly for MacMahon as he drove in his carriage from the palace. The Prussians generally felt annoyed that the Poles should have thus publicly and ostentatiously demonstrated their sympathy with France and their admiration of the French general who had defeated a German army. But except for this little ebullition of feeling, natural enough on both sides, MacMahon was a popular figure at the King's coronation; and before the ceremonies were over, the King himself had become anything but popular. The foreigners liked him for the most part because his manners were plain, frank, hearty, and agreeable, and to the foreigners it was a matter of little consequence what he said or did in the accepting of his crown. But the Germans winced under his blunt repudiation of the principle of popular sovereignty, and in the minds of some alarmists painful and odious memories began to revive and to transform themselves into terrible omens for the future.

For this pleasant, genial, gray-haired man, whose smile had so much of honest frankness and even a certain simple sweetness about it, had a grim and blood-stained history behind him. Not Napoleon the Third himself bore a more ominous record when he ascended the throne. The blood of the Berliners was purple on those hands which now gave so kindly and cheery a welcome to all comers. The revolutionists of Baden held in bitter hate the stern prince who was so unscrupulous in his mode of crushing out popular agitation. From Cologne to Königsberg, from Hamburg to Trieste, all Germans had for years had reason only too strong to regard William Prince of Prussia as the most resolute and relentless enemy of popular liberty. When the Pope was inspiring the hearts of freemen and patriots everywhere in Europe with sudden and splendid hopes doomed to speedy disappointment, the Prince of Prussia was execrated with the Hapsburgs, the Bourbons, and the Romanoffs. The one on.y thing commonly said in his favor was that he was honest and would keep his word. The late Earl of Clarendon, one of the most incautious and blundering of diplomatists (whom after his death the English newspapers have been eulogizing as a very sage and prince of statesmen), embodied this opinion sharply in a few words which he spoke to a friend of mine in Königsberg. Clarendon represented Queen Victoria at the coronation ceremonies, and my friend happened in conversation with him to be expressing a highly disparaging opinion of the King of Prussia. "There is just this to be said of him," the British Envoy remarked aloud in the centre of a somewhat miscellaneous group of listeners—"he is an honest man and a man of his word; he is not a Corsican conspirator."

Yes, this was and is the character of the King of Prussia. In good and evil he kept his word. You might trust him to do as he had said. During the greater part of his life the things he promised to do and did were not such as free men could approve. He set out in life with a genuine detestation of liberal principles and of anything that suggested popular revolution. William of Prussia is certainly not a man of intellect or broad intelligence or flexibility of mind. He would be in private life a respectable, steady, rather dull sort of man, honest as the sun, just as likely to go wrong as right in his opinions, perhaps indeed a shade more likely to go wrong than right, and sure to be doggedly obstinate in any opinion which he conceived to be founded on a principle. Horror of revolution was naturally his earliest public sentiment. He was one of the princes who entered Paris in 1815 with the allied sovereigns when they came to stamp out Bonapartism; and he seemed to have gone on to late manhood with the conviction that the mission of honest kings was to prevent popular agitation from threatening the divine right of the throne. Naturally enough, a man of such a character, whose chief merits were steadfastness and honesty, was much disgusted by the vacillation, the weakness, the half-unconscious deceitfulness of his brother, the late Frederick William. Poor Frederick William! well-meaning, ill-doing dreamer, "wind-changing" as Warwick, a sort of René of Anjou placed in a responsible position and cast into a stormy age. What blighted hopes and bloody streets were justly laid to his charge—to the charge of him who asked nothing better than to be able to oblige everybody and make all his people happy! Frederick William loved poetry and poets in a feeble, *dilettante* sort of way. He liked, one might say, to be thought to like the Muses and the Graces. He used to insist upon Tieck the poet reading aloud his new compositions to the royal circle of evenings; and when the bard began to read the King would immediately fall asleep, and nod until he nodded himself into wakefulness again; and then he would start up and say, "Bravo, Tieck! Delightful, Tieck! Go on reading, Tieck!" and then to sleep again. He liked in this sort of fashion the poetic and sentimental aspects of revolution, and he dandled popular movements on his royal knee until they became too demonstrative and frightened him, and then he shook them off and shrieked for the aid of his strong-nerved brother. One day Frederick William would be all for popular government and representative monarchy, and what not; the next day he became alarmed and receded, and was eager to crush the hopes he had himself awakened. He was always breaking his word to his people and his country, and yet he was not personally an untruthful man like English Charles the First. In private life he would have been amiable, respectable, gently æsthetical and sentimental; placed in a position of responsibility amid the seething passions and conflicting political currents of 1848, he proved himself a very dastard and caitiff. Germany could hardly have had upon the throne of Prussia a worse man for such a crisis. He was unlucky in every way; for his vacillation drew on him the repute of hypocrisy, and his whimsical excitable manners procured for him the reproach of intemperance. A sincerely pious man in his way, he was almost universally set down as a hypocrite; a sober man who only drank wine medicinally on the order of his physicians, he was favored throughout Europe with the nickname of "King Clicquot." His utter imbecility before and after the massacre of those whom he called his "beloved Berliners," made him more detestable to Berlin than was his blunt and stern brother, the present King, who gave with his own lips the orders which opened fire on the population. A more unkingly figure than that of poor, weak, well-intentioned, sentimental, lachrymose Frederick William, never in our days at least has been seen under a royal canopy.

It was but natural that such a character or no-character as this should disgust his brother and successor, the present King. Frederick William, as everybody knows, had no son to succeed him. The stout-hearted William would have liked his brother and sovereign to be one thing or the other; a despot of course he would have preferred, but he desired consistency and steadfastness on whatever side. William, it must be owned, was for many years a downright stupid, despotic old feudalist. At one of his brother's councils he flung his sword upon the table and vowed that he would rather appeal to that weapon than consent to rule over a people who dared to claim the right of voting their own taxes. He appears to have had the sincere stupid faith that Heaven directly tells or teaches kings how to rule, and that a king fails in his religious duty who takes counsel of aught save his own convictions. Perhaps a good many people in lowlier life are like William of Prussia in this respect. He certainly was not the only person in our time who habitually accepted his own likings and dislikings as the appointed ordinances of Heaven. In my own circle of acquaintance I think I have known such individuals.

Thus William of Prussia strode through life sword in hand menacing and, where he could, suppressing popular movement. Yet he was saved from utter detestation by the admitted integrity of his character—a virtue so dear to Germans, that for its sake they will pardon harshness and sometimes even stupidity. People disliked or dreaded him, but they despised his brother. There was a certain simplicity, too, always seen in William's mode of living which pleased the country. There was no affectation about him; he was almost as much of a plain, unpretending soldier as General Grant himself. Since he became King, anybody passing along the famous Unter den Linden might see the white-haired, simple old man writing or reading at the window of his palace. He was in this respect a sort of military Louis Philippe; a Louis Philippe with a strong purpose and without any craft. Therefore, when the death of his brother in 1861 called him to the throne, he found a people anxious to give him credit for every good quality and good purpose, willing to forget the past and look hopefully into the coming time. They only smiled at his renewal of the coronation ceremonies at Königsberg, believing that the old soldier thought there was something of a religious principle somehow mixed up in them, and that it was the imaginary piety, not the substantial pomp, which commended to his mind so gorgeous and costly an anachronism. After the coronation ceremonies, however, came back the old unpopularity. The King, people said, has learned nothing and forgotten nothing since he was Prince of Prussia. Every act he did after his accession to the crown seemed only more and more to confirm this impression. It was, I think, about this time that the celebrated "Diary" of Varnhagen von Ense was published by the niece of the deceased diplomatist; a diary full in itself of the most piquant interest, but made yet more piquant and interesting by the bitter and foolish persecution with which the King's officials endeavored to suppress the work and punish its publishers. I have not read or even seen the book for years, but the impression it made on me is almost as distinct just now as it was when I laid down the last of its many and vivacious volumes.

Varnhagen von Ense was a bitter creature, and the pen with which he wrote his diary seems to have been dipped in gall of special acridity. The diary goes over many years of Berlin court life, and the present King of Prussia is one of its central figures. The author does not seem to have had much respect for anybody; and King William was evidently an object of his particular detestation. All the doings of the days of 1848 are recorded or commented on, and the pages are interspersed with notices of the sharp ungenial things said by one royal personage of another. If the late Frederick William chose to say an ill-natured thing of Queen Victoria of England, down goes the remark in Varnhagen's pages, and it is chronicled for the perusal of all the world. We learn from the book that the present King of Prussia does not live on the most genial terms with his wife Augusta; that Augusta has rather a marked inclination towards Liberalism, and would find nothing more pleasant than a little coquetry with Revolution. Varnhagen intimates that the illustrious lady loved lions and novelties of any kind, and that at the time he writes she would have been particularly glad to make the acquaintance of Louis Blanc; and he more than hints at a decided inclination on her part to *porter le pantalon*—an inclination which her husband was not at all likely to gratify, consciously at least. Of the progressive wife Varnhagen speaks with no whit more respect than of the reactionary husband; and indeed he seems to look with irreverent and cynical eyes on everything royal that comes under his observation. Throughout the whole of the diary, the figure of the present King comes out consistently and distinctly. William is always the blunt, dull, wrong-headed, I might almost say pig-headed soldier-fanatic, who will do and suffer and make others do and suffer anything, in a cause which he believes to be right. With all Varnhagen von Ense's bitterness and scorn, he gives us no worse idea of King William than just this. But judging from the expression of the King's face, from his manner, and from what I have heard of him in Berlin and elsewhere, I should say there was a good deal of individual kindness and *bonhomie* in him for which the critic did not give him credit. I think he is, on the whole, better than Varnhagen von Ense chose to paint him or see him.

From Alexander Humboldt, as well as from Varnhagen von Ense, we learn a good deal of the inner life of kings and queens and princes in Berlin. There is something almost painful in reflecting on the kind of life which Humboldt must have led among these people, whom he so cordially despised, and whom in his private chroniclings he so held up to scorn. The great philosopher assuredly had a huge treasure of hatred locked up in his heart. He detested and scorned these royal personages, who so blandly patronized him, or were sometimes so rough in their condescending familiarity. Nothing takes the gilt off the life of courts so much as a perusal of what Humboldt has written about it. One hardly cares to think of so great, and on the whole so noble a man, living a life of what seems so like perpetual dissimulation; of his enduring these royal dullards and pert princesses, and doubtless seeming profoundly reverential, and then going home of nights to put down on paper his record of their vulgarity, and selfishness, and impertinence. Sometimes Humboldt was not able to contain himself within the limits of court politeness. The late King of Hanover (father of the now dethroned King George) was a rough brutal trooper, who had made himself odious in England as the Duke of Cumberland, and was accused by popular rumors of the darkest crimes—unjustly accused certainly, in the case where he was charged with the murder of his valet. The Duke did not make a very bad sort of King, as kings then went; but he retained all his roughness and coarseness of manner. He once accosted Humboldt in the palace of the late King of Prussia, and in his pleasant graceful way asked why it was that the Prussian court was always full of philosophers and loose women—describing the latter class of visitors by a very direct and expressive word. "Perhaps," replied Humboldt blandly, "the King invites the philosophers to meet me, and the other persons to please your Majesty!" Humboldt seems to have had little liking for any of the illustrious personages he met under the roof of the King of Prussia. A brief record he made of a conversation with the late Prince Albert (for whom he expressed a great contempt) went far when it was published to render the husband of Queen Victoria more unpopular and even detested in Ireland than another George the Fourth would have been. The Irish people will probably never forget that, accordiug to the statement of Humboldt, the Prince spoke contemptuously of Irish national aspirations, declared he had no sympathy with the Irish, and that they were as restless, idle, and unmanageable as the Poles—a pretty speech, the philosopher remarks, to be made by the husband of the Queen of Great Britain and Ireland. Some attempt was made when this record of Humboldt's came to light to dispute the truth of it; but Humboldt was certainly not a liar—and anyhow the Irish people believed the story and it did no little mischief; and Humboldt in his grave might have had the consolation of knowing that he had injured one prince at least.

What we learn of the King of Prussia through Humboldt is to the same effect as the teaching of Varnhagen's cynical spirit; and I think, if these keen irreverent critics did not do him wrong, his Majesty must have softened and improved with the responsibilities of royalty. In many respects one might be inclined to compare him with the English George the Third. Both were indeed dull, decent, and fanatical. But there are some wide differences. George the Third was obstinate in the worst sense; his was the obstinacy of a stupid, self-conceited man who believes himself wise and right in everything. Now, I fancy the King of Prussia is only obstinate in what he conceives, rightly or wrongly, to be questions of duty and of principle; and that there are many subjects, political and otherwise, of which he does not believe himself to be the mcst competent judge, and which therefore he is quite willing to leave to the consideration and decision of others. For instance, it was made evident that in the beginning of the transactions which were followed by (although they cannot be said to have caused) the present war, the King more than once expressed himself willing to do certain things, of which, however, Count von Bismarck subsequently disapproved; and the King quietly gave way. "You know better than I do; act as you think best," is, I believe, a quite common sentence on the lips of King William, when he is talking with this or that trusted minister. Then again it has been placed beyond all doubt that George the Third could be, when he thought fit, the most unabashed and unscrupulous of liars; and not even hatred itself will charge King William with any act or word of falsehood or duplicity.

Steadily did the King grow more and more unpopular after his coronation. All the old work of prosecuting newspapers and snubbing, or if possible punishing, free-spoken politicians, came into play again. The King quarrelled fiercely with his Parliament about the scheme of army reorganization. I think he was right as to the scheme, although terribly wrong-headed and high-handed in his way of forcing it down the throats of the people, and, aided by his House of Peers, he waged a sort of war upon the nation's representatives. Then first came to the front that extraordinary political figure, which before very long had cast into the shade every other in Europe, even including that of the Emperor Napoleon ; that marvellous compound of audacity and craft, candor and cunning, the profound sagacity of a Richelieu, the levity of a Palmerston ; imperturbably good-humored, illimitably unscrupulous ; a patriot without lofty emotion of any kind, a statesman who could sometimes condescend to be a juggler ; part bully, part buffoon, but always a man of supreme courage, inexhaustible resources of brain and tongue—always in short a man of genius. I need hardly add that I am speaking of the Count von Bismarck.

At the time of the Schleswig-Holstein campaign, there was probably no public man in Europe so generally unpopular as the King of Prussia, except perhaps his Minister, the Count von Bismarck. In England it was something like an article of faith to believe that the King was a bloodthirsty old tyrant, his Prime Minister a combination of Strafford and Sejanus, and his subjects generally a set of beer-bemuddled and servile blockheads. The dislike felt toward the King was extended to the members of his family, and the popular conviction in England was that the Princess Victoria, wife of the King's son, had a dull coarse drunkard for a husband. It is perfectly wonderful how soon an absurdly erroneous idea, if there is anything about it which jumps with the popular humor, takes hold of the public mind of England. The English people regarded the Prussians with utter detestation and contempt. Not only that, but they regarded it as quite a possible and even likely thing that poor brave little Denmark, with a population hardly larger than that of the city of New York, could hold her own, alone, against the combined forces of Austria and Prussia. One might have thought that there never was a Frederick the Great or an Archduke Charles ; that the only part ever played in history by Germans was that of impotent braggarts and stupid cowards. When there seemed some prospect of England's drawing the sword for Denmark, "Punch" published a cartoon which was very popular and successful. It represented an English sailor and soldier of the conventional dramatic style, looking with utter contempt at two awkward shambling boobies with long hair and huge meerschaums—one booby supposed to represent Prussia, the other Austria ; and Jack Tar says to his friend the red-coat: "They can't expect us to *fight* fellows like those, but we'll kick them, of course, with pleasure." This so fairly represented the average public opinion of England that there was positively some surprise felt in London when it was found that the Prussians really could fight at all. Towards the Austrians there was nothing like the same ill-feeling ; and when Bismarck's war against Austria (I cannot better describe it) broke out shortly after, the sympathy of England went almost unanimously with the enemy of Prussia. Ninety-nine men out of every hundred firmly believed that Austria would clutch Italy with one hand and Prussia with the other, and easily choke the life out of both. About the merits of the quarrel nobody in England outside the range of a very few politicians and journalists troubled himself at all. It was settled that Austria had somehow come to represent the cause of human freedom and progress ; that the King of Prussia was a stupid and brutal old trooper, hurried to his ruin by the evil counsels of a drunken Mephistopheles ; and that the Austrian forces would simply walk over the Prussians into Berlin. There was but one newspaper in London (and it has since died) which ventured to suggest, first, that perhaps the Prussians had the right side of the quarrel, and next, that perhaps they would have the better in the fight.

With the success of Prussia at Sadowa ended King William's personal unpopularity in Europe. Those who were prepared to take anything like a rational view of the situation began to see that there must be some manner of great cause behind such risks, sacrifices, and success. Those who disliked Prussia more than ever, as many in France did, were disposed to put the King out of their consideration altogether, and to turn their detestation wholly on the King's Minister. In fact, Bismarck so entirely eclipsed or occulted the King, that the latter may be said to have disappeared from the horizon of European politics. His good qualities or bad qualities no longer counted for aught in the estimation of foreigners. Bismarck was everything, the King was nothing. Now I wish the readers of THE GALAXY not to take this view of the matter. In everything which has been done by Prussia since his accession to the throne, King William has counted for something. His stern uncompromising truthfulness, seen as clearly in the despatches he sent from recent battle-fields as in any other deeds of his life, has always counted for much. So too has his narrow-minded dread of anything which he believes to savor of the revolution. So has his thorough and devoted Germanism. I am convinced that it would have been far more easy of late to induce Bismarck to make compromises with seemingly powerful enemies at the expense of German soil, than it would have been to persuade Bismarck's master to consent to such proposals. The King's is far more of a typical German character (except for its lack of intellect) than that of Bismarck, in whom there is so much of French audacity as well as of French humor. On the other hand, I would ask my readers not to rush into wild admiration of the King of Prussia, or to suppose that liberty owes him personally any direct thanks. King William's subjects know too well that they have little to thank him for on that score. Strange as the comparison may seem at first, it is not less true that the enthusiasm now felt by Germans for the King is derived from just the same source as the early enthusiasm of Frenchmen for the first Napoleon. In each man his people see the champion who has repelled the aggression of the insolent foreigner, and has been strong enough to pursue the foreigner into his own home and there chastise him for his aggression. The blind stupidity of Austria and the crimes of Bonapartism have made King William a patriot King. When Thiers wittily and bitterly said that the Second Empire had made two great statesmen, Cavour and Bismarck, he might have said with still closer accuracy that it had made one great sovereign, William of Prussia. Never man attained such a position as that lately won by King William with less of original "outfit" to qualify him for the place. Five or six years ago the King of Prussia was as much disliked and distrusted by his own subjects as ever the Emperor of the French was by the followers of the Left. Look back to the famous days when "Bockum-Dolff's hat" seemed likely to become a symbol of civil revolution in Germany. Look back to the time when the King's own son and heir apparent, the warrior Crown Prince who since has flamed across so many a field of blood, felt called upon to make formal protest in a public speech against the illiberal, repressive, and despotic policy of his father! Think of these things, and say whether any change could be more surprising than that which has converted King William into the typical champion and patriot of Germany; and when you seek the explanation of the change, you will simply find that the worst enemies of Prussia have been unwittingly the kindest friends and the best patrons of Prussia's honest and despotic old sovereign.

I think the King of Prussia's subjects were not wrong when they disliked and dreaded him, and I also think they are now not wrong when they trust and applaud him. It has been his great good fortune to reign during a period when the foreign policy of the State was of infinitely greater importance than its domestic management. It became the business of the King of Prussia to help his country to assert and to maintain a national existence. Nothing better was needed in the sovereign for this purpose than the qualities of a military dictator, and the King, in this case, was saved all trouble of thinking and planning. He had but to accept and agree to a certain line of policy—a certain set of national principles—and to put his foot down on these and see that they were carried through. For this object the really manly and sturdy nature of the King proved admirably adapted. He upheld manfully and firmly the standard of the nation. His defective qualities were rendered inactive, and had indeed no occasion or chance to display themselves, while all that was good of him came into full activity and bold relief. But I do not believe that the character of the King in any wise changed. He was a dull, honest, fanatical martinet when he turned his cannon against German liberals in 1848; he was a dull, honest, fanatical martinet when he unfurled the flag of Prussia against the Austrians in 1866 and against the French in 1870. The brave old man is only happy when doing what he thinks right; but he wants alike the intellect and the susceptibilities which enable people to distinguish right from wrong, despotism from justice, necessary firmness from stolid obstinacy. But for the wars and the great national issues which rose to claim instant decision, King William would have gone on dissolving Parliaments and punishing newspapers, levying taxes without the consent of representatives, and making the police-officer the master of Berlin. The vigor which was so popular when employed in resisting the French, would assuredly otherwise have found occupation in repressing the Prussians. I see nothing to admire in King William but his courage and his honesty. People who know him personally speak delightedly of his sweet and genial manners in private life; and I have observed that, like many another old *moustache*, he has the art of making himself highly popular with the ladies. There is a celebrated little *prima donna* as well known in London as in Berlin, who can only speak of the bluff monarch as *der süsse König*—"the sweet King." Indeed, there are not wanting people who hint that Queen Augusta is not always quite pleased at the manner in which the venerable soldier makes himself agreeable to dames and demoiselles. Certainly the ladies seem to be generally very enthusiastic about his Majesty when they come into acquaintanceship with him, and to the *prima donna* I have mentioned his kindness and courtesy have been only such as are well worthy of a gentleman and of a king. Still we all know that it does not take a great effort on the part of a sovereign to make people, especially women, think him very delightful. I do not, therefore, make much account of King William's courtesy and *bonhomie* in estimating his character. For all the service he has done to Germany let him have full thanks; but I cannot bring myself to any warmth of personal admiration for him. It is indeed hard to look at him without feeling for the moment some sentiment of genuine respect. The fine head and face, with its noble outlines and its frank pleasant smile, the stately, dignified form, which some seventy-five years have neither bowed nor enfeebled, make the King look like some splendid old paladin of the court of Charlemagne. He is, indeed, despite his years, the finest physical specimen of a sovereign Europe just now can show. Compare him with the Emperor Napoleon, so many years his junior—compare his soldierly presence, his manly bearing, his clear frank eyes, his simple and sincere expression, with the prematurely wasted and crippled frame, the face blotched and haggard, the lack-lustre eyes which seem always striving to avoid direct encounter with any other glance, the shambling gait, the sinister look of the nephew of the great Bonaparte, and you will say that the Prussians have at least had from the beginning of their antagonism an immense advantage over their rivals in the figurehead which their State was enabled to exhibit. But I cannot make a hero out of stout King William, although he has bravery enough of the common, military kind, to suit any of the heroes of the "Nibelungen Lied." He never would, if he could, render any service to liberty; he cannot understand the elements and first principles of popular freedom; to him the people is always, as a child, to be kept in leading strings and guided, and, if at all boisterous or naughty, smartly birched and put in a dark corner. There is nothing cruel about King William; that is to say, he would not willingly hurt any human creature, and is, indeed, rather kind-hearted and humane than otherwise. He is as utterly incapable of the mean spites and shabby cruelties of the great Frederick, whose statue stands so near his palace, as he is incapable of the savage brutalities and indecencies of Frederick's father. He is, in fact, simply a dull old disciplinarian, saturated through and through with the traditions of the feudal party of Germany, his highest merit being the fact that he keeps his word—that he is "a still strong man" who "cannot lie;" his noblest fortune being the happy chance which called on him to lead his country's battles, instead of leaving him free to contend against, and perhaps for the time to crush, his country's aspirations after domestic freedom. Kind Heaven has allowed him to become the champion and the representative of German unity—that unity which is Germany's immediate and supreme need, calling for the postponement of every other claim and desire; and this part he has played like a man, a soldier, and a king. But one can hardly be expected to forget all the past, to forget what Humboldt and Varnhagen von Ense wrote, what Jacobi and Waldeck spoke, what King William did in 1848, and what he said in 1861; and unless we forget all this and a great deal more to the same effect, we can hardly help acknowledging that but for the fortunate conditions which allowed him to prove himself the best friend of German unity, he would probably have proved himself the worst enemy of German liberty.

VICTOR EMANUEL, KING OF ITALY.

I HAVE before me just now a little silver coin picked up in Savoy very soon after Italy had become a kingdom, and Savoy had ceased to be part of it. That was in truth the only thing that made the coin in any way specially interesting—the fact that it happened to be in chance circulation through Savoy when Savoy had no longer any claim to it. So, for that little scrap of melancholy interest I have since kept the coin in my purse, and it has made many journeys with me in Europe and America; and I suppose I can never be utterly destitute while it remains in my possession. Now, the head which is displayed upon that coin is not of kingly mould. The mint has flattered its royal master much less than is usual with such portrait painters. An English silver or gold coin of this year's mintage will still represent Her Majesty Queen Victoria as a beautiful young woman of twenty, with features worthy of a Greek statue and a bust shapely enough for Dryden's Iphigenia. But the coin of King Victor Emanuel has little flattery in it. There is the coarse, bulldog cast of face; there are the heavy eye-brows, the unshapely nose, the hideous moustache, the receding forehead, and all the other beauties and graces of the "bloat King's" countenance. Certainly the face on the coin is not bloated enough, and there is too little animalism displayed in the back of the head, to do justice to the first King of Italy. Moreover, the coin gives somehow the idea of a small man, and the King of Italy finds it not easy to get a horse strong enough to bear the load of Antony. But for a coin it is a wonderfully honest and truthful piece of work, quite a model to other mints, and it gave when it was issued as fair an idea as a little piece of silver could well give of the head and face of Europe's most ill-favored sovereign.

What a chance Victor Emanuel had of being a hero of romance! No king perhaps ever had such a chance before, and missed it so persistently. Europe seemed at one time determined, whether he would or no, to make a hero, a knight, a *preux chevalier*, out of the son of Charles Albert. Not Charles Edward, the brilliant, unfortunate Stuart himself, not Gustavus Adolphus even seemed to have been surrounded by such a romantic rainbow of romance and of hope. When, after the crowning disaster of Novara, Victor Emanuel's weak, vacillating, unlucky, and not very trustworthy father abdicated the crown of Sardinia in favor of his son, the latter seemed in the eyes of liberal Europe to represent not merely the hopes of all true Italians, but the best hopes of liberty and progress all over the world. There was even then a vague idea afloat through Europe—although Europe did not know how Cavour had already accepted the idea as a principle of action—that with her tremendous defeats Piedmont had won the right to hoist the standard of one Italy. This then was the cause which the young King was taken to represent. He had been baptized in blood to that cause. He represented Italy united and free—free from Austrian and Pope, from political and religious despotism. He was at all events no carpet knight. He had fought bravely on more than one fearful field of battle; he had looked on death closely and undismayed; he had been wounded in fighting for Italy against the Austrian. It was said of the young sovereign—who was only Duke of Savoy then—that on the night of Novara, when all was over save retreat and humiliation, he shook his dripping sword at the ranks of the conquering Austrians and exclaimed, "Italy shall make herself for all that!"

Probably the story is substantially true, although Victor Emanuel may perhaps have used stronger expressions if he spoke at all; for no one ever doubted his courage and coolness in the hour of danger. But true or not, the anecdote exactly illustrated the light in which the world was prepared to regard the young sovereign of Sardinia—as the hope of Italy and of freedom, the representative of a defeat which he was determined and destined to convert into a victory.

Not many years after this, and while the lustre of his misfortunes and the brilliancy of his hopes still surrounded him, King Victor Emanuel visited England. He was welcomed everywhere with a cordiality of personal interest and admiration not often accorded by any people to a foreign king. Decidedly it was a hard thing to look at him and yet retain the thought of a hero of romance. He was not then nearly so bloated and burly as he is now; and he was at least some dozen or fourteen years younger. But even then how marvellously ill-favored he was; how rough and coarse-looking; how unattractive in manner; how brusque and uncouth in gesture and bearing; how liable to fits of an apparently stolid silence; how utterly devoid of grace and dignity! His huge straw-colored moustache, projecting about half a foot on each side of his face, was as unsightly a piece of manly decoration as ever royal countenance displayed. Yet the public tried to forget all those external defects and still regard him as a hero of romance somehow, anyhow. So fully was he believed to be a representative of civil and religious freedom in Italy, that one English religious society of some kind—I forget which it was—actually went the length of presenting an address to him, in which they flourished about the errors of Popery as freely as if they were appealing to an Oliver Cromwell or Frederick the Great. Cavour gave them very neatly and tersely the snub that their ignorance and presumption so well deserved; and their address did not obtain an honored place among Victor Emanuel's memorials of his visit to England.

He was very hospitably entertained by Queen Victoria, who is said to have suffered agonies of martrydom from her guest's everlasting cigar—the good soul detests tobacco as much as King James himself did—and even more from his occasional outbursts of roystering compliment and canteen love-making toward the ladies of her staid and modest court. One of the household edicts, I think, of Queen Elizabeth's court was that no gallant must "toy with the maids, under pain of fourpence." Poor Victor Emanuel's slender purse would have had to bear a good many deductions of fourpence, people used to hint, if this penal decree had prevailed in his time at Windsor or Osborne. But Queen Victoria was very patient and friendly. Cavour has left some pleasant descriptions of her easy, unaffected friendliness toward himself. Guizot, it will be remembered, has described her as the stiffest of the stiff, freezing into petrifaction a whole silent circle by her invincible coldness and formality. I cannot pretend to reconcile the conflicting accounts of these two eminent visitors, but certainly Cavour has drawn some animated and very attractive pictures of Queen Victoria's almost girlish good-humor and winning familiarity. However that may be, the whole heart of free England warmed to Victor Emanuel, and was ready to dub him in advance the chosen knight of liberty, the St. George of Italy, before whose resistless sword every dragon of despotism and superstition was to grovel in the dust.

So the King went his way, and the next thing the world heard of him was that he was in league with Louis Napoleon against the Austrian, and that the child his daughter was to be married to the obese and elderly Prince Napoleon, whose eccentric genius, varied accomplishments, and thrilling eloquence were then unrecognized and unknown. Then came the triumphs of Magenta and Solferino, and it was made plain once more to the world that Victor Emanuel had the courage of a true soldier. He actually took a personal share of the fighting when the Italians were in action. He did not sit on his horse, far away from the bullets, like his imperial ally, and direct the movements of the army by muttering "*C'est bien*," when an aide-de-camp galloped up to announce to him as a piece of solemn farce that this or that general had already accomplished this or that operation. No; Victor Emanuel took his share of the fighting like a king. In the affair of San Martino he led an attack himself, and encouraged his soldiers by bellowing in stentorian voice quite a clever joke for a king, just as he was about to charge. A crack regiment of French Zouaves (the French Zouaves were soldiers in those days) was so delighted with the Sardinian King that it elected him a corporal of the regiment on the field of battle—a quite wonderful piece of compliment from a Zouave regiment to a foreign sovereign. Not so long before had Lamoricière declared that "Italians don't fight," and here was a crack Zouave regiment enthusiastic about the fighting capacity of an Italian King. The irony of fate, it will be remembered, decreed soon after that Lamoricière should himself lay down his arms before an Italian general and Italian soldiers.

Out of that war, then, Victor Emanuel emerged still a hero. But the world soon began to think that he was only a hero in the field. The sale of Savoy and Nice much shocked the public sentiment of Europe. The house of Savoy, as an English orator observed, had sprung from the womb of the mountains which the unworthy heir of Savoy sold to a stranger. As the world had given to Victor Emanuel the credit of virtues which he never possessed, it was now ready to lay on him all the burden of deeds which were not his. Whether the cession of Savoy was right or wrong, Victor Emanuel was not to blame, under the hard circumstances, for withdrawing, according to the first Napoleon's phrase, "*sous les draps d'un roi constitutionnel*," and allowing his ministers to do the best they could. In fact, the thing was a necessity of the situation. Napoleon the Third had to make the demand to satisfy his own people, who never quite "seemed to see" the war for Italy. The Sardinian ministers had to yield to the demand to satisfy Napoleon the Third. Had Prussia been a raw, weak power in September, 1866, she must have ceded some territory to France. Sardinia or Italy was raw and weak in 1860, and had no choice but to submit. There were two things to be said for the bargain. First, Italy got good value for it. Next, the Savoyards and Nizzards never were good Italians. They rather piqued themselves on not being Italians. The Savoy delegates would not speak Italian in the old Turin Parliament. The ministers had to answer their French "interpellations" in French.

Still all this business did an immense harm to the reputation of King Victor Emanuel. He had acted like a quiet, sensible man—not in any way like a hero of romance, and Europe desired to see in him a hero of romance. Then he did not show himself, people said, very grateful to Garibaldi when the latter opened the way for the expulsion of the Bourbons from Naples, and did so much to crown Victor Emanuel King of Italy. Now I am a warm admirer of Garibaldi. I think his very weaknesses are noble and heroic. There is carefully preserved among the best household treasures of my family a vine leaf which Garibaldi once plucked and gave me as a *souvenir* for my wife. But I confess I should not like to be king of a new monarchy partly made by Garibaldi and with Garibaldi for a subject. The whole policy of Garibaldi proceeded on the gallant and generous assumption that Italy alone ought to be able to conquer all her enemies. We have since seen how little Italy availed against a mere fragment of the military power of Austria—that power which Prussia crushed like a nutshell. Events, I think, have vindicated the slower and less assuming policy of Victor Emanuel, or, I should say, the policy which Victor Emanuel consented to adopt at the bidding of Cavour.

But all the same the *prestige* of Victor Emanuel was gone. Then Europe began to look at the man coolly, and estimate him without glamour and without romance. Then it began to listen to the very many stories against him which his enemies could tell. Alas! these stories were not all untrue. Of course there were grotesque and hideous exaggerations. There are in Europe some three or four personages of the highest rank whom scandal delights to assail, and of whom it tells stories which common sense and common feeling alike compel us to reject. It would be wholly impossible even to hint at some of the charges which scandal in Europe persistently heaped on Victor Emanuel, the Emperor Napoleon III., Prince Napoleon, and the reigning King of the Netherlands. If one-half the stories told of these four men were true, then Europe would hold at present four personages of the highest rank who might have tutored Caligula in the arts of recondite debauchery, and have looked down on Alexander the Sixth as a prudish milksop. But I think no reasonable person will have much difficulty in sifting the probable truth out of the monstrous exaggerations. No one can doubt that Victor Emanuel is a man of gross habits and tastes, and is, or was, addicted to coarse and ignoble immoralities. "The manners of a mosstrooper and the morality of a he goat," was the description which my friend John Francis Maguire, the distinguished Roman Catholic member of the House of Commons, gave, in one of his Parliamentary speeches, of King Victor Emanuel. This was strong language, and it was the language of a prejudiced though honest political and religious partisan; but it was not, all things considered, a very bad description. Moreover, it was mildness, it was compliment—nay, it was base flattery—when compared with the hideous accusations publicly and distinctly made against Victor Emanuel by one of Garibaldi's sons, not to speak of other accusers, and privately whispered by slanderous gossip all over Europe. One peculiarity about Victor Emanuel worthy of notice is that he has no luxury in his tastes. He is, I believe, abstemious in eating and drinking, caring only for the homeliest fare. He has sat many times at the head of a grand state banquet, where the rarest viands, the most superb wines were abundant, and never removed the napkin from his plate, never tasted a morsel or emptied a glass. He had had his plain fare at an earlier hour, and cared nothing for the triumphs of cookery or the choicest products of the vine. He has thus sat, in good-humored silence, his hand leaning on the hilt of his sword, through a long, long banquet of seemingly endless courses, which to him was a pageant, a ceremonial duty, and nothing more. He delights in chamois-hunting—in hunting of almost any kind—in horses, in dogs, and in women of a certain coarse and gross description. There is nothing of the Richelieu or Lauzun, or even the Francis the First, about the dull, I had almost said harmless, immoralities of the King of Italy. Men in private and public station have done far greater harm, caused far more misery than ever he did, and yet escaped almost unwhipt of justice. The man has (or had, for people say he is reformed now) the coarse, easily-gratified tastes of a sailor turned ashore after a long cruise—and such tastes are not kingly; and that is about all that one feels fairly warranted in saying either to condemn or to palliate the vices of Victor Emanuel. He absolutely wants all element of greatness. He is not even a great soldier. He has boisterous animal courage, and finds the same excitement in leading a charge as in hunting the chamois. But he has nothing even of the very moderate degree of military capacity possessed by a dashing *sabreur* like Murat. It seems beyond doubt that it was the infatuation he displayed in attempting the personal direction of affairs which led to the breakdown at Custozza. The man is, in fact, like one of the rough jagers described in Schiller's "Wallenstein's Camp"—just this, and nothing more. When Garibaldi was in the zenith of his fortunes and fame in 1860, Victor Emanuel declared privately to a friend that the height of his ambition would be to follow the gallant guerilla leader as a mere soldier in the field. Certainly, when the two men entered Naples together, every one must have felt that their places ought to have been reversed. How like a king, an ideal king—a king of poetry and painting and romance—looked Garibaldi in the superb serenity of his untaught grace and sweetness and majesty. How rude, uncouth, clownish, even vulgar, looked the big, brawny, ungainly trooper whom people had to salute as King. When Garibaldi went to visit the hospitals where the wounded of the short struggle were lying, how womanlike he was in his sympathetic tenderness; how light and noiseless was his step; how gentle his every gesture; what a sweet word of genial compassion or encouragement he had for every sufferer. The burly King strode and clattered along like a dragoon swaggering through the crowd at a country fair. Not that Victor Emanuel wanted good nature, but that his rude *physique* had so little in it of the sympathetic or the tender.

Was there ever known such a whimsical, harmless, odd saturnalia as Naples presented during those extraordinary days? I am thinking now chiefly of the men who, mostly uncalled-for, "rallied round" the Revolution, and came from all manner of holes and corners to offer their services to Garibaldi, and to exhibit themselves in the capacity of freedom's friends, soldiers, and scholars. Hardly a hero, or crackbrain, or rantipole in Europe, one would think, but must have been then on exhibition somewhere in Naples. Father Gavazzi harangued from one position; Alexandre Dumas, accompanied by his faithful "Admiral Emile," directed affairs from another. Edwin James, then a British criminal lawyer and popular member of Parliament, was to be seen tearing round in a sort of semi-military costume, with pistols stuck in his belt. The worn, thoughtful, melancholy face of Mazzini was, for a short time at least, to be seen in juxtaposition with the cockney visage of an ambitious and restless common councilman from the city of London, who has lived all his life since on the glorious memories and honors of that good time. The House of Lords, the House of Commons, and the Guildhall of London were lavishly represented there. Men like Türr, the dashing Hungarian and Mieroslawski, the "Red" leader of Polish revolution—men to whom battle and danger were as the breath of their nostrils—were buttonholed and advised by heavy British vestrymen and pert Parisian journalists. Hardly any man or woman entered Naples from a foreign country at that astonishing time who did not believe that he or she had some special counsel to give, which Victor Emanuel or Garibaldi or some one of their immediate staff was bound to listen to and accept. Woman's Rights were pretty well represented in that pellmell. There was a Countess something or other—French, they said—who wore short petticoats and trousers, had silver-mounted pistols in her belt and silver spurs on her heels, and was generally believed to have done wonders in "the field"—what field no one would stop to ask. There was Jessie Mario White, modest, pleasant, fair-haired woman, wife of a gallant gentleman and soldier—Jessie White, who made no exhibition of herself, but did then and since faithful and valuable work for

Italian wounded, such as Italy ought not soon to forget. There was Mrs. Chambers—Mrs. Colonel Chambers—the Mrs. "Putney Giles" of Disraeli's "Lothair"—very prominent everywhere, sounding the special eulogies of Garibaldi with tireless tongue, and utterly overshadowing her quiet husband, who (the husband I mean) afterwards stood by Garibaldi's side at Aspromonte. Exeter Hall had sent out powerful delegations, in the firm faith apparently that Garibaldi would at their request order Naples forthwith to break up its shrines and images of saints and become Protestant; and that Naples would at once obey. Never was such a time of dreams and madness and fussiness, of splendid aspirations and silly self-seeking vanity, of chivalry and daring, and true wisdom and nonsense. It was a time naturally of many disappointments; and one disappointment to almost everybody was His Majesty King Victor Emanuel. His Majesty seemed at least not much to care about the whole affair from the beginning. He went through it as if he didn't quite understand what it was all about, and didn't think it worth the trouble of trying. People who saw him at that splendid moment when, the forces of Garibaldi joining with the regular Sardinian troops after all had been won, Garibaldi and the King met for the first time in that crisis, and the soldier hailed the sovereign as "King of Italy!"—people who saw and studied that picturesque historic meeting have told me that there was no more emotion of any kind on Victor Emanuel's face than if he were receiving a formal address from the mayor of a country town. "I thank you," were his only words of reply; and I am assured that it was not "I thank *you*," with emphasis on the last word to indicate that the King acknowledged how much he owed to his great soldier; but simply "I thank you," as he might have thanked a groom who opened a stable door for him. Perhaps the very depth and grandeur of the King's emotions rendered him incapable of finding any expression for them. Let us hope so. But I have had the positive assurances of some who saw the scene, that if any such emotions were felt the royal countenance concealed them as completely as though they never had been.

In truth, I presume that the whole thing really was a terrible bore to the royal Rawdon Crawley, who found himself compelled by cursed spite to play the part of a patriot king. The Pope, the ultramontane bishops, and the ultramontane press have always been ringing fierce changes on the inordinate and wicked ambition of Victor Emanuel. I am convinced the poor man has no more ambition than his horse. If he could have chalked out his own career for himself, he would probably have asked nothing better than to be allowed to devote his life to chamois-hunting, with a hunter's homely fare, and the companionship of a few friends (some fat ladies among the number) with whom he could talk and make jokes in the *patois* of Piedmont. This, and perhaps a battle-field and a dashing charge every now and then, would probably have realized his dreams of the *summum bonum*. But some implacable destiny, embodied in the form of a Cavour or a Garibaldi, was always driving on the stout King and bidding him get up and attempt great things—be a patriot and a hero. Fancy Rawdon Crawley impelled, or rather compelled by the inexorable command of Becky his wife, to go forth in quest of the Holy Grail, and one may perhaps be able to guess what Victor Emanuel's perplexity and reluctance were when he was bidden to set out for the accomplishment of the regeneration of Italy. "Honor to those to whom honor is due; honor to old Mother Baubo," says some one in "Faust." Honor on that principle, then, to King Victor Emanuel. He did get up and go forth and undertake to bear his part in the adventure. And here seriously let me speak of the one high merit of Victor Emanuel's career. He is not a hero; he is not a statesman or even a politician; he is not a patriot in any grand, exalted sense. He would like to be idle, and perhaps to be despotic. But he has proved that he understands the true responsibilities and duties of a constitutional King better than many sovereigns of higher intellect and better character. He always did go, or at least endeavor to go, where the promptings of his ministers, the commands of his one imperious minister, or the voice of the country directed. There must be a great struggle in the mind of Victor Emanuel between his duty as a king and his duty as a Roman Catholic, when he enters into antagonism with the Pope. Beyond doubt Victor Emanuel is a superstitious Catholic. Of late years his constitution has once or twice threatened to give way, and he is probably all the more anxious to be reconciled with the Church. Perhaps he would be glad enough to lay down the load of royalty altogether and become again an accepted and devoted Catholic, and hunt his chamois with a quieted conscience. But still, impelled by what must be some sort of patriotism and sense of duty, he accepts his uncongenial part of constitutional King, and strives to do all that the voice of his people demands. It is probable that at no time was the King personally much attached to his illustrious minister Cavour. The genius and soul of Cavour were too oppressively imperial, high-reaching, and energetic for the homely, plodding King. With all his external levity Count Cavour was terribly in earnest, and he must often have seemed a dreadful bore to his sovereign. Cavour knew himself the master, and did not always take pains to conceal his knowledge. He would sometimes adopt the most direct and vigorous language in remonstrating with the King if the latter did not act on valuable advice at the right moment. Sometimes, when things went decidedly against Cavour's wishes, the minister would take the monarch to task more roundly than even the most good-natured monarchs are likely to approve. When Napoleon the Third disappointed Cavour and all Italy by the sudden peace of Villafranca, I have heard that Cavour literally denounced Victor Emanuel for consenting to the arrangement. Count Arrivabene, an able writer, has given a very vivid and interesting description of Cavour's demeanor when he reached the Sardinian headquarters on his way to an interview with the King and learned what had been done. He was literally in a "tearing rage." He tore off his hat and dashed it down, he clenched his hands, he stamped wildly, gesticulated furiously, became red and purple, foamed at the mouth, and grew inarticulate for very passion. He believed that he and Italy were sold—as indeed they were; and it was while this temper was yet on him that he went to see the King, and denounced him, as I have said. Now this sort of thing certainly could not have been agreeable to Victor Emanuel; and yet he patiently accepted Cavour as a kind of glorious necessity. He never sought, as many another king in such *duresse* would have done, to weaken his minister's influence and authority by showing open sullenness and dissatisfaction. Ratazzi, with his pliable ways and his entire freedom from any wearisome earnestness or devotion to any particular cause, was naturally a far more companionable and agreeable minister for the King than the untiring and imperious Cavour. Accordingly, it was well known that Ratazzi was more of a personal favorite; but the King never seems to have acted otherwise than loyally and honestly toward Cavour. Ricasoli was all but intolerable to the King. Ricasoli was proud and stern; and he was, moreover, a somewhat rigid moralist, which Cavour hardly professed to be. The King writhed under the government of Ricasoli, and yet, despite all that was at the time whispered, he cannot, I think, be fairly accused of having done anything personally to rid himself of an obnoxious minister. Indeed, the single merit of Victor Emanuel's character, if we put aside the element of personal courage, is its rough integrity. He is a *galantuomo*, an honest man—in that sense, a man of his word. He gave his word to constitutional government and to Italy, and he appears to have kept the word in each case according to his lights.

But his popularity among his subjects, the interest felt in him by the world, have long been steadily on the wane. Years and years ago he ceased to retain the faintest gleam of the halo of romance that once was, despite of himself, thrown around him. His people care little or nothing for him. Why, indeed, should they care anything? The military *prestige* which he had won, such as it was, vanished at Custozza, and it was his evil destiny, hardly his fault, to be almost always placed in a position of antagonism to the one only Italian who since Cavour's death had an enthusiastic following in Italy. Aspromonte was a calamity for Victor Emanuel. One can hardly blame him; one can hardly see how he could have done otherwise. The greatest citizen or soldier in America or England, if he attempted to levy an army of his own, and make war from American or English territory upon a neighboring State, would surely have seen his bands dispersed and found himself arrested by order of his government; and it would never have occurred to any one to think that the government was doing a harsh, ungrateful, or improper thing. It would be the necessary, rightful execution of a disagreeable duty, and that is all. But the conditions of Garibaldi's case, like the one splendid service he had rendered, were so entirely abnormal and without precedent, the whole thing was from first to last so much more a matter of national sentiment than of political law, that national sentiment insisted on judging Garibaldi and the King in this case too, and at least a powerful, passionate minority declared Victor Emanuel an ingrate and a traitor. Mentana was almost as bad for the King as Custozza. The voice of the country, so far as one could understand its import, seemed to declare that when the King had once ordered the Italian troops to cross the frontier, he should have ordered them to go on; that if they had actually occupied Rome, France would have recognized accomplished facts; that as it was, Italy offended France and the Pope by stepping over the barrier of the convention of September, only to humiliate herself by stepping back again without having accomplished anything. Certainly the policy of the Italian Government at such a crisis was weak, miserable, even contemptible. Then indeed Italy might well have exclaimed, "Oh for one hour of Cavour!" One hour of the man of genius and courage, who, if he had moved forward, would not have darted back again! Perhaps it was unfair to hold the King responsible for the mistakes of his ministers. But when a once popular King has to be pleaded for on that sole ground, it is pretty clear that there is an end to his popularity. So with Victor Emanuel. The world began to forget him; his subjects began to despise him. Even the thrilling events that have lately taken place in Italy, the sudden crowning of the national edifice—the realization of that hope which so long appeared but a dream—which Cavour himself declared would be the most slow and difficult to realize of all Italy's hopes—even the possession of Rome hardly seems to have brought back one ray of the old popularity on the heavy head of King Victor Emanuel. Again the wonderful combination of good luck and bad—the good fortune which brought to the very door of the house of Savoy the sudden realization of its highest dreams—the misfortune which allowed that house no share in the true credit of having accomplished its destiny. What had Victor Emanuel to do with the sudden juncture of events which enabled Italy to take possession of her capital? Nothing whatever. His people have no more reason to thank him for Rome than they have to thank him for the rain or the sunshine, the olive and the vine. The King seems to have felt all this. His short visit to Rome, and the formal act of taking possession, may perhaps have been made so short because Victor Emanuel knew that he had little right to claim any honors or expect any popular enthusiasm. He entered Rome one day and went away the next. I confess, however, that I should not wonder if the visit was made so short merely because the whole thing was a bore to the honest King, and he could only make up his mind to endure a very few hours of it.

Victor Emanuel, King of United Italy, and welcomed by popular acclamation in Rome—his second son almost at the same moment proclaimed King of the Spaniards—his second daughter Queen of Portugal. How fortune seems to have delighted in honoring this house of Savoy. I only say "seems to have." I do not venture yet to regard the accession of King Amadeus to the crown of Spain as necessarily an honorable or a fortunate thing. Every one must wish the poor young prince well in such a situation; perhaps we should rather wish him well out of it. Never king assumed a crown with such ghastly omens to welcome him. Here is the King putting on his diadem; and yonder, lying dead by the hand of an assassin, is the man who gave him the diadem and made him King! But for Juan Prim there would be no Amadeus, King of the Spaniards; and for that reason Juan Prim lies dead. The young King must have needed all his hereditary courage to enable him to face calmly and bravely, as he seems to have done, so terrible a situation. Macaulay justly says that no danger is so trying to the nerves of a brave man as the danger of assassination. Men utterly reckless in battle—like "bonny Dundee" for example—have owned that the knowledge of the assassin's purpose and haunting presence was more than they could endure. The young Italian prince seems to have shown no sign of flinching. So far as anything indeed is known of him, he is favorably known to the world. He bore himself like a brave soldier at Custozza, and obtained the special commendation of the Austrian victor, the gallant old Archduke Albrecht. He married for love a lady of station decidedly inferior to that of a royal prince; the lady had the honor of being sneered at even in her honeymoon for the modest, inexpensive simplicity of her toilet, as she appeared with her young husband at one of the watering-places; he had not made himself before marriage the subject of as much scandal as used to follow and float around the bachelor reputation of his elder brother Humbert. He is believed to be honestly and manfully liberal in his views. He ought to make a good King as kings go—if the murderers of General Prim only give him the chance.

As I have mentioned the name of the man whose varied, brilliant, daring, and turbulent career has been so suddenly cut short, I may perhaps be excused for wandering a little out of the path of my subject to say that I think many of the American newspapers have hardly done justice to Prim. Some of them have written of him, even in announcing his death, as if it were not possible for a man to be honest and yet not to be a republican. In more than one instance the murder of Prim was treated as a sort of thing which, however painful to read of, was yet quite natural and even excusable in the case of a man who endeavored to give his country a King. There was a good deal too much of the "Sic semper tyrannis" tone and temper about some of the journals. Now, I do not believe that Prim was a patriot of that unselfish and lofty group to which William the Silent, and George Washington, and Daniel Manin belong. His was a very mixed character, and ambition had a large place in it. But I believe that he sincerely loved and tried to serve Spain; and I believe that in giving her a King he honestly thought he was doing for her the thing most suited to her tendencies and her interests. If Prim could have made Spain a republic, he could have made himself her President, even perhaps for life; while he could not venture, she being a kingdom, to constitute himself her King. Many times did Prim himself say to me, before the outbreak of his successful revolt, that he believed the republican to be the ultimate form of government everywhere, and that he would gladly see it in Spain; but that he did not believe Spain was yet suited for it, or numbered republicans enough. "To have a republic you must first have republicans," was a common saying of his. New England is a very different sort of place from Old Castile. At all events, Prim is not to be condemned as a traitor to his country and to liberty, even if it were true that he could have created a Spanish republic. We have to show first that he knew the thing was possible and refused to do it, for selfish or ignoble motives. This I am satisfied is not true. I think Prim believed a republic impossible in the Spain of to-day, and simply acted in accordance with his convictions. He came very near to being a great man; he wanted not much of being a great patriot. He was, I think, better than his fame. As Spain has decreed, he "deserved well of his country." It seems hardly reasonable or just to decry him or condemn him because he did not deserve better. Such as he was, he proved himself original. "He walked," as Carlyle says, "his own wild road, whither that led him." In an age very prolific of great political men, he made a distinct name and place for himself. "Name thou the best of German singers," exclaims Heine with pardonable pride, "and my name must be spoken among them." Name the half-dozen really great, originating characters in European politics during our time, and the name of Prim must come in among them.

But I was speaking of Victor Emanuel and his children. All I have heard then of the Duke of Aosta leads me to believe that he is qualified to make a respectable and loyal constitutional sovereign. High intellectual capacity no one expects from the house of Savoy, but there will probably be good sense, manly feeling, and no small share of political discretion. In the Duke of Aosta, too, Spain will have a King who can have no possible sympathy with slave systems and their products of whatever kind, and who can hardly have much inclination for the coercing and dragooning of reluctant populations. If Spain in his day and through his influence can get decently and honorably rid of Cuba, she will have entered upon a new chapter of her national existence, as important for her as that grand new volume which opens upon France when defeat has purged her of her thrice-accursed "militaryism." The dependencies have been a miserable misfortune to Spain. They have entangled her in all manner of complications; they have filled her with false principles; they have created whole corrupt classes among her soldiers and politicians. General Prim himself once assured me that the real revenues of Spain were in no wise the richer for her colonial possessions. Proconsuls made fortunes and spread corruption round them, and that was all. If her new King could only contrive to relieve Spain of this source of corruption and danger, he would be worth all the cost and labor of the revolution which gives him now a Spanish throne.

Why did fate decree that the very best of all the children of Victor Emanuel should have apparently the worst fortune? The Princess Clotilde is an exile from the country and the palace of her husband; and if the sweetness and virtue of one woman might have saved a court, the court of the Tuileries might have been saved by Victor Emanuel's eldest daughter. I have heard the Princess

Clotilde talked of by Ultramontanes, Legitimists, Orleanists, Republicans, Red Republicans (by some among the latter who firmly believed that the poor Empress Eugénie was wickeder than Messalina), and I never heard a word spoken of her that was not in her praise. Every one admitted that she was a pure and noble woman, a patient wife, a devoted mother; full of that unpretending simplicity which, let us own it frankly, is one of the graces which very high birth and old blood do sometimes bring. The Princess must in her secret soul have looked down on some of the odd *coteries* who were brought around her at the court of the Tuileries. She comes of a house in whose genealogy, to quote Disraeli's humorous words, "Chaos was a novel," and she found herself forced into companionship with ladies and gentlemen whose fathers and mothers, good lack! sometimes seemed to have omitted any baptismal registration whatever. I presume she was not ignorant of the parentage of De Morny, or Walewski, or Walewski's son, or the Jerome David class of people. I presume she heard what every one said of the Countess this and the Marchioness that, and so on. Of course the Princess Clotilde did not like these people—how could any decent woman like them?—but she accepted the necessities of her position with a self-possession and dignity which, offending no one, marked the line distinctly and honorably between her and them. Her joy was in her children. She loved to show them to friends, and to visitors even whom she felt that she could treat as friends. Perhaps she is not less happy now that the ill-omened, fateful splendors of the Palais Royal no longer help to make a gilded cage for the darlings of her nursery. Of the whole family, hers may be called the only career which has been doomed to what the world describes and pities as failure. It may well be that she is now happiest of all the children of the house of Savoy.

Meanwhile, Victor Emanuel has been welcomed at the Quirinal, and is indeed, at last, King of Italy. We may well say to him, as Banquo says of Macbeth, "Thou hast it all!" Lombardy, Tuscany, Parma, Modena, the Two Sicilies, Venetia, and Rome—what gathering within less than a fifth of an ordinary lifetime! And on the Quirinal Victor Emanuel may be said to have stood alone. Of all the men who mainly wrought to bring about that grand consummation, not one stood by his side. Daniel Manin, the pure, patient, fearless, patriot hero; Cavour, the consummate statesman; Massimo d'Azeglio, the Bayard or Lafayette of Italy's later days, the soldier, scholar, and lover of his country—these are dead, and rest with Dante. Mazzini is still a sort of exile—homeless, unshaken, seeing his prophecies fulfil themselves and his ideas come to light, while he abides in the gloom and shadow, and the world calls him a dreamer. Garibaldi is lending the aid of his restless sword to a cause which he cannot serve, and a people who never understood him; and he is getting sadly mixed up somehow in ordinary minds with General Cluseret and George Francis Train. Louis Napoleon, who, whatever his crimes, did something for the unity of Italy, is a broken man in captivity. Only Victor Emanuel, least gifted of all, utterly unworthy almost to be named in the same breath with any of them (save Louis Napoleon alone)—only he comes forward to receive the glories and stand up as the representative of one Italy! Let us do him the justice to acknowledge that he never sought the position or the glory. He accepted both as a necessity of his birth and his place, a formal duty and a bore. His was not the character which goes in quest of greatness. As Falstaff says of rebellion and the revolted English lord, greatness "lay in his way, and he found it."

LOUIS ADOLPHE THIERS.

GUIZOT quietly at work in the preparation of a history of France for the instruction of children—Thiers taking his place in a balloon to fly from one seat of government in France to another! Such were the occupations, at a given time in last November, of the two distinguished men whose rivalries and contentions disturbed the politics of France for so many years.

An ill-natured person might feel inclined to say that the adventures in the balloon were a proper crowning of the edifice of M. Thiers's fitful career. Was not his whole political life (*non meus hic sermo*, please to understand—it is the ill-natured person who says this) an enterprise in a balloon, high out of all the regions where common sense, consistency, and statesmanship are ruling elements? Did he not overleap with aëronautic flight when it so suited him, from liberalism to conservatism, from advocating freedom of thought to enforcing the harshest repression? Was not his literary reputation floated into high air by that most inflated and gaseous of all balloons, the "History of the Consulate and the Empire"? Thiers in a balloon is just where he ought to be, and where he ever has been. Condense into one meagre little person all the egotism, all the self-conceit, all the vainglory, all the incapacity for looking at anything whatever from the right point of view, which belong to the typical Frenchman of fiction and satire, and you have a pretty portrait of M. Thiers.

Doubtless, the ill-natured person who should say all this would be able to urge a good many plausible reasons in justification of his assertions. Still, one may be allowed to admire—one cannot help admiring—the astonishing energy and buoyancy which made M. Thiers, despite his seventy-three years, the most active emissary of the French Republic during the past autumn, the aëronautic rival of the vigorous young Corsican Gambetta, who was probably hardly grown enough for a merry-go-round in the Champs Elysées when Thiers was beginning to be regarded as an old fogy by the ardent revolutionists of 1848. About the middle of last September, a few days after the sudden creation of the French Republic, M. Thiers precipitated himself on London. An account in the newspapers described him as "accompanied by five ladies." Thus gracefully escorted, he marched on the English capital. He had interviews with Mr. Gladstone, Lord Granville, the French Ambassador, and divers other great personages. He was always rushing from diplomatic office to office. He "interviewed" everybody in London who could by any possibility be supposed capable of influencing in the slightest degree the fortunes of France. He never for a moment stopped talking. Great men excel each other in various qualities; but there never was a great man who could talk against M. Thiers. He could have shut up the late Lord Macaulay in no time; and I doubt whether Mr. Seward could have contrived to edge in a word while Thiers was in the same room. M. Thiers stayed in London little more than two days. He arrived, I think, on a Wednesday night, and left on the following Saturday. During that time he managed to do all the interviewing, and was likewise able to take his family to see the paintings in the National Gallery, where he was to be observed keenly eyeing the pictures, and eloquently laying down critical law and gospel on their merits, as if he had come over on a little autumnal holiday from a settled and peaceful country, which no longer needed looking after. Then he started from London in a steam-yacht, cruised about the North Sea and the

Baltic, dropped in upon the King of Denmark, sounded the views of Sweden, collected the general opinion of Finland, visited the Emperor of Russia and talked him into semi-bewilderment, and then travelled down by land to Vienna, where he used all his powers of persuasion on the Emperor Francis Joseph, and to Florence, where by the sheer force of argument and fluency he drove Victor Emanuel nearly out of his senses. Since that time, he all but concluded an armistice with Bismarck, and when last I heard of him (previous to this writing) he was, as I have said, going on a mission somewhere in a balloon.

During his recent diplomatic flights, M. Thiers constantly offered to encounter much greater fatigues and responsibilities if needful. He was ready to go anywhere and talk to anybody. He would have hunted up the Emperor of China or the Mikado of Japan, if either sovereign seemed in the remotest degree likely to intervene on the side of France. I believe I can say with confidence, that at the outset of his expedition he had no official authority or mission whatever from the Provisional Government. He told Jules Favre and the rest that he was about to start on a tour of inspection round the European cabinets, and that they had better let him try what he could do; and they did not refuse to let him try, and it would not have mattered in the least whether they refused or not. He came, in the first instance, altogether "on his own hook." Perhaps, at first, the Republican Government was not very anxious to accept the services of M. Thiers as a messenger of peace. No living Frenchman had done half so much to bring about the state of national feeling which enabled Louis Napoleon to precipitate the nation into a war against Prussia. Perhaps they thought the man whose bitterest complaint against the Emperor was that he failed to take advantage of the chance of crushing Prussia in 1866, was not the most likely emissary to conciliate victorious Prussia in 1870. But Thiers was determined to make himself useful, and the Republican Government had to give in at last, and concede some sort of official authority to him. Like the young lady who said she married the importunate suitor to get rid of him, Jules Favre and his colleagues probably accepted M. Thiers for their spokesman as the only way of escaping from his eloquence. His mission was heroic and patriotic, or egotistical and fussy, just as you are pleased to regard it. In certain lights Cardinal Richelieu looks wonderfully like Bottom the weaver. But it is impossible not to admire the energy and courage of the irrepressible, inexhaustible, fragile-looking, shabby old Orleanist. Thiers does not seem a personage capable of enduring fatigue. He appears a sapless, withered, wasted old creature. But the restless, fiery, exuberant, egotistical energy which carried him along so far and so fast in life, has apparently gained rather than lost in strength and resource during the forty years which have elapsed since the subject of this sketch, then editor of the "National," drew up in Paris the famous protest against the five infamous *ordonnances* of Charles the Tenth, and thus sounded the prelude to the Revolution of July.

It must have been no common stock of self-possession and self-complacency which enabled M. Thiers to present himself before the great Prussian Chancellor as a messenger of peace. Bismarck, who has a happy knack of apt Shakespearian quotation, might have accosted him in the words of Beatrice and said, "This is a man's office, but not yours." For M Thiers, throughout his whole career, devoted his brilliant gifts to the promotion of that spirit of narrow national vainglory which of late years has made France dreaded and detested in Germany. M. Thiers is like Æsop's trumpeter—guilty not of making war himself, but of blowing the blasts which set other men fighting. The very speech in which he protested last summer against the war initiated by the Imperial Government, was inspired by a principle more immoral, and more calculated to inflame Germany with resentment, than the very declaration of war itself. For Thiers only condemned the war on the ground that France was not properly prepared to crush Germany; that she had lost her opportunity by not falling on Prussia while the latter was in the death-grapple with Austria in 1866; and that as France had not done the thing at the right time, she had better not run the risk of doing it incompletely, by making the effort at an inopportune moment.

These considerations, however, did not trouble M. Thiers. He advanced to meet Count von Bismarck with the easy confidence of one who feels that he has a right to be treated as the best of friends and most appropriate of envoys. If, immediately after the conclusion of the American war, John Bright had been sent to Washington by England to endeavor to settle the Alabama dispute, he probably would not have approached the President with anything like the confident assurance of a genial welcome which inspired M. Thiers when he offered himself as a messenger to the Prussian statesman. This very sublimity of egotism is, and always was, one of the sources of the success of M. Thiers. No man could with more perfect composure and self-satisfaction dare to be inconsistent. His was the very audacity and Quixotism of inconsistency. In office to-day, he could advocate and enforce the very measures of repression which yesterday, out of office, he was the foremost to denounce—nay, which he obtained office by opposing and denouncing. He whose energetic action in protesting against the celebrated five *ordonnances* of Charles the Tenth did so much to bring about the Revolution of July, was himself the chief official author of the equally celebrated "laws of September," introduced in Louis Philippe's reign, which might have suited the administration ot a Peter the Great, or any other uncompromising despot. In practical politics, of course, almost every minister is occasionally compelled by the force of circumstances to do things which bear a considerable resemblance to acts warmly condemned by him while he sat in opposition. But M. Thiers invariably, when in power, exhibited himself as the author and champion of principles and policy which he had denounced with all the force of his eloquent tongue when he was the opponent of the Government. He seemed in fact to be two men rather than one, so entirely did Thiers in office contrast with Thiers in opposition. But Thiers himself never appeared conscious of inconsistency. Indeed, he was always consistent with his one grand essential principle and creed—faith in the inspiration and the destiny of M. Thiers.

To one other principle too let it be said in justice that this brilliant politician has always been faithful—the principle which maintains the right of France to throw her sword into the scale where every or any foreign question is to be weighed. When, after a long absence from the parliamentary arena, he entered the Imperial Corps Législatif as one of the deputies for Paris, he soon proved himself to be "old Cassius still." Age, study, experience, retirement, reflection, had in no wise dimmed the fire of his ardent nationalism. Eagerly as ever he contended for the sacred right of France to dragoon all Europe into obedience, to chop up the Continent into such symmetrical sections as might seem suitable to the taste and the convenience of French statesmen. Undoubtedly he was a sharp, tormenting thorn in the side of the Imperial Government when he returned to active political life. Louis Napoleon had no minister who could pretend to compare with Thiers in debate. He was an aggravating and exasperating enemy, against whom fluent and shallow men like Billault and Baroche, or even speakers of heavier calibre like Rouher, had no chance whatever. But there were times when to any impartial mind the invectives of Thiers made the Imperial policy look noble and enlightened in comparison with the canons of detestable egotism which he propounded as the true principles of government. I remember thinking more than once that if Louis Napoleon's Ministers could only have risen to the real height of the situation and appealed to whatever there was of lofty unselfish feeling in France, they might have overwhelmed their remorseless and envenomed critic. In 1866 and 1867, for example, Thiers made it a cardinal point of complaint and invective against the French Government that it had not prevented by force of arms the progress of Germany's unity. Nothing could be more pungent, brilliant, bitter, than the eloquence with which he proclaimed and advocated his doctrines of ignoble and unscrupulous selfishness. Why did not the Imperial spokesmen assume a virtue if they had it not, and boldly declare that the Government of France scorned the shallow and envious policy which sees calamity and danger in the union and growing strength of a neighboring people? Such a chord bravely struck would have awakened an echo in every true and generous heart. But the Imperial Ministers feebly tried to fight M. Thiers upon his own ground, to accept his principles as the conditions of contest. They endeavored in a paltering and limping way to show that the French Government had been selfish and only selfish, and had taken every care to keep Germany properly weak and divided. It was during one of these debates, thus provoked by M. Thiers, that occasion was given to Count von Bismarck for one of his most striking *coups de théâtre.* The French Minister (if I remember rightly, it was M. Rouher), tortured and baited by M. Thiers, stood at bay at last, and boldly declared that the Government of France had taken measures to render impossible any political cohesion of North and South Germany. A day or two after, Count von Bismarck effectively and contemptuously replied to this declaration by unfolding in the Prussian Chamber the treaties of alliance already concluded between his Government and the South German States.

It has always been a matter of surprise to me that Thiers did not prove a success at the bar, to which at first he applied his abilities. He seems to have the very gifts which would naturally have made a great pleader. All through his political career he displayed a wonderful capacity for making the worse appear the better cause. The adroitness which contends skilfully that black is white to-day, having argued with equal force and fluency that white was green yesterday, would have been highly appropriate and respectable in a legal advocate. But M. Thiers did not somehow get on at the bar, and having no influential friends (he was, I think, the son of a locksmith), but plenty of ambition, courage, and confidence, he strove to enter political life by the avenue of journalism. Much of Thiers's subsequent success as a debater was probably due to that skill which a practised journalist naturally acquires—the dexterity of arraying facts and arguments so as not to bear too long on any one part of the subject, and not to offer to the mind of the reader more than his patience and interest are willing to accept. Most of the events of his political career, up to his reappearance in public life in 1863, belong wholly to history and the past. His long rivalry with Guizot, his intrigues out of office, and his conduct as a Minister of Louis Philippe, have hardly a more direct and vital connection with the affairs of to-day than the statecraft of Mazarin or the political vicissitudes of Bolingbroke. One indeed of the projects of M. Thiers has now come rather unexpectedly into active operation. The fortifications of Paris were the offspring of the apprehension M. Thiers entertained, thirty years ago, that the Eastern question of that day might provoke another great European war. Since that time many critics sneered and laughed a good deal at M. Thiers's system of fortifications; but the whirligig of time has brought the statesman his revenge. No one could mistake the meaning of the smile of self-satisfaction which used last autumn to light up the unattractive features of the veteran Orleanist, as he made tour after tour of inspection around the defences of Paris. This chain of fortifications alone, one might almost say, connects the Thiers of the present generation with the Thiers of the past. There were malignant persons who did not scruple to say that the author of the scheme of defences was not altogether sorry for the national calamity which had brought them into use, and apparently justified their construction. It is very hard to be altogether sorry for even a domestic misfortune which gives one who is especially proud of his foresight and sagacity an opportunity of pointing out that the precautions which he recommended, and other members of the family scorned, are now eagerly adopted by unanimous concurrence. There certainly was something of the pardonable pride of the author of a long misprized invention visible in the face of M. Thiers as he used to gaze upon his beloved system of fortifications any time in last September. Little did even he himself think when, after Sadowa, he accused the Emperor's Government of having left itself no blunder more to commit, that it had yet to perpetrate one crowning and gigantic mistake, and that one effect at least of this stupendous error would be to compel Paris to treat *au sérieux*, and as a supreme necessity, that system of defences so long regarded as good for little else than to remind the present generation that Louis Adolphe Thiers was once Prime Minister of France.

Thiers was not far short of seventy years old when, in 1863, he entered upon a new chapter of his public life as one of the deputies for Paris in the Imperial Corps Législatif. A new generation had meantime arisen. Men were growing into fame as orators and politicians who were boys when Thiers was last heard as a parliamentary debater. He returned to political life at an eventful time and accompanied by some notable compeers. The elections which sent Thiers to represent the department of the Seine made the venerable and illustrious Berryer one of the delegates from Marseilles. I doubt whether the political life of any country has ever produced a purer, grander figure than that of Berryer; I am sure that an obsolete and hopeless cause never had a nobler advocate. The genius and the virtues of Berryer are indeed the loftiest claims modern French legitimacy can offer to the respect of posterity. I look back with a feeling of something like veneration to that grand and kingly form, to the sweet, serene, unaffected dignity of that august nature. Berryer belonged to a totally different political order from that of Thiers. As John Bright is to Disraeli, as John Henry Newman is to Monsignore Capel, as Montalembert was to Louis Veuillot, as Charles Sumner is to Seward, so was Berryer to Thiers. Of the oratorical merits of the two men I shall speak hereafter; now I refer to the relative value of their political characters. With Thiers and Berryer there came back to political life some men of mark and worth. Garnier-Pagès was one, the impulsive, true-hearted, not very strong-headed Republican; a man who might be a great leader if fine phrases and good intentions could rule the world. Carnot was another, not much perhaps in himself, but great as the son of the illustrious organizer of victory (oh, if France had lately had one hour of Carnot!), and personally very popular just then because of his scornful rejection of Louis Napoleon's offer to bring back the ashes of his father from Magdeburg in Prussia to France. Eugène Pelletan, who had been suffering savage persecution because of his fierce attack on the Empire in his book, "The New Babylon"; Jules Simon, a superior sort of French Tom Hughes—Tom Hughes with republican convictions and strong backbone—and several other men of name and fibre, were now companions in the Corps Législatif. All these, differing widely in personal opinions, and indeed representing every kind of political view, from the chivalrous and romantic legitimacy of Berryer to the republican religion or fetichism of Garnier-Pagès, combined to make up an opposition to the Imperial Government. Up to that time the opposition had consisted simply of five men. For years those five had fought a persevering and apparently hopeless fight against the strength of Imperial arms, Imperial gold, and the lungs of Imperial hirelings. Of the five the leader was Jules Favre. The second in command was Emile Ollivier, whose treason to liberty, truth, and peace has since been so sternly avenged by destiny. The other three were Picard, a member of the Republican Government of September, and MM. Darimon and Henon. Numerically the opposition, now strengthened by the new accessions, became quite respectable; morally and politically it wholly changed the situation. It was no longer a Leonidas or Horatius Cocles desperately holding a pass; it was an army encountering an army. The Imperialists of course still far outnumbered their opponents; but there were no men among the devotees of Imperialism who could even pretend to compare as orators with Berryer, Thiers, or Favre. Of these three men, it seems to me that Berryer was by far the greatest orator, but Thiers left him nowhere as a partisan leader. Thiers undoubtedly pushed Jules Favre aside and made him quite a secondary figure. Thiers delighted in worrying a ministry. He never needed, as Berryer did, the impulse of a great principle and a great purpose. He felt all the joy of the strife which distinguishes the born gladiator. He soon proved that his years had in no degree impaired his oratorical capacity. It became one of the grand events of Paris when Thiers was to speak. Owing to the peculiar regulations of the French Chamber, which required that those who meant to take part in a debate should inscribe their names beforehand in the book, and speak according to their turn—an odious usage, fatal to all genuine debate—it was always known in advance through Paris that to-morrow or the day after Thiers was to speak. Then came a struggle for places in what an Englishman would call the strangers' gallery. The Palais Bourbon, where the Corps Législatif held its sittings, opposite the Place de la Concorde, has the noble distinction of providing the least and worst accommodation for the public of any House of Assembly in the civilized world. The English House of Commons is miserably defective and niggardly in this respect, but it is liberal and lavish when compared with the French Corps Législatif. Therefore, when M. Thiers was about to speak, there was as much intriguing, clamoring, beseeching, wrangling, storming for seats in the public *tribunes* as would have sufficed to carry an English county election. The trouble had its reward. Nobody could be disappointed in M. Thiers who merely desired an intellectual exercise and treat. Thiers never was heavy or dull. He is, I think, the most interesting of all the great European debaters. I do not know whether I convey exactly the meaning I wish to express when I used the word "interesting." What I mean is that there is in M. Thiers an inexhaustible vivacity, freshness, and variety which never allows the attention to wander or flag. He never dwells too long on any one part of his subject; or if he has to dwell long anywhere, he enlivens the theme by a lavish copiousness of novel argument, application, and illustration, which is irresistibly piquant and fascinating. Reëntering public life in his old age, M. Thiers had physically something like the advantage which I have known to be possessed by certain mature actresses, who, never having had any claim to personal beauty in their youth, were visited with hardly any penalty of time when they began to descend into age. Thiers always had an insignificant presence, a dreadfully bad voice, and an unpleasant delivery. Time added nothing, and probably could add nothing, to these disadvantages. Already John Bright has lost, already Gladstone is losing, those magnificent qualities of voice and intonation which till lately distinguished both from all other living English orators. One of the only fine passages in Disraeli's "Life of Lord George Bentinck" is that in which he describes the melancholy sensation created in the House of Commons when Daniel O'Connell, feeble and broken down, tried vainly to raise above a mumbling murmur those accents which once could thrill and vibrate to the furthest corner of the most capacious hall. But the voice and delivery of Thiers at seventy were no whit worse than those of Thiers at forty; and in energy, vivacity, and variety, I think the opposition leader of 1866 had rather gained upon the Minister of 1836. In everything that makes a great orator he was far beneath Berryer. The latter had as commanding a presence as he had a superb voice, and a manner at once graceful and dignified. Berryer, too, had the sustaining strength of a profound conviction, pure and lofty as a faith. If Berryer was a political Don Quixote, Thiers was a political Gil Blas. Thiers was all sparkle, antithesis, audacity, sophistry. His *tours de force* were perfect masterpieces of fearless adroitness. He darted from point to point, from paradox to paradox, with the bewildering agility of a squirrel. He flashed through the heavy atmosphere of a dull debate with the scintillating radiancy of a firefly. He propounded sentiments of freedom which would positively have captivated you if you had not known a little of the antecedents of the orator. He threw off concise and luminous maxims of government which would have been precious guides if human politics could only be ruled by epigram. His long experience as a partisan leader, in and out of office, had made him master of a vast array of facts and dates, which he was expert to marshal in such a manner as often to bewilder his opponents. His knowledge of the mechanism and regulations of diplomatic and parliamentary practice was consummate. He was singularly clear and attractive in statement; his mode of putting a case had something in it that was positively fascinating. He was sharp and severe in retort, and there was a cold, self-complacent *hauteur* in his way of putting down an adversary, which occasionally reminded one of a peculiarity of Earl Russell's style when the latter was still a good parliamentary debater. M. Thiers had the great merit of never talking over the heads, above the understandings of his audience. His style of language was of the same character perhaps as that of Mr. Wendell Phillips. Of course no two men could possibly be more unlike in the manner of speaking, but the rhetorical vernacular of both has a considerable resemblance. The diction in each case is clear, incisive, penetrating—never, or hardly ever, rising to anything of exalted oratorical grandeur, never involved in mist or haze of any kind, and with the same habitual acidity and sharpness in it. I presume M. Thiers wrote the greater part of his speeches beforehand, but he evidently had the happy faculty, rare even among accomplished orators, which enables a speaker to blend the elaborately prepared portions of his discourse with the extemporaneous passages originated by the impulses and the incidents of the debate. Some of the cleverest arguments, and especially some of the cleverest sarcastic hits in M. Thiers's recent speeches, were provoked by questions and interruptions which must have been quite unexpected. But a strange peculiarity about the whole body of the speeches, the written parts as well as the extemporaneous, was that they bore no resemblance whatever to the glittering and gorgeous style which is so common and so objectionable in the pages of the author's history of the French Revolution, and of the Consulate and the Empire. I must say that I think M. Thiers's historical works are decidedly heavy reading. I think his speeches are more interesting and attractive to read than those of any political speaker of our day. As an orator I set him below Berryer, below Gladstone and Bright, below Wendell Phillips, and not above Disraeli. But as an interesting speaker—I can think of no better qualification for him—I place M. Thiers above any of those masters of the art of eloquence.

I have not compared M. Thiers with Jules Favre. Any juxtaposition of the two ought rather perhaps to be in the way of contrast than of comparison. Jules Favre is probably the most exquisite and perfect rhetorician practising in the public debates of our time. No one else can lend so brilliant an effect, so delightful an emphasis to words and phrases by the mere modulations of his tone. I once heard a French workingman say that Jules Favre *parlait comme un ange*—talked like an angel; and there was a simple appropriateness in the expression. An angel, if he had to address so unsympathetic and uncongenial an audience as the Imperial Corps Législatif, could hardly lend more musical effect to the meaning of his words than was given by Jules Favre's consummate rhetorical skill. But I must acknowledge that to me at least there never seemed to be much in what Jules Favre said. It seemed to me too often to want marrow and backbone. It was an eloquence of fine phrases and splendid vague generalities. "Flow on, thou shining river," one felt sometimes inclined to say as the bright, broad, shallow stream glided away. If Thiers spoke for half a day, and the discourse covered a dozen columns of the closely-printed "Moniteur," yet the listener or reader came away with the impression that the orator had crammed quite a surprising quantity of matter into his speech, and could have found ever so much more to say on the same subject. The impression produced on me at least by the speeches of Jules Favre was always of the very opposite character. They seemed to be all rhetoric and modulation; they were without depth and without fibre. The essentially declamatory character of Jules Favre's eloquence received its most complete illustration in that remarkable document—so painful and pathetic because of its obvious earnestness, so ludicrous and almost contemptible because of its turgid and extravagant outbursts—the report of his recent interviews with Count von Bismarck at the Prussian headquarters near Versailles. One must keep constantly in mind the awful seriousness of the situation, and the genuine suffering which it must have imposed upon Jules Favre, not to laugh outright or feel disgusted at the inflated, hyperbolical, and melodramatic style in which the Republican Minister describes his interview with the Prussian Chancellor. Now, whatever faults of style M. Thiers might commit, he never could thus make himself ridiculous. He never allows himself to be out of tune with the occasion and the audience. You may differ utterly from him, you may distrust and dislike him; but Thiers, the parliamentary orator, will not permit you to laugh at him.

Thiers was always very happy in his replies and retorts, and he never allowed if he could an interruption to one of his speeches in the Corps Législatif to pass without seizing its meaning and at once dissecting and demolishing it. He rejoiced in the light sword-play of such exercises. He would never have been contented with the superb quietness of contempt by which Berryer in one of his latest speeches crushed Granier de Cassagnac, the abject serf and hireling of Imperialism. While Berryer was speaking, Granier de Cassagnac suddenly expressed his coarse dissent from one of the orator's statements by crying out, "That is not true." Berryer was not certain as to the source of this insolent interruption. He gazed all round the assembly, and demanded in accents of subdued and noble indignation who had dared thus to challenge the truth of his statement. There was a dead pause. Even enemies looked up with reverence to the grand old orator, and were ashamed of the rude insult flung at him. De Cassagnac quailed, but every eye was on him, and he was compelled to declare himself. "It was I who spoke," said the Imperial servant. Berryer looked at him for a moment, and then said, "Oh, it was *you!*—then it is of no consequence," and calmly resumed the thread of his discourse. Nothing could have been finer, nothing more demolishing than the cold, grand contempt which branded De Cassagnac as a creature incapable of meriting, even by insult, the notice of a man of honor. But Thiers would never have been satisfied with such a mode of crushing an adversary; and indeed it needed all the majesty of Berryer's presence and the moral grandeur of his character to give it full force and emphasis. Thiers would have showered upon the head of the Imperial lacquey a whole fiery cornucopia of sarcasm and sharp invective, and De Cassagnac would have gone home rather proud of having drawn down upon his head the angry eloquence of the great Orleanist orator.

Thiers threw his whole soul into his speeches—not merely as to their preparation, but as to their revision and publication. According to the Imperial system, no independent reports of speeches in the Chambers were allowed to appear in print. The official stenographers noted down in full each day's debate, and the whole was published next day in the "Moniteur Universel." These reports professed to give every word and syllable of the speeches—every whisper of interruption. Sometimes, therefore, the "Moniteur" came out with twenty of its columns filled up with the dull maunderings of some provincial blockhead, for whom servility and money had secured an official candidature. Besides these stupendous reports, the Government furnished a somewhat condensed version, in which the twenty-column speech was reduced say to a dozen columns. Either of these reports the public journals might take, but none other; and no journal must alter or condense by the omission of a line or the substitution of a word the text thus officially furnished. When Thiers had spent the whole day in delivering a speech, he was accustomed to spend the whole night in reading over and correcting the proof-sheets of the official report. The venerable orator would hurry home when the sitting was over, change his clothes, get into his arm-chair before his desk, and set to work at the proof-sheets according as they came. Over these he would toil with the minute and patient inspection of a watchmaker or a lapidary, reading this or that passage many times, until he had satisfied himself that no error remained and that no turn of expression could well be improved. Before this task was done, the night had probably long faded and the early sun was already lighting Paris; but when the Corps Législatif came to assemble at noon, the inexhaustible septuagenarian was at his post again. That evening he would be found, the central figure of a group, in some salon, scattering his brilliant sayings and acrid sarcasms around him, and in all probability exercising his humor at the expense of the Imperial Ministers, the Empire, and even the Emperor himself. After 1866 he was exuberant in his *bons mots* about the humiliation of the Imperial Cabinet by Prussia. "Bismarck," he once declared, "is the best supporter of the French Government. He keeps it always in its place by first boxing it on one ear and then maintaining the equilibrium by boxing it on the other."

If one could have been present at the recent interviews between Count Bismarck and M. Thiers, he would doubtless have enjoyed a curious and edifying intellectual treat. Bismarck is a man of imperturbable good humor; Thiers a man of imperturbable self-conceit. Thiers has a tongue which never lacks a word, and that the most expressive word. Bismarck has a rare gift of shrewd satirical humor, and of phrases that stick to public memory. Each man would have regarded the other as a worthy antagonist in a duel of words. Neither would care to waste much time in lofty sentiment and grandiose appeals. Each would thoroughly understand that his best motto would be, "*A corsaire, corsaire et demi.*" Bismarck would find in Thiers no feather-headed Benedetti; assuredly, Thiers would favor Bismarck with none of Jules Favre's sighs and tears, and bravado and choking emotions. Thiers would have the greater part of the talk, that is certain; but Bismarck would probably contrive to compress a good deal of meaning and significance into his curt interjected sentences. Thiers assuredly must have long since worn out any freshness of surprise or thrilling emotion of any kind at the political convulsions of France. To him even the spectacle of the standard of Prussia hoisted on the pinnacles of Versailles could hardly have been an overpowering wonder. He had seen the soldiers of Prussia picketed in Paris; he could remember when a fickle Parisian populace, weary of war, had thronged into the streets to applaud the entrance of the conquering Czar of Russia. He had seen the Bourbon restored, and had helped to overthrow him. He had been twice the chief Minister of that Louis Philippe of Orleans, who in his youth had had to save the Princess his sister by carrying her off in her night-gown, without time to throw a shawl around her, and whose long years of exile had led him, in fulfilment of the prophecy of Danton, to the throne of France at last. He had helped towards the downfall of that same King his master, and had striven vainly at the end to stand between him and his fate. He had seen a second Republic rise and sink; he had now become the envoy of a third Republic. He had refused to serve an Imperial Napoleon, although his own teaching and preaching had been among the most effective agencies in debauching the mind and heart of the nation, and thus rendering a second Empire possible. People say M. Thiers has no feelings, and I shall not venture to contradict them—I have often heard the statement from those who know better than I can pretend to do. It would have been personally unfortunate for him in his interview with Count von Bismarck if he had been burthened with feelings. For he must surely in such a case have felt bitterly the consciousness that the misfortunes which had fallen on his country were in great measure the fruit of his own doctrines and his own labors. If the public conscience of France had not been seared and hardened against all sentiment of obligation to international principle, where French glory and French aggrandizement were concerned; if France had not learned to believe that no foreign nation had any rights which she was bound to respect; if she had not been saturated with the conviction that every benefit to a neighbor was an injury to herself; if she had not accepted these views as articles of national faith, and followed them out wherever she could to their uttermost consequences, then M. Thiers might be said to have written and spoken and lived in vain.

It is probable that a new career presents itself as a possibility to the indomitable energy, and, as many would say, the insatiable ambition of M. Thiers. Certainly, there seems not the faintest indication that the veteran believes himself to lag superfluous on the stage. It is likely that he rushed into the recent peace negotiations with the hope of playing over again the part so skilfully played by Talleyrand at the time of the Congress of Vienna, by virtue of which France obtained so much advantage which might hardly have been expected, and Germany got so little of what she might naturally have looked for. I certainly shall not venture to say whether M. Thiers may not even yet have an important official career before him. His recent enterprises and expeditions give evidence enough that he has nerve and physique for any undertaking likely to attract him, and I see no reason to doubt that his intellect is as fresh and active as it was thirty years ago. Thiers deserves nothing but honor for the unconquerable energy and courage which refuse to yield to years, and will not acknowledge the triumph of time. He would deserve far greater honor still if we could regard him as a disinterested patriot; highest honor of all if his principles were as wise and just as his ambition was unselfish. But charity itself could hardly hope to reconcile the facts of M. Thiers's long and varied career with any theory ascribing to the man himself a pure and disinterested purpose. That a statesman has changed his opinions is often his highest glory, if, as in the case of Mr. Gladstone, he has thereby grown into the light and the right. Noı is a change of views necessarily a reproach to a politician, even though he may have retrograded or gone wrong. But the man who is invariably a passionate liberal when out of office, and a severe conservative when in power; who makes it a regular practice to have one set of opinions while he leads the opposition, and another when he has succeeded in mounting to the lead of a ministry; such a man cannot possibly hope to obtain for such systematic alternations the credit of even a capricious and fantastic sincerity. No one who knows anything of M. Thiers would consent thus to exalt his heart at the expense of his head. When the late Lord Cardigan was, rightly or wrongly, accused of having returned rather too quickly from the famous charge of the Light Brigade at Balaklava, his lordship, among other things, alleged that his horse had run away with him. A bitter critic thereupon declared that Lord Cardigan could not be allowed thus unfairly to depreciate his consummate horsemanship. I am afraid we cannot allow M. Thiers's intelligence and shrewdness to be unjustly depreciated by the assumption that his political tergiversations were the result of meaningless caprice.

M. Thiers is one of the most gifted men of his day. But he is not, in my judgment, a great man. He wants altogether the grand and stable qualities of principle and judgment which are needed to constitute political greatness. His statesmanship is a sort of policy belonging apparently to the school of the Lower Empire; a Byzantine blending of intrigue and impudence. He has never had the faculty of reading the signs of the times, or of understanding that to-day is not necessarily like yesterday. But for the wonderful gifts of the man, there would seem to be something positively childish in the egotism which could believe that it lay in the power of France to maintain, despite of destiny, the petty princes of Germany and Italy, to arrange the political conditions of England, and prescribe to the United States how far their principle of internal coheson should reach. Victor Hugo is undoubtedly an egotistic Frenchman. Some of his recent utterances have been foolish and ridiculous. But the folly has been that of a great soul; the folly has consisted in appealing, out of all time and place, to sublime and impracticable sentiments of human brotherhood and love which ought to influence all human souls, but do not and probably never will. Far different is the egotism of Thiers. It is the egotism of selfishness, arrogance, and craft. In a sublime world, Victor Hugo's appeals would cease to be ridiculous; but the nobler the world, the more ignoble would seem the doctrines and the policy of Thiers. My own admiration of Thiers extends only to his skill as a debater and his marvellous intellectual vitality. The man who, despite the most disheartening disadvantages of presence, voice, and manner, is yet the most fascinating political debater of his time, the man who at seventy-three years of age can go up in a balloon in quest of a new career, must surely command some interest and admiration, let critical wisdom preach to us never so wisely. But the best days will have arisen for France when such a political character and such a literary career as those of M. Thiers shall have become an anachronism and an impossibility.

PRINCE NAPOLEON.

SOME few years ago, seven or eight perhaps, a certain sensation was created among artists, and journalists, and literary men, and connoisseurs, and critics, by one of Flandrin's best portraits. Undoubtedly, the portrait was an admirable likeness; no one who had ever seen the original could deny or question that; but yet there was an air, a character, a certain depth of idealized expression about it which seemed to present the subject in a new light, and threw one into a kind of doubt as to whether he had ever truly understood the original before. Either the painter had unduly glorified his sitter, or the sitter had impressed upon the artist a true idea of his character and intellect which had never before been revealed to the public at large. The portrait was that of a man of middle age, with a smooth, broad, thoughtful brow, a character of command about the finely-formed, somewhat sensuous lips; chin and nose beautifully moulded, in fact what ladies who write novels would call "chiselled;" a face degenerating a little into mere flesh, but still dignified and imposing. Everywhere over the face there was a tone of dissatisfaction, of disappointment, of sullenness mingling strangely with the sensuous characteristics, and conveying somehow the idea of great power and daring ambition unduly repressed by outward conditions, or rendered barren by inward defects, or actually frustrated by failure and fate. "A Cæsar out of employment!" exclaimed a celebrated French author and critic. So much there was of the Cæsar in the face that no school-boy, no Miss in her teens could have even glanced at it without saying, "That is the face of a Bonaparte!" Were not the features a little too massive, it might have passed for an admirable likeness of the victor of Austerlitz; or, at all events, of the Napoleon of Leipzig or the Hundred Days. Probably any ordinary observer would at once have set it down as a portrait of the great Napoleon, and never thought there could be any doubt about the matter. It was, in fact, the likeness of Napoleon-Jerome, son of the rattle-pate King of Westphalia—Prince Napoleon, as he is ordinarily called, the Plon-plon whom soldiers jeer at, the "Red Prince" whom priests and Legitimists denounce, the cousin of the Emperor of the French, the son-in-law of the King of Italy.

It was only somewhere about, or a little before the time of the Flandrin portrait, that Prince Napoleon had the honor of becoming a mystery in the eyes of the public. Up to 1860, his character was quite settled in public estimation, just as that of Louis Napoleon had been up to the time of the *coup d'etat.* Public opinion generally settles the characters of conspicuous men at first by the intuitive process—the most delightful and easy method possible, dispensing, as it does, with any necessity for studying the subject, or even knowing anything at all about it. When the intuitive process has once adjusted a man's character, it is not easy to get people to believe in any other adjustment. Still, there are some remarkable instances of a change in popular opinion. The case of Louis Napoleon, the Emperor, is one illustration; that of Prince Napoleon, his cousin, is another, not so remarkable, certainly, but still quite worthy of some attention.

Prince Napoleon had been before the world more or less since he appeared as representative of Corsica, in the Constituent Assembly of 1848. He was made conspicuous, in a negative sort of way, by having had no hand in the *coup d'etat,* or having even opposed it, although he did not scruple to profit by its success and enjoy its golden advantages. He had a command in the Crimean war; he was sent into Tuscany during the Italian campaign. All that time public opinion in Europe was unanimous about him. He was a sensualist, a coward, an imbecile, and a blockhead. He was a fat, stupid, muddle-headed Heliogabalus. Dulness, cowardice, and profligacy were his principal, perhaps his only characteristics. When the young Clotilde, of Savoy, was given to him for a wife, a positive cry of wonder and disgust went up from every country of Europe. In good truth, it was a scandalous thing to marry a young and innocent girl to a man nearly as old as her father; and who, undoubtedly, had been a *mauvais sujet*, and had led a life of dissipation so far. But Europe cried aloud as if three out of every four princely alliances were not made on the same principle and endowed with the same character. Had the Princess Clotilde been affianced to a hog or a gorilla, there could hardly have been greater wonder and horror expressed, so clear was the public mind about the stupidity and brutality of Prince Napoleon.

Certainly, if one looked a little deeper than mere public opinion, he would have found, even then, that here and there some men, not quite incapable of judging, did not accept the popular estimate of the Emperor's cousin. All through the memorable progress of the Congress of Paris—out of which sprang Italy—we find, by the documents subsequently made public, that Cavour was in close and frequent consultation with Prince Napoleon. Once we find Cavour saying that Prince Napoleon complains of his slowness, his too great moderation, and thinks he could serve the cause better by a little more boldness. "Perhaps he is right," says Cavour, in words to that effect; "but I fear I lack his force of character, his daringness of purpose." Richard Cobden makes the acquaintance of Prince Napoleon, and is surprised and delighted with his advanced opinions on the subject of free trade; and deliberately describes him (I heard Cobden use the words) as "one of the best informed, if not the very best informed, of all the public men of Europe." Kinglake observes the Prince during the Crimean campaign—where Napoleon-Jerome got his reputation for cowardice and his nick-name of Plon-plon—and finds in him a genius very like that of his uncle, the great Napoleon, especially a wonderful power of distinguishing at a glance between the essentials and the accidentals of any question or situation—and any one who has ever studied politics and public men will know how rare a faculty that is—and finally declares that he sees no reason to believe him inferior in courage to the conqueror of Marengo! Edmond About, not a very dull personage, and not quite given up to panegyric, bursts into a strain of almost lyrical enthusiasm about the wit, the brilliancy, the culture, the daring ambition of Prince Napoleon, and declares that the Prince is kept as much out of the way as possible, because a man endowed with a soul of such unresting energy, and the face of the great Emperor, is too formidable a personage to be seen hanging about the steps of a throne. To close this string of illustrations, Prince Napoleon is in somewhat frequent and confidential intercourse with Michel Chevalier, a man not likely to cultivate the society of heavy blockheads and dullards, even though these might happen to wear princely coronets. Clearly, public opinion here was even more directly at odds than it often is with the opinion of some whom we may call experts; and the difference was so great that there seemed no possible way of reconciling the two. A man may be a profligate and yet a man of genius, and even a patriot; but one cannot be a profligate blockhead and a man of genius, a Cloten and an Alcibiades, a Cæsar and a Pyrgopolinices at once.

It was in the early part of 1861 that Prince Napoleon contributed something of his own spontaneous motion to help in the solution of the enigma. That was the year when the Emperor removed the restriction which prevented both Chambers of the Legislature from freely debating the address, and the press from fully reporting the discussions. There was a remarkable debate in the Senate, ranging over a great variety of domestic and foreign questions, and one most memorable event of the debate was the brilliant, powerful and exhaustive oration delivered, with splendid energy and rhetorical effect, by Prince Napoleon. *Mon âne parle et même il parle bien*, declares the astonished Joan, in Voltaire's scandalous poem, "La Pucelle." Perhaps there was something of a similar wonder mingled with the burst of genuine admiration which went up first from Paris, then from France, and finally from Europe and America, when that magnificent democratic manifesto came to be read. Certainly, I remember no single speech which, during my time, created anything like the same sensation in Europe. For it took the outer world wholly by surprise. It was not a case like that of the sensation lately created by the florid and fervid eloquence of the young Spanish orator, Castellar. In this latter case the public were surprised and delighted to find that there was a master of thrilling rhetoric alive, and arrayed on the side of democratic freedom, of whose very existence most persons had been previously ignorant. But, in the case of Prince Napoleon, the surprise was, that a man whom the public had long known, and always set down as a stupid sensualist, should suddenly, and without any previous warning, turn out a great orator, whose eloquence had in it something so fresh, and genuine, and forcible that it recalled the memory of the most glorious days of the French Tribune. I write of this celebrated oration now only from recollection; and, of course, I did not hear it spoken. I say "of course," because the rules of the French Senate, unlike those of the Corps Legislatif, forbid the presence of any strangers during the debates. But those who heard it spoke enthusiastically of the force and freedom with which it was delivered; the sudden, impulsive fervor of occasional outbursts; and the wonderful readiness with which the speaker, when interrupted, as he was very frequently, passed from one topic to another in order to dispose of the interruption, and replied to sudden challenge with even prompter repartee. No one could read the speech without admiring the extent and variety of the political knowledge it displayed; the prodigality of illustration it flung over every argument; the thrilling power of some of its rhetorical "phrases;" the tone of sustained and passionate eloquence which made itself heard all throughout; and, perhaps above all, that flexible, spontaneous readiness of language and resource to which every interruption, every interjected question only acted like a spur to a generous horse, calling forth new and greater, and wholly unexpected efforts. In the French Senate I need, perhaps, hardly tell my readers, it is the habit to allow the utmost license of interruption, and Prince Napoleon's audacious onslaught on the reactionists and the *parti prêtre* called out even an unusual amount of impatient utterance. Those who interrupted took little by their motion. The energetic Prince tossed off his assailants as a bull flings the dogs away on the points of his horns. "Our principles are not yours," scornfully exclaims a Legitimist nobleman—the late Marquis de la Rochejaquelein, if I remember rightly. "Your principles are not ours!" vehemently replies the orator. "No, nor are your antecedents ours. Our pride is that our fathers fell on the battle-field resisting the foreign invaders whom your fathers brought in for the subjugation of France!" The speech is studded with sudden replies equally fervid and telling. Indeed, the whole material of the oration is rich, strong, and genuine. There seems to be in the eloquence of the French Chambers, of late, a certain want of freshness and natural power. I do not speak of Berryer—he had no such want. But Thiers—by far the ablest living debater who speaks only from preparation—with all his wonderful science and skill as an artist in debate, appears to be always somewhat artificial and elaborate. Jules Favre, with his exquisitely modulated tones, and his unrivalled choice of words, hardly ever appears to me to rise to that height where the orator, lost in his subject, compels his hearers to lose themselves also in it. Now, I cannot help thinking that the two or three really great speeches made by Prince Napoleon had in them more of the native fibre, force and passion of oratory than those of almost any Frenchman since the days of Mirabeau.

However that may be, the effect wrought on the public mind was unmistakable. Plon-plon had startled Europe. He entered the palace of the Luxembourg on that memorable day without any repute but that of a dullard and a sensualist; he came out of it a recognized orator. I have been told that he lay back in his open carriage and smoked his cigar, as he drove home from the Senate, to all appearance the same indolent, sullen, heavy apathetic personage whom all Paris had previously known and despised.

One notable effect of this famous speech was the reply which a certain passage in it drew from Louis Philippe's son, the Duc d'Aumale. Prince Napoleon had indulged in a bitter sneer or two against former dynasties, and the Duc d'Aumale, a man of great culture and ability, took up the quarrel fiercely. The Duke assailed Prince Napoleon in one of the keenest, most biting pamphlets which the political controversy of our day has produced. Among other things, the Duke replied to a supposed imputation on the weakness of Louis Philippe by admitting, frankly, that the *bourgeois* King had not dealt with enemies, when in his power, as a Bonaparte would have done. "*Et tenez*, Prince," wrote the Duke, "the only time when the word of a Bonaparte may be believed is when he avows that he will never spare a defenceless enemy." The pamphlet bristled with points equally sharp and envenomed. But the Duc d'Aumale was not content with written rejoinder. He sent a challenge to the Prince, and in serious earnest. The Prince, it need hardly be said, did not accept the challenge.

> Yes, like enough, high-battled Cæsar will
> Unstate his greatness, and be staged to the show
> Against a sworder!

Our Cæsar, though not "high-battled," was by no means likely to consent to be "staged against a sworder." The Emperor hastened to prevent any disastrous consequences, by insisting that the Prince must not accept the challenge—and there was no duel. People winked and sneered a good deal. It is said that the martial King Victor Emmanuel grumbled and chafed at his son-in-law; but there was no fight. Let me say, for my own part, that I think Prince Napoleon was quite right in not accepting the challenge, and that I do not believe him to be wanting in personal courage.

From that moment, Prince Napoleon became a conspicuous figure in European politics, and when any great question arose, men turned anxiously toward him, curious to know what he would do or say. In three or four successive sessions he spoke in the Senate, and even with the impression of the first surprise still strong on the public mind, the speeches preserved abundantly the reputation which the earliest of them had so suddenly created. He might be the *enfant terrible* of the Bonaparte family; he might be utterly wanting in statesmanship;

he might be insincere ; he might be physically a coward ; but all the world now admitted him to be an orator, and, in his way, a man of genius.

Then it became known to the public, all at once, that the Prince, whatever his failings, had some rare gifts besides that of eloquence. He was undoubtedly a man of exquisite taste in all things artistic ; he had an intelligent and liberal knowledge of practical science ; he had a great faculty of organization ; he was a keen humorist and wit. He loved the society of artists, and journalists, and literary men ; he associated with them *en bon camerade*, and he could talk with each upon his own subject ; his *bon mots* soon began to circulate far and wide. He was a patron of Revolution. In the innermost privacy of the Palais Royal men like Mieroslawski, the Polish Red Revolutionist, men like General Türr, unfolded and discussed their plans. Prince Gortschakoff, in his despatches at the time of the Polish Rebellion, distinctly pointed to the palace of Prince Napoleon as the headquarters of the insurrection. The "Red Prince" grew to be one of the mysterious figures in European policy. Was he in league with his cousin, the Emperor—or was he his cousin's enemy? Did he hope, on the strength of that Bonaparte face, and his secret league with Democracy, to mount one day from the steps of the throne to the throne itself? Between him and the succession to that throne intervened only the life of one frail boy. Was Prince Napoleon preparing for the day when he might play the part of a Gloster (without the smothering), and, pushing the boy aside, succeed to the crown of the great Emperor whom in face he so strikingly resembled?

At last came the celebrated Ajaccio speech. The Emperor had gone to visit Algeria ; the Prince went to deliver an oration at the inauguration of a monument to Napoleon I., at Ajaccio. The speech was, in brief, a powerful, passionate denunciation of Austria, and the principles which Austria represented before Sadowa taught her a lesson of tardy wisdom. Viewed as the exposition of a professor of history, one might fairly acknowledge the Prince's speech to have illustrated eloquently some solid and stern truths, which Europe would have done well even then to consider deeply. Subsequent events have justified and illuminated many of what then seemed the most startling utterances of the orator. Austria, for example, practically admits, by her present policy, the justice of much that Prince Napoleon pleaded against her. But as the speech of the Emperor's cousin ; of one who stood in near order of succession to the throne ; of one who had only just been raised to an office in the State so high that in the absence of the sovereign it made him seem the sovereign's proper representative, it was undoubtedly a piece of marvellous indiscretion. Europe stood amazed at its outspoken audacity. The Emperor could not overlook it ; and he publicly repudiated it. Prince Napoleon resigned his public offices—including that of President of the Commissioners of the International Exhibition, which undertaking suffered sadly from lack of his organizing capacity and his admirable taste and judgment—and the Imperial orator of Democracy disappeared from the public stage as suddenly, and amid as much tumult, as he had entered upon it.

Prince Napoleon has, indeed, been taken into favor since by his Imperial cousin, and has been sent on one or two missions, more or less important or mysterious ; but he has never, from the date of the Ajaccio speech up to the present moment, played any important part as a public man. He is not, however, "played out." His energy, his ambition, his ability, will assuredly bring him prominently before the public again. Let us, meanwhile, endeavor to set before the readers of THE GALAXY a fair and true picture of the man, free alike from the exaggerated proportions which wondering *quidnuncs* or parasites attribute to him, and from the distortions of unfriendly painters. Exaggeration of both kinds apart, Prince Napoleon is really one of the most remarkable figures on the present stage of French history. He is, at least, a man of great possibilities. Let us try to ascertain fairly what he is, and what are his chances for the future.

Born of a hair-brained, eccentric, adventure-seeking, negligent, selfish father, Prince Napoleon had little of the advantages of a home education. His boyhood, his youth, were passed in a vagrant kind of way, ranging from country to country, from court to court. He started in life with great natural talents, a strong tendency to something not very unlike rowdyism, an immense ambition, an almost equally vast indolence, a deep and genuine love of arts, letters, and luxury, an eccentric, fitful temper, and a predominant pride in that relationship to the great Emperor which is so plainly stamped upon his face. Without entering into any questions of current scandal, everybody must know that Napoleon III. has nothing of the Bonaparte in his face, a fact on which Prince Napoleon, in his earlier and wilder days, was not always very slow to comment. Indolence, love of luxury, and a capricious temper have, perhaps, been the chief enemies which have hitherto prevented the latter from fulfilling any high ambition. It would be affectation to ignore the fact that Prince Napoleon flung many years away in mere dissipation. Stories are told in Paris which would represent him almost as a Vitellius or an Egalité in profligacy—stories some of which simply transcend belief by their very monstrosity. Even to this day, to this hour, it is the firm conviction of the general public that the Emperor's cousin is steeped to the lips in sensuality. Now, rejecting, of course, a huge mass of this scandal, it is certain that Prince Napoleon was, for a long time, a downright *mauvais sujet;* it is by no means certain that he has, even at his present mature age, discarded all his evil habits. His temper is much against him. People habitually contrast the unvarying courtesy and self-control of the Emperor with the occasional brusqueness, and even rudeness, of the Prince. True that Prince Napoleon can be frankly and warmly familiar with his intimates, and even that, like Prince Hal, he sometimes encourages a degree of familiarity which hardly tends to mutual respect. But the outer world cannot always rely on him. He can be undiplomatically rough and hot, and he has a gift of biting jest which is perhaps one of the most dangerous qualities a statesman can cultivate. Then there is a personal restlessness about him which even princes cannot afford safely to indulge. He has hardly ever had any official position assigned to him which he did not sometime or other scornfully abandon on the spur of some sudden impulse. The Madrid embassy in former days, the Algerian administration, the Crimean command—these and other offices he only accepted to resign. He has wandered more widely over the face of the earth than any other living prince—probably than any other prince that ever lived. It used to be humorously said of him that he was qualifying to become a teacher of geography, in the event of fortune once more driving the race of Bonaparte into exile and obscurity. What port is there that has not sheltered his wandering yacht? He has pleasant dwellings enough to induce a man to stay at home. His Palais Royal is one of the most elegant and tasteful abodes belonging to a European prince. The stranger in Paris who is fortunate enough to obtain admission to it—and, indeed, admission is easy to procure—must be sadly wanting in taste if he does not admire the treasures of art and *vertu* which are laid up there, and the easy, graceful manner of their arrangement. Nothing of the air of the show-place is breathed there ; no rules, no conditions, no watchful, dogging lacqueys or sentinels make the visitor uncomfortable. Once admitted, the stranger goes where he will, and admires and examines what he pleases. He finds there curiosities and relics, medals and statues, bronzes and stones from every land in which history or romance takes any interest; he gazes on the latest artistic successes—Doré's magnificent lights and shadows, Gérome's audacious nudities; he observes autograph collections of value inestimable; he notices that on the tables, here and there, lie the newest triumphs or sensations of literature—the poem that every one is just talking of, the play that fills the theatres, George Sand's last novel, Rénan's new volume, Taine's freshest criticism: he is impressed everywhere with the conviction that he is in the house of a man of high culture and active intellect, who keeps up with the progress of the world in arts, and letters, and politics. Then there was, until lately, the famous Pompeiian Palace, in one of the avenues of the Champs Elysées, which ranked among the curiosities of Paris, but which Prince Napoleon has at last chosen, or been compelled, to sell. On the Swiss shore of the lake of Geneva, one of the most remarkable objects that attract the eye of the tourist who steams from Geneva to Lausanne, is La Bergerie, the palace of Prince Napoleon. But the owner of these palaces spends little of his time in them. His wife, the Princess Clotilde, stays at home and delights in her children, and shows them with pride to her visitors, while her restless husband is steaming in and out of the ports of the Mediterranean, the Black Sea, or the Baltic. Prince Napoleon has not found his place yet, say Edmond About and other admirers—when he does he will settle firmly to it. He is a restless, unmanageable idler and scamp, say his enemies—unstable as water, he shall not excel. Meanwhile years go by, and Prince Napoleon has long left even the latest verge of youth behind him; and he is only a possibility as yet, and is popular with no political party in France.

Strange that this avowed and ostentatious Democrat, this eloquent, powerful spokesman of French Radicalism, is not popular even with Democrats and Red Republicans. They do not trust him. They cannot understand how he can honestly extend one hand to Democracy, while in the other he receives the magnificent revenues assigned to him by Despotism. One might have thought that nothing would be more easy than for this man, with his daring, his ambition, his brilliant talents, his commanding eloquence, his democratic principles, and his Napoleon face, to make himself the idol of French Democracy. Yet he has utterly failed to do so. As a politician, he has almost invariably upheld the rightful cause, and accurately foretold the course of events. He believed in the possibility of Italy's resurrection long before there was any idea of his becoming son-in-law to a King of Italy; he has been one of the most earnest friends of the cause of Poland; he saw long ago what every one sees now, that the fall of the Austrian system was an absolute necessity to the progress of Europe; he was a steady supporter of the American Union, and when it was the fashion in France, as in England, to regard the independence of the Southern Confederacy as all but an accomplished fact, he remained firm in the conviction that the North was destined to triumph. With all his characteristic recklessness and impetuosity, he has many times shown a cool and penetrating judgment, hardly surpassed by that of any other European statesman. Yet the undeniable fact remains, that his opinion carries with it comparatively little weight, and that no party recognizes him as a leader.

Is he insincere? Most people say he is. They say that, with all his professions of democratic faith, he delights in his princely rank and his princely revenues; that he is selfish, grasping, luxurious, arrogant and deceitful. The army despises him; the populace do not trust him. Now, for myself, I do not accept this view of the character of Prince Napoleon. I think he is a sincere Democrat. a genuine lover of liberty and progress. But I think, at the same time, that he is cursed with some of the vices of Alcibiades, and some of the vices of Mirabeau; that he has the habitual indolence almost of a Vendôme, with Vendôme's occasional outbursts of sudden energy; that a love of luxury, and a restlessness of character, and fretfulness of temper stand in his way, and are his enemies. I doubt whether he will ever play a great historical part, whether he ever will do much more than he has done. His character wants that backbone of earnest, strong simplicity and faith, without which even the most brilliant talents can hardly achieve political greatness. He will probably rank in history among the Might-Have-Beens. Assuredly, he has in him the capacity to play a great part. In knowledge and culture, he is far, indeed, superior to his uncle, Napoleon I.; in justice of political conviction, he is a long way in advance of his cousin, Napoleon III. Taken for all in all, he is the most lavishly gifted of the race of the Bonapartes—and what a part in the cause of civilization and liberty might not be played by a Bonaparte endowed with genius and culture, and faithful to high and true convictions! But the time seems going by, if not gone by, when even admirers could expect to see Prince Napoleon play such a part. Probably the disturbing, distracting vein of unconquerable levity so conspicuous in the character of his father, is the marplot of the son's career, too. After all, Prince Napoleon is perhaps more of an Antony than a Cæsar—was not Antony, too, an orator, a wit, a lover of art and letters, a lover of luxury and free companionship, and woman? Doubtless Prince Napoleon will emerge again, some time and somehow, from his present condition of comparative obscurity. Any day, any crisis, any sudden impulse may bring him up to the front again. But I doubt whether the dynasty of the Bonapartes, the cause of democratic freedom, the destinies of France, will be influenced much for good or evil, by this man of rare and varied gifts—of almost measureless possibilities—the restless, reckless, eloquent, brilliant Imperial Democrat of the Palais Royal, and Red Republican of the Empire—the long misunderstood and yet scarcely comprehended Prince Napoleon.

THE DUKE OF CAMBRIDGE.

THERE used to be a story current in London, which I dare say is not true, to the effect that her gracious Majesty Queen Victoria once demurred to the Prince and Princess of Wales showing themselves too freely in society, and asked them angrily whether they meant to make themselves "as common as the Cambridges."

Certainly the Duke of Cambridge and his sister the Princess Mary, now Princess of Teck, were for a long time, if not exactly "common," if not precisely popular, the most social, the most easily approached, and the most often seen in public pageantry of all members of the royal family. The Princess Mary might perhaps fairly be called popular. The people liked her fine, winsome face, her plump and buxom form. If she has not a kindly, warm, and generous heart, then surely physiognomy is no index of character. But the Duke of Cambridge, although very commonly seen in public, and ready to give his presence and his support to almost any philanthropic meeting and institution which can claim to be fashionable, never seems to have attained any degree of popularity. Like his father, who enjoyed the repute of being the worst after-dinner speaker who ever opened his mouth, the Duke of Cambridge is to be found acting as chairman of some public banquet once a week on an average during the London season. He is president or patron of no end of public charities and other institutions. Yet the people do not seem to care anything about him, or even to like him. His appearance is not in his favor. He is handsome in a certain sense, but he is heavy, stolid, sensual-looking, and even gross in form and face. He has indeed nearly all the peculiarities of physiognomy which specially belong to the most typical members of the Guelph family, and there is, moreover, despite the obesity which usually suggests careless good-humor, something sinister or secret in his expression not pleasant to look upon. He seems to be a man of respectable average abilities. He is not a remarkably bad speaker. I think when he addresses the House of Lords, which he does rarely, or a public meeting or dinner-party, which he does often, he acquits himself rather better than the ordinary county member of Parliament. Judging by his apparent mental capacity and his style as a speaker, he ought to be rather popular than otherwise in England, for the English people like respectable mediocrity and not talent in their princes. "He is so respectable and such an ass," says Thackeray speaking of somebody, "that I positively wonder he didn't get on in England." The Duke of Cambridge is so respectable (in intellectual capacity) and so dull that I positively wonder he has not been popular in England. But popular he never has been. No such clamorous detestation follows him as used to pursue the late Duke of Cumberland, subsequently King of Hanover. No such accusations have been made against him as were familiarly pressed against the Duke of York. Even against the living Prince of Wales there are charges made by common scandal more serious than any that are usually talked of in regard to the Duke of Cambridge. But the English public likes the Duke as little as it could like any royal personage. England has lately been growing very jealous of the manner in which valuable appointments are heaped on members of the Queen's family. The Duke of Cambridge has long enjoyed some sinecure places of liberal revenue, and he holds one office of inestimable influence, for which he has never proved himself qualified, and for which common report declares him to be utterly disqualified. He is Commander-in-Chief of the British army; and that I believe to be his grand offence in the eyes of the British public. Many offences incident to his position are indeed charged upon him. It is said that he makes an unfair use, for purposes of favoritism, of the immense patronage which his office places at his disposal. Some years ago scandal used to charge him with advancing men out of the same motive which induced the Marquis of Steyne to obtain an appointment for Colonel Rawdon Crawley. The private life of the Duke is said to have been immoral, and unluckily for him it so happened that some of his closest friends and favorites became now and then involved in scandals of which the law courts had to take cognizance. But had none of these things been so, or been said, I think the Duke of Cambridge would have lacked popularity just as much as he does. The English people are silently angry with him, mainly because he is an anachronism—a man raised to the most influential public appointment the sovereign can bestow, for no other reason than because he is a member of the royal family. The Duke of Cambridge in the office of Commander-in-Chief is an anachronism at the head of an anomaly. The system is unfit for the army or the country; the man is incompetent to manage any military system, good or bad. As the question of army reorganization, now under debate in England, has a grand political importance, transcending by far its utmost possible military import, and as the position of the Duke of Cambridge is one of the peculiar and typical anomalies about to be abolished, it may surely interest American readers if I occupy a few pages in describing the man and the system. Altering slightly the words of Bugeaud to Louis Philippe in 1848, this reorganization of the army in England is not a reform, but a revolution. It strikes out the keystone from the arch of the fabric of English aristocracy.

The Duke of Cambridge is, as everybody knows, the first cousin of the Queen of England. He is about the same age as the Queen. When both were young it used to be said that he cherished hopes of becoming her husband. He is now himself one of the victims of the odious royal marriage act, which in England acknowledges as valid no marriage with a subject contracted by a member of the royal family without the consent of the sovereign. The Duke of Cambridge, it is well known, is privately married to a lady of respectable position and of character which has never been reproached, but whom, nevertheless, he cannot present to the world as his wife because the royal consent has not ratified the marriage. Many readers of THE GALAXY may perhaps remember that only four or five years ago there was some little commotion created in England by the report, never contradicted, that a princess of the royal house had set her heart upon marrying a young English nobleman who loved her, and that the Queen utterly refused to give her consent. Much sympathy was felt for the princess, because, as she was not a daughter of the Queen and was not young enough to be reasonably expected to acknowledge the control of any relative, this rigorous exercise of a merely technical power seemed particularly unjust and odious. It will be seen, therefore, that the objections raised against the Duke and his position in England are not founded on the belief that he is himself as an individual inordinately favored by the sovereign; but on the obvious fact that place and power are given to him because he is a member of the reigning family. The Duke of Cambridge has never shown the slightest military talent, the faintest capacity for the business of war. In his only campaign he proved worse than useless, and more than once made a humiliating exhibition, not of cowardice, but of utter incapacity and flaccid nervelessness. His warmest admirer never ventured to pretend that the Duke was personally the best man to take the place of Commander-in-Chief. While he was constantly accused by rumor and sometimes by public insinuation of blundering, of obstinacy, of ignorance, of gross favoritism, no defence ever made for him, no eulogy ever pronounced upon him, went the length of describing him as a well-qualified head of the military organization. His upholders and panegyrists were content with pleading virtually that he was by no means a bad sort of Commander-in-Chief; that he was not fairly responsible for this or that blunder or malversation; that on the whole there might have been men worse fitted than he for the place. The social vindication of the appointment was that which proved very naturally its worst offence in the eyes of the public—the fact that the sovereign and her family desired that the place should be given to the Duke of Cambridge, and that the ministers then in power either had not the courage or did not think it worth their while to resist the royal inclination.

The Duke, if he never proved himself much of a soldier, had at least opportunity enough to learn all the ordinary business of his profession. He actually is, and always has been, a professional soldier—not nominally an officer, as the late Prince Albert was, or as the Prince of Wales is, or as the Princess Victoria (Crown Princess of Prussia) may be said for that matter to be, the lady holding, I believe, an appointment as colonel of some regiment, and being doubtless just as well acquainted with her regimental duties as her fat and heavy brother. The Duke of Cambridge was made a colonel at the age of eighteen, and he did the ordinary barrack and garrison duties of his place. He used when young to be rather popular in garrison towns. In Dublin, for example, I think Prince George of Cambridge, as he was then called, was followed with glances of admiration by many hundred pairs of bright eyes. On the death of his father (whose after-dinner eloquence used to afford "Punch" a constant subject for mirth) Prince George became in 1850 Duke of Cambridge. He holds some appointments which I presume are sinecures to him; among the rest he is keeper of some of the royal parks (I don't know the precise title of his office), and the name of "George" may be seen appended to edicts inscribed on various placards on the trees and gates near Buckingham Palace. Nothing in particular was known about him as a soldier until the Crimean war. Indeed, up to that time there had been for many years as little chance for an English officer to prove his capacity as there was for a West Point man to show what he was worth in the period between the Mexican war and the attack on Fort Sumter. When the Crimean war broke out the Duke was appointed to the command of the first division of the army sent against the Russians. I believe it is beyond all doubt that he proved himself unfit for the business of war. He "lost his head," people say; he could not stand the sights and sounds of the battle-field. It required on one occasion—at Inkerman, I believe—the prompt and sharp interference of the late Lord Clyde, then Sir Colin Campbell, to prevent his Royal Highness from making a sad mess of his command. It is not likely that he wanted personal courage—few princes do; but his nerves gave way, and as he could be of no further use to anybody he was induced to return home. France and England each sent a fat prince, cousin of the reigning sovereign, to the Crimean war, and each prince rather suddenly came home again with the invidious whispers of the malign unpleasantly criticising his retreat from the field. After the Duke's return the corporation of Liverpool gave him (why, no man could well say) a grand triumphal entry, and I remember that an irreverent and cynical member of one of the local boards suggested that among the devices exhibited in honor of the illustrious visitor, a white feather would be an appropriate emblem. There the

Duke's active military career began and ended. He had not distinguished himself. Perhaps he had not disgraced himself; perhaps it was really only ill-health which prevented him from proving himself as genuine a warrior as his relative, the Crown Prince of Prussia. But the English people only saw that the Duke went out to the war and very quickly came back again. Julius Cæsar or the First Napoleon or General Sherman might have had to do the same thing under the same circumstances; but then these more lucky soldiers did not have to do it, and therefore were able to prove their military capacity. One thing very certain is, that without such good fortune and such proof of capacity neither Cæsar, Napoleon, nor Sherman would ever have been made commander-in-chief, and therein again they were unlike the Duke of Cambridge. For it was not long after the Duke's return home that on the death or resignation (I don't now quite remember which) of Viscount Hardinge, our heavy "George" was made Commander-in-Chief of the British army. I venture to think that, taking all the conditions of the time and the appointment into consideration, no more unreasonable, no more unjustifiable instance of military promotion was ever seen in England.

For observe, that the worst thing about the appointment of the Duke of Cambridge is not that an incompetent person obtains by virtue of his rank the highest military position in the State. If this were all, there might be just the same thing said of almost every other European country—indeed, of almost every other country. The King of Prussia was Commander-in-Chief of the armies of North Germany, but no one supposed that he was really competent to discharge all the duties of such a position. Abraham Lincoln was Commander-in-Chief of the Federal army, by virtue of his office of President; but no one supposed that his military knowledge and capacity would ever have recommended him to such a post. The appointment in each case was only nominal, and as a matter ot political convenience and propriety. It did not seem wise or even safe that the supreme military authority should be formally intrusted to any one but the ruler or the President. It was thoroughly understood that the duties of the office were discharged by some professional expert, for whose work the King or the President was responsible to the nation. But the office of Commander-in-Chief of the English army is something quite different from this. It is understood to be a genuine office, the occupant actually doing the work and having the authority. In the lifetime of the Duke of Wellington the country had the services of the very best Commander-in-Chief England could have selected. The sound and wise principle which dictated that appointment is really the principle on which the office is based in England. The Commander-in-Chief is not regarded, as on the Continent, in the light of an ornamental president of a great bureau whose duties are done by others, but as the most efficient military officer, the man best qualified to do the work. Marlborough was Commander-in-Chief, and so was Schomberg, and so was General Seymour Conway. When in 1828 the Duke of Wellington became Prime Minister, and therefore resigned the command of the army, Lord Hill was placed at the head of military affairs. The Duke of Wellington resumed the command in 1842 and held it to his death, when it was given to Viscount Hardinge, a capable man. The title of the office was not, I believe, actually "Commander-in-Chief," but "General Commanding-in-Chief." It was, if I remember rightly, owing to the disasters arising out of military mismanagement in the Crimea, that the changes were made which created a distinct Secretary of War and gave to the office of Commander-in-Chief its present title. Therefore it will be seen that the intrusting the command of the army to the Duke of Cambridge is not even justifiable on the ground that it follows an old established custom. It is, on the contrary, an innovation, and one which illustrates the worst possible principle. There is nothing to be said for it. No necessity justified or even excused it. When Viscount Hardinge died, if the principle adopted in his case—that of appointing the best man to the place—had been still in favor, there were many military generals in England, any one of whom would have filled the office with efficiency and credit. But the superstition of rank prevailed. The Duke of Wellington is believed to have once recommended that on his death Prince Albert, the Queen's husband, should be created Commander-in-Chief. Ridiculous as the suggestion may seem, it would probably have been a far better arrangement than that which was more recently adopted. Prince Albert could hardly have been called a professional soldier at all; and this would have been greatly in his favor. For he would have filled the place merely as the King of Prussia does; he would have intrusted the actual duties to some qualified man, and being endowed with remarkable judgment, temper, and discretion, he would doubtless have found the right man for the work. But the Duke of Cambridge, as a professional soldier, although a very indifferent one, is expected to perform and does perform the duties of his office, after his own fashion. He is too high in rank to be openly rebuked, contradicted, or called to account; he is not high enough to be accepted as a mere official ornament or figurehead. He is too much of a professional general to become willingly the pupil and instrument of a more skilled subordinate; too little of a professional general to render his authority of any real value, or to be properly qualified for any high military position. So the Duke of Cambridge did actually direct the affairs of the army, interfered in everything, was supreme in everything, and I think it is not too much to say mismanaged everything. He stood in the way of all useful reforms; he sheltered old abuses; he was as dictatorial as though he had the military genius of a Wellington or a Von Moltke; he was as independent of public opinion as the Mikado of Japan. The kind of mistakes which were made and abuses which were committed under his administration were not such as to attract much of the attention or interest of the newspapers. In England the press, moreover, is not supposed to be at liberty to criticise princes. Of late some little efforts at daring innovation are made in this direction; but as a rule, unless a prince does something very wrong indeed, he is secure from any censure or even criticism on the part of the newspapers. There was, besides, one great practical difficulty in the way of any one inclined to criticise the military administration of the Duke of Cambridge. The War Department in England had grown to be a kind of anomalous two-headed institution. There is a Secretary of War, who sits in the House of Lords or the House of Commons, as the case may be, and whom every one can challenge, criticise, and censure as he pleases. There is the Commander-in-Chief. Which of these two functionaries is the superior? The theory of course is that the Secretary of War is supreme; that he is responsible to Parliament, and that every official in the department is responsible to him. But everybody in England knows that this is not the actual case. There stands in Pall Mall, not far from the residence of the Prince of Wales, a plain business-like structure, with a statue of the late Lord Herbert of Lea (the Sidney Herbert of Crimean days) in front of it; and this is the War Office, where the Secretary of War is in power. But there is in Whitehall another building far better known to Londoners and strangers alike; an old-fashioned, unlovely, shabby-looking sort of barrack, with a clock in its shapeless cupola and two small arches in its front, in each of which enclosures sits all day a gigantic horseman in steel cuirass and high jack-boots. The country visitor comes here to wonder at the size and the accoutrements of the splendid soldiers; the nursery-maid loves the spot, and gazes with open mouth and sparkling eyes at the athletic cavaliers, and too often, like Hylas sent with his urn to the fountain, "*proposito florem prætulit officio,*" prefers looking at the gorgeous military carnation blazing before her to the duty of watching her infantile charge in the perambulator. This building is the famous "Horse Guards," where the Commander-in-Chief is enthroned. I suppose the theory of the thing was, that while the army system was to be shaped out and directed in the War Office, the actual details of practical administration were to be managed at the Horse Guards. But of late years the relations of the two departments appear to have got into an almost inextricable and hopeless muddle, so that no one can pretend to say where the responsibility of the War Office ends or the authority of the Horse Guards begins. The Duke of Cambridge, it is said, habitually acts upon his own authority and ignores the War Office altogether. Things are done by him of which the Secretary for War knows nothing until they are done. The late Sidney Herbert, a man devoted to the duties of the War Department, over which he presided for some years, once emphatically refused during a debate in the House of Commons to evade the responsibility of some step taken at the Horse Guards, by pleading that it was made without the knowledge of the War Office. He declared that he considered himself, as War Secretary, responsible to Parliament for everything done in any office of the War Department. But it was quite evident from the tone of his speech that the thing had been done without his knowledge or consent, and that if anybody but the Queen's cousin had done it there would have been a "row in the building." Now Sidney Herbert was an aristocrat of high rank, of splendid fortune, of unsurpassed social dignity and influence, of great political talents and reputation. If he then could not attempt to control and rebuke the Queen's cousin, how could such an attempt be expected from a man like Mr. Cardwell, the present War Secretary? Mr. Cardwell is a dull, steady-going, respectable man, who has no pretension to anything like the rank, social influence, or even popularity of Sidney Herbert. In fact, the War Secretaries stand sometimes in much the same relation toward the Duke of Cambridge that a New York judge occasionally holds toward one of the great leaders of the bar who pleads before him and is formally supposed to acknowledge his superior authority. The person holding the position nominally superior feels himself in reality quite "over-crowed," to use a Spenserian expression, by the influence, importance, and dignity of the other. Let any stranger in London who happens to be in the gallery of the House of Lords, observe the astonishing deference with which even a pure-blooded marquis or earl of antique title will receive the greeting of the Duke of Cambridge; and then say what chance there is of a War Secretary, who probably belongs to the middle or manufacturing classes, venturing to dictate to or rebuke so tremendous a *magnifico.* Lately an audacious critic of the Duke has started up in the person of a clever, vivacious young member of Parliament, George Otto Trevelyan, son of one of the ablest Indian administrators and nephew of Lord Macaulay. Trevelyan once held, I think, some subordinate place in the War Department, and he has lately been horrifying the conservatism and veneration of English society by boldly making speeches in which he attacks the Queen's cousin, declares that the latter is an injury and nuisance to the army system, that he stands in the way of all improvement, and that he ought to be abolished. But although most people dc profoundly and potently believe what this saucy Trevelyan says, yet his words find little echo in public debate, and his direct motions in the House of Commons have been unsuccessful. The Duke, I perceive, has lately, however, descended so far from his position of supreme dignity as to defend himself in a public speech, and to claim the merit of having always been a progressive and indeed rather daring army reformer. But I do not believe the English Government or Parliament would ever have ventured to take one step to lessen the Duke of Cambridge's power of doing harm to the military service, were it not for the pressure of events with which England had nothing directly to do, and which nevertheless have proved too strong for the resistance even of princes and of vested interests. The practical dethronement of the Duke of Cambridge I hold to be as certain as any mortal event still in the future can well be declared. The anomaly, the inconvenience, the degradation which English Governments and Parliaments would have endured forever if left to themselves, may be regarded as destined to be swept away by the same flood which overwhelmed the military organization of France, and washed the Bonapartes off the throne of the Tuileries. The Duke of Cambridge too had to surrender at Sedan.

For with the overwhelming successes of Prussia and the unparalleled collapse of France, there arose in England so loud and general a cry for the reorganization of the decaying old army system that no Government could possibly attempt to disregard it. Mr. Gladstone's Cabinet had the sense and spirit to see that no middle course of reform would be worth anything. *In medio tutissimus ibis* would never apply to this case. Any reform must count on the obstinate opposition of vested interests—a tremendous power in English affairs; and the only way to bear down that opposition would be by introducing a reform so thorough and grand as to carry with it the enthusiasm of popular support. Therefore the Government have undertaken a new work of revolution, certainly not less bold than that which overthrew the Irish Church, and destined perhaps to have a still more decisive influence on the political organization of English society. One of the many changes this measure will introduce—and it is certain to be carried, first or last—will be the extinction of the anomaly now represented by the position of the Duke of Cambridge. I shall not inflict any of the details of the measure upon my readers in THE GALAXY, and shall even give but slight attention to such of its main features as are of purely military character and import. But I shall endeavor briefly to make it clear that some of the changes it proposes to introduce will have a profound influence on the political and social condition of England, and are in fact steps in that great English revolution which is steadily marching on under our very eyes.

First comes the abolition of the purchase system as regards the commissions held by military officers. Except in certain regiments, and certain branches of the service outside England itself, the rule is that an officer obtains his commission by purchase. Promotion can be bought in the same way. A commission is a vested interest. The owner has paid so much for it, and expects to sell it for an equal sum. The regulation price recognized by law and the Horse Guards is by no means the actual price of the article. It is worth ever so much more to the holder, and he must of course have its real, not its regulation value. The pay in the English army is, for the officers, ridiculously small. The habits of the army, among officers, are ridiculously expensive. An officer is not expected to live upon his pay. Whether expected to do so or not, he could hardly accomplish the feat under any conditions; under the common conditions of an officers' mess-room the thing would be utterly impossible. Now let any reader ask himself what becomes of a department of the public service where you obtain admission by payment, and where when admitted you receive practically no remuneration? Of course it becomes a mere club and association for the wealthy and aristocratic; a brotherhood into which admission is sought for the sake of social distinction. Every man of rank in England will, as a matter of course, have one of his sons in the army. It is the right sort of thing to do, like hunting or going into the House of Commons. Then, on the other hand, every person who has made money sends one of his sons into the army, because thereby he acquires a stamp of gentility. Poverty and merit have no chance and no business there. It certainly is not true, as is commonly believed here, that promotion from the ranks never takes place; but speaking of the system as a whole, one may fairly say that promotion from the ranks is opposed to the ordinary regulation, and occurs so rarely that it need hardly be taken into our consideration here. Therefore the English army became an essentially aristocratic service. To be an officer was the right of the aristocratic, the luxury, ambition, and ornament of the wealthy. One is almost afraid now to venture on saying anything in praise of the French military system; but it had, if I do not greatly mistake, one regulation among others which honorably distinguished it from the English. I believe it was not permitted to a wealthy officer to distinguish himself from his fellows while in barracks by extravagance of expenditure. He had to live as the others lived. But the English system allowed full scope to wealth, and the result was that certain regiments prided themselves on luxury and ostentation, and a poor man, or even a man of moderate means, could not live in them. Add to all this that while the expenses were great and the pay next to nothing, there were certain valuable prizes, sinecures, and monopolies to be had in the army, which favoritism and family influence could procure, and which therefore rendered it additionally desirable that the control of the military organization should be retained in the hands of the aristocracy. John Bright described the military and diplomatic services of England as "a gigantic system of outdoor relief for the broken-down members of the British aristocracy." This was especially true of the military service, which had a large number of rich and pleasant prizes to be awarded at the uncontrolled discretion of the authorities. It might be fairly said that every aristocratic family had at least one scion in the army. Every aristocratic family had likewise one in the House of Commons; sometimes two, or three, or four sons and nephews. The mere numerical strength of the military officers who had seats in the House of Commons was enough to hold up a tremendous barrier in the way of army reform or political reform. It was as clear as light that a popular Parliament would among its very first works of reformation proceed to throw open the army to the competition of merit, independently of either aristocratic rank or moneyed influence. So the military men in the House of Commons were, with some few and remarkable exceptions, steady Tories and firm opponents of all reform either in the army or the political system. Year after year did gallant old De Lacy Evans bring forward his motion for the abolition of the purchase system in vain. He was always met by the supposed practical authority of the great bulk of the military members and by the dead weight of aristocratic influence and vested interests. The army, as then organized, was at once the fortress and the trophy of the English aristocracy. At last the effort at reform seemed to be given up altogether. Though humane reformers did at last succeed in getting rid of the detestable system of flogging in the army, the practice of trafficking in commissions seemed safer than ever. One difficulty in the way of its abolition was always pressed with special emphasis by persons who otherwise were prodigal enough of the public money—the cost such a measure would entail on the people of England. It would be impossible, of course, to abolish such a system without compensating those who had paid money for the commissions which thenceforward could be sold no more. The amount of money required for such compensation would be some forty millions of dollars. Moreover, when commissions are given away among all classes according to merit, the pay of officers will have to be raised. It would indeed be a cruel mockery to give poor Claude Melnotte an officer's rank if he does not at the same time get pay enough to enable him to live. Therefore for once the English aristocrats and Tories were heard to raise their voices in favor of the saving of public money; but they were only assuming the attitude of economists for the sake of upholding their own privileges and defending their vested interests. There will, of course, be a fierce and long fight made even still against the change, but the change, I take it, will be accomplished. The English army will cease to be an army officered exclusively from among the ranks of the aristocracy and the wealthy. Our time has seen no step attempted in English political affairs more distinctly democratic than this. I can hardly realize to my mind what England will be like when commissions and promotions in its military service are the recognized prizes of merit in whatever rank of life, and are won by open competition.

Next, the English Government, approaching rather delicately the difficulty about the Commander-in-Chief, propose to unite the two departments of the service under one roof. The Commander-in-Chief and his staff and offices will be transferred from the Horse Guards in Whitehall to the War Office in Pall Mall, and placed more directly under the control of the Secretary of War. This change must inevitably bring about the end at which it aims — the abolition of the embarrassing and injurious dualism of system now prevailing. It must indeed reduce the General commanding-in-chief to his proper position as the executive officer of the War Secretary, who is himself the servant of Parliament. Such a position would entail no restriction whatever on the military capacity or genius of the Commander-in-Chief were he another Marlborough; but it would make him responsible to somebody who is himself responsible to the House of Commons. I think it may be taken for granted that this will come to mean, sooner or later, the shelving of the Duke of Cambridge. It may be hoped that he will not consider it consistent with his dignity as a member of the royal family to remain in a position thus made virtually that of a subordinate. Some other place perhaps will be found for the cousin of the Queen. I have already heard some talk about the possibility and propriety of sending his Royal Highness as Lord Lieutenant to govern Ireland. Why not? There is a *vile corpus* convenient and ready to hand for any experiment. It would be quite in keeping with all the traditions of English rule, with the practice which was illustrated only a few years ago when the noisy and brainless scamp Sir Robert Peel, whom "Punch" christened "The Mountebank Member," was made Irish Secretary, if the Duke of Cambridge were allowed to soothe his offended dignity by practising his skilful hand on the government of Ireland.

Finally, the Government propose to introduce measures calculated to weld together as far as possible the regular and irregular forces of the country. There are in England three classes of soldiery—the regular army, the militia, and the volunteers. The militia constitute a force as nearly as possible corresponding with that in whose companionship Sir John Falstaff declined to march through Coventry. Bombastes Furioso or the Grande Duchesse hardly ever marshalled such a body of men as may be seen when a British militia regiment is turned out for exercise. Awkward country bumpkins and beer-swilling rowdies of the poacher class make up the bulk of the privates. They are a terror to any small town where they may happen to be exercising, and where not infrequently they finish up a day's drill by a general smashing of windows, sacking of shops, and plundering of inhabitants. The volunteers are a force composed of a much better class of men, and are capable, I think, of great military efficiency and service if properly organized. Of late the volunteer force has, I believe, been growing somewhat demoralized. The Government never gave it very cordial encouragement, its position was hardly defined, and the national enthusiasm out of which it sprang naturally began to languish. We in England have always owed our volunteer force to some sudden menace or dread of French invasion. It was so in the time of William Pitt. We all remember the famous sarcasm with which that statesman replied to the request of some volunteer regiments not to be sent out on foreign service. Pitt gravely assured them that they never should be sent out of the country unless in case of England's invasion. Erskine was a volunteer, and I think it was as an officer of volunteers that Gibbon said he acquired a practical knowledge of military affairs, which proved useful to him in describing the decline and fall of the Roman empire. Our present volunteer service originated in the last of the "three panics" described by Cobden—the fear of invasion by Louis Napoleon, the panic which Tennyson endeavored to foment by his weak and foolish "Form, form! Riflemen, form!" The volunteer force, however, continued to grow stronger and stronger long after the alarm had died away; and even though recently the progress of improvement seems to have been somewhat checked, and the volunteer body to have become lax in its organization, it appears to me that in its intelligence, its earnestness, and its physical capacity there exists the material out of which might be moulded a very valuable arm of the military service. The War Minister now proposes to take steps which shall render the militia a decent body, commanded by really qualified and responsible officers, which shall give better officers to the volunteers, and place these latter under more effective discipline, and which shall bring militia and volunteers into closer relationship with the regular army. How far these objects may be attained by the measures now under consideration I do not pretend to judge; but I cannot regard the present War Minister as a man highly qualified for the place he holds. Mr. Cardwell is an admirable clerk—patient, plodding, untiring; but I doubt whether he has any of the higher qualities of an administrator or much force of character. He is perhaps the very dullest speaker holding a marked position in the House of Commons. He is fluent, not as Gladstone and a river are fluent, but as the sand in an hour-glass is fluent. That sand itself is not more dull, colorless, monotonous, and dry, than is the eloquence of the War Minister. Mr. Cardwell is not always fortunate in his military prophecies. On the memorable night in last July when the news reached London that France had declared war against Prussia, Mr. Cardwell affirmed that that meant the occupation of Berlin by the French within a month. It must be remembered, however, as an excuse for the War Minister's unlucky prediction, that an English military commission sent to examine the two systems had shortly before reported wholly in favor of the French army organization and dead against that of Prussia.

The English Government, wisely, I think, decline to attempt the introduction of any measure for general and compulsory service, except as a last resource in desperate exigencies. The England of the future is not likely, I trust, to embroil herself much in Continental quarrels; and she may be quite expected to hold her own in the improbable event of any of her neighbors attempting to invade her. For myself, I can recollect no instance recorded by history of any foreign war wherein England took part, from which good temper, discretion, judgment, and justice would not alike have counselled her to hold aloof.

Such then are in substance the changes which are proposed for the reconstruction of the English army. The one grand reform or revolution is the abolition of the purchase system. This change will inevitably convert the army into a practical and regular profession, to which all classes will look as a possible means of providing for some of their children. It will have one advantage over the bar, that admission to the ranks of the officers will not necessarily involve the preliminary payment of any sum of money, however small. The profession will cease to be ornamental and aristocratic. It will no longer constitute one of the great props, one of the grand privileges, of the system of aristocracy. Its reorganization will be another and a bold step toward the establishment of that principle of equality which is of late years beginning to exercise so powerful a fascination over the popular mind of England. Caste had in Great Britain no such illustration and no such bulwark as the army system presented. I should be slow to undertake to limit the possible depth and extent of the influence which the impulse given by this reform may exercise over the political condition of England. I can hardly realize to myself by any effort of imagination the effect which such a change will work in what is called society in England, and in the literature, especially the romantic and satirical literature, of the country. Are we then no longer to have Rawdon Crawley, and Sir Derby Oaks, and "Captain Gandaw of the Pinks"? Was Black-Bottle Cardigan really the last of a race? Will people a generation hence fail to understand what was meant by the intimation that "the Tenth don't dance"? Is Guy Livingstone to become as utter a tradition and myth as Guy of Warwick? Is the English military officer to be henceforward simply a hard-working, well-qualified public servant, who obtains his place in open competition by virtue of his merits? Appreciate the full meaning of the change who can, it is too much for me; I can only wonder, admire, and hope. But it is surely not possible that the Duke of Cambridge, cousin of the Queen, can continue to preside over a service wherein the butcher, the baker, and the candlestick-maker have as good a chance of obtaining commissions for their sons as the marquis or the earl or the great millionaire. Only think of the flood of light which will be poured in upon all the details of the military organization, when once it becomes the direct interest of each of us to see that the profession is properly managed in which his own son, however poor in purse and humble in rank, has a chance of obtaining a commission! I believe the Duke of Cambridge had and has an honest hatred and contempt for the coarse and noisy interference of public and unprofessional criticism where the business of the sacred Horse Guards is concerned. Once, when goaded on to sheer desperation by comments in the papers, his Royal Highness actually wrote or dictated a letter of explanation to the "Times," signed with the monosyllabic grandeur of his name "George," we all held up the hands and eyes of wonder that such things had come to pass, that royal princes condescended to write to newspapers, and yet the world rolled on. I cannot think the Duke will abide the awful changes that are coming. He will probably pass into the twilight and repose of some dignified office, where blundering has no occupation and obstinacy can do no harm. Everything considered, I think we may say of him that he might have been a great deal worse than he was. My own impression is that he is rather better than his reputation. If the popular voice of England were to ask in the words of Shakespeare's "Lucio," "And was the Duke a fleshmonger, a fool, and a coward, as you then reported him to be?" I might answer, in the language of the pretended friar, "You must change persons with me ere you make that my report. You indeed spoke so of him, and much more, much worse."

BRIGHAM YOUNG.

THOSE among us who are not too young to have had "Evenings at Home" for a schoolday companion and instructor will remember the story called "Eyes and No Eyes" and its moral. They will remember that, of the two little boys who accomplished precisely the same walk at the same time, one saw all manner of delightful and wonderful things, while the other saw nothing whatever that was worth recollection or description. The former had eyes prepared to see, and the other had not; and that made all the difference. I have to confess that, during a recent visit to Salt Lake City—a visit lasting nearly as many days as that out of which my friend, Hepworth Dixon, made the better part of a volume—I must have been in the condition of the dull little reprobate who had no eyes to see the wonders which delighted his companion. For, so far as the city itself, its streets and its structures, are concerned, I really saw nothing in particular. A muddy little country town, with one or two tolerably decent streets, wherein a few handsome stores are mixed up with old shanties, is not much to see in any part of the civilized world. Other travellers have seen a wondrous sight on the very same spot. They have seen a large and beautiful city, with spacious, splendid streets, shaded by majestic trees and watered by silvery currents flowing in marble channels; they have seen a city combining the cleanliness and activity of young America with the picturesqueness and dignity of the Orient; a city which would be beautiful and wonderful anywhere, but which, raised up here on the bare bosom of the desert, is a phenomenon of apparently almost magical creation. Naturally, therefore, they have gone into raptures over the energy, and industry, and æstheticism of the Mormons; and, even while condemning sternly the doctrine and practice of polygamy, they have nevertheless been haunted by an uneasy doubt as to whether, after all, there is not some peculiar virtue in the having half a dozen wives together which endows a man with superhuman gifts as a builder of cities. Otherwise how comes this beautiful and perfect city, here on the unfriendly and unsheltering waste?

Well, I saw no beautiful and wonderful city, although I spent several days in the Mormon capital, and tramped every one of its streets, and lanes, and roads, scores of times over. Where others beheld the glorious virgin, Dulcinea del Toboso, radiant in beauty and bedight with queenly apparel, I saw only the homely milkmaid, with her red elbows and her russet gown. In plain words, the Mormon city appeared to me just a commonplace little country town, and no more. I saw in it no evidences of preternatural energy or skill. It has one decent street, wherein may be found, at most, half a dozen well-built and attractive-looking shops. It has a good many comfortable residences in the environs. It has two or three decentish hotels, like the hotels of any other fiftieth-class country town. It has the huge Tabernacle, a gigantic barn merely, a simple covering in and over of so much space—a thing in shape "very like a land turtle," as President George L. Smith, First Councillor of Brigham Young, observed to me. Salt Lake City has no lighting and no draining, except such draining as is done by the little runnels of water to be found in every street, and which remind one faintly and sadly of dear, quaint old Berne in Switzerland. At night you have to trudge along in the darkness and the mud, or slush, or dust, and it is a perilous quest the seeking of your way home, for at every crossing you must look or feel for the plank which bridges over the artificial brooklets already described, or you plunge helpless and hopeless into the little torrent. Decidedly, a "one-horse" place, in my estimation; I don't see how men endowed with average heads and arms could for twenty years have been occupied in the building of a city, and produced anything less creditable than this. I do not wonder at the complacency and self-conceit with which all the Mormon residents talk of the beauty of their city and the wonderful things they have accomplished, when Gentile travellers of credit and distinction have glorified this shabby, swampy, ricketty, common-place, vulgar, little hamlet into a town of sweetness and light, of symmetry and beauty. For my part, and for those who were with me, I can only say that we spent the first day or so in perpetual wonder as to whether this really could be the Mormon city of which we had read so many bewildering and glorious descriptions. And the theatre—oh, Hepworth Dixon, I like you much, and I think you are often abused and assailed most unjustly; but how could you write so about that theatre? Or was the beautiful temple of the drama which *you* saw here deliberately taken down, and did they raise in its place the big, gaunt, ugly, dirty, dismal structure which *I* saw, and in which I and my companions made part of a dreary dozen or two of audience, and blinked in the dim, depressing light of mediæval oil-lamps? I observe that, when driven to bay by sceptical inquiry, complacent Mormons generally fall back on the abundance of shade-trees in the streets. Let them have the full credit of this plantation. They have put trees in the streets, and the trees have grown; and, when we observe to a Mormon that we have seen rows of trees similarly growing in even smaller towns of the benighted European continent, he evidently thinks it is our monogamic perversity and prejudice which force us to deny the wondrous works of Mormonism. Making due allowance for every natural difficulty, remembering how nearly every implement, and utensil, and scrap of raw material had to be brought from across yonder rampart of mountains, and from hundreds of miles away, I yet fail to see anything very remarkable about this little Mormon town. Perhaps no other set of people could have made much more of the place; I cannot help thinking that no other set of people who were not Digger Indians could have made much less.

In fact, to retain the proper and picturesque ideas of Salt Lake City, one never ought to have entered the town at all. We ought to have remained on this hillside, from which you can look across that most lovely of all valleys on earth, cinctured as it is by a perfect girdle of mountains, the outlines of which are peerless and ineffable in their symmetry and beauty. The air is as clear, the skies are as blue, the grass as green as the dream of a poet or painter could show him. There below, fringed and mantled in the clustering green of its trees, you see the city, with the long, low, rounded dome or back of the Tabernacle rising broad and conspicuous. Looking down, you may well believe that the city thus exquisitely placed, thus deliciously shaded and surrounded, is itself a wonder of picturesqueness and symmetry. Why go down into the two or three dirty, irregular, shabby little streets, with their dust or mud for road pavement, their nozzling pigs trotting along the sidewalks, their dung-heaps and masses of decaying vegetable matter, their utterly commonplace, mean and disheartening aspect everywhere? But then we did go down—and where others had seen a fair and goodly, aye, and queenly city, we saw a muddy, uninteresting, straggling little village, disfiguring the lovely plain on which it stood.

Profound disappointment, then, is my first sensation in Salt Lake City. The place is so like any other place! Certainly, one receives a bracing little shock every now and then, which admonishes him that, despite the small, shabby stores, and the pigs, and the dunghills, he is not in the regions of merely commonplace dirt. For instance, we learn that the proprietor of the hotel where we are staying has four wives; and it is something odd to talk with a civil, respectable, burgess-like man, dressed in ordinary coat and pantaloons, and wearing mutton-chop whiskers—a sort of man who in England would probably be a church-warden—and who has more consorts than an average Turk. Then again it is startling to be asked, "Do you know Mr. ——?" and when I say "No, I don't," to be told, "Oh, you ought to know him. He came from England, and he has lately married two such nice English girls!" One morning, too, we have another kind of shock. There is a pretty little chambermaid in our hotel, a new-comer apparently, and she happens to find out that my wife and I had lived for many years in that part of the North of England from which she comes herself, whereupon she bursts into a perfect passion and tempest of tears, declares that she would rather be in her grave than in Salt Lake City, that she was deceived into coming, that the Mormonism she heard preached by the Mormon propaganda in England was a quite different thing from the Mormonism practised here, and that her only longing was to get out of the place, anyhow, forever. The girl seemed to be perfectly, passionately sincere. What could be done for her? Apparently nothing. She had spent all her money in coming out; and she seemed to be strongly under the conviction that, even if she had money, she could not get away. An influence was evidently over her which she had not the courage or strength of mind to attempt to resist, or even to elude. Doubtless, as she was a very pretty girl, she would be very soon sealed to some ruling elder. She said her sister had come with her, but the sister was in another part of the city, and since their arrival—only a few days, however—they had not met. My wife endeavored to console or encourage her, but the girl could only sob and protest that she never could learn to endure the place, but that she could not get away, and that she would rather be in her grave. We spoke of this case to one of the civil officers of the United States stationed in the city, and he shook his head and thought nothing could be done. The influence which enslaved this poor girl was not wholly that of force, but a power which worked upon her senses and her superstitions. I should think an underground railway would be a valuable institution to establish in connection with the Mormon city.

I well remember that when I lived in Liverpool, some ten or a dozen years ago, the Mormon propaganda, very active there, always kept the polygamy institution modestly in the background. Proselytes were courted and won by descriptions of a new Happy Valley, of a City of the Blest, where eternal summer shone, where the fruits were always ripe, where the earth smiled with a perpetual harvest, where labor and reward were plenty for all, and where the outworn toilers of Western Europe could renew their youth like the eagles. I remember, too, the remarkable case of a Liverpool family having a large business establishment in the most fashionable street of the great town, who were actually beguiled into selling off all their goods and property and migrating, parents, sons, and daughters, to the land of promise beyond the American wilderness, and how, before people had ceased to wonder at their folly, they all came back, humiliated, disgusted, cured. They had money and something like education, and they were a whole family, and so they were able, when they found themselves deceived, to effect a rapid retreat at the cost of nothing worse than disappointment and pecuniary loss. But for the poor, pretty serving-lass from Lancashire I do not know that there is much hope. Poverty and timidity and superstitious weakness will help to lock the Mormon chains around her. Perhaps she will get used to the place in time. Ought one to wish that she may—or rather to echo her own prayer, and petition that she may find an early grave? The grave-yards are densely planted with tombs here in this sacred city of Mormonism.

The place is unspeakably dreary. Hardly any women are ever seen in the streets, except on the Sunday, when all the families pour in to service in the huge Tabernacle. Most of the dwelling houses round the city are pent in behind walls. Most of the houses, too, have their dismal little *sucursales*, one or two or more, built on to the sides—and in each of these additions or wings to the original building a different wife and family are caged. There are no flower gardens anywhere. Children are bawling everywhere. Sometimes a wretched, slatternly, dispirited woman is seen lounging at the door or hanging over the gate of a house with a baby at her breast. More often, however, the house, or clump of houses, gives no external sign of life. It stands back gloomy in the sullen shade of its thick fruit trees, and might seem untenanted if one did not hear the incessant yelling of the children. We saw the women in hundreds, probably in thousands, at the Tabernacle on the Sunday—and what women they were! Such faces, so dispirited, depressed, shapeless, hopeless, soulless faces! No trace of woman's graceful pride and neatness in these slatternly, shabby, slouching, listless figures; no purple light of youth over these cheeks; no sparkle in these half-extinguished eyes. I protest that only in some of the *cretin* villages of the Swiss mountains have I seen creatures in female form so dull, miserable, moping, hopeless as the vast majority of these Mormon women. As we leave the Tabernacle, and walk slowly down the street amid the crowd, we see two prettily-dressed, lively-looking girls, who laugh with each other and are seemingly happy, and we thank Heaven that there are at least two merry, spirited girls in Salt Lake City. A few days after we meet our blithesome pair at Mintah station; and they are travelling with their father and mother on to San Francisco, whither we too are going—and we learn that they are not Mormons, but Gentiles—pleasant lasses from Philadelphia who had come with their parents to have a passing look at the externals of Mormonism.

My object, however, in writing this paper was to speak of the chief, Brigham Young himself, rather than of his city or his system. We saw Brigham Young, were admitted to prolonged speech of him, and received his parting benediction. The interview took place in the now famous house with the white walls and the gilded beehive on the top. We were received in a kind of office or parlor, hung round with oil paintings of the kind which in England we regard as "furniture," and which represented all the great captains and elders of Mormonism. Joseph Smith is there, and Brigham Young, and George L. Smith, now First Councillor; and various others whom to enumerate would be long, even if I knew or remembered their names. President Young was engaged just at the moment when we came, but his Secretary, a Scotchman, I think, and President George L. Smith, are very civil and cordial. George L. Smith is a huge, burly man, with a Friar Tuck joviality of paunch and visage, and a roll in his bright eye which, in some odd, undefined sort of way, suggests cakes and ale. He talks well, in a deep rolling voice, and with a dash of humor in his words and tone—he it is who irreverently but accurately likens the Tabernacle to a land-turtle. He speaks with immense admiration and reverence of Brigham Young, and specially commends his abstemiousness and hermit-like frugality in the matter of eating and drinking. Presently a door opens, and the oddest, most whimsical figure I have ever seen off the boards of an English country theatre stands in the room; and in a moment we are presented formally to Brigham Young.

There must be something of impressiveness and dignity about the man, for, odd as is his appearance and make up, one feels no inclination to laugh. But such a figure! Brigham Young wears a long-tailed. high-collared coat; the swallow-tails nearly touch the ground; the collar is about his ears. In shape the garment is like the swallow-tail coats which negro-melodists sometimes wear, or like the dandy English dress coat one can still see in prints in some of the shops of St. James street, London. But the material of Brigham's coat is some kind of rough, gray frieze, and the garment is adorned with huge brass buttons. The vest and trowsers are of the same material. Round the neck of the patriarch is some kind of bright crimson shawl, and on the patriarch's feet are natty little boots of the shiniest polished leather. I must say that the gray frieze coat of antique and wonderful construction, the gaudy crimson shawl, and the dandy boots make up an incongruous whole which irresistibly reminds one at first of the holiday get-up of some African King who adds to a great coat, preserved as an heirloom since Mungo Park's day, a pair of modern top-boots, and a lady's bonnet. The whole appearance of the patriarch, when one has got over the African monarch impression, is like that of a Suffolk farmer as presented on the boards of a Surrey theatre. But there is decidedly an amount of composure and even of dignity about Brigham Young which soon makes one forget the mere ludicrousness of the patriarch's external appearance. Young is a handsome man—much handsomer than his portrait on the wall would show him. Close upon seventy years of age, he has as clear an eye and as bright a complexion as if he were a hale English farmer of fifty-five. But there is something fox-like and cunning lurking under the superficial good-nature and kindliness of the face. He seems, when he speaks to you most effusively and plausibly, to be quietly studying your expression to see whether he is really talking you over or not. The expression of his face, especially of his eyes, strangely and provokingly reminds me of Kossuth. I think I have seen Kossuth thus watch the face of a listener to see whether or not the listener was conquered by his wonderful power of talk. Kossuth's face, apart from its intellectual qualities, appeared to me to express a strange blending of vanity, craft, and weakness; and Brigham Young's countenance now seems to show just such a mixture of qualities. Great force of character the man must surely have; great force of character Kossuth, too, had; but the face of neither man seemed to declare the possession of such a quality. Brigham Young decidedly does not impress me as a man of great ability; but rather as a man of great plausibility. I can at once understand how such a man, with such an eye and tongue, can easily exert an immense influence over women. Beyond doubt he is a man of genius; but his genius does not reveal itself, to me at least, in his face or his words. He speaks in a thin, clear, almost shrill tone, and with much apparent *bonhomie*. After a little commonplace conversation about the city, its improvements, approaches etc., the Prophet voluntarily goes on to speak of himself, his system, and his calumniators. His talk soon flows into a kind of monologue, and is indeed a curious rhapsody of religion, sentimentality, shrewdness and egotism. Sometimes several sentences succeed each other in which his hearers hardly seem to make out any meaning whatever, and Brigham Young appears a grotesque kind of Coleridge. Then again in a moment comes up a shrewd meaning very distinctly expressed, and with a dash of humor and sarcasm gleaming fantastically amid the scriptural allusions and the rhapsody of unctuous words. The purport of the whole is that Brigham Young has been misunderstood, misprized, and calumniated, even as Christ was; that were Christ to come up to-morrow in New York or London He would be misundertsood, misprized, and caluminated, even as Brigham Young now is; and that Brigham Young is not to be dismayed though the stars in their courses should fight against him. He protests with especial emphasis and at the same time especial meekness, with eyes half closed and delicately-modulated voice, against the false reports that any manner of force or influence whatever is, or ever was, exercised to keep men or women in Salt Lake City against their will. He appeals to the evidence of our own eyes, and asks us whether we have not seen for ourselves that the city is free to all to come and go as they will. At this time we had not heard the story told by the poor little maid at the hotel; but in any case the evidence of our eyes could go no farther than to prove that travellers like ourselves were free to enter and depart. We have, however, little occasion to trouble ourselves about answering; for the Prophet keeps the talk pretty well all to himself. His manner is certainly not that of a man of culture, but it has a good deal of the quiet grace and self-possession of what we call a gentleman. There is nothing *prononcé* or vulgar about him. Even when he is most rhapsodical his speech never loses its ease and gentleness of tone. He is bland, benevolent, sometimes quietly pathetic in manner. He poses himself *en victime*, but with the air of one who does this regretfully and only from a disinterested sense of duty. I begin very soon to find that there is no need of my troubling myself much to keep up the conversation; that my business is that of a listener; that the Prophet conceives himself to be addressing some portion of the English or American press through my humble medium. So I listen and my companion listens; and Brigham Young talks on; and I do declare and acknowledge that we are fast drifting into a hazy mental condition by virtue of which we begin to regard the Mormon President as a victim of cruel persecution, a suffering martyr and an injured angel!

Time, surely, that the interview should come to a close. We tear ourselves away, and the Prophet dismisses us with a fervent and effusive blessing. "Good-bye—do well, mean well, pray always. Christ be with you, God be with you, God bless you." All this, and a great deal more to the same effect, was uttered with no vulgar, maw-worm demonstrativeness of tone or gesture, no nasal twang, no uplifted hands; but quietly, earnestly, as if it came unaffectedly from the heart of the speaker. We took leave of Brigham Young, and came away a little puzzled as to whether we had been conversing with an impostor or a fanatic, a Peter the Hermit or a Tartuffe. One thing, however, is clear to me. I do not say that Brigham Young is a Tartuffe; but I know now how Tartuffe ought to be played so as to render the part more effective and more apparently natural and lifelike than I have ever seen it on French or English stage.

No one can doubt the sincerity of the homage which the Mormons in general pay to Brigham Young. One man, of the working class, apparently, with whom I talked at the gate of the Tabernacle, spoke almost with tears in his eyes of the condescension the Prophet always manifested. My informant told me that he was at one time disabled by some hurt or ailment; and, the first day that he was able to come into the street again, President Young happened to be passing in his carriage, and caught sight of the convalescent. "He stopped his carriage, sir, called me over to him, addressed me by my name, shook hands with me, asked me how I was getting on, and said he was glad to see me out again." The poor man was as proud of this as a French soldier might have been if the Little Corporal had recognized him and called him by his name. There is no flattery which the great can offer to the humble like this way of addressing the man by his right name, and thus proving that the identity of the small creature has lived clearly in the memory of the great being. Many a renowned commander has endeared himself to the soldiers whom he regarded and treated only as the instruments of his business, by the mere fact that he took care to remember men's names. They would gladly die for one who could be so nobly gracious, and could thus prove that they were regarded by him as worthy to occupy each a distinct place in his busy mind. The niggardliness and selfishness of John, Duke of Marlborough, the savage recklessness of Claverhouse, were easily forgotten by the poor private soldiers whom each commander made it his business, when occasion required, to address correctly by their appropriate names of Tom, Dick, or Harry. Lord Palmerston governed the House of Commons and most of those outside it with whom he usually came into contact, by just such little arts or courtesies as this. In one of Messrs. Erckmann and Chatrian's novels we read of a soldier who declares himself ready to go to the death for Marshal Ney because the Marshal, who originally belonged to the same district as himself, had just recognized his fellow-countryman and called him by his name. But the hero of the novel is somewhat grim and sarcastic, and he thinks it was not so wonderful a condescension that Ney should have recognized an old comrade and called him by his name. Perhaps the hero of the tale had not himself received any such recognition from Ney—perhaps if it had been vouchsafed to him he, too, would have been ready to go to the death. Anyhow, this correct calling of names, and quick recognition has always been a great power in the governing of men and women. "Deal you in words," is the advice of Mephistophiles to the student, in Faust, "and you may leave others to do the best they can with things." I was able to appreciate the governing power of Brigham Young all the better when I had heard the expression of this poor Mormon's gratitude and homage to the great President who had shaken hands with him and addressed him promptly and correctly by his name.

This same Mormon was very communicative. Indeed, as a rule, I found most of the men in Salt Lake City ready and even eager to discuss their "peculiar institution," and to invite Gentile opinion on it. He showed us his two wives, and declared that they lived together in perfect harmony and happiness; never had a word of quarrel, but were contented and loving as two sisters. He delivered a panegyric on the moral condition of Salt Lake City, where, he declared, there was no dishonesty, no drunkenness, and no prostitution. I believe he was correct in his description of the place. From many quite impartial authorities I heard the same accounts of the honesty of the Mormons. There certainly is no drunkenness to be observed anywhere openly, and I believe (although I have heard others assert the contrary) that Salt Lake City is really and truly free from this vice; and I suppose it goes without saying that there is little or no prostitution in a place where a man is expected to keep as many wives as his means will allow him. Intelligent Mormons rely immensely on this absence of prostitution as a justification of their system. They seem to think that when they have said, "We have no prostitutes," all is said; and that the Gentile, with the shames of London, Paris and New York burning in his memory and his conscience, must be left without a word of reply. Brigham Young, in conversation with me, dwelt much on this absence of prostitution. Orson Pratt preached in the Tabernacle during our stay a sermon obviously "at" the Gentile visitors, who were just then specially numerous; and he drew an emphatic contrast between the hideous profligacy of the Eastern cities and the purity of the Salt Lake community. I must say, for myself, that I do not think the question can thus be settled; I do not think prostitution so great an evil as polygamy. If this blunt declaration should shock anybody's moral feelings I am sorry for it; but it is none the less the expression of my sincere conviction. Pray do not set me down as excusing prostitution. I think it the worst of all social evils—except polygamy. I think polygamy the worse evil, because I am convinced that, regarded from a physiological, moral, religious, and even merely poetical and sentimental point of view, the only true social bond to be sought and maintained and justified is the loving union of one man with one woman—at least until death shall part the two. Now, I regard the existence of prostitution as a proof that some men and women fail to keep to the right path. I look on polygamy as a proof that a whole community is going directly the wrong way. No man proposes to himself to lead a life of profligacy. He falls into it. He would get out of it if he only could—if the world and the flesh and the devil were not now and then too strong for him. But the polygamist deliberately sets up and justifies and glorifies a system which is as false to physiology as it is to morals. Observe that I do not say the polygamist is necessarily an immoral man. Doubtless he is often—in Utah I really believe he is commonly—a sincere, devoted, mistaken man, who honestly believes himself to be doing right. But when he attempts to vindicate his system on the ground that it banishes prostitution, I, for myself, declare that I believe a society which has to put up with prostitution is in better case and hope than one which deliberately adopts polygamy. I am emphatic in expressing this opinion because, as I am opposed to any stronghanded or legal movement whatever to put down Brigham Young and his system, I desire to have it clearly understood that my opinions on the subject of polygamy are quite decided, and that no one who has clamored, or may hereafter clamor, for the uprooting of Mormonism by fire and sword, can have less sympathy than I have with Mormonism's peculiar institution.

Let me return to Brigham Young. I saw the Prophet but twice—once in the street and once in his own house, where the interview took place which I have described. The day after that on which I last saw him he left Salt Lake City and went into the country—some people said to avoid the necessity of meeting Mr. Colfax, who was just then expected to arrive with his party from the West. My impressions, therefore, of Brigham Young and his personal character are necessarily hasty, and probably superficial. I can only say that he did not impress me either as a man of great genius, or as a mere *charlatan*. My impression is that he is a sincere man—that is to say, a man who sincerely believes in himself, accepts his own impulses, prejudices and passions as divine instincts and intuitions to be the law of life for himself and others, and who, therefore, has attained that supreme condition of utterly unsparing and pitiless selfishness when the voice of self is listened to as the voice of God. With such a sincerity is quite consistent the adoption of every craft and trick in the government of men and women. Nobody can doubt that Napoleon I. was perfectly sincere as regards his faith in himself, his destiny, and his duty; and yet there was no trick of lawyer, or play-actor, or priest, of which he would not condescend to avail himself if it served his purpose. This is not the sincerity of a Pascal, or a Garibaldi, or a Garrison; but it is just as genuine and infinitely more common. It is the kind of sincerity which we meet every day in ordinary life, when we see some dogmatic, obstinate father of a family or sense-carrier of a small circle trying to mould every will and conscience and life under his control according to his own pedantic standard, and firmly confident all the time that his own perverseness and egotism are a guiding inspiration from heaven. After all, the downright, conventional stage-hypocrite is the rarest of all beings in real life. I sometimes doubt whether there ever was *in rerum naturâ* any one such creature. I suppose Tartuffe had persuaded himself into self-worship, into the conviction that everything he said and did must be right. I look upon Brigham Young as a man of such a temperament and character. Cunning and crafty he undoubtedly is, unless all evidences of eye, and lip, and voice belie him; but we all know that many a fanatic who boldly and cheerfully mounted the funeral pile or the scaffold for his creed had over and over again availed himself of all the tricks of craft and cunning to maintain his ascendancy over his followers. The fanatic is often crafty just as the madman is: the presence of craft in neither case disproves the existence of sincerity.

I believe Brigham Young to be simply a crafty fanatic. That he professes and leads his creed of Mormonism merely to obtain lands and beeves and wives, I do not believe, although this seems to be the general impression among the Gentiles who visit his city. I am convinced that he regards himself as a prophet and a heaven-appointed leader, and that this belief prevents him from seeing how selfish he is in one sense and how ridiculous in another. Any man who can deliberately put on such a coat in combination with such a pair of boots, as Brigham Young displayed during my interview with him, must have a faith in himself which would sustain him in anything. No human creature capable of looking at any two sides of a question where he himself was concerned, ever did or could present himself in public and expect to be reverenced when arrayed in such uncouth and preposterous toggery.

I cannot pretend to have had any extraordinary revelations of the inner mysteries or miseries of Mormonism made to me during my stay at Salt Lake City. Other travellers, nearly all other travellers indeed, have apparently been more fortunate or more pushing and persevering. I fancy it is rather difficult just now to get to know much of the interior of Mormon households; and I confess that I never could quite understand how people, otherwise honorable and upright, can think themselves justified in worming their way into Mormon confidences, and then making profit one way or another by revelations to the public. But one naturally and unavoidably hears, in Salt Lake City, of things which are deeply significant and which he may without scruple put into print. For example—there was a terrible pathos to my mind in the history of a respectable and intelligent woman who, years and years ago, when her life, now fading, was in its prime, married a man now a shining light of Mormonism, whose photograph you may see anywhere in Salt Lake City. She has been superseded since by divers successive wives; she is now striving in a condition far worse than widowhood to bring up her seven or eight children, and she has not been favored with even a passing call for more than a year and a half by the husband of her youth, who lives with the newest of his wives a few hundred yards away. I am told that such things are perfectly common; that the result of the system is to plant in Utah a number of families which may be described practically as households without husbands and fathers. I believe the lady of whom I have just spoken accepts her destiny with sad and firm resignation. Her faith in the religion of Mormonism is unshaken, and she regards her forlorn and widowed life as the heaven-appointed cross, by the bearing of which she is to win her eternal crown. Of course the Indian widows regard their bed of flames, the Russian women-fanatics behold their mutilated and mangled breasts with a similar enthusiasm of hope and superstition. But none the less ghastly and appalling is the monstrous faith which exacts and glorifies such unnatural sacrifices. These dreary homes, widowed not by death, seem to be the saddest, most shocking birth of Mormonism. After all, this is not the polygamy of the East, bad as that may be. "Give us," exclaimed M. Thiers in the French Chamber, three or four years ago, when Imperialism had reached the zenith of its despotic power—"give us liberty as in Austria!" So I can well imagine one of these superseded and lonely wives in Salt Lake City, crying aloud in the bitterness of her heart, "Give us polygamy as in Turkey!"

That the thing is a religion, however hideously it may show, I do not doubt. I mean that I feel no doubt that the great majority of the Mormon men are drawn to and kept in Mormonism by a belief in its truth and vital force as a religion. I do not believe that conscious and hypocritical sensuality is the leading impulse in making them or keeping them members of the Mormon church. I never heard of any community where a sensual man found any difficulty in gratifying his sensuality; nor are the vast majority of the Mormons men belonging to a class on whom a severe public opinion would bear so directly that they must necessarily wander thousands of miles away across the desert in order to be able comfortably to gratify their immoral propensities. To me, therefore, the possibility which appears most dangerous of all is the chance of any sudden crusade, legal or otherwise, being set on foot against this perverted and unfortunate people. Left to itself, I firmly believe that Mormonism will never long bear the glare of daylight, the throng of witnesses, the intelligent rivalry, the earnest and active criticism, poured in and forced in upon it by the Pacific railroads. But if it can bear all this then it can bear anything whatever which human ingenuity or force can put in arms against it; and it will run its course and have its day, let the Federal Hercules himself do what he may. Meanwhile it would be well to bear in mind that Mormonism has thus far cumbered the earth for comparatively a very few years; that all its members there in Utah counted together would hardly equal the population of a respectable street in London; and that at this moment the whole concern is ricketty and shaky, and threatens to tumble to pieces. I know that some of the ruling elders are panting for persecution; that they are openly doing their very best to "draw fire;" that they are daily endeavoring to work on the fears or the passions of Federal officials resident at Salt Lake by threats of terrible deeds to be done in the event of any attempt being made to interfere with Mormonism. Many of these Mormon apostles, dull, vulgar and clownish as they seem, have foresight enough to see that their system sadly needs just now the stimulus of a little persecution, and have fanatical courage enough to put themselves gladly in the front of any danger for the sake of sowing by their martyrdom the seed of the church. "That man," said William the Third of England, speaking of an inveterate conspirator against him "is determined to be made a victim, and I am determined not to make him one." I hope the United States will deal with the Mormons in a similar spirit. At the same time, I would ask my brothers of the pen whether those of them who have visited Salt Lake City have not made the place seem a good deal more wonderful, more alluringly mysterious, more grandly paradoxical in its nature, than it really is? I feel convinced that if people in Lancashire and Wales and Sweden had all been made distinctly aware that Salt Lake City is only a dusty or muddy little commonplace country hamlet, where labor is not less hard and is not any better paid than in dozens or scores of small hamlets this side the Missouri, one vast temptation to emigrate thither, the temptation supplied by morbid curiosity and ignorant wonder, would never have had any conquering power, and Mormonism would have been deprived of many thousand votaries. For, regarded in an artistic point of view, the City of the Saints is a vulgar sham; a trumpery humbug; and I verily believe that it has swelled into importance not more through the fanatical energy of its governing elders and the ignorance of their followers, than through the extravagant exaggeration and silly wonder of most of its hostile visitors and critics.

THE LIBERAL TRIUMVIRATE OF ENGLAND.

A YEAR ago I happened to be talking with some French friends at a dinner-table in Paris, about the Reform agitation then going on in England. "We admire your great orators and leaders," said an enthusiastic French gentleman; "your Bright, your Beales"—and he was warming to the subject when he saw that I was smiling, and he at once pulled up, and asked me earnestly whether he had said anything ridiculous. I endeavored to explain to him gently that in England we did not usually place our Bright and our Beales on exactly the same level—that the former was our greatest orator, our most powerful leader, and the latter a respectable, earnest gentleman of warm emotions and ordinary abilities whom chance had made the figure-head of a passing and vehement agitation, and who would probably be forgotten the day after to-morrow or thereabouts.

My French friend did not seem convinced. He had seen Mr. Beales's name in the London papers quite as often and as prominently for some months as Mr. Bright's; and, moreover, he had met Mr. Beales at dinner, and did not like to be told that he had not thereby made the acquaintance of a great tribune of the British people. So I dropped the subject and allowed our Bright and and our Beales to rank together without farther protest.

Here in New York, where English politics are understood infinitely better than in Paris, I have noticed not a little of this "Bright and Beales" classification when people talk of the leaders of English Liberalism. I have heard, with surprise, this or that respectable member of Parliament, who never for a moment dreamed of being classed among the chiefs of his party, exalted to a place of equality with Gladstone or Bright. In truth the English Liberal party (I mean now the advancing and popular party—not the old Whigs) has only three men who can be called leaders. After Gladstone, Bright, and Mill there comes a huge gap—and then follow the subalterns, of whom one might name half a dozen having about equal rank and influence, and of whom you may choose any favorite you like. Take, for example, Mr. W. E. Forster, Mr. Stansfeld, Mr. Thomas Hughes, the O'Donoghue, Mr. Coleridge (who, however, is marked out for the judicial bench, and therefore need hardly be counted), and one or two others, and you have the captains of the advanced Liberal party. The Liberals are not rich in rising talent; at least there seems no man of the younger political generation who gives any promise of commanding ability. They have many good debaters and clever politicians, but I see no "pony Gladstone" to succeed him who used to be called the "pony Peel;" and the man has yet to show himself in whom the House of Commons can hope for a future Bright. The great Liberals of our day have apparently not the gift of training disciples in order that the latter may become apostles in their time. Like Cavour, they are too earnest about the work and do too much of it themselves to have leisure or inclination for teaching and pushing others.

Officially Mr. Gladstone has been, of course, for several years the leader of the party. He is formally invested with all the insignia of command. He is indeed the only possible leader; for he is the only man who has the slightest chance just now of commanding the allegiance of the old Whigs with their dukes and earls, and the young Radicals with their philosophers, their Comtists, their Irish Nationalists, and their working men. But the true soul and voice and heart of the Liberal party pay silent allegiance to John Bright. He is, by universal acknowledgment, the maker of the Reform agitation and the Reform Bill.

Mr. Disraeli has over and over again flung in the face of Mr. Gladstone the fact that Bright, and not he, is the master spirit of Radicalism. Of late the Tories have taken to praising and courting Bright incessantly and ostentatiously, and contrasting his calm, consistent wisdom with Gladstone's impetuosity and fitfulness. Of course both Bright and Gladstone thoroughly understand the meaning of this, and smile at it and despise it. The obvious purpose is to try to set up a rivalry between the two. If Gladstone's authority could be damaged that would be quite enough; for it would be impossible at present to get the Whig dukes and earls to follow Bright, and the dethronement of Gladstone would be the break-up of the party. The trick is an utter failure. Bright is sincerely and generously loyal to Gladstone, and is a man as completely devoid of personal vanity or self-seeking as he is of fear. No personal question will ever divide these two men.

Gladstone is beyond doubt the most fluent and brilliant speaker in the English Parliament. No other man has anything like his inexhaustible flow and rush of varied and vivid expression. His memory is as surprising as his fluency. Grattan spoke of the eloquence of Fox as "rolling in resistless as the waves of the Atlantic." So far as this description conveys the idea of a vast volume of splendid words pouring unceasingly in, it may be applied to Gladstone. A listener new to the House is almost certain to prefer him to any other speaker there, and to regard him as the greatest English orator of the present generation. I was myself for a long time completely under the spell, and a little impatient of those who insisted on the superiority of Bright. But when one becomes accustomed to the speaking of the two men it is impossible not to find the fluency, the glitter, the impetuous volubility, the involved and complicated sentences, the Latinized, sesquipedalian words of Gladstone gradually losing their early charm and influence, just as the pure noble Saxon, the unforced energy, the exquisite simplicity, the perfect "fusion of reason and passion" which are the special characteristics of Bright's eloquence, grow more and more fascinating and commanding. Perhaps the same effect may be found to arise from a study or a contrast (if one must contrast them) between the political characters of the two men.

It is a somewhat singular fact that one English county has produced the three men who undoubtedly rank beyond all others in England as Parliamentary orators. The Earl of Derby, Mr. Gladstone, and Mr. Bright are all Lancashire men. But Gladstone is only Lancashire by birth. His shrewd old Scotch father came to Liverpool from across the Tweed, and made his money and founded his family in the great port of the Mersey. The Gladstones had, and have, large West Indian property; and when England emancipated her slaves by paying off the planters, the Gladstones came in for no small share of the national purchase-money. When the great Liberal orator came out so impetuously and unluckily with his celebrated panegyric on Jefferson Davis, a few years ago, some people shook their heads and remarked that the old planter spirit does not quite die out in the course of one generation; and I heard bitter allusion made to the celebrated declaration flung by Cooke, the great tragedian, in the face of an indignant theatre in Liverpool, that there was not a stone in the walls of that town which was not "cemented by the blood of Africans." But, indeed, Gladstone's outburst had no traditional, or hereditary, or other such source. It came straight from the impulsive heart and nature of the speaker. His strength and his weakness are alike illustrated by that sudden, indiscreet, unjustifiable, and repented outburst. Thus he every now and then disappoints his friends and shakes the confidence of his followers. A keen, intellectual, cynical member of the Liberal party, Mr. Grant Duff, not long since publicly reproached Mr. Gladstone with this trick of suddenly "turning round and firing his revolver in the face of his followers." Certain it is that there is little or no enthusiasm felt toward Gladstone personally, by his party. Admirers of Mr. Disraeli are usually devotees of the man himself. Young men, especially, delight in him and adore him. Mr. Gladstone is followed as a leader, admired as an orator; but I have heard very few of his followers ever express any personal affection or enthusiasm for him; but it is quite notorious in London that some of his adherents can hardly control their dislike of him. Mr. Bright, although a man of somewhat cold and reserved demeanor, and occasionally *brusque* in manner, is popular everywhere in the House. Mr. Gladstone is not personally popular even among his own followers. What is the reason? His enemies say that he has a bad temper and an unbending intellectual pride, which is as untrue as if they were to say he had a hoarse voice and a stammer. The obscurest man in the House of Commons is not more modest; and there is nothing ungenial in his manner or his temper. But the truth is that people cannot rely upon him, or think they cannot, which, so far as they are concerned, amounts to the same thing. His strongest passion in life—stronger than his love of figures, or of Homer, or even of liberty—is a love of argument. He is always ready to sacrifice his friend, or his party, or even his cause, to his argument. Add to this that he has a conscience so sensitive that it can hardly ever find any cause or deed smooth enough to be wholly satisfactory; add, moreover, that he has an eloquence so fluent as to flow literally away from him, or with him, and the wonder will be how such a man ever came to be the successful leader of a great party at all. He is always reconsidering what he has done, always penitent for something he has said, always turning up to-day the side of the question which everybody supposed was finally put away and done with yesterday.

You can read all this in his face. Furrowed with deep and rigid lines, it proclaims a certain self-torturing nature—the nature of the penitent, self-examining ascetic, whose heart is always vexed by doubts of his own worth and purity, and past and future. Decidedly, Gladstone wants force of character, and force of intellect as well. He is not a man of great thought. Every such man settles a question, so far as he is himself concerned, finally, one way or the other, before long; sees and accepts what the human limitations of thinking are; recognizes the necessity of being done with mere thinking about it, and so decides and is free to act. There is intellectual weakness in Gladstone's interminable consideration and reconsideration, qualification and requalification of every subject and branch of a subject. But there is also a strong, genuine, unmingled delight in mere argument—perhaps as barren a delight as human intellect can yield to.

Last year there were three Fenian prisoners lying under sentence of death in Manchester. Their crime was such as undoubtedly all civil governments are accustomed to punish by death. But there was considerable sympathy for them, partly because of their youth, partly because the deed they had done —the killing of a policeman in order to rescue a political conspirator—did not seem to be a mere base and malignant murder. Some eminent Liberals, Mr.

Bright among the rest, endeavored to obtain a mitigation of the sentence. The Tory Government refused; then a point of law was raised on their behalf, and argued in the House of Commons. The point was new, the Tory law-officers, dull men at the best, were taken by surprise, and broke down in reply. Yet there was a reply, and legally, a sufficient one. Mr. Gladstone saw it; saw where the point raised was defective, and how it might be disposed of. He sprang to his feet, pulled the Tory law-officers out of their difficulty, and upset the case for the Fenians. Now this must have seemed to a conscientious man quite the right thing to do. To a lover of argument the temptation of upsetting a defective plea was irresistible. But most of Mr. Gladstone's Irish followers, on whom he must needs rely, were surprised and angry, and even some of his English friends thought he might have left the Tories unaided to hang their own political prisoners. Gladstone's conduct was eminently characteristic. No impartial man could honestly say that he had done a wrong thing; but no one acquainted with political life could feel surprised that a leader who habitually does such things, is almost always being grumbled at by one or other section of his followers.

There is an obvious lack of directness as well as of robustness in the whole intellectual and political character of the man. I think it was Nathaniel Hawthorne who said of General McClellan that if he could only have shut one eye he might have gone straight into Richmond almost at any time during his command of the Army of the Potomac. I am sure if Gladstone would only close one eye now and then he might lead his party much more easily to splendid victory. With all his great, varied, comprehensive faculties, he is not a man to make a deep mark on the history of his country. He has to be driven on. Somebody must stand behind him. He is not self-sufficing. His style of eloquence is not straightforward, cleaving its way like an arrow. It goes round and round a subject, turning it up, holding it to the light, now this way, now that, examining and re-examining it. Even his reform speeches are as Disraeli once said very happily of Lord Palmerston, rather speeches about Reform than orations on behalf of it. He is indeed the brilliant Halifax of his age—at least he is a complete embodiment of Lord Macaulay's Halifax. A leader with so many splendid gifts and merits, no English parlimentary party of modern times has ever had. Taking manner, voice, elocution and all into account, as is but right in judging of a speaker, I think he is the most splendid of all English orators. Burke's manner and accent were terribly against him; Fox was full of repetition, and often stammered and stuttered in the very rush and tumult of his thoughts; Sheridan's glitter was sometimes tawdriness; both the Pitts were given to pompousness and affectation; Bright has neither the silver voice nor the varied information of Gladstone; Disraeli I do not rank among orators at all. Gladstone has none of the special defects of any of these men, yet I am convinced that Fox was a *greater* orator than Gladstone; I know that Bright is; while Burke's speeches are, as intellectual studies, incomparably beyond anything that Gladstone will ever bequeath to posterity; and as instruments to an end, some of Disraeli's speeches have been more effective and triumphant than anything ever spoken by his present rival.

In brief, Gladstone is not, to my thinking, a *great* orator; and I do not believe he is a great statesman. A great statesman, I presume, is tested by a crisis, and is greatest at a crisis. Such was Chatham; such was Washington; such was Napoleon Bonaparte; such was Cavour; such is Bismarck. All I have seen of Gladstone compels me to believe that he is not such a man. He s just the man to lead the Liberal party at this time; but I should despair of the triumph of that party for the present generation, if there were not stronger and simpler minds behind his to keep him in the right way, to drive him on—and, above all, to prevent him from recoiling after he has made an effective stride forward.

One of the great questions likely to arise soon in English political discussion is that of national education. On educational questions I fancy Mr. Gladstone is rather narrow-minded and old-fashioned; taking too much the tone and view of a college Don. His recent severance from the political representation of Oxford may have done something to release his mind from tradition and pedantry; but I much doubt whether he will not be found sadly wanting when a serious attempt is made to revolutionize the principles and the system of the English universities, and to substitute there (I quote again the language of Grant Duff) "the studies of men for the studies of children." Gladstone is a devotee of classical study; and his whole nature is under the influence of æstheticism, or of what is commonly called "sentiment." The sweet and genial traditions of the past have immense influence over him. His love of Greek poetry and of Italian art follow him into politics. With the Teuton, his poetry and his politics he has little or no sympathy; and I think the question to be decided shortly as regards the university system in England may be figuratively described as a question between Classic and Teuton. Gladstone is a profound Greek and Latin scholar—a master of Italian, a connoisseur of Italian art; he does not, I believe, know or care much about German literature. Accordingly, he was a devoted Philhellene and a passionate champion of Italian independence; while the outbreak of the recent struggle between the past and the present in Germany found him indifferent, and probably even ignorant. So it was in regard to the American crisis the other day. He knew little of American politics and national life; and the whole thing was a bewilderment and a surprise to him. If the Laocoon had been the work of a New England artist I think the North would have found at once a warm advocate in Mr. Gladstone.

Of a mould utterly different is John Bright, at the very root of whose character are found simplicity and straightforwardness. By simplicity I do not mean freedom from pretence or affectation; for no man can be more thoroughly unaffected and sincere than Gladstone. I mean that purely intellectual attribute which frees the judgment from the influence of complex emotions; which distinguishes at once essentials from non-essentials; which sees at a glance the true end and the real way to it, and can go directly onward. Men supremely gifted with this great practical quality are commonly set down as men of one idea. In this sense, undoubtedly, John Bright is a man of one idea; but the phrase does not justly describe him, or men like him, who are peculiar merely in having an accurate appreciation of what I may call political perspective, and thus knowing what proportion of public consideration certain objects ought, under certain circumstances, to obtain.

So far as ideas are the offspring of information, Mr. Bright has undoubtedly fewer ideas than some of his contemporaries. He is not a profound classical scholar like Gladstone; he has had nothing like the varied culture of Lowe; he makes, of course, no pretence to the attainments of Mill, who is at once a master of science, of classics, and of *belles-lettres*. But given a subject, almost any subject, coming at all within the domain of politics or economics, and time to think over it, and he is much more likely to be right in his judgment of it than any of the three men I have named. He is gifted beyond any Englishman now

.ıving with the rare and admirable faculty of seeing right into the heart of a subject, and discerning what it means and what it is worth. Nor is this ever a ucky jump at a conclusion. Bright never gives an opinion at random or off-nand. Some new policy is announced; some new subject is broached in the House of Commons; and Bright sits silent and listens. Friends and followers come round him and ask him what he thinks of it. "Wait until to-morrow and I will tell you," is almost invariably, in whatever form of words, the tenor ot his reply—and to-morrow's judgment is certain to be right. I can remember no great public question coming up in England for the past dozen years in regard to which Mr. Bright's deliberate judgment did not prove itself to be just.

This quality of sagacious judgment, however valuable and uncommon, would not of itself make a man a great statesman or even a great party leader; but it is only one of many remarkable attributes which are found harmoniously illustrated in the character of Mr. Bright. I do not mean, however, to dwell at any length here on the place John Bright holds in English political life or the qualities which have won him that place. He has lately been the subject of an article in this magazine, and he is indeed better known to American readers than any other English political man now living. One or two observations are all that just now seem necessary to make.

Men who have not heard Bright speak, and who only know him by repute as a powerful tribune of the people, a demagogue ("John of Bromwicham," Carlyle calls him, classing him with John of Leyden), are naturally apt to think of him as an impetuous, passionate, stormy orator, shaking people's souls with sound and fury. Almost anybody who only knew the two men vaguely and by rumor, would be likely to assume that the style of the classical Gladstone was stately, calm, and regular; that of the popular orator and democrat, impetuous, rugged, and vehement. Now, the great characteristic of Gladstone, after his fluency, is his impetuosity; that of Bright is his magnificent composure and self-control. Intensity is his great peculiarity. He never foams or froths or bellows, or wildly gesticulates. The heat of his oratorical passion is a white heat which consumes without flash or smoke or sputter. Some of his greatest effects have been produced by passages of pathetic appeal, of irony, or of invective, which were delivered with a calm intensity that might almost have seemed coldness, if the fire of genius and of eloquence did not burn beneath it. Another remark I should make is that Mr. Bright is the greatest master of pure Saxon English now speaking the English language. As the blind commonly have their sense of sound and of touch intensified, so it may be that Mr. Bright's comparative indifference to classic and foreign literature has tended to concentrate all his attention upon the culture of pure English, and given him a supreme faculty of appreciating and employing it. Certain it is that his unvarying choice of the very best Saxon word in every case seems to come from an instinct which is in itself something like genius.

Finally, let me remark, that the extent of Mr. Bright's democratic tendencies would probably disappoint some Americans. I may say now what I should probably have been laughed at for saying two or three years ago, that there is a good deal of the conservative about John Bright; that he is by nature disposed to shrink from innovation; that change for the mere sake of change is quite abhorrent to him; and that he is about the last man in England who would care to make political war for an idea. He seems to me to be the only one Englishman I have lately spoken with who retains any genuine feeling of personal loyalty toward the sovereign of England. But for his eloquence and his power, I fancy Mr. Bright would seem rather a slow sort of politician to many of the younger Radicals. The "Times" lately attributed Mr. Bright's conservatism to his advancing years. This was merely absurd. Mr. Bright is little older now than O'Connell was when he began his Parliamentary career. He is considerably younger than Disraeli, or Gladstone, or Mill. What Bright now is he always was. A dozen years ago he was defending the Queen and Prince Albert against the attacks of Tories and of some Radicals. He never was a Democrat in the French or Italian sense. He has always been wanting even, in sympathy, with popular revolution abroad. He never showed the slightest interest in speculative politics. I doubt if he ever talked of the "brotherhood of peoples." He has been driven into political agitation only because, like Schiller's Wilhelm Tell, he saw positive, practical, and pressing grievances bearing down upon his neighbors, which he felt called by duty to make war against. I have many times heard Mr. Bright say that he detests the House of Commons, and would be glad if it were permitted him never to mount a platform again.

But if Mr. Bright had little natural inclination for a Parliamentary career, what is one to say of Mr. John Stuart Mill's natural disinclination for such a path of life?

Physical constitution, intellectual peculiarities, temperament, habits—all seemed to mark out Mr. Mill as a man destined to close his career, as he had so long conducted it—in almost absolute seclusion. He is a silent, shy, shrinking man, of feeble frame and lonely ways. Until the general election of three years back, Mr. Mill was to his countrymen but as an oracle—as a voice—almost as a myth. The influence of his writings was immense. Personally he was but a name. He never came into any public place; he knew nobody. When the promoters of the movement to return him to Parliament came to canvass the Westminster electors, the great difficulty they had to contend with was, that three out of every four of the honest traders and shopkeepers had never heard of him; and the few who knew anything of his books had a vague impression that the author was dead years before. The very men who formed the executive of his committee could not say that they knew him, even by sight. Half in jest, half for a serious purpose, some of the Tories sent abroad over Westminster an awful report that there was no such man in existence as John Stuart Mill. "Did you ever see him?" was the bewildering question constantly put to this or that earnest canvasser, and invariably answered with an apologetic negative. I believe the services of my friend Dr. Chapman, editor of the "Westminster Review," were brought into pressing requisition, because he was one of the very few who really could boast a personal acquaintance with Stuart Mill. The day when the latter first entered the House of Commons was the first time he and Bright ever saw each other. I believe Cobden and Mill never met. Mill had no university acquaintances—he had never been to any university. He had no school friends—he had never been to a school. Perhaps the best educated man of his time in England, he owes his education to the personal care and teaching of his distinguished father, James Mill, who would have been illustrious if his son had not overshadowed his fame. Assuredly, to know James Mill intimately was, if I may thus apply Leigh Hunt's saying, in itself a liberal education. Following his father's steps at the India House, John Mill worked there methodically and quietly, until he rose to the highest position his father had occupied; and then he resigned his office, declined an offer of a seat at the Indian Council Board, subsequently made by Lord Stanley, and lapsed wholly into private life. Of late he rarely met even his close and early friends. Some estrangement, not necessary to dwell on, had taken place, I believe, between him and his old friend Thomas Carlyle, and I suppose they ceased to meet. After the death of the wife whom he so loved and revered, Mill lived almost always at Avignon, in the south of France, where she died, and where he raised a monument over her remains, which he visits and tends with a romantic devotion and constancy worthy of a Roland.

Only a profound sense of duty could drag such a man from his scholarly and sacred seclusion into the stress and storm of a parliamentary life. But it was urged upon Mill that he could do good to the popular cause by going into Parliament; and he is not a man to think anything of his personal preference in such a case. He accepted the contest and won. Some of his warmest admirers regretted that he had ever given his consent. They feared not so much that he might damage his reputation as that he might weaken the influence of his authority, and with it the strength of every great popular cause. Certainly those who thought thus, and who met Mr. Mill for the first time during the progress of the Westminester contest, did not feel much inclined to take a more encouraging view of the prospect.

Mr. Mill seems cut out by nature not to be a parliamentary success. He has a thin, fragile, awkward frame; he has a nervous, incessant twitching of the lips and eyes; he has a weak voice and a sort of stammer; he is over sixty years of age; he had never, so far as I know, addressed a political meeting of any kind up to the time of the Westminster contest. Yet with all these disadvantages, Mill has, as a political leader and speaker, been an undoubted success with the country, and a sort of success in the House. An orator of any kind he never could be. One might call him a wretchedly bad speaker, if his speaking were not so utterly unlike anybody else's, as to refuse to be classified with any other speaking, good or bad. But, so far as the best selection of words, the clearest style, the most coherent and convincing argument can constitute eloquence, Mill's speeches are eloquent. They are, of course, only spoken essays. They differ in no wise from the speaker's writings; and I need hardly say that a speech, to be effective, must never be just what the speaker would have written if it were to be consigned at once to print as a letter or an essay. As speeches, therefore, Mr. Mill's utterances in the House have little or no effect. Indeed, they are only listened to by a very few men of real intelligence and judgment on both sides. Some of the more boisterous of the Tories made many attempts to cough and laugh Mill into silence; indeed, there was obviously a deliberate plan of this kind in operation at one time. But Mill is a man whom nothing can deter from saying or doing what he thinks right. A more absolutely fearless being does not exist. He is even free from that fear which has sometimes paralyzed the boldest spirits, the fear of becoming ridiculous. So the Tory trick failed. Mill went on with patient, imperturbable, proud good-humor, despite all interruption—now and then paying off his Tory enemies by some keen contemptuous epigram or sarcasm, made all the more pungent by the thin, bland tone in which it was uttered. So the Tories gave up shouting, groaning and laughing; the more quickly because one at least of their chiefs, the Marquis of Salisbury (then in the House of Commons as Lord Cranbourne) had the spirit and sense to express openly and loudly his anger and disgust at the vulgar and brutal behaviour of some of his followers. Therefore Mr. Mill ceased to be interrupted; but he is not much listened to. That supreme, irrefutable evidence that a man fails to interest the House—the fact that a hum and buzz of conversation may be heard all the time he is speaking —is always fatally manifest when Mr. Mill addresses the Commons. But the House, after all, is only a platform from which a man endeavors to speak to the country, and if Mill does not always get the ear of the House, he never fails to be heard by the nation. I have no doubt that even the Tory members of the House read Mill's speeches when they appear in print; assuredly all intelligent Tories do. These speeches, in any case, are never lost on the country. They form at once a part of the really successful literature of each session. They always excite controversy of some kind—not even the great orations of Bright and Gladstone are more talked of.

So far they are a success, and there is something in the personal character of Mr. Mill himself, which makes him specially popular with the working classes of England. I doubt if there is now any Englishman whose name would be received with a more cordial outburst of applause at a popular meeting. Working-men, in fact, are very proud of Mr. Mill's scholarship, culture, and profundity. They can perceive easily enough that he is remarkable for just those intellectual qualities which the conventional demagogue never has. Tory newspapers and the "Saturday Review" sometimes affect to regard Mr. Bright as a man of defective education, but it is impossible to pretend to think that Mill is ignorant of Greek or superficial in his knowledge of history. When such a man makes himself especially the champion of working-men, the working-men think of him very much as the Irish peasants of '98 and '48 did of Edward Fitzgerald and Smith O'Brien, the aristocrats of birth and rank, who stepped down from their high places and gave themselves up to the cause of the unlettered and the poor.

There is something fascinating, moreover, about the singular blending of the emotional, and even the romantic, with the keen, vigorous, logical intellect, which is to be observed in Mill. Even political economy, in Mill's mind, is strangely guided and governed by mere feeling. Somebody said he was a combination of Ricardo and Tom Hughes—somebody else said, rather more happily, I think, that he is Adam Smith and Fénélon revived and rolled into one. The "Pall Mall Gazette" found his picture well painted in Lord Macaulay's analysis of the motives which influenced Edmund Burke, when he flung his soul into the impeachment of Warren Hastings. The mere eccentricities, the very defects of such a nature have in them something captivating. The admirers of Mr. Mill are therefore not unusually somewhat given to exalting admiration into idolatry. The classes who most admire him are the scholarly and adventurous young Radicals, who have a dash of Positivism in them; the extreme Radicals, who are prepared to go any and all lengths for the mere sake of change; and the working-men.

This is the Triumvirate of the English Liberal Party. Combined they represent, guide, and govern every section and fraction of that party that is worth taking into any consideration. Mr. Gladstone represents official Liberalism; Mr Bright speaks for and directs the old-fashioned, robust, popular Liberalism of which Manchester was the school; Mr. Mill is the exponent of the new Liberalism, the Liberalism of Idea and Logic. Bright's programme is a little ahead of Gladstone's, but Gladstone will probably be easily pulled up to it. Mill goes far beyond either, far beyond any point at which either is ever likely to arrive. Indeed, Mr. Mill may be fairly described by a phrase, which I believe is German, as a man in advance of every possible future—at least in England. But he is quite prepared to act loyally and steadily with his party and its leader on all momentous issues. On some minor questions he has lately gone widely away from them, and given thereby much offence; and indeed I am sure there are not a few of the old-fashioned Liberals and the Manchester men who would rather Mr. Mill had never come into Parliament and sat at their side. But on nearly all questions of Parliamentary Reform, and on that of the Irish Church, Mill and his Liberal colleagues will pull cordially together. So, too, on most economic questions, reduction of taxation, imposition of duties and the like. Where a sharp difference is likely to arise will only be in relation to some subject having an idea behind it—some question of foreign policy perhaps, something not at present imminent; and, let us hope, not destined in any case to be vital to the interests of the party. Only where an idea is involved will Mr. Mill refuse to allow his own judgment to bend to the general necessities of the party. It was his objection (a very unwise one, I think) to the idea behind the system of the ballot, which led him to separate himself sharply from Bright and other Liberals on that subject; it was the idea which lies at the bottom of a representation of minorities, which beguiled him into lending his advocacy to that most chimerical, awkward, and absurd piece of political mechanism which we know in England as the three-cornered constituency. The cohesion of Gladstone and Bright is decidedly more close and likely to endure than that between Bright and Mill. But on all immediate questions of great importance, these two men are sure to be found side by side. Mill has a deep and earnest admiration for Bright, who is sometimes, perhaps, a little impatient of the Politics of Idea.

During the session of 1868, I attended a meeting of a few representative Liberals of all classes, brought together to decide on some course of agitation with regard to Ireland. Mr. Mill was there, so were Professor Fawcett, Mr. Thomas Hughes, Lord Amberley, and other members of Parliament; Mr. Frederick Harrison, with some of his Positivist colleagues, and several representative working men. Mr. Bright was unable to attend. A certain course of action being recommended, Mr. Mill expressed his own approval of it, but emphatically declared that he considered Mr. Bright's judgment was entitled to be regarded as authoritative, and that should Mr. Bright recommend the meeting not to go on, the scheme had better be given up. Mr. Bright subsequently discouraged the scheme, and it was, on Mr. Mill's recommendation, at once abandoned. I mention this fact to illustrate the loyalty which Mr. Mill, with all his tendency to political eccentricity, usually displays toward the men whom he regards as the leaders of the party.

Mill and Bright are alike warm admirers of Gladstone and believers in him. Indeed one sometimes feels ashamed to doubt for a moment the steadfastness of a man in whom Bright and Mill put so full a faith.

Certainly the English Liberal has reason to congratulate himself, and feel proud when he remembers what sort of men his party's leaders used to be, and sees what men they are to-day. It will not do to study too closely the private characters of the chiefs of any political band in the House of Commons, from the days of Bolingbroke to those of Fox. The man who was not a sinecurist or a peculator was pretty sure to be a profligate or a gambler. Not a few eminent men were sinecurists, peculators, profligates, and gamblers. The political purity of the English Liberal leaders to-day is absolutely without the faintest shade of suspicion—it never even occurs to any one to suspect them, while their private lives, it may be said without indelicacy, are in pure and perfect accord with the noble principles they profess. Not often has there been a political triumvirate of greater men; of better men, never.

THE ENGLISH POSITIVISTS.

SOME few months ago, a little bubble of interest was made on the surface of London life, by a course of Sunday lectures of a peculiar kind.

These lectures were given in a small room in Bouverie street, off Fleet street—Bouverie street, sacred to publishing and newspaper offices—and only a very small stream of persons was drawn to the place. There was something very peculiar, however, about the lectures, the lecturer, and the audience, which might well have repaid a stranger in London for the trouble of going there. I doubt whether such a proportion of intellectual faces could have been seen among the congregation of any London church on these Sunday mornings; and I know one, at least, who attended the lectures, less for the sake of what he heard than because such listeners as the authoress of "Romola" were among the audience. The lecturer was Mr. Richard Congreve, and the subject of his discourses was the creed of Positivism.

I do not know how familiar Mr. Congreve and his writings and his doctrines are to the American public. In London, Mr. Congreve is, in a quiet way, a sort of celebrity or peculiarity. He is the head of the small, compact band of English Positivists. It is understood that he goes as far in the direction of the creed which was the dream of Auguste Comte's later years as any sane human creature can well go. I have, however, very little to say here of Mr. Congreve, individually; and I take his recent course of Sunday lectures only as a convenient starting point from which to begin a few remarks on the political principles, character, and influence of that small, resolute, aggressive body of intellectual, highly-educated and able men who are beginning to be known in the politics and society of England as the London Positivists.

A discourse on the principles of Positivism would be quite out of place here; but even those who understand the whole subject will, perhaps, allow me, for the benefit of those who do not, to explain very briefly what an English Positivist is. Positivism, it is known to my readers, is the name given to the philosophy which Auguste Comte, more than any other man, helped to reduce to a system. Regarded as a philosophy of history and human society, its grand and fundamental doctrine merely is that human life evolves itself in obedience to certain fixed laws, of which we could obtain a knowledge if only we applied ourselves to this study as we do to all other studies in practical science, by the patient observation of phenomena. Auguste Comte's reduction of this philosophical theory to a scientific system is undoubtedly one of the grandest achievements of human intellect. The philosophy did not begin with him or his generation, or, indeed, any generation of which we have authentic record. Whenever there were men capable of thinking at all, there must have been some whose minds were instinct with this doctrine; but Comte made it a system at once simple, grand, and fascinating, and he will always remain identified with its development, in the memory of the modern world. Unfortunately, Comte, in his later years, set to founding a *religion* also—a religion which has, perhaps, called down upon its founder and its followers more ridicule, contempt, and discredit than any vagary of human imagination in our day. I speak of all this only to explain to my readers that there is some little difficulty in defining what is meant by a Positivist. If we mean merely a believer in the philosophical theory of history, then Positivists are, indeed, to be named as legion, and their captains are among the greatest intellects of the world to-day. In England, we regard Mr. John Stuart Mill as, in this sense, the greatest Positivist, and undoubtedly he is so regarded here. But Mill utterly rejects and ridicules the fantastic religion which Comte, in his days of declining mental power, sought to graft on his grand philosophy. In his treatise on Comte, Mr. Mill showed no mercy to the Positivist religion, and, indeed, bitterly offended many of its votaries by his contemptuous exposure of its follies. What is said of Mill may be said of nineteen out of every twenty, at least, of the English followers of Comte. They accept the philosophy as grand, scientific, inexorable truth; they reject the religion with pity or with scorn, as a fantastic and barren chimera. Mr. Congreve is, in London, the leader of the small school who go for taking all or nothing, and to whom Auguste Comte is the prophet of a new and final religion, as well as the teacher of a new philosophy. Now this little school is the nucleus of the body of Englishmen of whom I write.

When I speak, therefore, of English Positivists, I do not mean the men who go no farther than John Stuart Mill does. These men are to be found everywhere; they are of all schools, and all religions. I mean the much smaller body of votaries who go, or feel inclined to go, much farther, and accept Comte's religious teaching as a law of life. It is quite probable that, even among the men who are now identified more or less, in the public mind, with Mr. Congreve and his school, there may be some who do not adopt, or even concern themselves about the religion of Positivism. A community of sentiment on historical and political questions, the habit of meeting together, consulting together, writing for publication together, might naturally bring into the group men who may not go the length of adopting the Comte worship. It is quite possible, therefore, that, in mentioning the names of English Positivists, I may happen to speak of some who have no more to do with that worship than I have.

I mean, then, only the group of men, most of whom are young, most of whom are highly cultured, many of whom are endowed with remarkable ability, who are to be found in a literary and political phalanstery with Mr. Congreve, and of whom the majority are understood to be actual votaries of the religion of Comte. Of course I have nothing to do here with their faith or their practices. If they adopt the worship of woman I think they do a better thing after all than the increasing and popular class of writers, whose principal business in life is to persuade us that our wives and sisters are all Messalinas in heart and nearly all Messalinas in practice. If, when they pray, they touch certain cranial bumps at certain passages of the prayer, I do not see that they institute anything worse than the genuflections of the Ritualist or the breast-beating of the Roman Catholics. If, finally, one is sometimes a little puzzled when he receives a letter from a Positivist friend, and finds it dated "5th Marcus Aurelius," or "12th Auguste Comte," instead of July or December, as the case may be, one must remember that there never yet was a young sect which did not delight in puzzling outsiders by a new and peculiar nomenclature. I never heard anything worse charged against the Positivists than that they worship woman, touch their foreheads when they pray, and arrange the calendar according to a plan of their own invention; except, of course, the general charge of Atheism; but as that is made in England against anybody whom all his neighbors do not quite understand, I hardly think it worth discussing in this particular instance. We are all Atheists in England in the estimation of our neighbors, whose political opinions are different from our own.

The English Positivists, then, are beginning to stand out sharply against the common background of political life. They are a little school; as distinctly a school for their time and chances as the Girondists were, or the Manchester school, or the Massachusetts Abolitionists, or the Boston Transcendentalists. They are Radical, of course, but their Radicalism has a curious twist in it. On any given question of Radicalism they go as far as any practical politician does; but then they also go in most cases so very much farther that they often alarm the practical politician out of his ordinary composure. They are generally incisive of speech, aggressive of purpose, defiant of political prudery, and even of political prudence. Their politics are always politics of idea.

Some three or four years ago the Positivists published a large and ponderous volume of essays on subjects of international policy. Each man who contributed an essay signed his name, and although a general community of idea and principle pervaded the book, it was not understood that everybody who wrote necessarily adopted all the views of his associates. The book, in fact, was constructed on the model of the famous "Essays and Reviews" which had sent such a thrill through the religious world a few years before. The political essays naturally failed to create anything like the sensation which was produced by their theological predecessors; but they did excite considerable attention, and awoke the echoes. They astonished a good many Liberal politicians of the steady old school, and they set many men thinking. What surprised people at first was the singular combination of literary culture and ultra-Radical opinion. Literary young men in England, of late, are generally to be divided into two classes—the smart writers for periodicals, the minor novelists and dramatists, and so forth, who know no more and care no more about politics than ballet girls do, and the University men, the men of "culture," who affect Toryism as something fine and distinguished, and profess a patrician horror of democracy and the "mob." If at the time this volume was published one had taken aside some practical politician in London and said, "Here is a collection of practical essays written by a cluster of young men who all have University degrees after their names—will you read it?" the answer would certainly have been—"Not I, it's sure to be some contemptible sham Tory rubbish; some 'blood-and-culture' trash; some schoolboy impertinence about demagoguism and the mob." Therefore the surprise was not slight to such men when they read the book and found that its central idea, its connecting thread, was a Radicalism which might well be called thorough; a Radicalism which made Bright look like a steady old Conservative; invited Mill to push his ideas a little farther; and poured scorn upon the Radical press for its slowness and its timidity. A simple, startling foreign policy was prescribed to England. Its gospel, after all, was but an old one—so old that it had been forgotten in English politics. It was merely—Be just and fear not. Renounce all aggression; give back the spoils of conquest Give Gibraltar back to the Spaniards who own it; prepare to cast loose your colonial dependencies; prepare even to quit your loved India; ask the Irish people fairly and clearly what they want, and if they desire to be free of your rule, bid them go and be free and Godspeed. All the old traditional policies seemed to these men only obsolete and odious superstitions. They would have England, the State, to stand up and act precisely as an Englishman of honor and conscience would do, and they treated with utter contempt any policy of expediency or any policy whatever that aimed at any end but that of finding out the right thing to do and then doing it at once This seemed to me, studying the school quite as an outside observer, its one great central idea; and it would of course be impossible not to honor the body of writers who proposed to show how it was to be accomplished.

But no school lives on one grand idea ; and this school had its chimeras and crotchets—almost its crazes. For example, the leader of the Positivist band took great trouble to argue that Europe ought to form herself into a noble federation of States, to the exclusion of Russia, which was to be regarded as an Oriental, barbarous, unmanageable, intolerable sort of thing, and pushed out of the European system altogether. Then a good many of the leading minds of the school are imbued with a passionate love for a sort of celestial despotism, an ideal imperialism which the people are first to create and then to obey—which is to teach them, house them, keep them in employment, keep them in health, and leave them nothing to do for themselves, while yet securing to them the most absolute freedom. To some of these men the condition of New York, where the State does hardly anything for the individual, would seem as distressing and objectionable as that of despotic Paris or even Constantinople. A distinguished member of the school declared that nothing was to him more odious than any manner of voluntaryism, and that he hoped to see State operation introduced into every department of English social organization. The connection of this theory with the principle of Positivism, which would mould all men into a sort of hierarchy, is natural and obvious enough, and there is, to support it, a certain reaction now in England against the voluntary principle, in education and in public charities. But, as it is put forward and argued by men of the school I describe, it may be taken as one of the most remarkable points of departure from the common tendency of thought in England. The Positivists are all, indeed, un-English, in the common use of a phrase which is ceasing of late to be so dreaded a stigma as it once used to be in British politics. They are, as I have already said, a somewhat aggressive body, and are imbued with a contempt, which they never care to conceal, for the average public opinion of the British Philistine, whether he present himself as a West End tradesman or a West End Peer.

The Positivists are almost always to be found in antagonism with this sort of public opinion. They attack the Philistine, and they attack no less readily the dainty scholar and critic who lately gave the Philistine his name, and whose over-refining love of sweetness and light is so terribly offended by the rough and earnest work of Radical politics. Whatever way average opinion tends, the influence of the Positivists is sure to tend the other way.

There was a time, nearly two years ago, when the average English mind was suddenly seized with a passion of blended hate, fear, and contempt for Fenianism. The thing was first beginning to show itself in a serious light and it had not gone far enough to show what it really was. It looked more formidable than it proved to be, and it seemed less like an ordinary rebellious organization than like some mysterious and demoniacal league against property and public security. When I say it seemed, I mean it seemed to the average English mind, to the ordinary swell and the ordinary shopkeeper. Just at this time the Positivists drew up a petition to be presented to the House of Commons, in which they called upon the House to insist that lenity should be shown to all Fenian prisoners, that they should be regarded as men driven into rebellion by a deep sense of injustice, and that measures should be taken to prevent the British troops from committing such excesses in Ireland as had been perpetrated in the suppression of the Indian mutiny, and more lately in Jamaica. Now, if there was anything peculiarly calculated to vex and aggravate the House of Commons and the English public generally, it was such a view of the business as this. Fenianism had not acquired the solemn and tragic interest which it obtained a few months afterward. It is only just to say that Englishmen in general began to look with pity and a sort of respect on Fenianism, once it became clear that it had among its followers men who, to quote the language of one of the least sympathetic of London newspapers, "knew how to die." But, at the time I speak of, Fenianism was a vague, mystic, accursed thing, which it was proper to regard as utterly detestable and contemptible. Imagine then what the feeling of the English county member must have been when he learned that there were actually in London a set of educated Englishmen, nearly all trained in the universities and nearly all moving in good society, who regarded the Fenians just as he himself regarded rebels against the Emperor of Austria or the Pope of Rome, and who not merely asked that consideration should be shown toward them, but went on to talk of the necessity of protecting them against the brutality of the loyal British soldier! The petition was signed by all who had a share in its preparation. Such men as Richard Congreve, T. M. Ludlow, Frederick Harrison and Professor Beesly, were among the petitioners who risked their admission into respectable society by signing the document. The petitioners did not feel quite sure about getting any one of mark to present their appeal; and it is certain that a good many professed Liberals, of advanced opinions and full of sympathy with foreign rebels of any class or character, would have promptly refused to accept the ungenial office. The petitioners, however, applied to one who was not likely to be influenced by any considerations but those of right and justice, and whom, moreover, no body in the House of Commons would think of trying to put down. They asked Mr. Bright to present their petition, and there was, of course, no hesitation on his part. Mr. Bright not merely presented the petition, but read it amid the angry and impatient murmurs of an amazed and indignant House; and he declared, in tones of measured and impressive calmness, that he entirely approved of and adopted the sentiments which the petitioners expressed. There was, of course, a storm of indignation, and some members went the length of recommending that the petition should not even be received—an extreme and indeed extravagant course in a country where the right of petitition is supposed to be held sacred, and which the good sense even of some Tory members promptly repudiated. Mr. Disraeli did his very best to aggravate the feeling of the House against the petitioners. During the Indian mutiny he had himself loudly protested against the spirit of vengeance which our press encouraged; asked whether we meant to make Nana Sahib the model for a British officer, and whether Moloch or Christ was our divinity. Yet he now declared that the language of the petition was a libel on the Indian army, and that nothing had ever occurred during the Bengal outbreak to warrant the imputations cast on the humanity of our soldiers.

I suppose it is not easy to convey to an American reader a correct idea of the degree of boldness involved in the presentation of this celebrated petition. It really was a very bold thing to do. It was running right in the very teeth of the public opinion of all the classes which are called respectable in England. It was, however, strictly characteristic of the men who signed it. Most, if not all of them, took a prominent part in the prosecution of Governor Eyre of Jamaica, for the lawless execution of George William Gordon and the wholesale and merciless floggings and hangings by which order was made to reign in the island. Most of them, indeed, have a pretty spirit of contradiction of their own, and a pretty gift of sarcasm. I think I hardly remember any man who received, during an equal length of time, a greater amount of abuse from the press than Professor Beesly drew down on himself not very long ago. It was at the time when the public mind was in its wildest thrill of horror at the really fearful revelations of organized murder in connection with the Sawgrinders' Union in Sheffield. The whole question of trades' union organization had been under discussion; and even before the Sheffield revelations came out, the general voice of English respectability was against the workmen's societies altogether. But when the disclosures of organized murder in connection with one union came out, a sort of panic took possession of the public mind. The first, and not unnatural impulse was to assume that all trades' unions must be very much the same sort of thing, and that the societies of workmen were little better than organized Thuggism. Now, Professor Beesly, Mr. Frederick Harrison and other signers of the petition for the Fenians, had long been prominent and influential advocates of the trades' union principle. They had been to the English artisan something like what the Boston Abolitionist was so long to the negro. The trades' union bodies, who felt aggrieved at the unjust suspicion which made them a party to hideous crimes they abhorred, began to hold public meetings to repudiate the charge, and record their detestation of the Sheffield outrages. Professor Beesly attended one of these meetings in London. He made a speech, in which he told the working men that he thought enough had been done in the way of disavowing crimes which no one had a right to impute to them; that there was no need of their further humiliating themselves; and that it was rather odd the English Aristocracy had such a horror of murderers among the poorer classes, seeing how very fond they were of men like Eyre, of Jamaica! In fact, Professor Beesly uplifted his voice very honestly, but rather recklessly and out of time, against the social hypocrisy which is the stain and curse of London society, and which is never so happy as when it can find some chance of denouncing sin or crime among Republicans, or Irishmen, or workingmen. There was nothing Professor Beesly said which had not sense and truth in it; but it might have been said more discreetly and at a better time; and it was said with a sarcastic and scornful bitterness which is one of the characteristics of the speaker. For several days the London press literally raged at the professor. "Punch" persevered for a long time in calling him "Professor Beastly;" a a strong effort was made to obtain his expulsion from the college in which he has a chair. He was talked of and written of as if he were the advocate and the accomplice of assassins, instead of being, as he is, an honorable gentleman and an enlightened scholar, whose great influence over the working classes had always been exerted in the cause of peaceful progress and good order. It was a common thing, for days and weeks, to see the names of Broadhead and Beesly coupled with ostentatious malignity in the leading columns of London newspapers.

I give these random illustrations only to show in what manner the school of writers and thinkers I speak of usually present themselves before the English public. Now Mr. Harrison devotes himself to a pertinacious, powerful series of attacks on Eyre, of Jamaica, at a time when that personage is the hero and pet martyr of English society; now Professor Beesly horrifies British respectability by pointing out that there are respectable murderers who are quite as bad as Broadhead; now Mr. John Morley undertakes even to criticise the Queen; now Mr. Congreve assails the anonymous writers of the London press as hired and masked assassins; now the whole band unite in the defence of Fenians. This sort of thing has a startling effect upon the steady public mind of England;

and it is thus, and not otherwise, that the public mind of England ever comes to hear of these really gifted and honest, but very antagonistic and somewhat crochetty men. Several of them are brilliant and powerful writers. Professor Beesly writes with a keen, caustic, bitter force which has something Parisian in it. I know of no writer in English journalism who more closely resembles in style a certain type of the literary gladiator of French controversy. He has much of Eugene Pelletan in him, and something of Henri Rochefort, blended with a good deal that reminds one of Jules Simon. Frederick Harrison is fast becoming a power in the Radical politics and literature of England. John Morley is a young man of great culture, and who writes with a quite remarkable freshness and force. I could mention many other men of the same school (I have already said that I do not know whether each and every one of these is or is not a professed Positivist) who would be distinguished as scholars and writers in the literature of any country. However they may differ on minor points, however they may differ in ability, in experience, in discretion, they have one peculiarity in common: they are to be found foremost in every liberal and radical cause; they are always to be found on the side of the weak, and standing up for the oppressed; they are inveterate enemies of cant; they hate vulgar idolatry and vulgar idols. Looking back a few years, I can remember that almost, if not quite, every man I have alluded to was a fearless and outspoken advocate of the cause of the North, at a time when it was *de rigueur* among men of "culture" in London to champion the cause of the South. Some of the men I have named were indefatigable workers at that time on the unfashionable side. They wrote pamphlets; they wrote leading articles; they made speeches; they delivered lectures in out-of-the-way quarters to workingmen and poor men of all kinds; they hardly came, in any prominent way, before the public, in most of this work. It brought them, probably, no notoriety or recognition whatever on this side of the ocean; but their work was a power in England. I feel convinced that, in any case, the English workingmen would have gone right on such a question as that which was at issue between North and South. As Mr. Motley truly said in his address to the New York Historical Society, the workers and the thinkers were never misled; but I am bound to say that the admirable knowledge of the realities of the subject; the clear, quick, and penetrating judgment, and the patient, unswerving hope and confidence which were so signally displayed by the London workingmen from first to last of that great struggle, were in no slight degree the result of the teaching and the labor of men like Professor Beesly and Frederick Harrison.

If I were to set up a typical Positivist, in order to make my American reader more readily and completely familiar with the picture which the word calls up in the minds of Londoners, I should do it in the following way: I should exhibit my model Positivist as a man still young for anything like prominence in English public life, but not actually young in years—say thirty-eight or forty. He has had a training at one of the great historical Universities, or at all events at the modern and popular University of London. He is a barrister, but does not practise much, and has probably a modest competence on which he can live without working for the sake of living, and can indulge his own tastes in literature and politics. He has immense earnestness and great self-conceit. He has an utter contempt for dull men and timid or half-measure men, and he scorns Whigs even more than Tories. He devotes much of his time generously and patiently to the political and other instruction of working men. He writes in the "Fortnightly Review," and sometimes in "MacMillan," and sometimes in the "Westminster Review." He plunges into gallant and fearless controversy with the "Pall Mall Gazette," and he is not easily worsted, for his pen is sharp and his ink very acrid. Nevertheless, is any great question stirring, with a serious principle or a deep human interest at the heart of it, he is sure to be found on the right side. Where the controversy is of a smaller kind and admits of crotchet, then he is pretty sure to bring out a crotchet of some kind. He is perpetually giving the "Saturday Review" an opportunity to ridicule him and abuse him, and he does not care. He writes pamphlets and goes to immense trouble to get up the facts, and expense to give them to the world, and he never grudges trouble or money, where any cause or even any crotchet is to be served. He is ready to stand up alone, against all the world if needs be, for his opinions or his friends. Benevolent schemes which are of the nature of mere charity he never concerns himself about. I never heard of him on a platform with the Earl of Shaftesbury, and I fancy he has a contempt for all patronage of the poor or projects of an eleemosynary character. He is for giving men their political rights and educating them—if necessary compelling them to be educated; and he has little faith in any other way of doing good. He has, of course, a high admiration for and faith in Mr. Mill. His nature is not quite reverential—in general he is rather inclined to sit in the chair of the scorner; but if he reverenced any living man it would be Mill. He admires the manly, noble character of Bright, and his calm, strong eloquence. I do not think he cares much about Gladstone—I rather fancy our Positivist looks upon Gladstone as somewhat weak and unsteady—and with him to be weak is indeed to be miserable. Disraeli is to him an object of entire scorn and detestation, for he can endure no one who has not deeply-rooted principles of some kind. He has a crotchet about Russia, a theory about China; he gets quite beside himself in his anger over the anonymous leading articles of the London press. He is not an English type of man at all, in the present and conventional sense. He cares not a rush about tradition, and mocks at the wisdom of our ancestors. The bare fact that some custom, or institution, or way of thinking has been sanctioned and hallowed by long generations of usage, is in his eyes rather a *prima facie* reason for despising it than otherwise. He is pitilessly intolerant of all superstitions—save his own—that is to say, he is intolerant in words and logic and ridicule, for the wildest superstition would find him its defender, if it once came to be practically oppressed or even threatened. He is "ever a fighter," like one of Browning's heroes; he is the knight-errant, the Quixote of modern English politics. He admires George Eliot in literature, and, I should say, he regards Charles Dickens as a sort of person who does very well to amuse idlers and ignorant people. I do not hear of his going much to the theatre, and it is a doubt to me if he has yet heard of the "Grande Duchesse." Life with him is a very earnest business, and, although he has a pretty gift of sarcasm, which he uses as a weapon of offence against his enemies, I cannot, with any effort of imagination, picture him to myself as in the act of making a joke.

A small drawing-room would assuredly hold all the London Positivists who make themselves effective in English politics. Yet I do not hesitate to say that they are becoming—that they have already become—a power which no one, calculating on the chances of any coming struggle, can afford to leave out of his consideration. Their public influence thus far has been wholly for good; and they set up no propaganda that I have ever seen or heard of, as regards either philosophy or religion. The course of lectures I have already mentioned was the nearest approach to any public diffusion of their peculiar doctrines which I can remember, and it created little or no sensation in London. Indeed, little or no publicity was sought for it. I have read lately somewhere that a newspaper, specially devoted to the propagation and vindication of Positivism, is about to be, or has been started in London. I do not know whether this is true or not; but for any such journal I should anticipate a very small circulation, and an existence only to be maintained by continual subsidy.

So quietly have these men hitherto pursued their course, whatever it may be, in religion or religious philosophy, that it was long indeed before any idea got abroad that the cluster of highly-educated, ultra-radical thinkers, who were to be found sharpshooting on the side of every great human principle and every oppressed cause, and who seemed positively to delight in standing up against the vulgar rush of public opinion, were anything more than chance associates, or were bound by any tie more close and firm than that of general political sympathy. Even now that people are beginning to know them, and to classify them, in a vague sort of way, as "those Positivists," they make so little parade of any peculiarity of faith that, without precise and personal knowledge, it would be rash to say for certain that this or that member of the group is or is not an actual professor of the Comtist religion. I read a few days ago, in one of the few sensible books written on America by an Englishman, some remarks made about a peculiar view of Europe's duty to Egypt, which was described as being held by "the Comtists." I do not know whether the men referred to hold the view ascribed to them or not; but, assuredly, if they do, the fact has no more direct connection with their Comtism than Bright's free-trade views have with Bright's Quakerism. An illustration, however, will serve well enough as an example of the vague and careless sort of way in which doctrines and the men who profess them get mixed up together insolubly in the public mind. The Sultan of a generation back, who told the European diplomatist that if he changed his religion at all he would become a Roman Catholic, because he observed that Roman Catholic people always grew the best wine, was not more unreasonable in his logic than many well-informed men when they are striving to connect cause and effect in dealing with the religion of others.

I do not myself make any attempt to explain why a follower of Comte's worship should, at least in England, be always on the side of liberty and equality and human progress. Indeed, if inclined to discuss such a question at all, I should rather be disposed to put it the other way and ask how it happens that men so enlightened and liberal in education and principles should yield a moment's obedience to the ghostly shadow of Roman Catholic superstition, which Auguste Comte, in the decaying years of his noble intellect, conjured up to form a new religion. But I am quite content to let the question go unanswered—and should be willing, indeed, to leave it unasked. I wish just now to do nothing more than to direct the attention of American readers to the fact that a new set or sect has arisen to influence English politics, and that their influence and its origin are different from anything which, judging by the history of previous generations, one might naturally have been led to expect. "Culture" in England has, of late years, almost invariably ranked itself on the side of privilege. The Oxford undergraduate shouts himself hoarse in cheering for Disraeli and groaning for Bright. Oxford rejects Gladstone the moment he becomes a Liberal. The vigorous Radicalism of Thorold Rogers costs him his chair as professor of political economy, although no man in England is a more perfect master of some of the more important branches of that science. The journals which are started for the sake of being read by men of "culture" are sure to throw their influence, nine times out of ten, into the cause of privilege and class ascendency. The "Saturday Review" does this deliberately; the "Pall Mall Gazette" does it instinctively. Suddenly there comes out from the bosom of the universities themselves a band of keen, acute, fearless gladiators, who throw themselves into the van of every great movement which works for democracy, equality and freedom. They invade the press and the platform; they write in this journal and in that; they are always writing, always printing; they are ready for any assailant, however big, they are willing to work with any ally, however small; they shrink from no logical consequence or practical inconvenience of any argument or opinion; they take the working man by the hand and talk to him and tell him all they know—and it is something worth studying, the fact that their scholarship and his no-scholarship so often come to the same conclusion. They will work with anybody, because they go farther than almost anybody; and they will allow anybody the full swing of his own crotchet, even though he be not so willing to give them scope enough for theirs. Thus they are commonly associated with Goldwin Smith, who has a perfect horror of French Democracy and French Imperialism, and who sees in Mirabeau only a "Voltairean debauchee;" with Tom Hughes, who is a sturdy member of the Church of England, and does not, I fancy, care three straws about the policy of ideas; with Bright, whose somewhat Puritanical mind draws back with a kind of dread from anything that savors of free-thinking; with Auberon Herbert, the mild young aristocrat, converted from Toryism by pure sentimentalism and philanthropy; with Connolly, the eloquent Irish plasterer, whose vigorous stump oratory aroused the warm admiration of Louis Blanc. It would be impossible that such a knot of men, so gifted and so fearless, so independent and so unresting, so keen of pen, and so unsparing of logic, should be without a clear and marked influence on the politics of England. It is quite a curious phenomenon that such a group of men should be found in close and constant co-operation with the English artisan, his trades' union organizations, and his political cause. Frederick Harrison represented the working men in the Parliamentary commission lately held to inquire into the whole operation of the trades' unions. Professor Beesly writes continually in the "Beehive," the newspaper which is the organ of George Potter and the trades' societies. I cannot see how the cause of Democracy can fail to derive strength and help from this sort of alliance, and I therefore welcome the influence upon English politics of the little group of Positivist penmen, believing that it will have a deeper reach than most people now imagine, and that where it operates effectively at all, it will be for good.

ENGLISH TORYISM AND ITS LEADERS.

SIR JOHN MANDEVILLE tells a story of a man who set out on a voyage of discovery, and sailing on and on in a westerly direction, at last touched a land where he was surprised to find a climate the same as his own; animals like those he had left behind; men and women not only having the same dress and complexion, but actually speaking the same language as the people of his own country. He was so struck with this unexpected and wonderful discovery, that he took to his ship again without delay, and sailed back eastward to impart to his own people the news that in a far-off, strange, western sea he had found a race identical with themselves. The truth was that the simple voyager had gone round the world, reached his own country without recognizing it, and then went round the world again to get home.

If the voyage were made in our time, and the explorer were a British Tory who had left England in the opening of the year 1867, and after unconsciously sailing round the world had fallen in with British Tories again in the autumn of the same year, one could easily excuse his failing to recognize his own people. For in the interval of time from February to August, British Toryism underwent the most sudden and complete transformation known outside the sphere of Ovid's Metamorphoses. If any of my American readers will try to imagine a whole political party, great in numbers, greater still in wealth, station and influence, suddenly performing just such a turn-round as the "New York Herald" accomplished at a certain early crisis of the late civil war, he will have some idea of the marvellous and unprecedented feat which was executed by the English Tories, when, renouncing all their time-honored traditions, watchwords and principles, they changed a limited and oligarchical franchise into household suffrage. It is singular, indeed, that such a thing should have been done. It is more singular still that it should have been done, as it most assuredly was done, in order that one man should be kept in power. It is even more singular yet that it should have been done by a party of men individually high principled, honorable, unselfish, incapable of any deliberate meanness—and of whom many if not most actually disliked and distrusted the man in whose interest and by whose influence the surrender of principle was made.

Perhaps when I have said a little about the leadership of the English Tories, the phenomenon will appear less wonderful or at least more intelligible. It was not a mere epigram which Mr. Mill uttered when he described the Tories as the stupid party. An average Tory really is a stupid man. He is a gentleman in all the ordinary acceptation of the word. He has been to Oxford or Cambridge; he has received a decent classical education; he has travelled along the beaten tracks—made what would have been called in Mary Wortley Montague's day "the grand tour;" he has birth and high breeding; he is a good fellow, with manly, honorable ways, and that genial consideration for the feelings of others which is the fundamental condition, the vital element of gentlemanly breeding. But he is, with all this, stupid. His mind is narrow, dull, inflexible; he cannot connect cause with effect, or see that a change is coming, or why it should come; with him *post hoc* always means *propter hoc;* he cannot account for Goodwin Sands otherwise than because of Tenterden steeple. You cannot help liking him, and sometimes laughing at him. It may seem paradoxical, but I at least am unable to get out of my mind the conviction that there is a solid basis of stupidity in the mind of the great Conservative Chief, Lord Derby. Let me explain what I mean. The Earl of Derby is in one sense a highly accomplished man. He is a good classical scholar, and can make a speech in Latin. He has produced some very spirited translations from Horace; and I like his version of the Iliad better on the whole than any other I know. He is a splendid debater—Macaulay said very truly that with Lord Derby the science of debate was an instinct. He will roll out resonant, rotund, verbose sentences by the hour, by the yard; he is great at making hits and points; he has immense power of reply and repartee—of a certain easy and obvious kind; his voice is fine, his manner is noble, his invective is powerful. But he has no ideas. The light he throws out is a polarized light. He adds nothing new to the political thought of the age. I have heard many of his finest speeches; and I can remember that they were then very telling, in a Parliamentary point of view; but I cannot remember anything he said. He is always interpreting into eloquent and effective words the commonplace Philistine notions, the hereditary conventionalities of his party—and nothing more. His mind is not open to new impressions, and he is not able to appreciate the cause, the purpose or the tendency of change. This I hold to be the essential characteristic of stupidity; and this is an attribute of Lord Derby, with all his Greek, his Latin, his impetuous rhetoric, his debating skill and his audacious blunders, which sometimes almost deceive one into thinking him a man of genius. Now the Earl of Derby is the greatest Tory living; and if I have fairly described the highest type of Tory, one can easily form some conception of what the average Tory must be. Every one likes Lord Derby, and I fully believe it to be the fact that those who know him best like him best. I cannot imagine Lord Derby doing a mean thing; I cannot imagine him haughty to a poor man, or patronizingly offensive to a timid visitor of humble birth. Look at Lord Derby through the wrong end of the intellectual telescope and you have the average British Tory. The Tory's knowledge is confined to classics and field sports—when he knows anything. Even Lord Derby has been guilty of the most flagrant mistakes in geography and modern history. People are never tired of alluding to a famous blunder of his about Tambov in Russia. It is also told of him that he once spoke in Parliament of Demerara as an island; and when one of his colleagues afterward remonstrated with him on the mistake, he asked with ingenuousness and *naïveté* "How on earth was I to know that Demerara was not an island?" He once, at a public meeting, spoke of himself very frankly as having been born "in the pre-scientific period"—the period but too recently closed, when English Universities and high class schools troubled themselves only about Greek and Latin, and thought it beneath their dignity to show much interest in such vulgar, practical studies as chemistry and natural history, to say nothing of that ungentlemanly and ungenerous study, the science of political economy. The average British Tory is a Lord Derby without eloquence, brains, official habits and political experience.

How, then, do the Tories exist as a party? How do they continue to believe themselves to be Tories, and speak of themselves as Tories, when they have surrendered all, or nearly all, the great principles which are the creed and faith, and business of Toryism? Because they have, in our times, never had Tories for leaders. A man is not a Tory merely because he fights the Tory battles, any more than a captain of the Irish Brigade was a Frenchman because he fought for King Louis, or Hobart Pasha is a Turk because he commands the

Ottoman navy. The Tory party has always, of late years, had to call in the aid of brilliant outsiders, political renegades, refugees from broken-down agitations, disappointed and cynical deserters from the Liberal camp, or mere adventurers, to fight their battles for them. It used to be quite a curious sight, some three or four years ago, when the Tories were, as they are now again, in opposition, to look down from the gallery of the House of Commons and see the men who did gladiatorial duty for the party. Along the back benches, above and below the "gangway," were stretched out huge at length the stalwart, handsome, manly country gentlemen, the bone and sinew of the Tory party—the only real Tories to be found in the House. But *they* did not bear the brunt of debate. They could cheer splendidly, and vote in platoons; but you don't suppose they were just the sort of men to confront Gladstone, and reply to Bright? Not they; and they knew it. There sat Disraeli, the brilliant renegade from Radicalism, who was ready to think for them and talk for them: and who were his lieutenants? Cairns, the successful, adroit, eloquent lawyer, a North of Ireland man, with about as much of the genuine British Tory in him as there is in Disraeli himself; Seymour Fitzgerald, the clever, pushing Irishman, also a lawyer; Whiteside, the voluble, eloquent, rather boisterous advocate, also a lawyer, and also an Irishman; smart, saucy Pope Hennessy, a young Irish adventurer, who had taken up with Toryism and ultramontanism as the best way of making a career, and who would, at the slightest hint from his chief, have risen, utterly ignorant of the subject under debate, and challenged Gladstone's finance or Roundel Palmer's law. These men, and such men—these and no others—did the debating and the fighting for the great Tory party of England at a most critical period of that party's existence. Needless to say that the party who were compelled by their own poverty of idea, their own stupidity, to have these men for their representatives, were stupid enough to be led anywhere and into anything by the force of a little dexterity and daring on the part of the one man into whose hands they had confided their destinies.

In speaking, therefore, of the leaders of Toryism, I must distinctly say that I am not speaking of Tories. The rank and file are Tories; the general and officers belong to another race. Mr. Disraeli is so well known on this side of the Atlantic that I need not occupy much time or space in describing him. He is the most brilliant specimen of the adventurer or political soldier of fortune known to English public life in our days. I do not suppose anybody believes Mr. Disraeli's Toryism to be a genuine faith. This is not merely because he has changed his opinions so completely since the time when he came out as a Radical, under the patronage of O'Connell, and wrote to William Johnson Fox, the Democratic orator, a famous letter, in which he, Disraeli, boasted that "his forte was revolution." Men have changed their views as completely, and even as suddenly, and yet obtained credit for sincerity and integrity. It is not even because, in all of Mr. Disraeli's novels, a prime and favorite personage is a daring political adventurer, who carries all before him by the audacity of his genius and his unscrupulousness; it is not even that Mr. Disraeli, in private life, frequently speaks of success in politics as the one grand object worth striving for or living for. "What do you and I come to this House of Commons night after night for?" said Mr. Disraeli once to a great Englishman, and when the latter failed to reply very quickly, he answered his own question by saying, "You know we come here for fame." The man to whom he spoke declared, in all truthfulness, that he did not follow a political career for the sake of fame. But Disraeli was quite incredulous, and probably could not, by any earnestness and apparent sincerity of asseveration, be got to believe that there lives a being who could sacrifice time, and money, and intellect, and eloquence merely for the sake of serving the public. Yet it is not alone this cynical avowal of selfishness which makes people so profoundly sceptical as to Mr. Disraeli's Toryism. It is the fact that he always escapes into Liberalism whenever he has an opportunity; that he lives by hawking Toryism, not by imbibing it himself; that he is ready to sell it, or betray it, or drag it in the dirt whenever he can safely serve himself by doing so; that he can become the most ardent of Freetraders, the most uncompromising champion of a Popular Suffrage to-day, when it is for his interest, after having fought fiercely against both yesterday, when to fight against them was for his interest. Mr. Disraeli is decidedly a man without scruple. Those who have read his "Vivian Grey" will remember with what zest and unction he describes his hero bewildering a company and dumbfoundering a scientific authority by extemporizing an imaginary quotation from a book which he holds in his hand, and from which he pretends to read the passage he is reciting. It is not long since Mr. Disraeli himself publicly ventured on a bold little experiment of a somewhat similar kind. The story is curious, and worth hearing; and it is certain that it cannot be contradicted.

Three or four years ago, a bitter factious attack was made in the House of Commons upon Mr. Stansfeld, then holding office in the Liberal government, because of his open and avowed friendship for, and intimacy with Mazzini. This was at a time when the French government were endeavoring to connect Mazzini with a plot to assassinate the Emperor Napoleon. Mr. Disraeli was very stern in his condemnation of Mr. Stansfeld for his friendship with one who, twenty odd years before, had encouraged a young enthusiast (as the enthusiast said) in a design to kill Charles Albert, King of Sardinia. Mr. Bright, in a moderate and kindly speech, deprecated the idea of making unpardonable crimes out of the hotheaded follies of enthusiastic men in their young days; and he added that he believed there would be found in a certain poem, written by Disraeli himself some twenty-five or thirty years before, and called "A Revolutionary Epick," some lines of eloquent apostrophe in praise of tyrannicide. Up sprang Mr. Disraeli, indignant and excited, and vehemently denied that any such sentiment, any such line, could be found in the poem. Mr. Bright at once accepted the assurance; said he had never seen the poem himself, but only heard that there was such a passage in it; apologized for the mistake—and there most people thought the matter would have ended. In truth, the volume which Mr. Disraeli had published a generation before, with the grandiloquent title, "A Revolutionary Epick" (not "epic," in the common way, but dignified, old-fashioned "epick"), was a piece of youthful, bombastic folly long out of print, and almost wholly forgotten. But Disraeli chose to attach great importance to the charge he supposed to be made against him; and he declared that he felt himself bound to refute it utterly by more than a mere denial. Accordingly, in a few weeks, there came out a new edition of the Epick, with a dedication to Lord Stanley, and a preface explaining that, as the first edition was out of print, and as a charge founded on a passage in it had been made against the author, said author felt bound to issue this new edition, that all the world might see how unfounded was the accusation. Sure enough, the publication did seem to dispose of the charge effectually. There was only one passage which in any way bore on the subject of tyrannicide, and that certainly did not express approval. What could be more satisfactory? Unluckily, however, the gentleman on whose hint Mr. Bright spoke, happened to possess one copy of the original edition. He compared this, to make assurance doubly sure, with the copy at the British Museum, the only other copy accessible to him, and he found that the passage which contained the praise of tyrannicide had been partly altered, partly suppressed, in the new edition specially issued by Mr. Disraeli, in order to prove to the world that he had not written a line in the poem to imply that he sanctioned the slaying of a tyrant. Now, this was a small and trifling affair ; but just see how significant and characteristic it was ! It surely did not make much matter whether Mr. Disraeli, in his young, nonsensical days, had or had not indulged in a burst of enthusiasm about the slaying of tyrants, in a poem so bombastical that no rational man could think of it with any seriousness. But Mr. Disraeli chose to regard his reputation as seriously assailed ; and what did he do to vindicate himself? He published a new edition, which he trumpeted as not merely authentic, but as issued for the sole purpose of proving that he had not praised tyrannicide, and he deliberately excised the lines which contained the passage in question ! The controversy turned on some two lines and a half; and of these Mr. Disraeli cut out all the dangerous words and gave the garbled version to the world as his authoritative reply to the charge made against him ! This, too, after the famous "annexation" of one of Thiers's speeches, and the delivery of it as a panegyric on the memory of the Duke of Wellington, and after the appropriation of a page or two out of an essay by Macaulay, and its introduction wholesale, as original, into one of Mr. Disraeli's novels.

The truth is that Disraeli is so reckless a gladiator that he will catch up any weapon of defence, use any means of evasion and escape ; will fight anyhow, and win anyhow. In political affairs, at least, he has no moral sense whatever ; and the public seems to tolerate him on that understanding. Certainly, escapades and practices which would ruin the reputation of any other public man do not seem to bring Disraeli into serious disrepute. The few high-toned men of his own party and the other who hold all trickery in detestation, had made up their minds about him long ago ; and nothing could hurt him more in their esteem—the great majority of politicians laugh at the whole thing, and take no thought. The feeling seems to be, "We don't expect grave and severe virtue from this man ; we take him as he is. It would be ridiculous to apply a grave moral test to anything he may say or do." In Lockhart's "Life of Walter Scott," it is told that the great novelist went one morning very early to call on a certain friend. The friend was in bed, and Scott, pushing into the room familiarly, found that his friend was—not alone, as he expected him to be. Scott was a highly moral man, and he would have turned his back indignantly on any other of his friends whom he found guilty of vice ; but his biographer says that he took the discovery he had made very lightly in this instance ; and he afterward explained that the delinquent was so ridiculously without depth of character it would be absurd to find serious fault with anything he did. Perhaps it is in a similar spirit that the British public regard Mr. Disraeli. He delivered a memorable peroration one night last year in the House of Commons, the utterance and the language of which were so peculiar that charity itself could not affect to be ignorant of the stimulating cause which sent forth such extraordinary eloquence. Yet hardly anybody seemed to regard it as more than a good joke ; and the newspapers which were most indignant and most scandalized over Andrew Johnson's celebrated inaugural address made no allusion whatever to Mr. Disraeli's bewildering outburst. One reason, probably, is that Disraeli, in private, is much liked. He is very kindly ; he is a good friend ; he is sympathetic in his dealings with young politicians, and is always glad to give a helping hand to a young man of talent. Personal ambition, which, in Mr. Bright's eyes, is something despicable, and which Mr. Gladstone probably regards as a sin, is, in Disraeli's acceptation, something generous and elevating, something to be fostered and encouraged. Therefore, young men of talent admire Disraeli, and are glad and proud to gather round him. The men who have any brains in the Tory ranks are usually of the adventurer class; and they form a phalanx by the aid of which Disraeli can do great things. No matter how the honest, dull bulk of his party may distrust him, they cannot do without him and his phalanx; and they allow him to win his battles by the force of their votes, and they think he is winning their battles all the time.

One young man of brains there was on the Tory side of the House of Commons, who did not like Disraeli, and never professed to like him. This was Lord Robert Cecil, who subsequently became Viscount Cranbourne, and now sits in the House of Lords as Marquis of Salisbury. Lord Robert Cecil was by far the ablest scion of noble Toryism in the House of Commons. Younger than Lord Stanley he had not Lord Stanley's solidity and caution; but he had much more of original ability; he had brilliant ideas, great readiness in debate, and a perfect genius for saying bitter things in the bitterest tone. The younger son of a wealthy peer, he had, in consequence of a dispute with his father, manfully accepted honorable poverty, and was glad, for no short time, to help out his means by the use of his pen. He wrote in the "Quarterly Review," the time-honored organ of Toryism; and after a while certain political articles regularly appearing in that periodical became identified with his name. One great object of these articles seemed to be to denounce Mr. Disraeli and warn the Tory party against him as a traitor, certain in the end to sell and surrender their principles. Lord Robert Cecil was an ultra-Tory—or at least thought himself so—I feel convinced that his intellect and his experience will set him free one day. He was a Tory on principle and would listen to no compromise. People did not at first see how much ability there was in him—very few indeed saw how much of genuine manhood and nobleness there was in him. His tall, bent, awkward figure; his prematurely bald crown, his face with an outline and a beard that reminded one of a Jew pedler from the Minories, his ungainly gestures, his unmelodious voice, and the extraordinary and wanton bitterness of his tongue, set the ordinary observer strongly against him. He seemed to delight in being gratuitously offensive. Let me give one illustration. He assailed Mr. Gladstone's financial policy one night, and said it was like the practice of a pettifogging attorney. This was rather coarse and it was received with loud murmurs of disapprobation, but Lord Robert went on unheeding. Next night, however, when the debate was resumed, he rose and said he feared he had used language the previous evening which was calculated to give offence, and which he could not justify. There were murmurs of encouraging applause—nothing delights the House of Commons like an unsolicited and manly apology. Yes, he had, on the previous night, in a moment of excitement, compared the policy of the Chancellor of the Exchequer to the practice of a pettifogging attorney. That was language which on sober consideration he felt he could not justify and ought not to have used, "and therefore," said Lord Robert, "I beg leave to offer my sincere apology"—here Mr. Gladstone half rose from his seat, with face of eager generosity, ready to pardon even before fully asked—"I beg leave to tender my sincere apology—to the attorneys!" Half the House roared with laughter, the other half with anger—and Gladstone threw himself back in his seat with an expression of mingled disappointment, pity and scorn, on his pallid, noble features.

There was something so wanton, something so nearly approaching to outrageous buffoonery, in conduct like this, on the part of Lord Robert Cecil, that it was long before impartial observers came to recognize the fine intellect and the manly character that were disguised under such an unprepossessing exterior. When the Tories came into power, the great place of Secretary for India was given to Lord Robert, who had then become Viscount Cranbourne, and the responsibilities of office wrought as complete a change in him as the wearing of the crown did in Harry the Fifth. No man ever displayed in so short a time greater aptitude for the duties of the office he had undertaken, or a loftier sense of its tremendous moral and political responsibility, than did Lord Cranbourne during his too brief tenure of the Indian Secretaryship. The cynic had become a statesman, the intellectual gladiator an earnest champion of exalted political principle. The license of tongue, in which Lord Cranbourne had revelled while yet a free lance, he absolutely renounced when he became a responsible minister. He extorted the respect and admiration of Gladstone and Bright, and indeed of every one who took the slightest interest in the condition and the future of India. The manner of his leaving office became him, too, almost as much as his occupation of it. He was sincerely opposed to a sudden lowering of the franchise, and he insisted that his party ought to think nothing of power when compared with principle. He found that Disraeli was determined to surrender anything rather than power, and he withdrew from the uncongenial companionship. He resigned office, and dropped into the ranks once more, never hesitating to express his conviction of the utter insincerity of the Conservative leader. He would have been a sharp and stinging thorn in Disraeli's side, only that death intervened and took away, not him, but his father. The death of his elder brother had made Lord Robert Cecil, Viscount Cranbourne; the death of his father now converted Viscount Cranbourne into the Marquis of Salisbury, and condemned him to the languid, inert, lifeless atmosphere of the House of Peers. The sincere pity of all who admired him followed the brilliant Salisbury in his melancholy descent. I should despair of conveying to an American reader unacquainted with English politics any adequate idea of the profundity and hopelessness of the fall which precipitates a young, ardent and gifted politician from the brilliant battle-ground of the House of Commons into the lifeless, Lethean pool of the House of Lords.

Still, the Tory party may be led, as it has been, by a chief in the House of Lords, although its great and splendid fights must be fought in the Commons. If then, in our time, Toryism ever should again become a principle which a man of genius and high character could fairly fight for, it has a leader ready to its hand in the Marquis of Salisbury. For the present it has Lord Cairns. The Earl of Derby's health no longer allows him to undertake the serious and laborious duties of party leadership. When he withdrew from the front, an attempt was made to put up with Lord Malmesbury. But Malmesbury is stupid and muddle-headed to a degree which even Tory peers cannot endure in a Tory peer; and it has somehow been "borne in upon him" that he had better leave the place to some one really qualified to fill it. Now, the Tories in the House of Commons, the country gentlemen of England, the men whose ancestors came over, perhaps, with the Conqueror, the men who imbibed family Toryism from the breasts of their mothers, are driven, when they want a capable leader, to follow a renegade Radical, the son of a middle-class Jew. In like manner the Tory Lords, also sadly needing an efficient leader, are compelled to take up with a lawyer from Belfast, the son of middle-class parents in the North of Ireland, who has fought his way by sheer talent and energy into the front rank of the bar, into the front bench of the Parliamentary Opposition, and at last into a peerage. Lord Cairns is a very capable man; his sudden rise into high place and influence proves the fact of itself, for he was not a young man when he entered Parliament, obscure and unknown, and he is now only in the prime of life, while he leads the Opposition in the House of Lords. He is one of the most fluent and effective debaters in either House; he has great command of telling argument; his training at the bar gives him the faculty of making the very most, and at the shortest notice, of all the knowledge and all the facts he can bring to bear on any question. He has shown more than once that he is capable of pouring forth a powerful, almost indeed, a passionate invective. An orator in the highest sense he certainly is not. No gleam of the poetic softens or brightens his lithe and nervous logic; no deep feeling animates, inspires and sanctifies it. He has made no speeches which anybody hereafter will care to read. He has made, he will make, no mark upon his age. When he dies, he wholly dies. But living, he is a skilful and a capable man—far better qualified to be a party leader than an Erskine or a Grattan would be. A North of Ireland Presbyterian, he has made his way to a peerage, and now to be the leader of peers, with less of native genius than that which conducted Wolfe Tone, another North of Ireland Presbyterian, to rebellion and failure and a bloody death. He has, above all things, skill and discretion; and he can lead the Tory party well, so long as no great cause has to be vindicated, no splendid phantom of a principle maintained. His name and his antecedents are useful to us now, inasmuch as they serve still farther to illustrate the fact that Toryism is not led by Tories.

In speaking of Tory leaders one ought not, of course, to leave out the name of Lord Stanley. But Lord Stanley is only a Tory *ex officio*, and by virtue of his position as the eldest son and heir of the great Earl of Derby. I have never heard of Lord Stanley's uttering a Tory sentiment, even when he had to play a Tory part. His speeches are all the speeches of a steady, respectable, thoughtful sort of Liberal, inclined to study carefully both or all sides of a question, and opposed to extreme opinions either way. He will never, it is quite clear, be guilty of the audacity of openly breaking with his party while his father lives; and perhaps when he becomes Earl of Derby, there may be nothing distinctively Tory worth fighting about. Lord Stanley is indeed totally devoid of that generous ardor which makes men open converts. He is no longer young, and he will probably remain all his life where he stands at present. But a genuine Tory he is not. I confess that at one time I looked to him with great hope, as a man likely to develop into statesmanship of the highest order, and to announce himself as a votary of political and intellectual progress. Some years ago I wrote an article in the "Westminster Review," the object of which was to point to Lord Stanley as the future colleague of Gladstone in a great and a really liberal government. I have changed my opinion since. Lord Stanley wants, not the brains, but the heart for such a place. He has not the spirit to step out of his hereditary way. He is one of the sort of men of whom Goethe used to say, "If only they would commit an extravagance even, I should have some hope for them." He seems to care for little beyond accuracy of judgment and propriety; and I do not suppose accuracy of judgment and propriety ever made a great statesman. There is nothing venturesome about Lord Stanley—therefore there is nothing great. A man to be great must brave being ridiculous; and I do not remember that Lord Stanley has ever run the risk of being ridiculous. One of the finest and most celebrated passages of modern Parliamentary eloquence is that in which George Canning, vindicating his recognition of the South American republics, proclaimed that he had called in the New World to redress the balance of the Old. I once heard a member of the House of Lords, now dead, who sat in the House of Commons near Canning, when Canning spoke that famous speech, say that when the orator came to the great climax the House was actually breaking into a titter, so absurd then did any grandiloquence about South American republics seem; and it was only the earnestness and resolve of his manner that commanded a respectful attention, and thus compelled the House to recognize the genuine grandeur of the idea, and to break into a tempest of applause. I have heard something the same told of one of the grandest passages in any of Bright's speeches—that in one of his orations against the Crimean War, in which he declared that he already heard, during the debate, the beating of the wings of the Angel of Death. The House was under the influence of a war fever, and disposed to scoff at all appeals to prudence or to pity; and it was just on the verge of a laugh at the orator's majestic apostrophe, when his earnestness conquered, the grandeur of the moment was recognized, and a peal of irrepressible applause proclaimed the triumph of his eloquence. Now, these are the risks that a man like Lord Stanley never will run. Only genius makes such ventures. He is always safe: great statesmen must sometimes brave terrible hazards. In England he has received immense praise for the part he took in averting a war between France and Prussia on the Luxembourg question. Now, it is quite true that he did much; that, in fact, he lent all the influence of England to the mode of arrangement by which both the contending Powers were enabled to back decently out of a dangerous and painful position. But the idea of such a mode of settlement did not come from him. It was originated by Baron von Beust, the Austrian Prime Minister, and it was quietly urged a good deal before Lord Stanley saw it. Von Beust, who has a keener wit than Stanley, knew that if the proposition came directly from him it would, *ipso facto*, be odious to Prussia; and he was, therefore, rejoiced when Lord Stanley took it up and adopted it as his own and England's. Von Beust was well content, and so was Lord Stanley—just as Cuddie Headrigg, in "Old Mortality," is content that John Gudyill shall have the responsibility and the honor of the shot which the latter never fired. The one original thing which Lord Stanley did during the controversy was to write a dispatch to Prussia recommending her to come to terms, because of the superior navy of France, and the certainty, in the event of war, that France would have the best of it at sea.

Now, this was a capital argument to influence a man like Lord Stanley himself—calm, cold-blooded, utterly rational. But human ingenuity could hardly have devised an appeal less likely to influence Prussia in the way of peace. Prussia, flushed with her splendid victories over Austria, and deeply offended by the arrogant and dictatorial conduct of France, was much more likely to be stung by such an argument, if it affected her at all, into flinging down the gauntlet at once, and inviting France to come if she dared. The use of such a mode of persuasion is, indeed, an adequate illustration of the whole character of Lord Stanley. Cool, prudent, and rational, he is capable enough of weighing things fairly when they are presented to him; but he can neither create an opportunity nor run a risk. Therefore, he remains officially a Tory, mentally a Liberal, politically neither the one nor the other. His bones are marrowless, his blood is cold. He can forfeit his own career, and hazard his reputation for his party; but that is all. He cannot give his mind to it, and he cannot redeem himself from his futile bondage to it. He is a respectable speaker, despite his defective articulation and his lifeless manner; he will be a respectable politician, despite his want of faith in, or zeal for the cause he tries to follow. That is his career; that is the doom to which he voluntarily condemns himself.

I do not know that there are any other Tory chiefs worth talking about. Sir Stafford Northcote looks like a Bonn or Heidelberg professor, and has a fair average intellect, fit for commonplace finance and elementary politics; there is not a ghost of an idea in him. Walpole is a pompous, well-meaning, gentlemanlike imbecile. Gathorne Hardy is fluent, as the sand in an hourglass is fluent—he can pour out words and serve to mark the passing of time. Sir John Pakington is an educated Dogberry, a respectable Justice Shallow. Not upon men like these do the political fortunes of the Tory party of our day depend, although Walpole and Pakington fairly represent the sincerity, the manhood, and the respectability of Toryism.

I come back to the point from which I started—that Toryism, in itself, is only another word for stupidity, and that any triumphs the party have won or may win are secured by the surrender of the principle they profess to be fighting for, and by the skilful management of men whose conscience permits them to adapt the means unscrupulously to the end. Were the Tory party led by genuine Tories it would have been extinct long ago. It lives and looks upon the earth, it has its triumphs and its gains, its present and its future, only because by very virtue of its own dulness it has allowed itself to be led by men whom it ought to detest, whom it sometimes does distrust, but who have the wit to sell principle in the dearest market, and buy reputation in the cheapest.

"GEORGE ELIOT" AND GEORGE LEWES.

LITERARY reputations are, in one respect, like wines—some are greatly improved by a long voyage, while others lose all zest and strength in the process of crossing the ocean. There ought to be hardly any difference, one would think, between the literary taste of the public of London and that of the public of New York; and yet it is certain that an author or a book may be positively celebrated in the one city and only barely known and coldly recognized in the other. Every one, of course, has noticed the fact that certain English authors are better known and appreciated in New York than in London; certain American writers more talked of in London than in New York. The general public of England do not seem to me to appreciate the true position of Whittier and Lowell among American poets. The average Englishman knows hardly anything of any American poet but Longfellow, who receives, I venture to think, a far more wholesale and enthusiastic admiration in England than in his own country. Robert Buchanan, the Scottish poet, lately, I have read, described "Evangeline" as a far finer poem than Goethe's "Hermann und Dorothea," a judgment which I presume and hope it would be impossible to get any American scholar and critic to indorse or even to consider seriously. On the other hand, it is well known that both the Brownings—certainly Mrs. Browning—found quicker and more cordial appreciation in America than in England. Lately, we in London have taken to discussing and debating over Walt Whitman with a warmth and interest which people in New York do not seem to manifest in regard to the author of "Leaves of Grass." Charles Dickens appears to me to have more devoted admirers among the best class of readers here than he has in his own country. Of course, it would be hardly possible for any man to be more popular and more successful than Dickens is in England; but New York journals quote him and draw illustrations from him much more frequently than London papers do—I do not think any day has passed since first I came to this country, six or seven months ago, that I have not seen at least two or three allusions to Dickens in the leading articles of the daily papers—and I question whether, among critics standing as high in London as George William Curtis does here, Dickens could find the enthusiastic, the almost lyrical devotion of Curtis's admiration. Charles Reade, again, is more generally and warmly admired here than in England. Am I wrong in supposing that the reverse is the case with regard to the authoress of "Romola" and "The Mill on the Floss?" All American critics and all American readers of taste, have doubtless testified practically their recognition of the genius of this extraordinary woman; but there seems to me to be relatively less admiration for her in New York than in London. The general verdict of English criticism would, I feel no doubt, place George Eliot on a higher pedestal than Charles Dickens. We regard her as belonging to a higher school of art, as more nearly affined to the great immortal few whose genius and fame transcend the fashion of the age and defy the caprice of public taste. So far as I have been able to observe, I do not think this is the opinion of American criticism.

In any case, the mere question will excuse my writing a few pages about a woman whom I regard as the greatest living novelist of England; as, on the whole, the greatest woman now engaged in European literature. Only George Sand and Harriet Martineau could fairly be compared with her; and, while Miss

Martineau, of course, is far inferior in all the higher gifts of imagination and the higher faculties of art, George Sand, with all her passion, her rich fancy, and daring, subtle analysis of certain natures, has never exhibited the serene, symmetrical power displayed in "Romola" and in "Silas Marner." Mrs. Lewes (it would be affectation to try to assume that there is still any mystery about the identity of "George Eliot") is what George Sand is not—a great writer, merely as a writer. Few, indeed, are the beings who have ever combined so many high qualities in one person as Mrs. Lewes does. Her literary career began as a translator and an essayist. Her tastes seemed then to lead her wholly into the somewhat barren fields where German metaphysics endeavor to come to the relief or the confusion of German theology. She became a contributor to the "Westminster Review;" then she became its assistant editor, and worked assiduously for it under the direction of Dr. John Chapman, the editor, with whose family she lived for a time, and in whose house she first met George Henry Lewes. She is an accomplished linguist, a brilliant talker, a musician of extraordinary skill. She has a musical sense so delicate and exquisite that there are tender, simple, true ballad melodies which fill her with a pathetic pain almost too keen to bear; and yet she has the firm, strong command of tone and touch, without which a really scientific musician cannot be made. I do not think this exceeding sensibility of nature is often to be found in combination with a genuine mastery of the practical science of music. But Mrs. Lewes has mastered many sciences as well as literatures. Probably no other novel writer, since novel writing became a business, ever possessed one tithe of her scientific knowledge. Indeed, hardly anything is rarer than the union of the scientific and the literary or artistic temperaments. So rare is it, that the exceptional, the almost solitary instance of Goethe comes up at once, distinct and striking, to the mind. English novelists are even less likely to have anything of a scientific taste than French or German. Dickens knows nothing of science, and has, indeed, as little knowledge of any kind, save that which is derived from observation, as any respectable Englishman could well have. Thackeray was a man of varied reading, versed in the lighter literature of several languages, and strongly imbued with artistic tastes; but he had no care for science, and knew nothing of it but just what every one has to learn at school. Lord Lytton's science is a mere sham. Charlotte Brontë was all genius and ignorance. Mrs. Lewes is all genius and culture. Had she never written a page of fiction, nay, had she never written a line of poetry or prose, she must have been regarded with wonder and admiration by all who knew her as a woman of vast and varied knowledge; a woman who could think deeply and talk brilliantly, who could play high and severe classical music like a professional performer, and could bring forth the most delicate and tender aroma of nature and poetry lying deep in the heart of some simple, old-fashioned Scotch or English ballad. Nature, indeed, seemed to have given to this extraordinary woman all the gifts a woman could ask or have—save one. It will not, I hope, be considered a piece of gossipping personality if I allude to a fact which must, some day or other, be part of literary history. Mrs. Lewes is not beautiful. In her appearance there is nothing whatever to attract admiration. Hers is not even a face like that of Charlotte Cushman, which, at least, must make a deep impression, and seize at once the attention of the gazer. Nor does it seem, like that of Madame de Staël or Elizabeth Barrett Browning, informed and illuminated by the light of genius. Mrs. Lewes is what we in England call decidedly plain—what people in New York call homely; and what persons who did not care to soften the force of an unpleasant truth would describe probably by a still harder and more emphatic adjective.

This woman, thus rarely gifted with poetry and music and imagination—thus disciplined in man's highest studies and accustomed to the most laborious of man's literary drudgery—does not seem to have found out, until she had passed what is conventionally regarded as the age of romance, that she had in her, transcendent above all other gifts, the faculty of the novelist. When an author who is not very young makes a great hit at last, we soon begin to learn that he had already made many attempts in the same direction, and his publishers find an eager demand for the stories and sketches which, when they first appeared, utterly failed to attract attention. Thackeray's early efforts, Trollope's, Charles Reade's, Nathaniel Hawthorne's, all these have been lighted into success by the blaze of the later triumph. But it does not seem that Miss Marion Evans, as she then was, ever published anything in the way of fiction previous to the series of sketches which appeared in "Blackwood's Magazine," and were called "Scenes of Clerical Life." These sketches attracted considerable attention, and were much admired; but I do not think many people saw in them the capacity which produced "Adam Bede" and "Romola." With the publication of "Adam Bede" came a complete triumph. The author was elevated at once and by acclamation to the highest rank among living novelists. I think it was in the very first number of the "Cornhill Magazine" that Thackeray, in a gossiping paragraph about novelists of the day, whom he mentioned alphabetically and by their initials, spoke of "E" as a "star of the first magnitude just risen on the horizon." Thackeray, it will be remembered, was one of the first, if not, indeed, the very first, to recognize the genius manifested in "Jane Eyre." The publishers sent him some of the proof sheets for his advice, and Thackeray saw in them the work of a great novelist.

The place which Mrs. Lewes thus so suddenly won, she has, of course, always maintained. Her position of absolute supremacy over all other women writers in England is something peculiar and curious. She is first—and there is no second. No living authoress in Britain is ever now compared with her. I read, not long since, in a New York paper, a sentence which spoke of George Eliot and Miss Mulock as being the greatest English authoresses in the field of fiction. It seemed very odd and funny to me. Certainly, an English critic would never have thought of bracketing together such a pair. Miss Mulock is a graceful, true-hearted, good writer; but Miss Mulock and George Eliot! Robert Lytton and Robert Browning! "A. K. H. B." (I think these are the initials) and John Stuart Mill! Mark Lemon's novels and Charles Dickens's! Mrs. Lewes has made people read novels who perhaps never read fiction from any other pen. She has made the novel the companion and friend and study of scholars and thinkers and statesmen. Her books are discussed by the gravest critics as productions of the highest school of art. Men and journals which have always regarded, or affected to regard, Thackeray as a mere cynic, and Dickens as little better than a professional buffoon, have discussed "The Mill on the Floss" and "Romola" as if these novels were already classic. Of course it would be a very doubtful kind of merit which commanded the admiration of literary prigs or pedants; but that is not the merit of George Eliot. Her books find their way to all hearts and intelligences, but it is their peculiarity that they compel, they extort the admiration of men who would disparage all novels, if they could, as frivolous and worthless, but who are forced even by their own canons and principles to recognize the deep clear thought, the noble culture, the penetrating, analytical power, which are evident in almost every chapter of these stories. Most of our novelists write in a slipslop, careless style. Dickens is worthless, if regarded merely as a prose writer; Trollope hardly cares about grammar; Charles Reade, with all his masculine force and clearness, is terribly irregular and rugged. The woman writers have seldom any style at all. George Eliot's prose might be the study of a scholar anxious to acquire and appreciate a noble English style. It is as luminous as the language of Mill; far more truly picturesque than that of Ruskin; capable of forcible, memorable expression as the robust Saxon of Bright. I am not going into a criticism of George Eliot, who has been, no doubt, fully criticised in America already. I am merely engaged in pointing out the special reasons why she has won in England a certain kind of admiration which, it seems to me, hardly any novelist ever has had before. I think she has infused into the novel some elements it never had before, and so thoroughly infused them that they blend with all the other materials, and do not form anywhere a solid lump or mass distinguishable from the rest. There are philosophical novels—"Wilhelm Meister," for example—which are weighed down and loaded with the philosophy, and which the world admires in spite of the philosophy. There are political novels—Disraeli's, for instance—which are only intelligible to those who make politics and political personalities a study, and which viewed merely as stories would not be worth speaking about. There are novels with a great direct purpose in them, such as "Uncle Tom's Cabin," or "Bleak House," or Charles Reade's "Hard Cash;" but these, after all, are only magnificent pamphlets, splendidly illustrated diatribes. The deep philosophic thought of George Eliot's novels suffuses and illumines them everywhere. You can point to no sermon here, no lecture there, no solid mass interposing between this incident and that, no ponderous moral hung around the neck of this or that personage. Only you feel that you are under the control of one who is not merely a great story-teller but who is also a deep thinker.

It is not, perhaps, unnecessary to say to American readers that George Eliot is the only novelist who can paint such English people as the Poysers and the Tullivers just as they really are. She looks into the very souls of these people. She tracks out their slow peculiar mental processes; she reproduces them fresh and firm from very life. Mere realism, mere photographing, even from the life, is not in art a very great triumph. But George Eliot can make her dullest people interesting and dramatically effective. She can paint two dull people with quite different ways of dulness—say a dull man and a dull woman, for example —and you are astonished to find how utterly distinct the two kinds of stupidity are—and how intensely amusing both can be made. Look at the two pedantic, pompous, dull advocates in the later part of Robert Browning's "The Ring and the Book." How distinct they are; how different, how unlike, and how true, are the two portraits. But then it must be owned that the poet is himself terribly tedious just there. His pedants are quite as tiresome as they would be in real life, if each successively held you by the button. George Eliot never is guilty of this great artistic fault. You never want to be rid of Mrs. Poyser or Aunt Glegg, or the prattling Florentines in "Romola." It is almost superfluous to say that there never was or could be a Mark Tapley, or a Sam Weller. We put up with these impossibilities and delight in them, because they are so amusing and so full of fantastic humor. But Mrs. Poyser lives, and I have met Aunt Glegg often; and poor Mrs. Tulliver's cares and hopes, and little fears, and pitiful reasonings, are animating scores of Mrs. Tullivers all over England to-day. I would propose a safe and easy test to any American or other "foreigner" (I am supposing myself now again in England), who is curious to know how much he understands of the English character. Let him read any of George Eliot's novels—even "Felix Holt," which is so decidedly inferior to the rest—and if he fails to follow, with thorough appreciation, the talk and the ways of the Poysers and such like personages, he may be assured he does not understand one great phase of English life.

Are these novels popular in England? Educated public opinion, I repeat, ranks them higher than the novels of any other living author. But they are not popular—that is, as Wilkie Collins or Miss Braddon is popular; and I do not mean to say anything slighting of either Wilkie Collins or Miss Braddon, both of whom I think possess very great talents, and have been treated with quite too much of the *de haut en bas* mood of the great critics. George Eliot's novels certainly are not run after and devoured by the average circulating library readers, as "The Woman in White," and "Lady Audley's Secret" were. She has, of course, nothing like the number of readers who follow Charles Dickens; nor even, I should say, nearly as many as Anthony Trollope. When "Romola," which the "Saturday Review" justly pronounced to be, if not the greatest, certainly the noblest romance of modern days, was being published as a serial in the "Cornhill Magazine," it was comparatively a failure, in the circulating library sense; and even when it appeared in its complete form, and the public could better appreciate its artistic perfection, it was anything but a splendid success, as regarded from the publisher's point of view. Perhaps this may be partly accounted for by the nature of the subject, the scene and the time; but even the warmest admirer of George Eliot may freely admit that "Romola" lacks a little of that passionate heat which is needed to make a writer of fiction thoroughly popular. When a statue of pure and perfect marble attracts as great a crowd of gazers as a glowing picture, then a novel like "Romola" will have as many admirers as a novel like "Consuelo" or "Villette."

I am not one of the admirers of George Eliot who regret that she ventured on the production of a long poem. I think "The Spanish Gypsy" a true and a fine poem, although I do not place it so high in artistic rank as the best of the author's prose writings. But I believe it to be the greatest story in verse ever produced by an Englishwoman. This is not, perhaps, very high praise, for Englishwomen have seldom done much in the higher fields of poetry; but we have "Aurora Leigh;" and I think "The Spanish Gypsy," on the whole, a finer piece of work. Most of our English critics fell to discussing the question whether "The Spanish Gypsy" was to be regarded as poetry at all, or only as a story put into verse; and in this futile and vexatious controversy the artistic value of the work itself almost escaped analysis. I own that I think criticism shows to little advantage when it occupies itself in considering whether a work of art is to be called by this name or that; and I am rather impatient of the critic who comes with his canons of art, his Thirty-Nine articles of literary dogma, and judges a book, not by what it is in itself, but by the answer it gives to his self-invented catechism. I do not believe that the art of man ever can invent—I know it never has invented—any set of rules or formulas by which you can decide, off-hand and with certainty, that a great story in verse, which you admit to have power and beauty and pathos and melody, does not belong to true poetry. One great school of critics discovered, by the application of such high rules and canons that Shakespeare, though a great genius was not a great poet; a later school made a similar discovery with regard to Schiller; a certain body of critics now say the same of Byron. I don't think it matters much what you call the work. "The Spanish Gypsy" has imagination and beauty; it has exquisite pictures and lofty thoughts; it has melody and music. Admitting this much, and the most depreciating critics did admit it, I think it hardly worth considering what name we are to apply to the book. Such, however, was the sort of controversy in which all deep and true consideration of the artistic value of "The Spanish Gypsy" evaporated. I am not sorry Mrs. Lewes published the poem; but I am sorry she put her literary name to it in the first instance. Had it appeared anonymously it would have astonished and delighted the world. But people compared "The Spanish Gypsy" with the author's prose works, and were disappointed because the woman who surpassed Dickens in fiction did not likewise surpass Tennyson and Browning in poetry. Thus, and in no other sense, was "The Spanish Gypsy" a failure. No woman had written anything of the same kind to surpass it; but some men, even of our own day, had—and no man of our day has written novels which excel those of George Eliot. Mrs. Lewes will probably not write any more long poems; but I think English poetry has gained something by her one venture.

Mrs. Lewes's mind is of a class which, however varied its power, is not fairly described by the word "versatile." Versatility is a smaller kind of faculty, a dexterity of intellect and capacity—the property of a mind of the second order. If we want a perfect type and pattern of versatility, we may find it very close to the authoress of "Silas Marner," in the person of her husband, George Henry Lewes. What man of our day has done so many things and done them so well? He is the biographer of Goethe and of Robespierre; he has compiled the "History of Philosophy," in which he has something really his own to say of every great philosopher, from Thales to Schelling; he has translated Spinoza; he has published various scientific works; he has written at least two novels; he has made one of the most successful dramatic adaptations known to our stage; he is an accomplished theatrical critic; he was at one time so successful as an amateur actor that he seriously contemplated taking to the stage as a profession, in the full conviction, which he did not hesitate frankly to avow, that he was destined to be the successor to Macready. He did actually join a company at one of the Manchester theatres, and perform there for some time under a feigned name; but the amount of encouragement he received from the public did not stimulate him to continue on the boards, although I believe his confidence in his own capacity to succeed Macready remained unshaken. Mr. Lewes was always remarkable for a frank and fearless self-conceit, which, by its very sincerity and audacity, almost disarmed criticism. Indeed, I do not suppose any man less gifted with self-confidence would have even attempted to do half the things which George Henry Lewes has done well. Margaret Fuller was very unfavorably impressed by Lewes when she met him at Thomas Carlyle's house, and she wrote of him contemptuously and angrily. But these were the days of Lewes's Bohemianism; days of an audacity and a self-conceit unsubdued as yet by experience and the world, and some saddening and some refining influences; and Margaret Fuller failed to appreciate the amount of intellect and manliness that was in him. Charlotte Brontë, on the other hand, was quite enthusiastic about Lewes, and wrote to him and of him with an almost amusing veneration. Indeed, he is a man of ability and versatility that may fairly be called extraordinary. His merit is not that he has written books on a great variety of subjects. London has many hack writers who could go to work at any publisher's order and produce successively an epic poem, a novel, a treatise on the philosophy of the conditioned, a handbook of astronomy, a farce, a life of Julius Cæsar, a history of African explorations, and a volume of sermons. But none of these productions would have one gleam of genuine native vitality about it. The moment it had served its purpose in the literary market it would go, dead, down to the dead. Lewes's works are of quite a different style. They have positive merit and value of their own, and they live. It was a characteristically audacious thing to attempt to cram the history of philosophy into a couple of medium-sized volumes, polishing off each philosopher in a few pages—draining him, plucking out the heart of his mystery and his system, and stowing him away in the glass jar designed to exhibit him to an edified class of students. But it must be avowed that Lewes's has been a marvellously clever and successful attempt. He certainly crumples up the whole science of metaphysics, sweeps away transcendental philosophy, and demolishes *a priori* reasoning, in a manner which strongly reminds one of Arthur Pendennis upsetting, in a dashing criticism and on the faith of an hour's reading in an encyclopædia, some great scientific theory of which he had never heard previously, and the development of which had been the life's labor of a sage. But Lewes does, somehow or other, very often come to a right conclusion, and measure great theories and men with accurate estimate; and the work is immensely interesting, and it is not easy to see how anybody could have done it better. His "Life of Goethe" is undoubtedly a very successful, symmetrical, and comprehensive piece of biography. Some of his scientific studies have a genuine value, and they are all fascinating. One of his pieces—adapted from the French, of course, as most so-called English pieces are—will always be played while Charles Mathews lives, or while there are actors who can play in Charles Mathews's style. I wonder whether any of the readers of THE GALAXY read, or having read remember, Lewes's novels? I only recollect two of them, and I do not know whether he wrote any others. One was called "Ranthorpe," and it had, in its day, quite a sort of success. How long ago was it published? Fully twenty years, I should think: I remember quite well being thrown into youthful raptures with it at the time. But I do not go upon my boyish admiration for it. I came across it somewhere much more recently, and read it through. There was a good deal of inflation, and audacity, and nonsense in it; but at the same time it showed more of brains and artistic impulse and constructive power than nine out of every ten novels published in England to-day. It was all about a young poet, who came to London and made, for a moment, a great success, and was dazzled by it, and became intoxicated with love for a lustrous beauty of high rank, who only played with him; and how he forgot, for a time, the modest, delightful, simple girl to whom he was pledged at home; and how he did not get on, and the public and the *salons* grew tired of him; and he became miserable, and was going to drown himself (I think), but was prevented by some wise and timely person; and how, of course, it all came right in the end, and he was redeemed. This outline, probably, will not suggest much of originality to any reader; but there was a great deal of freshness and thought in the book, some of the incidents and one or two of the characters had a flavor of originality about them; and the style was, for the most part, animated and attractive. It was the work of a man of brains, and culture, and taste; and one felt this all through, and was not ashamed of the time spent in reading it. The other of Lewes's novels was called "Rose, Blanche, and Violet." It charmed me a good deal when I read it; but I have not read it lately, and so I forbear giving any decided opinion as to its merits. It is, of course, quite settled now that George Lewes had not in him the materials to make a successful novelist; but men of far less talent have produced far worse novels than his, and been, in their way, successful.

Lewes first became prominent in literature as a contributor to the "Leader," a very remarkable weekly organ of advanced opinions on all questions, which was started in London seventeen or eighteen years ago, and died, after much flickering and lingering, in 1861 or thereabouts. The "Leader," in its early and best days, fairly sparkled all over with talent, originality and audacity. It was to extreme philosophical radicalism, (with a dash of something like atheism) what the "Saturday Review" now is to cultured swelldom and Belgravian Sadduceeism. Miss Martineau wrote for it. Lewes and Thornton Hunt (they were then intimates, unfortunately for Lewes) were among its principal contributors; Edward Whitty flung over its pages the brilliant eccentric light which was destined to immature and melancholy extinction. Lewes's theatrical criticisms, which he used to sign "Vivian," were inimitable in their vivacity, their wit, and their keenness, even when their soundness of judgment was most open to question. Poor Charles Kean was an especial object of Lewes's detestation, and was accordingly pelted and peppered with torturingly clever and piquant pasquinades in the form of criticism. Lewes has got wonderfully sober and grave in style since those wild days, and his occasional contributions in the shape of dramatic criticism to the "Pall Mall Gazette" are doubtless more generally accurate, are certainly much more thoughtful, but are far less amusing than the admirable fooling of days gone by. It was in the "Leader," I think, that Lewes carried on his famous controversy with Charles Dickens on the possibility of such spontaneous combustion as that of the old brute in "Bleak House," and it was in the "Leader" that he made an equally famous exposure of a sham spiritualist medium, about whom London was then much agitated. The "Leader," probably, never paid; it was far too iconoclastic and eccentric to be a commercial success, but it made quite a mark and will always be a memory. It did not succeed in its object; but, like the arrow of the hero in Virgil, it left a long line of sparkles and light behind it. Lewes has abandoned Bohemia long since, and Edward Whitty is dead, and Thornton Hunt has come to nothing—and there is another "Leader" now in London which bears about as much resemblance to the original and real "Leader" as Richard Cromwell did to Oliver, or Charles Kean to Edmund.

Bohemianism, and novel-writing, and amateur acting, and persiflage, and epigram, are all gone by now with Lewes. He has settled into a grave and steady writer, for the most part of late confining himself to scientific subjects. A few years ago he started the "Fortnightly Review," in the hope of establishing in England a counterpart of the "Revue des Deux Mondes." The first number was enriched by one of the most thoughtful, subtle, beautiful essays lately contributed to literature; and it bore the signature of George Eliot. Lewes himself wrote a series of essays on "The Principles of Success in Literature," very good, very sound, but not very lively reading. A great English novelist was pleased graciously to say, *apropos* of these essays, "Success in literature! What does Lewes know about success in literature?" and the small devotees of the great successful novelist laughed and repeated the joke. It is certain that the "Fortnightly Review" was not a success under the editorship of George Henry Lewes; and people said, I do not know how truly, that a good deal of the nobly-earned money paid for "Silas Marner" and the "Mill on the Floss" disappeared in the attempt to erect a British "Revue des Deux Mondes." The "Fortnightly" lives still, and is called "Fortnightly" still, although it now only comes out once a month, but Lewes has long ceased to edit it. I think the present editor, John Morley, a young man of great ability and promise, is better suited for the work than Lewes was—indeed I doubt whether Lewes, with all his varied gifts and acquirements, possesses the peculiar qualities which make a man a genuine editor. But the difference between wild Hal, the Prince of Gadshill, and grave, wise Henry the Fifth, could hardly be greater than that between the Vivian of the "Leader" and the late editor of the solemn, ponderous "Fortnightly Review."

Lewes wrote at one time a great deal for the "Westminster Review." It was during his connection with it that he became acquainted, at Dr. Chapman's house, with Marion Evans. There was a great similarity between their tastes. Both loved the study of languages, and of philosophical thought, and of literature and science generally. Both were splendid in conversation, brilliant in epigram; both loved music and were intensely susceptible to its influence. The mind of the woman was, I need hardly say, far the stronger, wider, deeper of the two; but the affinity was clear and close. A great misfortune had fallen on Lewes; and he was probably in that condition of mind which makes a man not unlikely to lose his faith in everything and drift into hopeless, perpetual cynicism. From this, if this impended over him, Lewes was saved by his intercourse with the rarely-gifted woman he had met in so timely an hour. The result is, as every one knows, a companionship and union unusual indeed in literary life. Very seldom has a distinguished author had for wife a distinguished authoress, or *vice versa*; indeed, it used to be one of the dear delightful theories of blockheads that such unions, if they could take place, would be miserably unhappy. This theory, so soothing to complacent dulness, was hardly borne out in the instance of the Brownings; it is just as little corroborated by the example of "George Eliot" and George Lewes. I believe, too, the example of George Eliot is highly unsatisfactory to the devotees of that other theory, so long cherished by dolts of both sexes, that a woman of talent and culture can never do anything in the way of mending or making, of cooking a chop or ordering a household. People tell us they can trace the influence of Lewes's varied scholarship and critical judgment in the novels of George Eliot. It is hardly possible to doubt that some such influence must be there, but I certainly never saw it anywhere distinctly and openly evident. It would be poor art which allowed a thin stream of Lewes to be seen sparkling through the broad, deep, luminous lake which mirrors the genius of George Eliot. I am, however, rather inclined to fancy that Lewes, in general, abstains from critical *surveillance* or restraint over the productions of his greater companion, believing, perhaps, that the higher mind had better be a law to itself. If this be so, I think it is a wholesome principle pushed sometimes too far, for one can hardly believe that the calm judgment of any sincere and qualified adviser would not have discouraged and condemned the painful, unnecessary underplot of past intrigue and sin which is so great a blot in "Felix Holt," or suggested a rapider dramatic movement in some passages of "The Spanish Gypsy." Lewes once wrote to Charlotte Brontë that he would rather be the author of Miss Austen's stories than of the whole of the Waverley Novels. I certainly do not agree with him in that opinion; but it is strange that one who held it should not have endeavored to prevent an authoress greater than Miss Austen, and far more directly under his influence than Charlotte Brontë, from sinking, in one or two instances, into faults which neither Miss Austen nor Miss Brontë would ever have committed. Many things are strange about this literary and domestic companionship; this comparatively trifling fact seems to me not the least strange.

Finally let me say that I fully expect George Eliot yet to give to the world some work of art even greater than any she has already produced. She is not a woman to close with even a comparative failure. Her maxim, I feel confident, would be that of the Emperor Napoleon—offer terms of peace and repose after a great victory; never otherwise.

GEORGE SAND.

WE are all of us probably inclined now and then to waste a little time in vaguely speculating on what might have happened if this or that particular event had not given a special direction to the career of some great man or woman. If there had been an inch of difference in the size of Cleopatra's nose; if Hannibal had not lingered at Capua; if Cromwell had carried out his idea of emigration; if Napoleon Bonaparte had taken service under the Turk—and so on through all the old familiar illustrations dear to the minor essayist and the debating society. I have sometimes felt tempted thus to lose myself in speculating on what might have happened if the woman whom all the world knows as George Sand had been happily married in her youth to the husband of her choice. Would she ever have taken to literature at all? Would she, loving as she does, and as Frenchwomen so rarely do, the changing face of inanimate nature—the fields, the flowers, and the brooks—have lived a peaceful and obscure life in some happy country place, and been content with home, and family, and love, and never thought of fame? Or if, thus happily married, she still had allowed her genius to find an expression in literature, would she have written books with no passionate purpose in them—books which might have seemed like those of a good Miss Mulock made perfect—books which Podsnap might have read with approval and put without a scruple into the hands of that modest young person, his daughter? Certainly one cannot but think that a different kind of early life would have given a quite different complexion to the literary individuality of George Sand.

Bulwer Lytton, in one of his novels, insists that true genius is always quite independent of the individual sufferings or joys of its possessor, and describes some inspired youth in the novel as sitting down while sorrow is in his heart and hunger gnawing at his vitals, to throw off a sparkling and gladsome little fairy tale. Now this is undoubtedly true in general of any high order of genius; but there are at least some great and striking exceptions. Rousseau and Byron are, in modern days, remarkable illustrations of genius, admittedly of a very high rank, governed and guided almost wholly by the individual fortunes of the men themselves. So too must we speak of the genius of George Sand. Not Rousseau, not even Byron, was in this sense more egotistic than the woman who broke the chains of her ill-assorted marriage with a crash that made its echoes heard at last in every civilized country in the world. Just as people are constantly quoting *nous avons changé tout cela* who never read a page of Molière, or *pour encourager les autres* without even being aware that there is a story of Voltaire's called "Candide," so there have been thousands of passionate protests uttered in America and Europe for the last twenty years by people who never saw a volume of George Sand, and yet are only echoing her sentiments and even repeating her words.

In a former number of THE GALAXY I expressed casually the opinion that George Sand is probably the most influential writer of our day. I am still, and deliberately, of the same opinion. It must be remembered that very few English or American authors have any wide or deep influence over peoples who do not speak English. Even of the very greatest authors this is true. Compare, for example, the literary dominion of Shakespeare with that of Cervantes. All nations who read Shakespeare read Cervantes: in Stratford-upon-Avon itself Don Quixote is probably as familiar a figure in people's minds as Falstaff; but Shakespeare is little known indeed to the vast majority of readers in the country of Cervantes, in the land of Dante, or in that of Racine and Victor Hugo. In something of the same way we may compare the influence of George Sand with that of even the greatest living authors of England and America. What influence has Charles Dickens or George Eliot outside the range of the English tongue? But George Sand's genius has been felt as a power in every country of the world where people read any manner of books. It has been felt almost as Rousseau's once was felt; it has aroused anger, terror, pity, or wild and rapturous excitement and admiration; it has rallied around it every instinct in man or woman which is revolutionary; it has ranged against it all that is conservative. It is not so much a literary influence as a great disorganizing force, riving the rocks of custom, resolving into their original elements the social combinations which tradition and convention would declare to be indissoluble. I am not now speaking merely of the sentiments which George Sand does or did entertain on the subject of marriage. Divested of all startling effects and thrilling dramatic illustrations, these sentiments probably amounted to nothing more dreadful than the belief that an unwedded union between two people who love and are true to each other is less immoral than the legal marriage of two uncongenial creatures who do not love and probably are not true to each other. But the grand, revolutionary idea which George Sand announced was that of the social independence and equality of woman—the principle that woman is not made for man in any other sense than as man is made for woman. For the first time in the history of the world woman spoke out for herself with a voice as powerful as that of man. For the first time in the history of the world woman spoke out as woman, not as the servant, the satellite, the pupil, the plaything, or the goddess of man.

Now I intend at present to write of George Sand rather as an individual, or an influence, than as the author of certain works of fiction. Criticism would now be superfluously bestowed on the literary merits and peculiarities of the great woman whose astonishing intellectual activity has never ceased to produce, during the last thirty years, works which take already a classical place in French literature. If any reputation of our day may be looked upon as established, we may thus regard the reputation of George Sand. She is, beyond comparison, the greatest living novelist of France. She has won this position by the most legitimate application of the gifts of an artist. With all her marvellous fecundity, she has hardly ever given to the world any work which does not seem at least to have been the subject of the most elaborate and patient care. The greatest temptation which tries a story-teller is perhaps the temptation to rely on the attractiveness of story-telling, and to pay little or no attention to style. Walter Scott's prose, for example, if regarded as mere prose, is rambling, irregular, and almost worthless. Dickens's prose is as bad a model for imitation as a musical performance which is out of tune. Of course, I need hardly say that attention to style is almost as characteristic of French authors in general, as the lack of it is characteristic of English authors; but even in France, the prose of George Sand stands out conspicuous for its wonderful expressiveness and force, its almost perfect beauty. Then of all modern French authors—I might perhaps say of all modern novelists of any country—George Sand has added to fiction, has annexed from the worlds of reality and of imagination, the greatest number of original characters—of what Emerson calls new organic creations. Moreover, George Sand is, after Rousseau, the one only great French author who has looked directly and lovingly into the face of Nature, and learned the secrets which skies and waters, fields and lanes, can teach to the heart that loves them. Gifts such as these have won her the almost unrivalled place which she holds in living literature, and she has conquered at last even the public opinion which once detested and proscribed her. I could therefore hope to add nothing to what has been already said by criticism in regard to her merits as a novelist. Indeed, I think it probable that the majority of readers in this country know more of George Sand through the interpretation of the critics than through the pages of her books. And in her case criticism is so nearly unanimous as to her literary merits, that I may safely assume the public in general to have in their minds a just recognition of her position as a novelist. My object is rather to say something about the place which George Sand has taken as a social revolutionist, about the influence she has so long exercised over the world, and about the woman herself. For she is assuredly the greatest champion of woman's rights, in one sense, that the world has ever seen; and she is, on the other hand, the one woman out of all the world who has been most commonly pointed to as the appalling example to scare doubtful and fluttering womanhood back into its sheepfold of submissiveness and conventionality. There is hardly a woman's heart anywhere in the civilized world which has not felt the vibration of George Sand's thrilling voice. Women who never saw one of her books, nay, who never heard even her *nom de plume*, have been stirred by emotions of doubt or fear or repining or ambition, which they never would have known but for George Sand, and perhaps but for George Sand's uncongenial marriage. For indeed there is not now, and has not been for twenty years, I venture to think, a single "revolutionary" idea, as slow and steady-going people would call it, afloat anywhere in Europe or America, on the subject of woman's relations to man, society, and destiny, which is not due immediately to the influence of George Sand, and to the influence of George Sand's unhappy marriage upon George Sand herself.

The world has of late years grown used to this extraordinary woman, and has lost much of the wonder and terror with which it once regarded her. I can quite remember—younger people than I can remember—the time when all good and proper personages in England regarded the authoress of "Indiana" as a sort of feminine fiend, endowed with a hideous power for the destruction of souls and an inextinguishable thirst for the slaughter of virtuous beliefs. I fancy a good deal of this sentiment was due to the fearful reports wafted across the seas, that this terrible woman had not merely repudiated the marriage bond, but had actually put off the garments sacred to womanhood. That George Sand appeared in men's clothes was an outrage upon consecrated proprieties far more astonishing than any theoretical onslaught upon old opinions could be. Reformers indeed should always, if they are wise in their generation, have a care of the proprieties. Many worthy people can listen with comparative fortitude when sacred and eternal truths are assailed, who are stricken with horror when the ark of propriety is never so lightly touched. George Sand's pantaloons were therefore regarded as the most appalling illustration of George Sand's wickedness. I well remember what excitement, scandal, and horror were created in the provincial town where I lived some twenty years ago, when the editor of a local Panjandrum (to borrow Mr. Trollope's word) insulted the feelings and the morals of his constituents and subscribers by polluting his pages with a translation from one of George Sand's shorter novels. Ah me, the little novel might, so far as morality was concerned, have been written every word by

Miss Phelps, or the authoress of the "Heir of Redcliffe"; it had not a word, from beginning to end, which might not have been read out to a Sunday school of girls; the translation was made by a woman of the purest soul, and in her own locality the highest name; and yet how virtue did shriek out against the publication! The editor persevered in the publishing of the novel, spurred on to boldness by some of his very young and therefore fearless coadjutors, who thought it delightful to confront public opinion, and liked the notion of the stars in their courses fighting against Sisera, and Sisera not being dismayed. That charming, tender, touching little story! I would submit it to-day cheerfully to the verdict of a jury of matrons, confident that it would be declared a fit and proper publication. But at that time it was enough that the story bore the odious name of George Sand; public opinion condemned it, and sent the magazine which ventured to translate it to an early and dishonored grave. I remember reading about that time a short notice of George Sand by an English authoress of some talent and culture, in which the Frenchwoman's novels were described as so abominably filthy, that even the denizens of the Paris brothels were ashamed to be caught reading them. Now this declaration was made in all good faith, in the simple good faith of that class of persons who will pass wholesale and emphatic judgment upon works of which they have never read a single page. For I need hardly tell any intelligent person of to-day, that whatever may be said of George Sand's doctrines, she is no more open to the charge of indelicacy than the authoress of "Romola." I cannot myself remember any passage in George Sand's novels which can be called indelicate; and indeed her severest and most hostile critics are fond of saying, not without a certain justice, that one of the worst characteristics of her works is the delicacy and beauty of her style, which thus commends to pure and innocent minds certain doctrines that, broadly stated, would repel and shock them. Were I one of George Sand's inveterate opponents, this, or something like it, is the ground I would take up. I would say: "The welfare of the human family demands that a marriage, legally made, shall never be questioned or undone. Marriage is not a union depending on love or congeniality, or any such condition. It is just as sacred when made for money, or for ambition, or for lust of the flesh, or for any other pupose, however ignoble and base, as when contracted in the spirit of the purest mutual love. Here is a woman of great power and daring genius, who says that the essential condition of marriage is love and natural fitness; that a legal union of man and woman without this is no marriage at all, but a detestable and disgusting sin. Now the more delicately, modestly, plausibly she can put this revolutionary and pernicious doctrine, the more dangerous she becomes, and the more earnestly we ought to denounce her." This was in fact what a great many persons did say; and the protest was at least consistent and logical.

But horror is an emotion which cannot long live on the old fuel, and even the world of English Philistinism soon ceased to regard George Sand as a mere monster. Any one now taking up "Indiana," for example, would perhaps find it not quite easy to understand how the book produced such an effect. Our novel-writing women of to-day commonly feed us on more fiery stuff than this. Not to speak of such accomplished artists in impurity as the lady who calls herself Ouida, and one or two others of the same school, we have young women only just promoted from pantalettes, who can throw you off such glowing chapters of passion and young desire as would make the rhapsodies of "Indiana" seem very feeble milk-and-water brewage by comparison. Indeed, except for some of the descriptions in the opening chapters, I fail to see any extraordinary merit in "Indiana"; and toward the end it seems to me to grow verbose, weak, and tiresome. "Leone Leoni" opens with one of the finest dramatic outbursts of emotion known to the literature of modern fiction; but it soon wanders away into discursive weakness, and only just toward the close brightens up into a burst of lurid splendor. It is not those which I may call the questionable novels of George Sand—the novels which were believed to illustrate in naked and appalling simplicity her doctrines and her life—that will bear up her fame through succeeding generations. If every one of the novels which thus in their time drew down the thunders of society's denunciation were to be swept into the wallet wherein Time, according to Shakespeare, carries scraps for oblivion, George Sand would still remain where she now is, at the head of the French fiction of her day. It is true, as Goethe says, that "miracle-working pictures are rarely works of art." The books which make the hair of the respectable public stand on end, are not often the works by which the fame of the author is preserved for posterity.

It is a curious fact that at the early time to which I have been alluding, little or nothing was known in England (or, I presume, in America) of the real life of Aurore Amandine Dupin, who had been pleased to call herself George Sand. People knew, or had heard, that she had separated from her husband, that she had written novels which depreciated the sanctity of legal marriage, and that she sometimes wore male costume in the streets. This was enough. In England, at least, we were ready to infer any enormity regarding a woman who was unsound on the legal marriage question, and who did not wear petticoats. What would have been said had people then commonly known half the stories which were circulated in Paris; half the extravagances into which a passionate soul and the stimulus of sudden emancipation from restraint had hurried the authoress of "Indiana" and "Lucrezia Floriani"? For it must be owned that the life of that woman was, in its earlier years, a strange and wild phenomenon, hardly to be comprehended perhaps by American or English natures. I have heard George Sand bitterly arraigned even by persons who protested that they were at one with her as regards the early sentiments which used to excite such odium. I have heard her described by such as a sort of Lamia of literature and passion; a creature who could seize some noble, generous, youthful heart, drain it of its love, its aspirations, its profoundest emotions, and then fling it, squeezed and lifeless, away. I have heard it declared that George Sand made "copy" of the fierce and passionate loves which she knew so well how to awaken and to foster; that she distilled the life-blood of youth to obtain the mixture out of which she derived her inspiration. The charge so commonly (I think unjustly) made against Goethe, that he played with the girlish love of Bettina and of others in order to obtain a subject for literary dissection, is vehemently and deliberately urged in an aggravated form, in many aggravated forms, against George Sand. Where, such accusers ask, is that young poet, endowed with a lyrical genius rare indeed in the France of later days, that young poet whose imagination was at once so daring and so subtle; who might have been Béranger and Heine in one, and have risen to an atmosphere in which neither Béranger nor Heine ever floated? Where is he, and what evil influence was it which sapped the strength of his nature, corrupted his genius, and prepared for him a premature and shameful grave? Where is that young musician, whose pure, tender, and lofty strains sound sweetly and sadly in the ears, as the very hymn and music of the Might-Have-Been—where is he now, and what was the seductive power which made a plaything of him and then flung him away? Here and there some man of stronger mould is pointed out as one who was at the first conquered, and then deceived and trifled with, but who ordered his stout heart to bear, and rose superior to the hour, and lived to retrieve his nature and make himself a name of respect; but the others, of more sensitive and perhaps finer organizations, are only the more to be pitied because they were so terribly in earnest. Seldom, even in the literary history of modern France, has there been a more strange and shocking episode than the publication by George Sand of the little book called "Elle et Lui," and the rejoinder to it by Paul de Musset called "Lui et Elle." I can hardly be accused of straying into the regions of private scandal when I speak of two books which had a wide circulation, are still being read, and may be had, I presume, in any New York bookstore where French literature is sold. The former of the two books, "She and He," was a story, or something which purported to be a story, by George Sand, telling of two ill-assorted beings whom fate had thrown together for a while, and of whom the woman was all tenderness, love, patience, the man all egotism, selfishness, sensuousness, and eccentricity. The point of the whole business was to show how sublimely the woman suffered, and how wantonly the man flung happiness away. Had it been merely a piece of fiction, it must have been regarded by any healthy mind as a morbid, unwholesome, disagreeable production; a sin of the highest æsthetic kind against true art, which must always, even in its pathos and its tragedy, leave on the mind exalted and delightful impressions. But every one in Paris at once hailed the story as a chapter of autobiography, as the author's vindication of one episode in her own career—a vindication at the expense of a man who had gone down, ruined and lost, to an early grave. Therefore the brother of the dead man flung into literature a little book called "He and She," in which a story, substantially the same in its outlines, is so told as exactly to reverse the conditions under which the verdict of public opinion was sought. Very curious indeed was the manner in which the same substance of facts was made to present the two principal figures with complexions and characters so strangely altered. In the woman's book, the woman was made the patient, loving, suffering victim; in the man's reply, this same woman was depicted as the most utterly selfish and depraved creature the human imagination could conceive. Even if one had no other means whatever of forming an estimate of the character of George Sand, it would be hardly possible to accept as her likeness the hideous picture sketched by Paul de Musset. No woman, I am glad to believe, ever existed in real life so utterly selfish, base, and wicked as his bitter pen has drawn. I must say that the thing is very cleverly done. The picture is at least consistent with itself. As a character in romance it might be pronounced original, bold, brilliant, and, in an artistic sense, quite natural. There is something thoroughly French in the easy and delicate force of the final touch with which de Musset dismisses his hideous subject. Having sketched this woman in tints that seem to flame across the eyes of the reader; having described with wonderful realism and power her affectation, her deceit, her reckless caprices, her base and cruel coquetries, her devouring wantonness, her soul-destroying arts, her unutterable selfishness and egotism; having, to use a vulgar phrase, "turned her inside out," and told her story backwards, the author calmly explains that the hero of the narrative in his dying hour called his brother to his bedside, and enjoined him, if occasion should ever arise, if the partner of his sin should ever calumniate him in his grave, to vindicate his memory and avenge the treason practised upon him. "Of course," adds the narrator, "the brother made the promise—and I have since heard that he has kept his word." I can hardly hope to convey to the reader any adequate idea of the effect produced on the mind by these few simple words of compressed, whispered hatred and triumph, closing a philippic, or a revelation, or a libel of such extraordinary bitterness and ferocity. The whole episode is, I believe and earnestly hope, without precedent or imitation in literary controversy. Never, that I know of, has a living woman been publicly exhibited to the world in a portraiture so hideous as that which Paul de Musset drew of George Sand. Never, that I know of, has any woman gone so near to deserving and justifying such a measure of retaliation.

For if it be assumed—and I suppose it never has been disputed—that in writing "Elle et Lui" George Sand meant to describe herself and Alfred de Musset, it is hard to conceive of any sin against taste and feeling, against art and morals, more flagrant than such a publication. The practice, to which French writers are so much addicted, of making "copy" of the private lives, characters, and relationships of themselves and their friends, seems to me in all cases utterly detestable. Lamartine's sins of this kind were grievous and glaring; but were they red as scarlet, they would seem whiter than snow when compared with the lurid monstrosity of George Sand's assault on the memory of the dead poet who was once her favorite. The whole affair indeed is so unlike anything which could occur in America or in England, that we can hardly find any canons by which to try it, or any standard of punishment by which to regulate its censure. I allude to it now because it is the only substantial evidence I know of which does fairly seem to justify the worst of the accusations brought against George Sand; and I do not think it right, when writing for grown men and women, who are supposed to have sense and judgment, to affect not to know that such accusations are made, or to pretend to think that it would be proper not to allude to them. They have been put forward, replied to, urged again, made the theme of all manner of controversy in scores of French and in some English publications. Pray let it be distinctly understood that I am not entering into any criticism of the morality of any part of George Sand's private life. With that we have nothing here to do. I am now dealing with the question, fairly belonging to public controversy, whether the great artist did not deliberately deal with human hearts as the painter of old is said to have done with a purchased slave—inflicting torture in order the better to learn how to depict the struggles and contortions of mortal agony. In answer to such a question I can only point to "Lucrezia Floriani" and to "Elle et Lui," and say that unless the universal opinion of qualified critics be wrong these books, and others too, owe their piquancy and their dramatic force to the anatomization of dead passions and discarded lovers. We have all laughed over the pedantic surgeon in Molière's "Malade Imaginaire," who invites his *fiancée* as a delightful treat to see him dissect the body of a woman. I am afraid that George Sand did sometimes invite an admiring public to an exhibition yet more ghastly and revolting—the dissection of the heart of a dead lover.

But in truth we shall never judge George Sand and her writings at all if we insist on criticising them from any point of view set up by the proprieties or even the moralities of Old England or New England. When the passionate young woman, in whose veins ran the wild blood of Marshal Saxe, found herself surrendered by legality and prescription to a marriage bond against which her soul revolted, society seemed for her to have resolved itself into its original elements. Its conventionalities and traditions contained nothing which she held herself bound to respect. The world was not her friend, nor the world's law. By one great decisive step she sundered herself forever from the bonds of what we call society. She had shaken the dust of convention from her feet; the world was all before her where to choose. No creature on earth is so absolutely free as the Frenchwoman who has broken with society. There, then, stood this daring young woman, on the threshold of a new, fresh, and illimitable world; a young woman gifted with genius such as our later years have rarely seen, and blessed or cursed with a nature so strangely uniting the most characteristic qualities of man and woman as to be in itself quite unparalleled and unique. Just think of it—try to think of it! Society and the world had no longer any laws which she recognized. Nothing was sacred; nothing was settled. She had to evolve from her own heart and brain her own law of life. What wonder if she made some sad mistakes? Nay, is it not rather a theme for wonder and admiration that she did somehow come right at last? I know of no one who seems to me to have been open at once to the temptations of woman's nature and man's nature except this George Sand. Her soul, her brain, her style may be described, from one point of view, as exuberantly and splendidly feminine; yet no other woman has ever shown the same power of understanding and entering into the nature of a man. If Balzac is the only man who has ever thoroughly mastered the mysteries of a woman's heart, George Sand is the only woman, so far as I know, who has ever shown that she could feel as a man can feel. I have read stray passages in her novels which I would confidently submit to the criticism of any intelligent men unacquainted with the text, convinced that they would declare that only a man could have thus analyzed the emotions of manhood. I have in my mind just now especially a passage in the novel "Piccinino" which, were the authorship unknown, would, I am satisfied, secure the decision of a jury of literary experts that the author must be a man. Now this gift of entire appreciation of the feelings of a different sex or race is, I take it, one of the rarest and highest dramatic qualities. Especially is it difficult for a woman, as our social life goes, to enter into the feelings of a man. While men and women alike admit the accuracy of certain pictures of women drawn by such artists as Cervantes, Molière, Balzac, and Thackeray, there are few women—indeed, perhaps there are no women but one—by whom a man has been so painted as to challenge and compel the recognition and acknowledgment of men. In THE GALAXY some months ago I wrote of a great Englishwoman, the authoress of "Romola," and I expressed my conviction that on the whole she is entitled to higher rank as a novelist than even the authoress of "Consuelo." Many, very many men and women, for whose judgment I have the highest respect, differed from me in this opinion. I still hold it, nevertheless; but I freely admit that George Eliot has nothing like the dramatic insight which enables George Sand to enter into the feelings and the experiences of a man. I go so far as to say that, having some knowledge of the literature of fiction in most countries, I am not aware of the existence of any woman but this one who could draw a real, living, struggling, passion-tortured man. All other novelists of George Sand's sex—even including Charlotte Brontë—draw only what I may call "women's men." If ever the two natures could be united in one form, if ever a single human being could have the soul of man and the soul of woman at once, George Sand might be described as that physical and psychological phenomenon. Now the point to which I wish to direct attention is the peculiarity of the temptation to which a nature such as this was necessarily exposed at every turn when, free of all restraint and a rebel against all conventionality, it confronted the world and the world's law, and stood up, itself alone, against the domination of custom and the majesty of tradition. I claim, then, that when we have taken all these considerations into account, we are bound to admit that Aurora Dudevant deserves the generous recognition of the world for the use which she made of her splendid gifts. Her influence on French literature has been on the whole a purifying and strengthening power. The cynicism, the recklessness, the wanton, licentious disregard of any manner of principle, the debasing parade of disbelief in any higher purpose or nobler restraint, which are the shame and curse of modern French fiction, find no sanction in the pages of George Sand. I remember no passage in her works which gives the slightest encouragement to the "nothing new, and nothing true, and it don't signify" code of ethics which has been so much in fashion of late years. I find nothing in George Sand which does not do homage to the existence of a principle and a law in everything. This daring woman, who broke with society so early and so conspicuously, has always insisted, through every illustration, character, and catastrophe in her books, that the one only reality, the one only thing that can endure, is the rule of right and of virtue. Nor has she ever, that I can recollect, fallen into the enfeebling and sentimental theory so commonly expressed in the works of Victor Hugo, that the vague abstraction society is always to bear the blame of the faults committed by the individual man or woman. Of all persons in the world Aurora Dudevant might be supposed most likely to adopt this easy and complacent theory as her guiding principle. She had every excuse, every reason for endeavoring to preach up the doctrine that our errors are society's and our virtues our own. But I am not aware that she ever taught any lesson save the lesson that men and women must endeavor to be heroes and heroines for themselves, heroes and heroines though all the world else were craven and weak and selfish and unprincipled. Even that wretched and lamentable "Elle et Lui" affair, utterly inexcusable as it is when we read between the lines its secret history, has at least the merit of being an earnest and powerful protest against the egotistical and debasing indulgence of moral weaknesses and eccentricities which mean and vulgar minds are apt to regard as the privilege of genius. "Stand upon your own ground; be your own ruler; look to yourself, not to your stars, for your failure or success; always make your standard a lofty ideal, and try persistently to reach it, though all the temptations of earth and all the power of darkness strive against you"—this and nothing else, if I have read her books rightly, is the moral taught by George Sand. She may be wrong in her principle sometimes, but at least she always has a principle. She has a profound and generous faith in the possibilities of human nature; in the capacity of man's heart for purity, self-sacrifice, and self-redemption. Indeed, so far is she from holding counsel with wilful weakness or sin, that I think she sometimes falls into the noble error of painting her heroes as too glorious in their triumph over temptation, in their subjugation of every passion and interest to the dictates of duty and of honor. Take, for instance, that extraordinary book which has just been given to the American public in Miss Virginia Vaughan's excellent translation, "Mauprat." If I understand that magnificent romance at all, its purport is to prove that no human nature is ever plunged into temptation beyond its own strength to resist, provided that it really wills resistance; that no character is irretrievable, no error inexpiable, where there is sincere resolve to expiate and longing desire to retrieve. Take again that exquisite little story, "La Dernière Aldini"; I do not know where one could find a finer illustration of the entire sacrifice of man's natural impulse, passion, interest, to what might almost be called an abstract idea of honor and principle. I have never read this little story without wondering how many men one ever has known who, placed in the same situation as that of Nello, the hero, would have done the same thing; and yet so simply and naturally are the characters wrought out and the incidents described, that the idea of pompous, dramatic self-sacrifice never enters the mind of the reader, and it seems to him that Nello could not do otherwise than as he is doing. I speak of these two stories particularly, because in both of them there is a good deal of the world and the flesh; that is, both are stories of strong human passion and temptation. Many of George Sand's novels, the shorter ones especially, are as absolutely pure in moral tone, as entirely free from even a taint or suggestion of impurity, as they are perfect in style. Now, if we cannot help knowing that much of this great woman's life was far from being irreproachable, are we not bound to give her all the fuller credit because her genius at least kept so far the whiteness of its soul? Revolutions are not to be made with rose water; you cannot have omelettes without breaking of eggs. I am afraid that great social revolutionists are not often creatures of the most pure and perfect nature. It is not to patient Griselda you must look for any protest against even the uttermost tyranny of social conventions. One thing I think may at least be admitted as part of George Sand's vindication—that the marriage system in France is the most debased and debasing institution existing in civilized society, now that the buying and selling of slaves has ceased to be a tolerated system. I hold that the most ardent advocates of the irrevocable endurance of the marriage bond are bound by their very principles to admit that in protesting against the so-called marriage system of France George Sand stood on the side of purity and right. Assuredly she often went into extravagances in the other direction. It seems to be the fate of all French reformers to rush suddenly to extremes; and we must remember that George Sand was not a Bristol Quakeress or a Boston transcendentalist, but a passionate Frenchwoman, the descendant of one of the maddest votaries of love and war who ever stormed across the stage of European history.

Regarding George Sand then as an influence in literature and on society, I claim for her at least four great and special merits. First, she insisted on calling public attention to the true principle of marriage; that is to say, she put the question as it had not been put before. Of course, the fundamental principle she would have enforced is always being urged more or less feebly, more or less sincerely; but she made it her own question, and illuminated it by the fervid, fierce rays of her genius and her passion. Secondly, her works are an exposition of the tremendous reality of the feelings which people who call themselves practical are apt to regard with indifference or contempt as mere sentiments. In the long run the passions decide the life-question one way or the other. They are the tide which, as you know or do not know how to use it, will either turn your mill and float your boat, or drown your fields and sweep away your dwellings. Life and society receive no impulse and no direction from the influences out of which the novels of Dickens or even of Thackeray are made up. These are but pleasant or tender toying with the playthings and puppets of existence. George Sand constrains us to look at the realities through the medium of her fiction. Thirdly, she insists that man can and shall make his own career; not whine to the stars and rail out against the powers above, when he has weakly or wantonly marred his own destiny. Fourthly—and this ought not to be considered her least service to the literature of her country—she has tried to teach people to look at nature with their own eyes, and to invite the true love of her to flow into their hearts. The great service which Ruskin, with all his eccentricities and extravagances, has rendered to English-speaking peoples by teaching them to use their own eyes when they look at clouds, and waters, and grasses, and hills, George Sand has rendered to France.

I hold that these are virtues and services which ought to outweigh even very grave personal and artistic errors. We often hear that this or that great poet or romancist has painted men as they are; this other as they ought to be. I think George Sand paints men as they are, and also not merely as they ought to be, but as they can be. The sum of the lesson taught by her books is one of confidence in man's possibilities, and hope in his steady progress. At the same time she is entirely practical in her faith and her aspirations. She never expects that the trees are to grow up into the heavens, that men and women are to be other than men and women. She does not want them to be other; she finds the springs and sources of their social regeneration in the fact that they are just what they are, to begin with. I am afraid some of the ladies who seem to base their scheme of woman's emancipation and equality on the assumption that, by some development of time or process of schooling, a condition of things is to be brought about where difference of sex is no longer to be a disturbing power, will find small comfort or encouragement in the writings of George Sand. She deals in realities altogether; the realities of life, even when they are such as to shallow minds may seem mere sentiments and ecstasies; the realities of society, of suffering, of passion, of inanimate nature. There is in her nothing unmeaning, nothing untrue; there is in her much error, doubtless, but no sham.

I believe George Sand is growing into a quiet and beautiful old age. After a life of storm and stress, a life which, metaphorically at least, was "worn by war and passion," her closing years seem likely to be gilded with the calm glory of an autumnal sunset. One is glad to think of her thus happy and peaceful, accepting so tranquilly the reality of old age, still laboring with her unwearied pen, still delighting in books, and landscapes, and friends, and work. The world can well afford to forget as soon as possible her literary and other errors. Of the vast mass of romances, stories, plays, sketches, criticisms, pamphlets, political articles, even, it is said, ministerial manifestoes of republican days, which she poured out, only a few comparatively will perhaps be always treasured by posterity; but these will be enough to secure her a classic place. And she will not be remembered by her writings alone. Hers is probably the most powerful individuality displayed by any modern Frenchwoman. The influence of Madame Roland was but a glittering unreality, that of Madame de Staël only a boudoir and coterie success, when compared with the power exercised over literature, human feeling, and social law, by the energy, the courage, the genius, even the very errors and extravagances of George Sand.

EDWARD BULWER, LORD LYTTON.

TEN years ago an important political question was agitating the English House of Commons and the English public. It was the old question of Parliamentary Reform in a new shape. Thirty years before Lord John Russell had pleaded the right of the middle classes to have a voice in the election of their Parliamentary representatives; this time he was asserting a similar right for the working population. Then he had to contend against the opposition of the aristocracy only; this time he had to fight against the combined antagonism of the aristocracy and the middle classes, the latter having made common cause with their old enemies to preserve a monopoly of their new privileges. The debate in the House of Commons on the proposed Reform Bill of 1860 was long and bitter. When it was reaching its height, a speaker arose on the Tory side of the House whose appearance on the scene of the debate lent a new and piquant interest to the night's discussion. He sat on the front bench of the Opposition, quite near to Disraeli himself. The moment he rose, every head craned forward to see him; the moment he began to speak, every ear was strained with keen curiosity to hear him. The ears were for a while sorely tried and perplexed. What was he saying—nay, what language was he speaking? What extraordinary, indescribable sounds were those which were heard issuing from his lips? Were they articulate sounds at all? For some minutes certainly those who like myself had never heard the speaker before were utterly bewildered. We could only hear what seemed to us an incoherent, inarticulate guttural jabber, like the efforts at speech of somebody with a mutilated tongue or excided palate. Anything like it I never heard before or since; for no subsequent listening to the same speaker ever produced nearly the same impression: either he had greatly improved in elocution, or his listener had grown used to him. But the night of this famous speech, nothing could have exceeded the extraordinary nature of the sensations produced on those who heard the orator for the first time. After a while we began to detect articulate sounds; then we guessed at and recognized words; then whole sentences began to shape themselves out of the guttural fag; and at last we grew to understand that, with an elocution the most defective and abominable ever possessed by mortal orator, this Tory speaker was really delivering a speech of astonishing brilliancy, ingenuity, and power. The sentences had a magnificent, almost majestic rotundity, energy, and power; they reminded one of something cut out of solid and glittering marble, at once so dazzling and so impressive. The speech was from first to last an aristocratic argument against the fitness of the working man to be anything but a political serf. In the true fashion of the aristocrat, the speaker was for patronizing the working man in every possible way; behaving to him as a kind and friendly master; seeing that he had a decent home to live in and coals and blankets in winter; but all the time insisting that the ruin of England must follow any successful attempt to place political power in the hands of "poverty and passion." The speech overflowed with illustration, ingenious analogy, felicitous quotation, brilliant epigram, and political paradoxes that were made to sound wondrously like maxims of wisdom. Despite all its hideous defects of delivery, this speech was, beyond the most distant comparison, the finest delivered on the Tory side during the whole of that long and memorable debate. For a time one was almost cheated into the belief that that elaborate and splendid diction, now so stately and now so sparkling, was genuine eloquence. Yet to the last the listener was frequently baffled by some uncouth, semi-articulate, hardly intelligible sound. "What on earth does he mean," asked a puzzled and indeed agonized reporter of some laboring brother, "by talking so often about the political authority of Joe Miller?" Careful inquiry elicited the fact that the name of the political authority to which the orator had been alluding was John Mill. Fortunately for his readers and his fame, the speaker had taken good care to write out his oration and send the manuscript to the newspapers.

Now this inarticulate orator, this Demosthenes without the pebble-training, was, as my readers have already guessed, Edward Bulwer-Lytton, then a baronet and a member of the House of Commons, now a peer. Undoubtedly he succeeded, by this and one or two other speeches, in securing for himself a place among the few great Parliamentary debaters of the day. Despite of physical defects which would have discouraged almost any other man from entering into public life at all, he had succeeded in winning a reputation as a great speaker in a debate where Palmerston, Gladstone, Bright, and Disraeli were champions. So deaf that he could not hear the arguments of his opponents, so defective in utterance as to become often almost unintelligible, he actually made the House of Commons doubt for a while whether a new great orator had not come among them. It was not great oratory after all; it was not true oratory of any kind; but it was a splendid imitation of the real thing—the finest electro-plate anywhere to be found. "If it is not Bran, it is Bran's brother," says a Scottish proverb. If this speech of Bulwer-Lytton's was not true oratory, it was oratory's illegitimate brother.

Nearly a whole generation before the winning of that late success, Bulwer-Lytton had tried the House of Commons, and miserably, ludicrously failed. The young Tory members who vociferously cheered his great anti-reform speech of 1860, were in their cradles when Bulwer-Lytton first addressed the House of Commons, and having signally failed withdrew, as people supposed, altogether from Parliamentary life. His failure was even more complete than that of his friend Disraeli, and he took the failure more to heart. Rumor affirms that the first serious quarrel between Bulwer and his wife arose out of her vexation and disappointment at his break-down, and the bitter, provoking taunts with which she gave vent to her anger. I know no other instance of a rhetorical triumph so long delayed, and at length so completely effected. Nor can one learn that it was by any intervening practice or training that Bulwer in his declining years atoned for the failure of his youth. He was never that I know of a public speaker; he won his Parliametary success in defiance of Charles James Fox's famous axiom, that a speaker can only improve himself at the expense of his audiences. Between his failure and his triumph Bulwer-Lytton may be said to have had no political audience.

A statesman Bulwer-Lytton never became, although he held high office in a Tory Cabinet. He did little or nothing to distinguish himself, unless there be distinction in writing some high-flown, eloquent despatches, such as Ernest Maltravers might have penned, to the discontented islanders of Ionia; and it was he, if I remember rightly, who thought of sending out "Gladstone the Philhellene" on that mission of futile conciliation which only misled the Ionians and amused England. It always seemed to me that in his political career Bulwer acted just as one of the heroes of his own romances might have done. Having suffered defeat and humiliation, he vowed a vow to wrest from Fate a victory upon the very spot which had seen his discomfiture; and he kept his word, won his victory, and then calmly quitted the field forever. A more prosaic explanation might perhaps be found in the fact that weak physical health rendered it impossible for Bulwer to encounter the severe continuous labor which English political life exacts. But I prefer for myself the more romantic and less commonplace explanation, and I hope my readers will do likewise. I prefer to think of the great romancist retrieving after thirty years of silence his Parliamentary defeat, and then, having reconciled himself with Destiny, retiring from the scene contented, to struggle in that arena no more. In all seriousness, there must be some quality of greatness in the man who, after bearing such a defeat for so many years, can struggle with Fate again, and accomplish so conspicuous a success.

Now this is in fact one grand explanation of Bulwer-Lytton's rank in English literature. He has the self-reliance, the patience, the courage so rare among literary men, by which one is enabled to extract their full and utter value from whatsoever intellectual endowments he may possess. Bulwer-Lytton alone among all famous English authors of our days has apparently done all that he could possibly do—obtained from his faculties their entire tribute. Readers of the letters of poor Charlotte Brontë may remember the impatience with which she occasionally complained that her idol Thackeray would not put forth his whole strength. No such fault could possibly be found with Bulwer-Lytton. Sooner or later he always put forth his whole strength. He had many failures, but, as in the case of his political discomfiture, he had always the art of learning from failure the way how to succeed, and accordingly succeeding. When he wrote his wretched "Sea Captain," the critics all told him he could not produce a successful drama. Bulwer thought he could. He thought the very failure of that attempt would show him how to succeed another time. He was determined not to give in until he had satisfied himself as to his fitness, one way or the other, and so he persevered. Now observe the character of the man, and see how much superior he himself is to his works, and how much of their success the works owe to the man's peculiar temper. We all know what authors usually are, and how they receive criticism. In ordinary cases, when the critics declare some piece of work a failure, the author either is crushed for the time by the fiat, or he insists that the critics are idiots, hired assassins, personal enemies, and so forth; he defiantly adheres to his own notions and his own method—and he probably fails. Bulwer-Lytton looked at the matter in quite a different light. He said, apparently, to himself: "The critics only know what I have done; I know what I can do. From their point of view they are quite right—this thing is a failure. But I know that it is a failure only because I went to work the wrong way. I *can* do something infinitely better. Their experience and their comments have given me some valuable hints; I will forthwith go to work on a better principle." So Bulwer-Lytton wrote "Richelieu," "Money," and the "Lady of Lyons"—the last probably the most successful acting drama produced in England since the days of Shakespeare, and the first hardly below it in stage success. Of course I am not claiming for either of these plays a high and genuine dramatic value. They probably bear the same resemblance to the true drama that their author's Parliamentary speech-making does to true eloquence. But of their popularity and their transcendent technical success there cannot be the slightest doubt. Bulwer-Lytton proved to his critics that he could do better than any other living man the very thing they said he could never do—write a play that should conquer the public and hold the stage. So to those who affirmed that, whatever else he might do, he never could be a Parliamentary speaker, he replied by standing up when approaching the very brink of old age, and delivering speeches which won the willing and generous applause of Disraeli, and extorted the reluctant but manly and frank recognition of such an opponent as John Bright.

Bulwer-Lytton once insisted, in an address delivered to some English literary institution, that the word "versatile" is generally used wrongly when we speak of men who do a great many things well; that it is a comprehensive, not merely a versatile mind, each of these men has; not a knack of adroitly turning himself to many heterogeneous labors, but a capacity so wide that it unfolds quite naturally many fields of labor. In this sense Bulwer-Lytton has undoubtedly a more comprehensive mind than any of his English contemporaries. He has written the most successful dramas and some of the most successful novels of his day; and he has so varied the method of his novel-writing that he may be said to have at least three distinct and separate principles of construction. Some of his poetic translations seem to me almost absolutely the best done in England of late years; many of his essays approach a true literary value, while all or nearly all of them are attractive reading; his satire, "The New Timon," is the only thing of the kind which is likely to outlive his age; and his political speeches are what I have already described. Now, to estimate the personal value of these successes, let us not fail to remember that their author never was placed in a condition to make literary or other labor a necessity, and that for nearly a whole generation he has been in the enjoyment of actual wealth; that in England literature adds little or no social distinction to a man of Bulwer-Lytton's rank; and that during a considerable portion of his life the author of "The Caxtons" and "My Novel" has been tortured by almost incessant ill-health. Almost everything that could tend to make a man shun continuous and patient labor (opulence and ill-health would be quite enough to make most of us shun it) combined to render Bulwer-Lytton an idle or at least an indolent man. Yet almost all the literary success he attained was due to a patient toil which would have wearied out a penny-a-liner, and a laborious self-study and self-culture which might have overtaxed the nerves of a Königsberg professor. "Easy writing is cursed hard reading," is a maxim which Bulwer-Lytton fully understood, and of which he showed his appreciation in his personal practice.

Bulwer-Lytton was born on the fringe of the aristocratic region. He can hardly be said to belong to the genuine aristocracy, although of late, thanks to his political opinions and his peerage, he has come to be ranked among aristocrats. He is the brother of a distinguished diplomatist, Sir Henry Bulwer, and the father of a somewhat promising diplomatist, not quite unknown to Washington people, Robert Lytton, "Owen Meredith." Bulwer-Lytton had advanced tolerably far upon his career when he inherited through his mother a magnificent estate, which enabled him to set up for an aristocrat. His baronetcy had been conferred upon him by the Crown, as his peerage lately was. He started in political life, like Mr. Disraeli, as a Liberal; indeed, it was, if I am not greatly mistaken, on the introduction of Bulwer-Lytton that Disraeli obtained the early patronage of Daniel O'Connell, which he so soon forfeited by the political tergiversation that drew down from the great Agitator the famous outburst of fierce and savage scorn wherein, alluding to Disraeli's boasted Jewish origin, he proclaimed him evidently descended in a right line from the blasphemous thief who died impenitent on the cross. Disraeli's apostasy was sudden and glaring, and he kept the field. Bulwer-Lytton soon faded out of politics altogether for nearly thirty years, and when he reappeared in the House of Commons and wore the garb of a Tory, his old friend and political patron O'Connell had long become a mere tradition. Nearly all of those who listened with curiosity to Bulwer-Lytton's speeches in 1859 and 1860, were curious only to hear how a great romancist and dramatist would acquit himself in a part which, so far as they were concerned, was entirely a new appearance. They had no personal memory of his former efforts; no recollection of the time when the young author of the sparkling, piquant, and successful "Pelham" endeavored to take London by storm as a political orator, and failed in the enterprise.

In one peculiarity, at least, Bulwer-Lytton the novelist surpassed all his rivals and contemporaries. His range was so wide as to take in all circles and classes of English readers. He wrote fashionable novels, historical novels, political novels, metaphysical novels, psychological novels, moral-purpose novels, immoral-purpose novels. "Wilhelm Meister" was not too heavy nor "Tristram Shandy" too light for him. He tried to rival Scott in the historical romance; he strove hard to be another Goethe in his "Ernest Maltravers"; he quite surpassed Ainsworth's "Jack Sheppard," and the general run of what we in England call "thieves' literature," in his "Paul Clifford"; he became a sort of pinchbeck Sterne in "The Caxtons," and was severely classical in "The Last Days of Pompeii." One might divide his novels into at least half a dozen classes, each class quite distinct and different from all the rest, and yet the one author, the one Bulwer-Lytton, showing and shining through them all. Bulwer is always there. He is masquerading now in the garb of a mediæval baron, and now in that of an old Roman dandy; anon he is disguised as a thief from St. Giles's, and again as a full-blooded aristocrat from the region of St. James's. But he is the same man always, and you can hardly fail to recognize him even in his cleverest disguise. It may be questioned whether there is one spark of true and original genius in Bulwer. Certain ideas commonly floating about in this or that year he collects and brings to a focus, and by their aid he burns a distinct impression into the public mind. Just as he expressed the thin and spurious classicism of one period in his Pompeian romance, so he made copy out of the pseudo-science and bastard psychology of a later day in his "Strange Story." Never was there in literature a more masterly and wonderful mechanic. Many-sided he never was, although probably the fame of many-sidedness (if one may use so ungraceful an expression) is the renown which he specially coveted and most strenuously strove to win. Only genius can be many-sided, and Bulwer-Lytton's marvellous capability never can be confounded with genius. The nearest approach to genius in all his works may be found in their occasional outbursts and flashes of audacious, preposterous absurdity. The power which could palm off such outrageous nonsense as in some instances he has done on two or three generations of novel-readers, which could compel the public to swallow it and delight in it, despite all that the satire of a Thackeray or a Jerrold could do, must surely, one would almost say, have had something in it savoring of a sort of genius. For there are in some even of the very best and purest of Bulwer's novels whole scenes and characters which it seems almost utterly impossible that any reader whatever could follow without laughter. I protest that I think the author of "Ernest Maltravers" owed much of his success to the daring which assumed that anything might be imposed on the public, and to the absence of that sense of the ludicrous which might have made a man of a different stamp laugh at his own nonsense. I assume that Bulwer wrote in perfect faith and seriousness, honestly believing them to be fine, the most ridiculous, bombastic, fantastic passages in all his novels. I take it for granted that Mr. Morris's sad hero, "The Man who never Laughed Again," must have been frivolity itself when compared with Bulwer-Lytton at work upon a novel. The sensitive distrust of one's own capacity, the high-minded doubt of the value of one's own works, which is probably the companion, the Mentor, the tormentor often, and not unfrequently the conqueror and destroyer of true genius, never seems to have vexed the author of "Eugene Aram" and "Godolphin." Bulwer-Lytton won a great name partly because he was not a man of genius. The kind of thing he tried to do could not have been done truly and successfully, in the high artistic sense, by any one with a capacity below that of a Shakespeare, or at least a Goethe. A man of genius, but inferior genius, would have made a wretched failure of it. Between the two stools of popularity and art, of time and eternity, he must have fallen to the ground. But where genius might fail to achieve a splendid success, talent and audacity might turn out a magnificent sham. This is the sort of success, this and none other, which I believe Bulwer-Lytton to have achieved. He is the finest *faiseur* in the literature of to-day. His waxwork gallery surpasses Madame Tussaud's; or rather his sham art is as much superior to that of a James or an Ainsworth as Madame Tussaud's gallery is to Mrs. Jarley's show. That sort of sentiment which lies somewhere down in the heart of every one, however commonplace, or busy, or cynical—the sentiment which is represented by the applause of the galleries in a popular theatre, and which cultivated audiences are usually ashamed to acknowledge—was the feeling which Bulwer-Lytton could always reach and draw forth. He had so much at least of the true artistic instinct as to recognize that the strongest element of popularity is the sentimental; and he knew that out of ten persons who openly laugh at such a thing, nine are secretly touched by it. Bulwer-Lytton found much of his stock and capital in the human emotions which sympathize with youthful ambition and youthful love, just as Dickens makes perpetual play with the feelings which are touched by the death of children. When Claude Melnotte, transfigured into the splendid Colonel Morier, rushes forward just at the critical moment, outbids yon sordid huckster for his priceless jewel Pauline, flings down the purse containing double the needful sum, declares that he has bought every coin of it in the cause of nations with a Frenchman's blood, and sweeps away his ransomed bride amid the thunder of the galleries, of course we all know that sort of thing is not poetry, or high art, or anything but splendiferous rubbish. Yet it does touch most of us somehow. I know I always feel divided between laughter and enthusiastic sympathy even still, when I see it for the hundred and fiftieth time or so. In the same way, when Paul Clifford charges on society the crimes of his outlaw career; when Rienzi vows vengeance for his brother's blood; when Zanoni resigns his immortal youth that "the flower at his feet may a little longer drink the dew"; when Ernest Maltravers silently laments amid all his splendor of success the obscure Arcadia of his boyish love, we can all see at a glance how bombastic, gaudy, melodramatic, is the style in which the author works out his ideas; how utterly unlike the simple, strong majesty of true art the whole thing is; but yet we must acknowledge that the author understands thoroughly how to touch a certain vein of what may be called elementary emotion, common almost to all minds, which it is the object of society to repress or suppress, and the object of the popular artist to stir up into activity. Preach, advise, remonstrate, demonstrate as you will, the majority of us will always feel inclined to give alms to beggar-women and whining little children in the snowy streets. We know we are doing unwisely, and perhaps even wrongly; we know that the misery which touches us is probably a trumped-up and sham misery; we know that whatever we give to the undeserving and the insincere is practically withdrawn from the deserving and the sincere; we are ashamed to be seen giving the money, and yet we do give it whenever we can. Because, after all, our common emotion of sympathy with the more obvious, intelligible, and I would almost say vulgar forms of human suffering, are far too strong for our moderating maxims and our more refined mental conditions. So of the sympathies which heroes and heroines, aspirations and agonies of the style of Bulwer-Lytton awaken in us. Virtue cannot so inoculate our old stock but we shall relish it; and is not he something of an artist who recognizes this great fact in human nature, and plays upon that vibrating, imperishable chord, and compels it to give him back such an applauding echo? After all, I think there is just as much of sham and of Madame Tussaud, and of the beggar-child in the snow, about Paul Dombey's deathbed and Little Dorrit's filial devotion, as about the mock heroics of Claude Melnotte or the domestic virtues of the Caxtons. Of course I am not comparing Bulwer-Lytton with Dickens. The latter was a man of genius, and one of the greatest humorists known at least to modern literature. But nearly all the pathetic side of Dickens seems to me of much the same origin as the heroic side of Bulwer-Lytton, and I question whether the greater part of the popularity won by the author of "Bleak House" has not been gained by a mastery of the very same kind of art as that which sets galleries applauding for Claude Melnotte, and young women in tears for Eugene Aram.

There are, moreover, two points of superiority in artistic purpose which may be claimed for Bulwer-Lytton over either Dickens or Thackeray. They do not, perhaps, "amount to much" in any case; but they are worth mentioning. Bulwer-Lytton has more than once drawn to the best of his power a gentleman, and he has often drawn, or tried to draw, a man possessed by some great, impersonal, unselfish object in life. The former of these personages Dickens never seemed to have known or believed in; the latter, Thackeray never even attempted to paint. Why has Dickens never drawn a gentleman? I am not using the word in the artificial, conventional, snobbish sense. I mean by a gentleman a creature with intellect as well as heart, with refined and cultivated tastes, with something of personal dignity about him. I do not care from what origin he may have sprung, or to what class he may have belonged: there is no reason, even in England, why a man born in a garret might not acquire all the ways, and thoughts, and refinements of a gentleman. Among the class to which most of Dickens's heroes are represented as belonging, have we not all in England known gentlemen of intellect and culture? Yet Dickens has never painted such a being. Nicholas Nickleby is a plucky, honest, good-hearted blockhead; Tom Pinch is a benevolent idiot; Eugene Wrayburn is a low-bred, impertinent snob—a mere "cad," as Londoners would say. I have had no sympathy with the "Saturday Review" in its perpetual accusations of vulgarity against Dickens; and I think a recent English critic was pleasantly and purposely extravagant when he charged the author of the "Christmas Carol" with having no loftier idea of human happiness than the eating of plum pudding and kissing girls under the mistletoe. But I do say that Dickens never drew a cultivated English gentleman or lady—a cultivated and refined English man or woman, if you will; and yet I know that there are such personages to be found without troublesome quest among the very classes of society which he was always describing.

Now Thackeray could draw and has drawn English gentlemen and gentlewomen; but has he ever drawn a high-minded, self-forgetting man or woman devoted to some, to any, great object, or cause, or purpose of any kind in life—absorbed by it and faithful to it? Is it true that even in London society men are wholly given up to dining, and paying visits, and making and spending money? Is it true that all men, even in London society, pass their lives in a purposeless, drifting way, making good resolves and not carrying them out; doing good things now and then out of easy, generous impulse; loving lightly, and recovering from love quickly? Are there in London society, on the one hand, no passions; on the other hand, no simple, strong, consistent, unselfish, high-minded lives? Assuredly there are; but Thackeray, the greatest painter of English society England has ever had, chose, for some reason or another, to ignore them. Only when he comes to speak of artists, more especially of painters, does he ever hint that he is aware of the existence of men whose lives are consistent, steadfast, and unselfish. Surely this is a great omission. One does not care to drag into this discussion the names of living illustrations; but I should like to have pointed Thackeray's attention to this and that and the other man whom, to my certain knowledge, he knew and warmly, fully appreciated, and asked him, "Why, when you were painting with such incomparable fidelity such illustrations of English life as you chose to select, did you not think fit to picture such a simple, strong, consistent, magnanimous, self-forgetting, self-devoting nature as that, or that, or that?"—and so on, through many examples which I or anybody could have named. I suppose the honest answer would have been, "I cannot draw that kind of character; I cannot quite enter into its experiences and make it look life-like as I see it; it is not in my line, and I prefer not to attempt it." Now, I think it to the credit of Bulwer-Lytton, as a mere artist, that he did include such figures even in his wax-work gallery. He could not make them look like life; but he showed at least that he was aware of their existence, and that he did his best to teach the world to recognize them.

Thus then, using with inexhaustible energy and perseverance his wonderful gifts as an intellectual mechanician, Edward Bulwer-Lytton went on from 1828 to 1860 grinding out of his mill an almost unbroken succession of novels and romances to suit all changes in public taste. I do not believe he changed his themes and ways of treating them purposely, to suit the changes of public taste; but rather that, being a man of no true original and creative power, his style and his views were modified by the modifying conditions of successive years. Some new idea, some new way of looking at this or that question of human life came up, and it attracted him who was always a close and diligent student of the world and its fashions; and he made it into a romance. Whatever new schools of fiction came into existence, Bulwer-Lytton, always directing the new ideas into the channel where popular and elementary sympathies flowed freely, succeeded in turning each change to advantage, and keeping his place. Dickens sprang up and founded a school; and yet Bulwer-Lytton held his own. Thackeray arose and established a new school, and Bulwer-Lytton, whom no human being would have thought of comparing with either as a man of genius, did not lose a reader. Charlotte Brontë came like a shadow, and so departed; George Eliot gave a new lift and life to romance; the realistic school was followed by the sensational school; the Literature of Adultery ran its vulgar course—and Bulwer-Lytton remained where he always had been, and moulted no feather.

It is not likely that any true critic ever thought very highly of him, or indeed took him quite seriously; but for many, many years criticism, which had so scoffed and girded at him once, had only civil words and applauding smiles for him. How Thackeray once did make savage fun of "Bullwig," and more lately how Thackeray praised him! Charles Dickens—what an enthusiastic admirer of the genius of his friend Lytton he too became! And Tennyson—what a fierce passage of arms that was long ago between Bulwer and him; and now what cordial mutual admiration! Fonblanque and Forster, the "Athenæum" and "Punch," Tray, Blanche, and Sweetheart—how they all welcomed in chorus each new effort of genius by the great romancist who was once the stock butt of all lively satirists. How did this happy change come about? Nobody ever had harder dealing at the hands of the critics than Bulwer when his powers were really most fresh and forcible; nobody ever had more general and genial commendation than shone of late years around his sunny way. How was this? Did the critics really find that they had been mistaken and own themselves conquered by his transcendent merit? Did he "win the wise who frowned before to smile at last"? To some extent, yes. He showed that he was not to be written down; that no critical article could snuff him out; that he really had some stuff in him and plenty of mettle and perseverance; and he soon became a literary institution, an accomplished fact which criticism could not help recognizing. But there was much more than this operating towards Bulwer-Lytton's reconciliation with criticism. He became a wealthy man, a man of fashion, a sort of aristocrat, with yet a sincere love for the society of authors and artists, with a taste for encouraging private theatricals and endowing literary institutions, and with a splendid country house. He became a genial, golden link between literature and society. Even Bohemia was enabled by his liberal and courteous good-will to penetrate sometimes into the regions of Belgravia. The critics began to fall in love with him. I do not believe that Lord Lytton made himself thus agreeable to his literary brethren out of any motive whatever but that of honest goodfellowship and kindness. I have heard too many instances of his frank and brotherly friendliness to utterly obscure writers, who could be of no sort of service to him or to anybody, not to feel satisfied of his unselfish good-nature and his thorough loyalty to that which ought to be the *esprit de corps* of the literary profession. But it is certain that he thus converted enemies into friends, and stole the gall out of many an inkstand, and the poison from many a penman's feathered dart. Not that the critics simply sold their birthright of bitterness for an invitation to dinner or the kindly smile of a literary Peer. But you cannot, I suppose, deal very rigidly with the works of a man who is uniformly kind to you; who brings you into a sort of society which otherwise you would probably never have a chance of seeing; who, being himself a lord, treats you, poor critic, as a friend and brother; and whose works, moreover, are certain to have a great public success, no matter what you say or leave unsaid. The temptation to look for and discover merit in such books is strong indeed—perhaps too strong for frail critical nature. Thus arises the great sin of English criticism. It is certainly not venal; it is hardly ever malign. Mere ill-nature, or impatience, or the human delight of showing one's strength, may often induce a London critic to deal too sharply with some new and nameless author; but although we who write books are each and all of us delighted to persuade ourselves that any disparaging criticism must be the result of some personal hatred, I cannot remember ever having had serious reason to believe that a London critic had attacked a book because of his personal ill-will to the author. The sin is quite of another kind—a tendency to praise the books of certain authors merely because the critic knows the men so intimately, and likes them so well, that he is at once naturally prejudiced in their favor, and disinclined to say anything which could hurt or injure them. Thus of late criticism has had hardly anything to say of Lord Lytton, except in the way of praise. He is the head, and patron, and ornament of a great London literary "Ring." I use this word because none other could so well convey to a reader in New York a clear idea of the friendly professional unity of the coterie I desire to describe; but I wish it to be distinctly understood that I do not attribute anything like venality or hired partisanship of any kind to the literary Ring of which Lord Lytton is the sparkling gem. Of course it has become, as such cliques always must become, somewhat of a Mutual Admiration Society; and it is certain that a place in that brotherhood secures a man against much disparaging criticism. There are indeed literary cliques in London, of a somewhat lower range than this, where the influence of personal friendships does operate in a manner that closely borders upon a sort of literary corruption. But Lord Lytton and his friends and admirers are not of that sort. They are friends together, and they do admire each other, and I suppose everybody (save one person) likes Lord Lytton now; and so it is only in the rare case of a fresh, independent outsider, like the critic who wrote in the "Westminster Review" some two years ago, that a really impartial, keen, artistic survey is taken of the works of him that was "Bullwig." When Lytton published his "Caxtons," the reviewer of the "Examiner," even up to that time a journal of great influence and prestige, having nearly exhausted all possible modes of panegyric, bethought himself that some unappreciative and cynical persons might possibly think there was a lack of originality in a work so obviously constructed after the model of "Tristram Shandy." So he hastened to confute or convince all such persons by pointing out that in this very fact consisted the special claim of "The Caxtons" to absolute originality. The original genius of Lytton was proved by his producing so excellent a copy. Don't you see? You don't, perhaps. But then if you were intimate with Lord Lytton, and were liked by him, and were a performer in the private theatricals at Knebworth, his country seat, you would probably see it quite clearly, and agree with it, every word.

There was one person indeed who had no toleration for Lord Lytton, or for his friendly critics. That was Lord Lytton's wife. There really is no scandal in alluding to a conjugal quarrel which was brought so persistently under public notice by one of the parties as that between Bulwer-Lytton and his wife. I do not know whether I ought to call it a quarrel. Can that be called a fight, piteously asks the man in Juvenal, where my enemy only beats and I am merely beaten? Can that be called a quarrel in which, so far as the public could judge, the wife did all the denunciation, and the husband made no reply? Lady Lytton wrote novels for the purpose of satirizing her husband and his friends—his parasites, she called them. Bulwer-Lytton she gracefully described as having "the head of a goat on the body of a grasshopper"—a description which has just enough of comical truthfulness in its savage ferocity to make it specially cruel to the victim of the satire, and amusing to the unconcerned public. Lady Lytton attributed to her husband the most odious meannesses, vices, and cruelties; but the public, with all its love of scandal, seems to have steadfastly refused to take her ladyship's word for these accusations. Dickens she denounced and vilified as a mere parasite and sycophant of her husband. At one time she poured out a gush of fulsome eulogy on Thackeray because he apparently was not one of Lytton's friends; afterwards, when the relationship between "Pelham" and "Pendennis" became friendly, she changed her tune and tried to bite the file, to satirize the great satirist. Disraeli she caricatured under the title of "Jericho Jabber." This sort of thing she kept always going on. Sometimes she issued pamphlets addressed to the women of England, calling on them to take up her quarrel—which somehow they did not seem inclined to do. Once when Lord Lytton, then only Sir Edward, was on the hustings, addressing his constituents at a county election, her ladyship suddenly mounted the platform and "went for" him. Sir Edward and his friends prudently and quietly withdrew. I do not know anything of the merits of the quarrel, and have always been disposed to think that something like insanity must have been the explanation of much of Lady Lytton's conduct. But it is beyond doubt that her husband's demeanor was remarkable for its quiet, indomitable patience and dignity. Lately the public has happily heard little of Lady Lytton's complaints. I did not even know whether she was still living, until I saw a little book announced the other day by some publisher, which bore her name. Let her pass—with the one remark that her long succession of bitter attacks upon her husband does not seem to have done him any damage in the estimation of the world.

It is not likely that posterity will preserve much of Lord Lytton's writings. They do not, I think, add to literature one original character. Even the glorified murderer or robber, the Eugene Aram or Paul Clifford sort of person, had been done and done much better by Schiller, by Godwin, and by others, before Bulwer-Lytton tried him at second hand. As pictures of English society, those of them which profess to deal with modern English life have no value whatever. The historical novels, the classical novels, are glaringly false in their color and tone. Some of the personages in "The Last Days of Pompeii" are a good deal more like modern English dandies than most of the people who are given out as such in "Pelham." The attempts at political satire in "Paul Clifford," at broad humor in "Eugene Aram" (the Corporal and his cat for example), are feeble and miserable. There is hardly one touch of refined and genuine pathos —of pathos drawn from other than the old stock conventional sources—in the whole of the romances, plays, and poems. The one great faculty which the author possessed was the capacity to burnish up and display the absolutely commonplace, the merely conventional, the utterly unreal, so that it looked new, original, and real in the eyes of the ordinary public, and sometimes even succeeded, for the hour, in deceiving the expert. Bulwer-Lytton's romance is only the romance of the London "Family Herald" or the "New York Ledger," plus high intellectual culture and an intimate acquaintance with the best spheres of letters, art, and fashion. I own that I have considerable admiration for the man who, with so small an original outfit, accomplished so much. So successful a romancist; occasionally almost a sort of poet; a perfect master of the art of writing plays to catch audiences; so skilful an imitator of oratory that, despite almost unparalleled physical defects, he once nearly persuaded the world that his was genuine eloquence—who shall say that the capacity which can do all this is not something to be admired? It is a clever thing to be able to make ornaments of paste which shall pass with the world for diamonds; mock-turtle soup which shall taste like real; wax figures which look at first as if they were alive. Of the literary art which is akin to this, our common literature has probably never had so great a master as Lord Lytton. Such a man is especially the one to stand up as the appropriate representative of literature in such an assembly as the English House of Lords. I should be sorry to see a Browning, a Thackeray, a Carlyle, a Tennyson, a Dickens there; but I think Lord Lytton is in his right place—a splendid sham author in a splendid sham legislative assembly.

"PAR NOBILE FRATRUM—THE TWO NEWMANS."

"THE truth, friend," exclaims Mr. Arthur Pendennis, debating some question with his comrade Warrington; "where is the truth? Show it me. I see it on both sides. I see it in this man who worships by act of Parliament, and is rewarded with a silk apron and five thousand a year; in that man who, driven fatally by the remorseless logic of his creed, gives up everything, friends, fame, dearest ties, closest vanities, the respect of an army of churchmen, the recognized position of a leader, and passes over, truth-impelled, to the enemy in whose ranks he is ready to serve henceforth as a nameless private soldier; I see the truth in that man as I do in his brother, whose logic drives him to quite a different conclusion, and who, after having passed a life in vain endeavors to reconcile an irreconcilable book, flings it at last down in despair, and declares, with tearful eyes and hands up to heaven, his revolt and recantation."

Perhaps many American readers, meeting with this passage, may have supposed that the two brothers here described were merely typical figures, invented almost at random by Thackeray to enable Pendennis to point his moral But in England people know that the two brothers are real personages, and still live. I saw one of them a few nights ago, the one last mentioned by Arthur Pendennis. I saw him, as he is indeed often to be seen, the centre and leader of a little group or knot, a hopeless minority, vainly striving by force of argument and logic, of almost unlimited erudition, and a keen bright intellect, to obtain public attention for something which the public persisted in regarding as an idle crotchet, an impotent craze. The other brother, the elder, is a man whose secession from the Church of England has lately been described by Disraeli, in the preface to the collected edition of his works, as having "dealt a blow to the Church under which it still reels." "That extraordinary event," says Disraeli, "has been 'apologized for' but has never been explained. It was a mistake and a misfortune." Probably no reader of "The Galaxy" will now need to be told that the typical brothers alluded to by Pendennis are John Henry and Francis W. Newman.

The Atlantic deals curiously and capriciously with reputations. Both these brothers Newman seem to me to be less known in America than they deserve to be. John Henry in especial I found to be thus comparatively ignored in the United States. He is beyond doubt one of the greatest, certainly one of the most influential Englishmen of our time. He has engraved his name deeply on the history of his age. He has led perhaps the most remarkable religious movement known to England for generations. He is one of the very few men whose lofty and commanding intellect has been acknowledged and admired by all sects and parties. Gather together any company of eminent Englishmen, however select in its composition, however splendid in its members, and John Henry Newman will be among the few especially conspicuous.

Perhaps most of my readers will be of opinion that Newman's intellect has been sadly misused; that his influence has been for the most part disastrous. But no one who knows anything of the subject can deny the greatness alike of the intellect and of the influence. Let me add, too, that no enemy ever yet called into question the simple sincerity, the blameless purity of John Henry Newman's purposes and character. Of later years he has been rarely seen in London, for his duties keep him in Birmingham, where he is at the head of a religious and educational institution. I have heard that years are telling heavily on him, and that when he now preaches he is listened to with the kind of half-melancholy reverence which hangs on the words of a great man who is already beginning to be a portion of the past. But his influence was a power almost unequalled in its day, and that day has not yet wholly faded.

The Newman brothers are Londoners by birth, sons of a wealthy banker of Lombard street—the British Wall street. Both were educated at Ealing school, and both went to the University of Oxford. John Henry is by some four years the senior of Francis, who was born in 1805, and who now looks at least a dozen or fifteen years younger than his distinguished brother. Both men were endowed with remarkable gifts; both had a splendid faculty of acquiring knowledge. John Henry Newman became a clergyman of the Established Church. He was a close and intimate friend of Keble, of Pusey, and of Manning. He grew to be regarded as one of the rising stars of Protestantism. No name, soon, stood higher than his. His friends loved him, and Protestant England began to revere him. Now observe the change that came on these two brothers, alike so gifted and earnest, alike so wooed by the promise of brilliant worldly career. Two movements of thought, having perhaps a common origin in the dissatisfaction with the existing intellectual stagnation of the Church, but tending in widely different directions, carried the brothers along with them—"seized," to use the words of Richter, "their bleeding hearts and flung them different ways." The younger brother found himself drawn toward rationalism. He could not subscribe the Thirty-Nine Articles for his degree as a Master; he left Oxford. He wandered for years in the East, endeavoring, not very successfully, to teach Christianity on its broadest basis to the Mohammedans; and he finally returned to England to take his place among the leaders of that school of free thought which the ignorant, the careless, or the malignant set down as infidelity. In the mean time his brother became one of the pioneers of a still more unexpected movement. In the English Church for a long time everything had seemed to be settled and at rest. The old controversy with Rome appeared out of date, unnecessary, and perhaps vulgar. Everything was just as it should be—stable and respectable. But it suddenly occurred to some earnest, unresting souls, like that of Keble—souls "without haste and without rest," like Goethe's star—to insist that the Church of England had higher claims and nobler duties than those of preaching harmless sermons and enriching bishops. Keble could not bear to think of the Church taking pleasure since all is well. He urged on some of the more vigorous and thoughtful minds around him that they should reclaim for the Church the place which ought to be hers as the true successor of the Apostles. He claimed for her that she, and she alone, was the real Catholic Church, authorized to teach all nations, and that Rome had wandered away from the right path, foregone the glorious mission which she might have maintained. One of Keble's closest and dearest friends was John Henry Newman, and Keble regarded Newman as a man qualified beyond all others to become the teacher and leader of the new movement. Keble preached a famous sermon in 1833, and inaugurated the publication of a series of tracts designed to vindicate the real mission of the Church of England. This was the Tractarian movement, which had early, various, and memorable results. John Henry Newman wrote the most celebrated of all the tracts, the famous "No. 90," which drew down the censure of the University authorities on the ground that it actually tended to abolish all difference between the Church of England and the Church of Rome. Yet a little, and the gradual workings of Newman's mind became evident to all the world. The brightest and most penetrating intellect in the English Protestant Church was publicly and deliberately withdrawn from her service, and John Henry Newman became a priest of the Church of Rome. To this had the inquiry conducted him which led his friend Dr. Pusey merely to endeavor to incorporate some of the mysticism and the symbols of Rome with the practice and the progress of the English Church; which had led Dr. Keble only to a more liberal and truly Christianlike temper of Protestant faith; which had sent Francis Newman into radical rationalism. The two brothers were intellectually divided forever. Each renounced a career rich in promise for mere conscience' sake; and the one went this way, the other that.

Disraeli has in no wise exaggerated the depth and painfulness of the sensation produced among English Protestants by the secession of John Henry Newman. It was of course received upon the opposite side with corresponding exultation. No man, indeed, could be less qualified than Mr. Disraeli to understand the tremendous, the irresistible force of conviction in a nature like that of Newman. The brilliant master of political tactics has made it evident that he did not understand the motive of Newman's secession any more than he did the meaning of the title of Newman's celebrated book, "Apologia pro Vitâ suâ." "That extraordinary event," says Disraeli, speaking of the secession, "has been apologized for, but has never been explained." Evidently Disraeli believed that the English word "apology" is the correct translation of the Latinized Greek word "apologia," which it most certainly is not. Nothing could have been further from Newman's mind or from the purpose, or indeed from the title of his book, than to apologize for his secession. On the contrary, the book is sharply and pertinaciously aggressive. It was called forth by an attack made on Dr. Newman by the Rev. Charles Kingsley. I think Kingsley was in the main right in his views, but he was rough and blundering in his expression of them, and he is about as well qualified to carry on a controversy with John Henry Newman as Governor Hoffman would be to undertake a rhetorical competition with Mr. Wendell Phillips. Kingsley's bluff, rude, illogical way of fighting, his "wild and skipping spirit," were placed at ludicrous and fearful disadvantage. Newman "went for him" unsparingly, and literally tore him with the beak and claws of logic, satire, and invective. One was reminded of Pascal's attacks on the Jesuits—only that this time the wit and power were on the side which might fairly be called Jesuitical. Out of this merciless onslaught on Kingsley came the "Apologia pro Vitâ suâ," in which Newman endeavored to vindicate and glorify, not excuse or apologize for, his strange secession. The book is well worth reading, if only as a curious illustration of the utter inadequacy of human intellect and human logic to secure a soul from the strangest wandering, the saddest possible illusion. You cannot read a page of it without admiration for the intellect of the author, and without pity for the poverty even of the richest intellectual gifts where guidance is sought in a faith and in things which transcend the limits of human logic.

John Henry Newman threw his whole soul, energy, genius, and fame into the cause of the Roman Catholic Church. Rome welcomed him with that cordial welcome she always gives to a new-comer, and she utilized him and set work for him to do. Macaulay has shown very effectively in one of his essays how the Roman Church seldom loses any one it has gained, because it is so skilful in finding for everybody his proper place, and assigning him in her service the task he is best qualified to do, so that her ambition becomes his ambition, her interest his interest, her conquests his conquests. Newman appears to have been made a sort of missionary from Rome to the intellect and culture of the English people. Within the Church to which he had gone over he became an immense influence and almost unequalled power. The Catholics delighted to have a leader whose intellect no one could pretend to despise, whose gifts and culture had been panegyrized in the most glowing terms, over and over again, by the foremost statesmen and divines of the Protestant Church. Newman was appointed head of the oratory of St. Philip Neri at Birmingham, and was for some years rector of the Roman Catholic University of Dublin. He rarely came before the public. In all the arts that make an orator or a great preacher he is strikingly deficient. His manner is constrained, awkward, and even ungainly; his voice is thin and weak. His bearing is not impressive. His gaunt, emaciated figure, his sharp, eagle face, his cold, meditative eye, rather repel than attract those who see him for the first time. The matter of his discourse, whether sermon, speech, or lecture, is always admirable, and the language is concise, scholarly, expressive—perhaps a little overweighted with thought; but there is nothing there of the orator. It is as a writer, and as an "influence"—I don't know how better to express it—that Newman has become famous. I doubt if we have many better prose writers. He is full of keen, pungent, satirical humor; and there is, on the other hand, a subtle vein of poetry and of pathos suffusing nearly all he writes. One of the finest and one of the most frequently quoted passages in modern English literature is Newman's touching and noble apostrophe to England's "Saxon Bible." He has published volumes of verse which I think belong to the very highest order of verse-making that is not genuine poetry. They are full of thought, feeling, pathos, tenderness, beauty of illustration; they are all that verse can be made by one who just fails to be a poet. An English critical review not long since classed the poetical works of Dr. Newman and George Eliot together, as the nearest approach which intellect and culture have made in our days toward the production of genuine poetry. When Newman made his famous attack on Dr. Achilli, an Italian priest who had renounced the Roman Church, and whom Newman publicly accused of many crimes, the judge who had to sentence the accuser to the payment of a fine for libel pronounced a panegyric on his intellect and his character such as is rarely heard from an English judgment seat. Not long after, when the subject came up somehow in the House of Commons, Mr. Gladstone broke into an encomium of John Henry Newman which might have seemed poetical by hyperbole to those who did not know the merits of the one man and the conscientious truthfulness of the other. We have heard the testimony borne by Mr. Disraeli to the importance of Newman's intellect as a support of the English Church, and the shock which was caused by his withdrawal. Seldom, indeed, has a man seceded from one church and become the aggressive, unsparing, intolerant champion of its enemy, and yet retained the esteem and the affection of those whom he abandoned, as this good, great, mistaken Englishman has done.

The two brothers then are hopelessly divided. One consorts with the Pope and Cardinal Wiseman and Archbishop Manning, and is the idol and saint of the Ultramontanes, and devotes his noble intellect to the task of making the Irish Catholic a more bigoted Catholic than ever. The other falls in with the little band, that once seemed a forlorn hope, of what we may call the philosophical radicals of England. He becomes a professor of the rationalistic University of London, and a contributor to the free-thinking "Westminster Review." Judging each brother's success merely by what each sought to do, I suppose the career of the Catholic has been the more successful. Not that I think he has made much way toward the conversion of England to Catholicism. With all its Puseyism and ritualism, England seems to have little real inclination toward the doctrines of Rome. There is indeed a distinguished "convert" every now and then—the Marquis of Bute some two years ago, Lord Robert Montagu last year; but the great mass of the English people remain obstinately anti-papal. The tendency is far more toward Rationalism than toward Romanism; with the Newman who withdrew from all churches rather than with the Newman who renounced one church to enter another. Therefore, when I say that the career of John Newman appears to me to have been more successful than that of Francis, I mean only that he has been a greater influence, a more powerful instrument of his cause than his brother ever has been. The boast was made unjustly for Voltaire that he almost arrested the progress of Christianity in Europe. I think the admirers of John Newman might claim for him that he actually did for a time at least arrest the progress of Protestantism in England. He had indeed the great advantage of passing from one organization to another. Like Coriolanus, when he seceded he became the leader of the enemy's army. It was quite otherwise with his brother, who leaving the English Church was thenceforward only an individual, and for the most part an isolated worker. But indeed, with all his intellect, his high culture, and his indomitable courage, Francis Newman has never been an influential man in English politics. It may be that his keen logic is too uncompromising; and there can be no practical statesmanship without compromise. It may be that there is something eccentric, egotistic (in the less offensive sense), and crotchety in that sharp, independent, and self-sufficing intelligence. Whatever the reason, nine out of ten men in London set down Francis Newman as hopelessly given over to crotchets, while the tenth man, admiring however much his character and his capacity, is sometimes grieved and sometimes provoked that both together do not make him a greater power in the nation. I never remember Francis Newman to have been in accord with what I may call the average public opinion of English political life, except in one instance; and in that case I believe him to have been wrong. He was in favor of the Crimean war; and for this once therefore he found himself on the side of the majority. As if to mark the contrast of views which it has been the fate of these two brothers to present during their lives, it so happened that, so far as John Henry's opinions on the subject could be learned by the public, they were against the war. At least they were decidedly against the Turks. I remember hearing him deliver at that time a course of lectures in an educational institution, having for their subject the origin and the results of the Ottoman settlement in Europe. I well remember how effectively and vividly he argued, with his thin voice and his constrained, ungraceful action, that the Turk had no greater moral right to the territory he occupies, but does not cultivate and improve, than the pirate has to the sea over which he sails. But Francis Newman was then for once mixed up with the majority; and I doubt whether he could have much liked the unwonted position. He certainly took care to explain more than once that his reasons for taking that side were not those of the average Englishman. He thus might have given some of his casual associates occasion to say of him, as Charles Mathews says of woman in general, that even when he is right he is right in a wrong sort of way. For myself I am inclined to reverse the saying, and declare of Francis Newman that even when he is wrong he is wrong in a right sort of way. He was right, and in a very right sort of way, when he came out from his habitual seclusion during the American civil war, and stood up on many a platform for the cause of the Union. Like his brother, he is a poor public speaker. At his very best he is the professor talking to his class, not the orator addressing a crowd. His manner is singularly constrained, ineffective, and even awkward; his voice is thin and weak. There is a certain very small and rare class of bad speakers, which has yet a virtue and charm of its own almost equal to eloquence. I am now thinking of men utterly wanting in all the arts and graces, in all the power and effect of rhetorical delivery, but who yet with whatever defect of manner can say such striking things, can put such noble thoughts into expressive words, can be so entirely original and so completely masters of their subject, that they seem to be orators in all but voice and manner. Horace Greeley always is, to me at least, such a speaker; so is Stuart Mill. These are bad speakers as Jane Eyre or Consuelo may have been an unlovely woman; all the rules declare against them, all the intelligences and sympathies are in their favor. But Francis Newman is not a speaker of this kind. He is feeble, ineffective, and often even commonplace. Nature has denied to him the faculty of adequately expressing himself in spoken words. He is almost as much out of his element when addressing a public meeting as he would be if he were singing in an opera. Few Englishmen living can claim to be the intellectual superiors of Francis Newman; but you would never know Francis Newman by hearing him speak on a platform. The last time I heard him address a public meeting was on an occasion to which I have already alluded. He was presiding over an assemblage called together to protest against compulsory vaccination. The Government and Parliament have lately made very stringent the enactment for compulsory vaccination, in consequence of the terrible increase of small-pox. There is in London, as in all other great capitals, a certain knot of persons who would refuse to wash their faces or kiss their wives if Government ordered or even recommended either performance. Therefore there was a small agitation got up against vaccination, and Francis Newman consented to become the president of one of its meetings. This meeting was held in Exeter Hall—not indeed in the vast hall where the oratorios are performed, and where once upon a time Henry Ward Beecher pleaded the cause of the Union; but in the "lower hall," as it is called, a little subterranean den. Some eminent classic person, I really forget who, being reproached with the small size of his apartments, declared that he should be only too glad if he could fill his rooms, small as they were, with men his friends. The organizers of this meeting might have been content if they could have filled the hall, small as it was, with men and women their friends. The attendance was not nearly up to the size of the room. There on the platform sat the good, the gifted, and the fearless Francis Newman; and immediately around him were some dozen embodied and living crotchets and crazes. There was this learned physician who has communication with the spirit-world regularly. There was this other eminent person who has long been trying in vain to teach an apathetic Government how to cure crime on phrenological principles. There was Smith, who is opposed to all wars; Brown, who firmly believes that every disease comes from the use of salt; Jones, who has at his own expense put into circulation thousands of copies of his work against the employment of medical men in puerperal cases· Robinson, who is ready to spend his last coin for the purpose of proving that vaccination and original sin are one and the same thing. How often, oh, how often have I not heard those theories expounded! How often have I marvelled at the extraordinary perversion of ingenuity by which figures, facts, philosophy, and Scripture are jumbled up together to convince you that the moon is made of green cheese! We just wanted on this memorable occasion the awful persons who prove to you that the earth is flat, and the indefatigable ladies who expound their claims to the British crown feloniously usurped by Queen Victoria. There sat Francis Newman presiding over this preposterous little conclave, and having of course what seemed to him satisfactory and just reasons for the position he occupied. He spoke rather better than usual, and there was a bewildering bravery of paradox writhing through his speech which must have delighted his listeners. The meeting came to nothing. The papers took hardly any notice of it (London papers were never in my time so entirely conventional, respectable, and Philistinish as they are just now); and Newman's effort went wholly in vain. I have mentioned it only because it was illustrative or typical of so much in the man's whole career. So much of lovely independence; such a disdain of public opinion and public ridicule; such an absence of all perception of the ridiculous! Thus it was that he endeavored to rouse up the English public, who except for the extreme democracy always have had a strong hankering for the Austrian Government, to a sense of the crimes of the House of Hapsburg against its subjects. Thus he was for reform in Parliament when Parliamentary reform was a theme supposed to be dead and buried; when Palmerston had trampled on its ashes, and Disraeli had made merry over its coffin. Thus he came out for the American Union when John Bright stood almost alone in the House of Commons, and Mill and Goldwin Smith and two or three others were trying to organize public opinion outside the House. The same qualities after all which made Newman nearly sublime in these latter instances, were just those which made him well nigh ridiculous in the anti-vaccination business. But in all the instances alike the same thing can be said of Francis Newman. There is a turn or twist of some kind in his nature and intellect which always seems to mar his best efforts at practical accomplishment. Even his purely literary and scholastic productions are marked by the same fatal characteristic. All the outfit, all the materials are there in surprising profusion. There is the culture, there is the intellect, the patience, the sincerity. But the result is not in proportion to the value of the materials. The blending is not complete, is not effectual. Something has always intervened or been wanting. Francis Newman has never done and probably never will do anything equal to his strength and his capacity.

I am not inviting a comparison between these two brothers, so alike in their sincerity, their devotion, their courage, and their gifts—so singularly unlike, so utterly divided, in their creeds and their careers. My own sympathies, of course, naturally go with Francis Newman, who has in a vast majority of instances been a teacher of some opinion, a champion of some political cause of which I am proud to be a disciple and a follower. But I suppose the greater intellect and the richer gifts were those which were given up so meekly and wholly to the service of the dogmatism of the Roman Catholic Church. The career of John Henry Newman may probably be regarded as having practically closed. His latest work of note, "The Grammar of Assent," does not indeed seem to show any falling away of his intellectual powers; but I have heard that his physical strength has suffered severely with years, and he never was a strong man. He is now in his seventieth year, and it is therefore only reasonable to regard him as one who has done his work and whose life is fully open to the judgment of his time. May I be allowed to say that I think he has done some good even to that English Church to which his secession struck so heavy a blow? Newman was really the mainspring of that movement which proposed to rescue the Church from apathy, from dull easy-going quiescence, from the perfunctory discharge of formal duties, and to quicken her once again with the spirit of a priesthood, to arouse her to the living work, physical and spiritual, of an ecclesiastical sovereignty. The impulse indeed overshot itself in his case, and was misdirected in the case of Dr. Pusey, plunging blindly into Romanism with the one, degenerating into a somewhat barren symbolism with the other. But throughout the English Church in general there has been surely a higher spirit at work since that famous Oxford movement which was inspired by John Henry Newman. I think its influence has been more active, more beneficent, more human, and yet at the same time more spiritual, since that sudden and startling impulse was given. For the man himself little more needs to be said. Every one acknowledges his gifts and his virtues. No one doubts that in his marvellous change he sought only the pure truth. His theology, I presume, is not that of the readers of "The Galaxy" in general, any more than it is mine; but I trust there is none of us so narrowed to his own form of Christianity as to refuse his respect and admiration to one so highly lifted above the average of men in goodness and intellect, even though his career may have been sacrificed at the shrine of a faith that is not ours. For me, I am sometimes lost in wonder at the sacrifice, but I can only think with respect and even veneration of the man.

The younger brother needs no apology or vindication, in the United States especially. He is, be it understood, a thoroughly religious man. He has never sunk into materialism or frittered away his earnestness in mere skepticism. He is not orthodox—he has gone his own way as regards church dogma and discipline; but except in the vulgarest and narrowest application of the word, he is no "infidel." The United States owe him some good feeling, for he was one of the few eminent men in England who never were faithless to the cause of the Union, and never doubted of its ultimate triumph. I have now before me one of the most powerful arguments addressed to an English audience for the Union and against secession that reason, justice, and eloquence could frame. It is a pamphlet published in 1863 by "F. W. Newman, late Professor at University College, London," in the form of a "Letter to a Friend who had joined the Southern Independence Association." How wonderful it seems now that such arguments ever should have been needed; how few there were then in England who regarded them; how completely time has justified and sealed them as true, right, and prophetic. I read the pages over, and all the old struggle comes back with its rancors and its dangers, and I honor anew the brave man who was not afraid to stand as one of a little group, isolated, denounced, and laughed at, confiding always in justice and time.

The story of these two brothers is on the whole as strange a chapter as any I know in the biography of human intellect and creed. I think it may at least teach us a lesson of toleration, if nothing better. The very pride of intellect itself can hardly pretend to look down with mere scorn upon beliefs or errors which have carried off in contrary directions these two Newmans. The sternest bigot can scarcely refuse to admit that truthfulness and goodness may abide without the limits of his own creed, when he remembers the high and noble example of pure, true, and disinterested lives which these intellectually-sundered brothers alike have given to their fellow-men

ARCHBISHOP MANNING.

ST. JAMES'S HALL, London, is primarily a place for concerts and singers, as Exeter Hall is. But, like its venerable predecessor, St. James's Hall has come to be identified with political meetings of a certain class. Exeter Hall, a huge, gaunt, unadorned, and dreary room in the Strand, is resorted to for the most part as the arena and platform of ultra-Protestantism. St. James's Hall, a beautiful and almost lavishly ornate structure in Piccadilly, is commonly used by the leading Roman Catholics of London when they desire to make a demonstration. There are political classes which will use either place indifferently; but Exeter Hall has usually a tinge of Protestant exclusiveness about its political expression, while the ceiling of the other building has rung alike to the thrilling music of John Bright's voice, to the strident vehemence of Mr. Bradlaugh, the humdrum humming of Mr. Odger, and the clear, delicate, tremulous intonations of Stuart Mill. But I never heard of a Roman Catholic meeting of great importance being held anywhere in London lately, except in St. James's Hall.

Let us attend such a meeting there. The hall is a huge oblong, with galleries around three of the sides, and a platform bearing a splendid organ on the fourth. The room is brilliantly lighted, and the mode of lighting is peculiar and picturesque. The platform, the galleries, the body of the hall alike are crowded. This is a meeting held to make a demonstration in favor of some Roman Catholic demand—say for separate education. On the platform are the great Catholic peers, most of them men of lineage stretching back to years when Catholicism was yet unsuspicious of any possible rivalry in England. There are the Norfolks, the Denbighs, the Dormers, the Petres, the Staffords; there are such later accessions to Catholicism as the Marquis of Bute, whose change created such a sensation, and Lord Robert Montagu, who "went over" only last year. There are some recent accessions of the peerage also—Lord Acton, for instance, head of a distinguished and ancient family, but only lately called to the Upper House, and who, when Sir John Acton, won honorable fame as a writer and scholar. Lord Acton not many years ago started the "Home and Foreign Review," a quarterly periodical which endeavored to reconcile Catholicism with liberalism and science. The universal opinion of England and of Europe declared the "Home and Foreign Review" to be unsurpassed for ability, scholarship, and political information by any publication in the world. It leaped at one bound to a level with the "Edinburgh," the "Quarterly," and the "Revue des Deux Mondes." But the Pope thought the Review too liberal, and intimated that it ought to be suppressed; and Lord Acton meekly bowed his head and suppressed it in all the bloom of its growing fame. Some Irish members of Parliament are on the platform—men of station and wealth like Munsell, men of energy and brains like John Francis Maguire; perhaps, too, the handsome, brilliant-minded O'Donoghue, with his picturesque pedigree and his broken fortunes. But in general there is not a very cordial *rapprochement* between the English Catholic peers and the Irish Catholic members. Of all slow, cold, stately Conservatives in the world, the slowest, coldest, and stateliest is the English Catholic peer. Only the common bond of religion brings these two sets of men together now and then. They meet, but do not blend. In the body of the hall are the middle-class Catholics of London, the shopkeepers and clerks, mostly Irish or of Irish parentage. In the galleries are swarming the genuine Irishmen of London, the Paddies who are always threatening to interrupt Garibaldian gatherings in the parks, and who throw up their hats at the prospect of any "row" on behalf of the Pope. The chair is taken by some duke or earl, who is listened to respectfully, but without any special fervor of admiration. The English Catholics are undemonstrative in any case, and Irish Paddy does not care much about a chilly English peer. But a speaker is presently introduced who has only to make his appearance in front of the platform in order to awaken one universal burst of applause. Paddy and the Duke of Norfolk vie with each other; the steady English shopkeeper from Islington is as demonstrative as any O'Donoghue or Maguire. The meeting is wide awake and informed by one spirit and soul at last.

The man who has aroused all this emotion shrinks back almost as if he were afraid of it, although it is surely not new to him. He is a tall thin personage, some sixty-two years of age. His face is bloodless—pale as a ghost, one might say. He is so thin as to look almost cadaverous. The outlines of the face are handsome and dignified. There is much of courtly grace and refinement about the bearing and gestures of this pale, weak, and wasted man. He wears a long robe of violet silk, with some kind of dark cape or collar, and has a massive gold chain round his neck, holding attached to it a great gold cross. There is a certain nervous quivering about his eyes and lips, but otherwise he is perfectly collected and master of the occasion. His voice is thin, but wonderfully clear and penetrating. It is heard all through this great hall—a moment ago so noisy, now so silent. The words fall with a slow, quiet force, like drops of water. Whatever your opinion may be, you cannot choose but listen; and, indeed, you want only to listen and see. For this is the foremost man in the Catholic Church of England. This is the Cardinal Grandison of Disraeli's "Lothair"—Dr. Henry Edward Manning, Roman Catholic Archbishop of Westminster, successor in that office of the late Cardinal Wiseman.

It is no wonder that the Irishmen at the meeting are enthusiastic about Archbishop Manning. An Englishman of Englishmen, with no drop of Irish blood in his veins, he is more Hibernian than the Hibernians themselves in his sympathies with Ireland. A man of social position, of old family, of the highest education and the most refined instincts, he would leave the Catholic noblemen at any time to go down to his Irish teetotallers at the East End of London. He firmly believes that the salvation of England is yet to be accomplished through the influence of that religious devotion which is at the bottom of the Irish nature, and which some of us call superstition. He loves his own country dearly, but turns away from her present condition of industrial prosperity to the days before the Reformation, when yet saints trod the English soil. "In England there has been no saint since the Reformation," he said the other day, in sad, sweet tones, to one of wholly different opinions, who listened with a mingling of amazement and reverence. No views that I have ever heard put into living words embodied to anything like the same extent the full claims and pretensions of Ultramontanism. It is quite wonderful to sit and listen. One cannot but be impressed by the sweetness, the thoughtfulness, the dignity, I had almost said the sanctity of the man who thus pours forth, with a manner full of the most tranquil conviction, opinions which proclaim all modern progress a failure, and glorify the Roman priest or the Irish peasant as the true herald and repositary of light, liberty, and regeneration to a sinking and degraded world,

Years ago, Henry Edward Manning was one of the brilliant lights of the English Protestant Church. Just twenty years back he was appointed to the high place of Archdeacon of Chichester, having also, according to the manner in which the English State Church rewards its dignitaries, more than one other ecclesiastical appointment at the same time. Dr. Manning had distinguished himself highly during his career at the University of Oxford. His father was a member of the House of Commons, and Manning on starting into life had many friends and very bright prospects. Nothing would have been easier, nothing seemingly would have been more natural than for him to tread the way so plainly opened before him, and to rise to higher and higher dignity, until at last perhaps the princely renown of a bishopric and a seat in the House of Lords would have been his reward. But Dr. Manning's career was cast in a time of stress and trial for the English State Church. I have described briefly in a former article the origin, growth, and effects of that remarkable movement which, beginning within the Church itself and seeking to establish loftier claims for her than she had long put forward, ended by convulsing her in a manner more troublous than any religious crisis which had occurred since the Reformation. Dr. Manning's is evidently a nature which must have been specially allured by what I may be allowed to call the supernatural claims put forward on behalf of the Church of England. He was of course correspondingly disappointed by what he considered the failure of those claims. As Coleridge says that every man is born an Aristotelian or a Platonist, so it may perhaps be said that every man is born with a predisposition to lean either on natural or supernatural laws in the direct guidance of life. I am not now raising any religious question whatever. What I say may be said of members of the same sect or church—of any sect, of any church. One man, as faithful and devout a believer as any, is yet content to go through his daily duties and fulfil his career trusting to his religious principles, his insight, and his reason, without requiring at every moment the light of spiritual or supernatural guidance. Another must always have his world in direct communion with the spiritual, or it is no world of faith to him. Now it is impossible to look in Dr. Manning's face without seeing that his is one of those sensitive, spiritual, I had almost said morbid natures, which can find no endurable existence without a close and constant communion with the supernatural. Keble, Newman, Time and the Hour, called out for the assertion of the claim that the Church of England was the true heir of the apostolic succession. Such a nature as Manning's must have delightedly welcomed the claim. But the mere investigation sent, as I have already explained, one Newman to Catholicism and the other to Rationalism. Dr. Manning, too, felt compelled to ask himself whether the Church could make good its claim, and whether, if it could not, he had any longer a place within its walls. The change does not appear to have come so rapidly to fulfilment with him as with John Henry Newman. Dr. Manning seems to me to have a less aggressive temperament than his distinguished predecessor in secession. There is more about him of the quietist, of the ecstatic, so far as religious thought is concerned, while it is possible that he may be a more practical and influential guide in the mere policy of the church to which he belongs. There is an amount of scorn in Newman's nature which sometimes reminds one of Pascal, and which I have not observed in Dr. Manning or in his writings. I cannot imagine Dr. Manning, for example, pelting Charles Kingsley with sarcasms and overwhelming him with contempt, as Dr. Newman evidently delighted to do in the famous controversy which was provoked by the apostle of Muscular Christianity. I suppose therefore that Dr. Manning clung for a long time to the faith in which he was bred. But his whole nature is evidently cast in the mould which makes Roman Catholic devotees. He is a man of the type which perhaps found in Fénelon its most illustrious example. I think it is not too much to say that to him that light of private judgment which some of us regard as man's grandest and most peculiarly divine attribute, must always have presented itself as something abhorrent to his nature. I am judging, of course, as an outsider and as one little acquainted with theological subjects; but my impression of the two men would be that Dr. Newman joined the Roman Catholic Church in obedience to some compulsion of reason, acting in what must seem to most of us an inscrutable manner, and that Dr. Manning never would have been a Protestant at all if he had not believed that the Protestant Church was truly all which its rival claims to be.

Dr. Manning in fact did not leave the Church. The Church left him. He had misunderstood it. It became revealed at last as it really is, a church founded on the right of private judgment, and Manning was appalled and turned away from it. Something that may almost be called accident brought home to his mind the true character of the Church to which he belonged. Many readers of "The Galaxy" may have some recollection of the once celebrated Gorham case in England—a case which I shall not now describe any further than by saying that it raised the question whether the Church of England can prescribe the religion of the State. Had the Church the right to decide whether certain doctrine taught by one of its clergy was heretical, and to condemn it if so declared? In England, Church and State are so bound up together, that it is practically the State and not the Church which decides whether this or that teaching is heresy or true religion. A lord chancellor who may be an infidel, and two or three "law lords" who may be anything or nothing, settle the question in the end. We all remember the epigram about Lord Chancellor Westbury, the least godly of men, having "dismissed Hell with costs," and taken away from the English Protestant "his last hope of damnation." The Gorham case, twenty years ago, showed that the Church, as an ecclesiastical body, had no power to condemn heresy. This, to men like Stuart Mill, appears on the whole a satisfactory condition of things so long as there is a State Church, for the plain reason which he gives—namely, that the State in England is now far more liberal than the Church. But to Dr. Manning the idea of the Church thus abdicating its function of interpreting and declaring doctrine was equivalent to the renunciation of its right to existence. He strove hard to bring about an organized and solemn declaration and protest from the Church—a declaration of doctrine, a protest against secular control. He became the leader of an effort in this direction. The effort met with little support. The then Bishop of London did indeed introduce a bill into the House of Lords for the purpose of enacting that in matters of doctrine, as distinct from questions of mere law, the final decision should rest with the prelates. Dr. Manning sat in the gallery of the House of Lords on that memorable night. The Bishop of London wholly failed. The House of Lords scouted the idea of liberal England tolerating a sort of ecclesiastical inquisition. Every one admitted the anomalous condition in which things then were placed; but few indeed would think of enacting a dogma of infallibility in favor of the bishops of the Church. Lord Brougham spoke against the bill with what Dr. Manning himself admits to be plain English common sense. He said the House of Lords through its law peers could decide questions of mere ecclesiastical law, and the decisions would carry weight and authority; but neither peers nor bishops could in England decide a question of doctrine. Suppose, he asked, the bishops were divided equally on such a question, where would the decision be then? Suppose there was a very small majority, who would accept such a decision? Or even suppose there was a large majority, but that the minority comprised the few men of greatest knowledge, ability, and authority, what value would attach to the judgment of such a majority? The bill was a hopeless failure. Dr. Manning has himself described with equal candor and clearness the effect which the debate had upon him. He mentally supplemented Lord Brougham's questions by one other. Suppose that all the bishops of the Church of England should decide unanimously on any doctrine, would any one receive the decision as infallible? He was compelled to answer, "No one." The Church of England had no pretension to be the infallible spiritual guide of men. Were she to raise any such pretension, it would be rejected with contempt by the common mind of the nation. Hear then how this conviction affected the man who up to that time had had no thought but for the interests and duties of the English Church. "To those," he has himself told us, "who believed that God has established upon the earth a divine and therefore an unerring guardian and teacher of his faith, this event demonstrated that the Church of England could not be that guardian and teacher."

While Dr. Manning was still uncertain whither to turn, the celebrated "Papal aggression" took place. Cardinal Wiseman was sent to England by the Pope, with the title of Archbishop of Westminster. All England raged. Earl Russell wrote his famous "Durham Letter." The Lord Chancellor Campbell, at a public dinner in the city of London, called up a storm of enthusiasm by quoting the line from Shakespeare, which declares that

Under our feet we'll stamp the cardinal's hat.

Protestant zealots in Stockport belabored the Roman Catholics and sacked their houses; Irish laborers in Birkenhead retorted upon the Protestants. The Government brought in the Ecclesiastical Titles Bill—a measure making it penal for any Catholic prelate to call himself archbishop or bishop of any place in England. Let him be "Archbishop Wiseman" or "Cardinal Wiseman, Archbishop of Mesopotamia," as long as he liked—but not Archbishop of Westminster or Tuam. The bill was powerfully, splendidly opposed by Gladstone, Bright, and Cobden, on the broad ground that it invaded the precincts of religious liberty; but it was carried and made law. There it remained. There never was the slightest attempt made to enforce it. The Catholic prelates held to the titles the Pope had given them; and no English court, judge, magistrate or policeman ever offered to prevent or punish them. So ludicrous, so barren a proceeding as the carrying of that measure has not been known in the England of our time.

Cardinal Wiseman was an able and a discreet man. He was calm, plausible, powerful. He was very earnest in the cause of his Church, but he seemed much more like a man of the world than Newman or Dr. Manning. There was little of the loftily spiritual in his manner or appearance. His bulky person and swollen face suggested at the first glance a sort of Abbot Boniface; he was, I believe, in reality an ascetic. The corpulence which seemed the result of good living was only the effect of ill health. He had a persuasive and an imposing way. His ability was singularly flexible. His eloquence was often too gorgeous and ornamental for a pure taste, but when the occasion needed he could address an audience in language of the simplest and most practical common sense. The same adaptability, if I may use such a word, was evident in all he did. He would talk with a cabinet minister on terms of calm equality, as if his rank must be self-evident, and he delighted to set a band of poor school children playing around him. He was a cosmopolitan—English and Irish by extraction, Spanish by birth, Roman by education. When he spoke English he was exactly like what a portly, dignified British bishop ought to be—a John Bull in every respect. When he spoke Italian at Rome he fell instinctively and at once into all the peculiarities of intonation and gesture which distinguish the people of Italy from all other races. When he conversed in Spanish he subsided into the grave, somewhat saturnine dignity and repose of the true Castilian. All this, I presume, was but the natural effect of that flexibility of temperament I have attempted to describe. I had but slight personal acquaintance with Cardinal Wiseman, and I paint him only as he impressed me, a casual observer. I am satisfied that he was a profoundly earnest and single-minded man; the testimony of many whom I know and who knew him well compels me to that conviction. But such was not the impression he would have left on a mere acquaintance. He seemed rather one who could, for a purpose which he believed great, be all things to all men. He impressed me quite differently from the manner in which I have been impressed by John Henry Newman and by Archbishop Manning. He reminded one of some great, capable, worldly-wise, astute Prince of the Church of other generations, politician rather than priest, more ready to sustain and skilled to defend the temporal power of the Papacy than to illustrate its highest spiritual influence.

The events which brought Cardinal Wiseman to England had naturally a powerful effect upon the mind of Dr. Manning. It was the renewed claim of the Roman Church to enfold England in its spiritual jurisdiction. For Dr. Manning, who had just seen what he regarded as the voluntary abdication of the English Church, the claim would in any case have probably been decisive. It "stepped between him and his fighting soul." But the personal influence of Cardinal Wiseman had likewise an immense weight and force. Dr. Manning ever since that time entertained a feeling of the profoundest devotion and reverence for Cardinal Wiseman. The change was consummated in 1851, and one of the first practical comments upon the value of the Ecclesiastical Titles Act was the announcement that a scholar and divine of whom the Protestant Church had long been especially proud had resigned his preferments, his dignities, and his prospects, and passed over to the Church of Rome. I cannot better illustrate the effect produced on the public mind than by saying that even the secession of John Henry Newman hardly made a deeper impression.

Dr. Manning, of course, rose to high rank in the church of his adoption He became Roman of the Romans—Ultramontane of the Ultramontanes. On the death of his friend and leader, Cardinal Wiseman, whose funeral sermon he preached, Henry Manning became Archbishop of Westminster. Except for his frequent journeys to Rome, he has always since his appointment lived in London. Although a good deal of an ascetic, as his emaciated face and figure would testify, he is nothing of a hermit. He mingles to a certain extent in society, he takes part in many public movements, and he has doubtless given Mr. Disraeli ample opportunity of studying his manner and bearing. I don't believe Mr. Disraeli capable of understanding the profound devotion and single-minded sincerity of the man. A more singular, striking, marvellous figure does not stand out, I think, in our English society. Everything that an ordinary Englishman or American would regard as admirable and auspicious in the progress of our civilization, Dr. Manning calmly looks upon as lamentable and evil-omened. What we call progress is to his mind decay. What we call light is to him darkness. What we reverence as individual liberty he deplores as spiritual slavery. The mere fact that a man gives reasons for his faith seems shocking to this strangely-gifted apostle of unconditional belief. Though you were to accept on bended knees ninety-nine of the decrees of Rome, you would still be in his mind a heretic if you paused to consider as to the acceptance of the hundredth dogma. All the peculiarly modern changes in the legislation of England, the admission of Jews to Parliament, the introduction of the principle of divorce, the practical recognition of the English divine's right of private judgment, are painful and odious to him. I have never heard from any other source anything so clear, complete, and astonishing as his cordial acceptance of the uttermost claims of Rome; the prostration of all reason and judgment before the supposed supernatural attributes of the Papal throne. In one of the finest passages of his own writings he says: "My love for England begins with the England of St. Bede. Saxon England, with all its tumults, seems to me saintly and beautiful. Norman England I have always loved less, because, although majestic, it became continually less Catholic, until the evil spirit of the world broke off the light yoke of faith at the so-called Reformation. Still I loved the Christian England which survived, and all the lingering outlines of diocese and parishes, cathedrals and churches, with the names of saints upon them. It is this vision of the past which still hovers over England and makes it beautiful and full of the memories of the kingdom of God. Nay, I loved the parish church of my childhood and the college chapel of my youth, and the little church under a green hillside where the morning and evening prayers and the music of the English Bible for seventeen years became a part of my soul. Nothing is more beautiful in the natural order, and if there were no eternal world I could have made it my home." To Dr. Manning the time when saints walked the earth of England is more of a reality than the day before yesterday to most of us. Where the ordinary eye sees only a poor, ignorant Irish peasant, Dr. Manning discerns a heaven-commissioned bearer of light and truth, destined by the power of his unquestioning faith to redeem perhaps, in the end, even English philosophers and statesmen. When it was said in the praise of the murdered Archbishop of Paris that he was disposed to regret the introduction of the dogma of infallibility, Archbishop Manning came eagerly to the rescue of his friend's memory, and as one would vindicate a person unjustly accused of crime, he vindicated the dead Archbishop from the stigma of having for a moment dared to have an opinion of his own on such a subject. Of course, if Dr. Manning were an ordinary theological devotee or fanatic, there would be nothing remarkable in all this. But he is a man of the widest culture, of high intellectual gifts, of keen and penetrating judgment in all ordinary affairs, remarkable for his close and logical argument, his persuasive reasoning, and for a genial, quiet kind of humor which seems especially calculated to dissolve sophistry by its action. He is an English gentleman, a man of the world; he was educated at Oxford with Arthur Pendennis and young Lord Magnus Charters; he lives at York Place in the London of to-day; he drives down to the House of Commons and talks politics in the lobby with Gladstone and Lowe; he meets Disraeli at dinner parties, and is on friendly terms, I dare say, with Huxley and Herbert Spencer; he reads the newspapers, and I make no doubt is now well acquainted with the history of the agitation against Tammany and Boss Tweed. I think such a man is a marvellous phenomenon in our age. It is as if one of the mediæval saints from the stained windows of a church should suddenly become infused with life and take a part in all the ways of our present world, I can understand the long-abiding power of the Catholic Church when I remember that I have heard and seen and talked with Henry Edward Manning.

Dr. Manning is not, I fancy, very much of a political reformer. His inclinations would probably be rather conservative than otherwise. He is drawn toward Gladstone and the Liberal party less by distinct political affinity, of which there is but little, than by his hope and belief that through Gladstone something will be done for that Ireland which to this Oxford scholar is still the "island of the saints." The Catholic members of Parliament, whether English or Irish, consult Archbishop Manning constantly upon all questions connected with education or religion. His parlor in York Place—not far from where Mme. Tussaud's wax-work exhibition attracts the country visitor—is the frequent scene of conferences which have their influence upon the action of the House of Commons. He is a devoted upholder of the doctrine of total abstinence from intoxicating drinks; and he is the only Englishman of real influence and ability, except Francis Newman, who is in favor of prohibitory legislation. He is the medium of communication between Rome and England; the living link of connection between the English Catholic peer and the Irish Catholic bricklayer. The position which he occupies is at all events quite distinctive. There is nobody else in England who could set up the faintest claim to any such place. It would be superfluous to remark that I do not expect the readers of "The Galaxy" to have any sympathy with the opinions, theological or political, of such a man. But the man himself is worthy of profound interest, of study, and even of admiration. He is the spirit, the soul, the ideal of mediæval faith embodied in the form of a living English scholar and gentleman. He represents and illustrates a movement the most remarkable, possibly the most portentous, which has disturbed England and the English Church since the time of Wyckliffe. No one can have any real knowledge of the influences at work in English life to-day, no one can understand the history of the past twenty years, or even pretend to conjecture as to the possibilities of the future, who has not paid some attention to the movement which has Dr. Manning for one of its most distinguished leaders, and to the position and character of Manning himself.

JOHN RUSKIN.

ANY one who has visited the National Gallery in London must have seen, and seeing must have studied, the contrasted paintings placed side by side of Turner and of Claude. They will attract attention if only because the two Turners are thus placed apart from the rooms used as a Turner Gallery, and containing the great collection of the master's works. The pictures of which I am now speaking are hung in a room principally occupied by the paintings of Murillo. As you enter you are at once attracted by four large pictures which hang on either side of the door opposite. On the right are Turner's "Dido Building Carthage," and Claude's "Embarkation of the Queen of Sheba." On the left are a "Landscape with the Sun Rising" by Turner, and "The Marriage of Isaac and Rebecca" by Claude. Nobody could fail to observe that the pictures are thus arranged for some distinct purpose. They are in fact placed side by side for the sake of comparison and contrast. They are all eminently characteristic; they have the peculiar faults and the peculiar merits of the artists. In the Claudes we have even one of those yellow trunks which are the abomination of the critic I am about to speak of, and one might almost suppose that the Queen of Sheba was embarking for Saratoga. I do not propose to criticise the pictures; but in them you have, to the full, Turner and Claude.

Now in the contrast between these pictures may be found, symbolically at least, the origin and motive of John Ruskin's career. He sprang into literary life simply as a vindicator of the fame and genius of Turner. But as he went on with his task he found, or at least he convinced himself, that the vindication of the great painter was essentially a vindication of all true art. Still further proceeding with his self-imposed task, he persuaded himself that the cause of true art was identical with the cause of truth, and that truth, from Ruskin's point of view, enclosed in the same rules and principles all the morals, all the politics, all the science, industry, and daily business of life. Therefore from an art-critic he became a moralist, a political economist, a philosopher, a statesman, a preacher—anything, everything that human intelligence can impel a man to be. All that he has written since his first appeal to the public has been inspired by this conviction—that an appreciation of the truth in art reveals to him who has it the truth in everything. This belief has been the source of Mr. Ruskin's greatest successes and of his most complete and ludicrous failures. It has made him the admiration of the world one week, and the object of its placid pity or broad laughter the next. A being who could be Joan of Arc to-day and Voltaire's Pucelle to-morrow would hardly exhibit a stronger psychical paradox than the eccentric genius of Mr. Ruskin commonly displays. But in order to understand him, or to do him common justice—in order not to regard him as a mere erratic utterer of eloquent contradictions, poured out on the impulse of each moment's new freak of fancy—we must always bear in mind this fundamental faith of the man. Extravagant as this or that doctrine may be, outrageous as to-day's contradiction of yesterday's assertion may be, yet the whole career is consistent with its essential principles and belief.

Ruskin was singularly fitted by fortune to live for a purpose; to consecrate his life to the cause of art and of what he considered truth. As everybody knows, he was born to wealth so considerable as to allow him to indulge all his tastes and whims, and to write without any regard for money profit. I hardly know of any other author of eminence who in our time has worked with so complete an independence of publisher, public, or paymaster. I do not suppose Ruskin ever wrote one line for money. Some of his works must have brought him in a good return of mere pounds and shillings; but they would have been written just the same if they had never paid for printing; and indeed the author is always spending money on some benevolent crotchet. He was born in London, and he himself attributes much of his early love for nature to the fact that he was "accustomed for two or three years to no other prospect than that of the brick walls over the way," and that he had "no brothers nor sisters nor companions." I question whether anybody not acquainted with London can understand how completely one can be shut in from the pure face of free nature in that vast city. In New York one can hardly walk far in any direction without catching glimpses of the water and the shores of New Jersey or Long Island. But in some of the most respectable middle-class regions of London, you might drudge away or dream away your life and never have one sight of open nature unless you made a regular expedition to find her. Ruskin speaks somewhere of the strange and exquisite delight which the cockney feels when he treads on grass; and every biographical sketch of him recalls that passage in his writings which tells us of the first thing he could remember as an event in his life—his being taken by his nurse to the brow of one of the crags overlooking Derwentwater, and the "intense joy, mingled with awe, that I had in looking through the hollows in the mossy roots over the crag into the dark lake, and which has associated itself more or less with all twining roots of trees ever since." Ruskin travelled much, and at a very early age, through Europe. He became familiar with most of the beautiful show-places of the European Continent when a boy, and I believe he never extended the sphere of his travels. About his early life there is little to be said. He completed his education at Oxford, and, more successful than Arthur Pendennis, he went in for a prize poem and won the prize. He visited the Continent, more especially Switzerland and Italy, again and again. He married a Scottish lady, and the marriage was not a happy one. I don't propose to go into any of the scandal and talk which the events created; but I may say that the marriage was dissolved without any moral blame resting on or even imputed to either of the parties, and that the lady afterwards became the wife of Mr. Millais. Since then Mr. Ruskin has led a secluded rather than a lonely life. His constitution is feeble; he has as little robustness of *physique* as can well be conceived, and no kind of excitement is suitable for him. Only the other day he sank into a condition of such exhaustion that for a while it was believed impossible he could recover. At one time he used to appear in public rather often; and was ready to deliver lectures on the ethics of art wherever he thought his teaching could benefit the ignorant or the poor. He was especially ready to address assemblages of workingmen, the pupils of charitable institutions for the teaching of drawing. I cannot remember his ever having taken part in any fashionable pageant or demonstration of any kind. Of late he has ceased to show himself at any manner of public meeting, and he addresses his favorite workingmen through the medium of an irregular little publication, a sort of periodical or tract which he calls "Fors Clavigera." Of this publication "I send a copy," he announces, "to each of the principal journals and periodicals, to be noticed or not at their pleasure; otherwise, I shall use no advertisements." The author also informs us that "the tracts will be sold for sevenpence each, without abatement on quantity." I doubt whether many sales have taken place, or whether the reference to purchase in quantity was at all necessary, or whether indeed the author cared one way or the other. In one of these printed letters he says: "The scientific men are busy as ants, examining the sun and the moon and the seven stars; and can tell me all about them, I believe, by this time, and how they move and what they are made of. And I do not care, for my part, two copper spangles how they move nor what they are made of. I can't move them any other way than they go, nor make them of anything else better than they are made." This might sound wonderfully sharp and practical, if, a few pages on, Mr. Ruskin did not broach his proposition for the founding of a little model colony of labor in England, where boys and girls alike are to be taught agriculture, vocal music, Latin, and the history of five cities—Athens, Rome, Venice, Florence, and London. This scheme was broached last August, and it is rather soon yet even to ask whether any steps have been taken to put it into execution; but Mr. Ruskin has already given five thousand dollars to begin with, and will probably give a good deal more before he acknowledges the inevitable failure. Ruskin lives in one of the most beautiful of London suburbs, on Denmark Hill, at the south side of the river, near Dulwich and the exquisite Sydenham slopes where the Crystal Palace stands. Here he indulges his love of pictures and statues, and of rest—when he is not in the mood for unrest—and nourishes philanthropic schemes of eccentric kinds, and is altogether about the nearest approach to an independent, self-sufficing philosopher our modern days have known. Of his life as a private citizen this much is about all that it concerns us to hear.

Twenty-eight years have passed away since Mr. Ruskin leaped into the critical arena, with a spring as bold and startling as that of Edward Kean on the Kemble-haunted stage. The little volume, so modest in its appearance, so self-sufficient in its tone, which the author defiantly flung down like a gage of battle before the world, was entitled "Modern Painters: their Superiority in the Art of Landscape Painting to all the Ancient Masters. By a Graduate of Oxford." I was a boy of thirteen, living in a small provincial town, when this book made its first appearance, but it seems to me that the echo of the sensation it created still rings in my ears. It was a challenge to all established beliefs and prejudices; and the challenge was delivered in the tones of one who felt confident that he could make good his words against any and all opponents. If there was one thing that more than another seemed to have been fixed and rooted in the English mind, it was that Claude and one or two other of the old masters possessed the secret of landscape painting. When, therefore, this bold young dogmatist involved in one common denunciation "Claude, Gaspar Poussin, Salvator Rosa, Ruysdael, Paul Potter, Cavaletto, and the various Van-Somethings and Koek-Somethings, more especially and malignantly those who have libelled the sea," it was no wonder that affronted authority raised its indignant voice and thundered at him. Affronted authority, however, gained little by its thunder. The young Oxford graduate possessed, along with genius and profound conviction, an imperturbable and magnificent self-conceit, against which the surges of angry criticism dashed themselves in vain. Mr. Ruskin, when putting on his armor, had boasted himself as one who takes it off; but in his case there proved to be little rashness in the premature fortification. For assuredly that book overrode and bore down its critics. I need not follow it through its various editions, its successive volumes, its amplifications, wherein at last the original design, the vindication of Turner, swelled into an enunciation and illustration of the true principles of landscape art. Nor do

I mean to say that the book carried all its points. Far from it. Claude still lives, and Salvator Rosa has his admirers, among whom most of us are very glad to enroll ourselves; and Ruskin himself has since that time pointed out many serious defects in Turner, and has unsaid a great deal of what he then proclaimed. But if the Oxford graduate had been wrong in every illustration of his principal doctrine, I should still hold that the doctrine itself was true and of inestimable value, and that the book was a triumph. For, I think, it proclaimed and firmly established the true point of view from which we must judge of the art of painting in all its departments. In plain words, Ruskin taught the English public that they must look at nature with their own eyes, and judge of art by the help of nature. Up to the publication of that book England, at least, had been falling into the way of regarding art as a sort of polite school to which it was our duty to endeavor to make nature conform. Conventionality and apathy had sunk apparently into the very souls of men and women. Hardly one in ten thousand ever really saw a landscape, a wave, a ray of the sun as it is. Nobody used his own eyes. Every one was content to think that he saw what the painters told him he saw. Ruskin himself tells us somewhere about a test question which used to be put to young landscape painters by one who was supposed to be a master of the craft: "Where do you put your brown tree?" The question illustrates the whole theory and school of conventionality. Conventionality had decreed first that there are brown trees, and next that there cannot be a respectable landscape without a brown tree. Long after the teaching of Ruskin had well-nigh revolutionized opinion in England, I stood once with a lover of art of the old-fashioned school, looking on one of the most beautiful and famous scenes in England. The tender autumn season, the melancholy woods in the background, the little lake, the half-ruined abbey, did not even need the halo of poetic and romantic association which hung around them in order to render the scene a very temptation, one might have thought, to the true artist. I suggested something of the kind. My companion shook his head almost contemptuously. "You could never make a picture of that," he said. I pressed him to tell me why so picturesque a scene could not be represented somehow in a picture. He did not care evidently to argue with ignorance, and he even endeavored to concede something to my untutored whim. "Perhaps," he began with hesitation, "if one were to put a large dark tree in there to the left, one might make something of it. But no" (he had done his best and could not humor me any further), "it is out of the question; there couldn't be a picture made out of *that*." How could I illustrate more clearly the kind of thing which Ruskin came to put down and did put down in England?

Of course Mr. Ruskin was never a man to do anything by halves, and having once laid down the canon that nature and truth are to be the guides of the artist, he soon began to write and to think as if nature and truth alone were concerned. He seemed to have taken no account of the fact that one great object of art is simply to give delight, and that however natural and truthful an artist may be, yet he is to bear in mind this one purpose of his work, or he might almost as well let it alone. Nature and truth are to be his guides to the delighting of men; to show him how he is to give a delight which shall be pure and genuine. A single inaccuracy as to fact seems at one time to have spoiled all Mr. Ruskin's enjoyment of a painting, and filled him with a feeling of scorn and detestation for it. He denounces Raphael's "Charge to Peter," on the ground that the apostles are not dressed as men of that time and place would have been when going out fishing; and he makes no allowance for the fact, pointed out by M. Taine, that Raphael's design first of all was to represent a group of noble, serious men, majestic and picturesque, and that mere realism entered little into his purpose. It may seem the oddest thing to compare Ruskin with Macaulay, but it is certain that the very kind of objection which the former urges against the paintings of Raphael the latter brings forward against one of the poems of Goldsmith. "What would be thought of a painter," asks Macaulay, "who would mix January and August in one landscape, who would introduce a frozen river into a harvest scene? Would it be a sufficient defence of such a picture to say that every part was exquisitely colored; that the green hedges, the apple trees loaded with fruit, the wagons reeling under the yellow sheaves, and the sunburned reapers wiping their foreheads, were very fine; and that the ice and the boys sliding were also very fine? To such a picture the 'Deserted Village' bears a great resemblance." Now it would indeed be an incomprehensible mistake if a painter were to mix up August and January as Macaulay suggests, or to depict the apostles like a group of Greek philosophers, as in Ruskin's opinion Raphael did. But I venture to think that even the extraordinary blunder mentioned in the first part of the sentence would not necessarily condemn a picture to utter contempt. It was a great mistake to make Dido and Iulus contemporaries; a great mistake to represent angels employing gunpowder for the suppression of Lucifer's insurrection; a great mistake to talk of the clock having struck in the time of Julius Cæsar. Yet I suppose Virgil and Milton and Shakespeare were great poets, and that the very passages in which those errors occur are nevertheless genuine poetry. Now Ruskin criticises Raphael and Claude on precisely the principle which would declare Virgil, Milton, and Shakespeare worthless because of the errors I have mentioned. The errors are errors no doubt, and ought to be pointed out, and there an end. Virgil was not writing a history of the foundation of Carthage. Shakespeare was not describing the social life of Rome under Julius Cæsar. Milton was not a gazetteer of the revolt of Lucifer and his angels. Mr. Ruskin might as well dispose of a sculptured group of Centaurs by remarking that there never were Centaurs, or of the famous hermaphrodite in the Louvre by explaining that hermaphrodites of that perfect order are unknown to physiology. The beauty of color and contour, the effect of graceful grouping, the reach of poetic imagination, the dignity of embodied thought, outlive all such criticism even when in its way it is just, for they bear in themselves the vindication of their existence. But Ruskin's criticism is the legitimate result of the cardinal error of his career—the belief that the morality of art exactly corresponds with the morality of human life; that there is a central law of right and wrong for everything, like Stephen Pearl Andrews's universal science, of which when you have once got the key you can open every lock—which is the solving word of every enigma, the standard by which everything is finally to be judged. I need not show how he followed out that creed and gave it a new application in "The Seven Lamps of Architecture" and the "Stones of Venice." In these masterpieces of eloquent declamation, the building of houses was brought up to be tried according to Mr. Ruskin's self-constructed canons of æsthetic and architectural morality. No one, I venture to think, cares much about the doctrine; everybody is carried away by the eloquence, the originality, and the feeling. Later still Mr. Ruskin applied the same central, all-pervading principle to the condemnation of fluttering ribbons in a woman's bonnet. The stucco of a house he set down as false and immoral, like the painting of a meretricious cheek. His æsthetic transcendentalism soon ceased to have any practical influence. It would be idle to try to persuade English house-builders that the attributes of a building are moral qualities, and that the component parts of a London residence ought to symbolize and embody "action," "voice," and "beauty." It may be doubted whether a single architect was ever practically influenced by the dogmatic eloquence of Mr. Ruskin. In fact the architects, above all other men, rebelled against the books and scorned them. But the books made their way with the public, who, caring nothing about the principles of morality which underlie the construction of houses, were charmed by the dazzling rhetoric, the wealth of gorgeous imagery, the interesting and animated digressions, the frequent flashes of vigorous good sense, and the lofty thought whose only fault was that which least affected the ordinary reader—its utter inapplicability to the practical subject of the books.

It was about the year 1849 that that great secession movement in art broke out to which its leaders chose to give the title of pre-Raphaelite. The principal founder of the movement has since been almost forgotten as an artist, but has come into a sort of celebrity as a poet—Mr. Dante Gabriel Rossetti. With him were allied, it is almost needless to say, the two now famous and successful painters, Holman Hunt and Millais. Decidedly that was the most thriving controversy in the world of art and letters during our time. It was the only battle of schools which could tell us what the war for and against the Sturm-und-Drang school in Germany, the Byron epoch in England, the struggle of the Classicists and Romanticists in France, must have been like. The pre-Raphaelite dispute has long ceased to be heard. Years ago Mr. Ruskin himself, the prophet and apostle of the new sect, described the defection of its greatest pupil as "not a fall, but a catastrophe." Rossetti's sonnets are criticised, but not his paintings. "Are not you still a pre-Raphaelite?" asked an inquisitive person lately of the sonneteer. "I am not an 'ite' of any kind," was the answer; "I am an artist." John Everett Millais is among the most fortunate and fashionable painters of the day. Those who saw his wonderful "Somnambulist" in last season's exhibition of the London Royal Academy would have found in it little of the harsh and "crawling realism" which distinguished the "Beauty in Bricks Brotherhood," as somebody called the rebellious school of twenty years ago. A London comic paper lately published a capital likeness of Mr. Millais, handsome, respectable, tending to stoutness and baldness, and described the portrait as that of the converted pre-Raphaelite. The progress of things was exactly similar to that which goes on in the English political world so often. A fiery young Radical member of Parliament begins by denouncing the Government and the constitution. He wins first notoriety, and then, if he has any real stuff in him, reputation; and then he is invited to office, and he takes it and becomes respectable, wealthy, and fashionable; and his rebellion is all over, and the world goes on just as before. Such was, so far as individuals are concerned, the course of the pre-Raphaelite rebellion; undoubtedly the movement did some good; most rebellions do. It was a protest against the vague and feeble generalizations and the vapid classicism which were growing too common in art. Ruskin himself has happily described the generalized and conventional way of painting trees and shrubs which was growing to be common and tolerated, and which he says was no less absurd than if a painter were to depict some anomalous animal, and defend it as a generalization of pig and pony. Anything which teaches a careful and rigid study of nature must do good. The pre-Raphaelite school was excellent discipline for its young scholars. Probably even those of Millais's paintings which bear on the face of them least evident traces of that early school, might have been far inferior to what they are, were it not for the slow and severe study which the original principles of the movement demanded. The present interest which the secession has for me is less on its own account than because of the vigorous, ingenious, and eloquent pages which Ruskin poured forth in its vindication. He gave it meanings which it never had; found out truth and beauty in its most prosaic details such as its working scholars never meant to symbolize; he explained and expounded it as Johnson did the meaning of the word "slow" in the opening line of the "Traveller," and in fact well-nigh persuaded himself and the world that a new priesthood had arisen to teach the divinity of art. But even he could not write pre-Raphaelitism into popularity and vitality. The common instinct of human nature, which looks to art as the representative of beauty, pathos, humor, and passion, could not be talked into an acceptance of ignoble and ugly realisms. It may be an error to depict a Judean fisherman like a stately Greek philosopher; but error for error, it is far less gross and grievous than to paint the exquisite heroine of Keats's lovely poem as a lank and scraggy spinster, with high cheek bones like one of Walter Scott's fishwives, undressing herself in a green moonlight, and displaying a neck and shoulders worthy of Miss Miggs, and stays and petticoat that bring to mind Tilly Slowboy.

The pre-Raphaelite mania faded away, but Ruskin's vindication endures; just as the letters of Pascal are still read by every one, although nobody cares "two copper spangles" about the controversy which provoked them. Mr. Ruskin's mental energy did not long lie fallow. Turning the bull's-eye of his central theory upon other subjects, he dragged political economy up for judgment. Who can forget the whimsical sensation produced by the appearance in the "Cornhill Magazine" of the letters entitled "Unto this Last"? I need not say much about them. They were a series of fantastic sermons, sometimes eloquent and instructive, sometimes turgid and absurd, on the moral duty of man. They had literally nothing to do with the subject of political economy. The political economists were talking of one thing, and Mr. Ruskin was talking of another and a totally different thing. The value of an article is what it will bring in the market, say the economists. "For shame!" cries Mr. Ruskin; "is the value of her rudder to a ship at sea in a tempest only what it would be bought for at home in Wapping?" So on through the whole, the two disputants talking on quite different subjects. Mr. Ruskin might just as reasonably have interrupted a medical professor lecturing to his class on the effects and uses of castor oil, by telling him in eloquent verbiage that castor oil will not make men virtuous and nations great. Nobody ever said it would; but it is important to explain the properties of castor oil for all that. It would be a grand thing of course if, as Mr. Ruskin prayed, England would "cast all thoughts of possessive wealth back to the barbaric nations among whom they first arose," and leave "the sands of the Indus and the adamant of Golconda" to "stiffen the housings of the charger, and flash from the turban of the slave." This would be ever so much finer than opening banks, making railways (which Mr. Ruskin specially detests), and dealing in stocks. But it has nothing to do, good or bad, with the practical exposition of the economic laws of banking and exchange. It is about as effective a refutation of the political economist's doctrines as a tract from the Peace Society denouncing all war would be to a lecture from Von Moltke on the practical science of campaigning. But Mr. Ruskin never saw this, and never was disconcerted. He turned to other missions with the firm conviction that he had finished off political economy, as a clever free-thinking London lady calmly announced a few years back to her friends that she had abolished Christianity. Then Mr. Ruskin condemned mines and factories, railways and engines. With all the same strenuous and ornate eloquence he passed sentence on London pantomimes and "cascades of girls," and the too liberal exposure of "lower limbs" by the young ladies composing those cascades. Nothing is too trivial for the omniscient philosopher, and nothing is too great. The moral government of a nation is decreed by the same voice and on the same principles as those which have prescribed the length of a lady's waist-ribbon and the shape of a door-scraper. The first Napoleon never claimed for himself the divine right of intermeddling with and arranging everything more complacently than does the mild and fragile philosopher of Denmark Hill. Be it observed that his absolute ignorance of a subject never deters Mr. Ruskin from pronouncing prompt judgment upon it. It may be some complicated question of foreign, say of American politics, on which men of good ability, who have mastered all the facts and studied the arguments on both sides, are slow to pronounce. Mr. Ruskin, boldly acknowledging that until this morning he never heard of the subject, settles it out of hand and delivers final judgment. Sometimes his restless impulses and his extravagant way of plunging at conclusions and conjecturing facts lead him into unpleasant predicaments. He delivered a manifesto some years ago upon the brutality of the lower orders of Englishmen, founded on certain extraordinary persecutions inflicted on his friend Thomas Carlyle. Behold Carlyle himself coming out with a letter in which he declares that all these stories of persecution were not only untrue, but were "curiously the reverse of truth." Of course every one knew that Ruskin believed them to be true; that he half heard something, conjectured something else, jumped at a conclusion, and as usual regarded himself as an inspired prophet, compelled by his mission to come forward and deliver judgment on a sinful people.

Mr. Ruskin's devotion to Carlyle has been unfortunate for him, as it has for so many others. For that which is reality in Carlyle is only echo and imitation in Ruskin, and the latter has power enough and a field wide enough of his own to render inexcusable the attempt to follow slavishly another man. Moreover, Carlyle's utterances, right or wrong, have meaning and practical application; but when Ruskin repeats them they become meaningless and inapplicable. Mr. Ruskin endeavoring to apply Carlyle's dogmas to the business of art and social life and politics often reminds one of the humorous Hindoo story of the Gooroo Simple and his followers, who went through life making the most outrageous blunders, because they would insist on the literal application of their traditional maxims of wisdom to every common incident of existence. When a self-conceited man ever consents to make another man his idol, even his very self-conceit only tends to render him more awkwardly and unconditionally devoted and servile. The amount of nonsense that Ruskin has talked and written, under the evident conviction that thus and not otherwise would Thomas Carlyle have dealt with the subject, is something almost inconceivable. I never heard of Ruskin taking up any political question without being on the wrong side of it. I am not merely speaking of what I personally consider the wrong side; I am alluding to questions which history and hard fact and the common voice and feeling of humanity have since decided. Against every movement to give political freedom to his countrymen, against every movement to do common justice to the negro race, against every effort to secure fair play for a democratic cause, Mr. Ruskin has peremptorily arrayed himself. "I am a Kingsman and no Mobsman," he declares; and this declaration seems in his mind to settle the question and to justify his vindication of every despotism of caste or sovereignty. To this has his doctrine of æsthetic moral law, to this has his worship of Carlyle, conducted him.

For myself, I doubt whether Mr. Ruskin has any great qualities but his eloquence, and his true, honest love of Nature. As a man to stand up before a society of which one part was fashionably languid and the other part only too busy and greedy, and preach to it of Nature's immortal beauty and of the true way to do her reverence, I think Ruskin had and has a place almost worthy the dignity of a prophet. I think, too, that he has the capacity to fill the place, to fulfil its every duty. Surely this ought to be enough for the work and for the praise of any man. But the womanish restlessness of Ruskin's temperament, combined with the extraordinary self-sufficiency which contributed so much to his success when he was master of a subject, sent him perpetually intruding into fields where he was unfit to labor, and enterprises which he had no capacity to conduct. No man has ever contradicted himself so often, so recklessly, so complacently, as Mr. Ruskin has done. It is absurd to call him a great critic even in art, for he seldom expresses any opinion one day without flatly contradicting it the next. He is a great writer, as Rousseau was—fresh, eloquent, audacious, writing out of the fulness of the present mood, and heedless how far the impulse of to-day may contravene that of yesterday; but as Rousseau was always faithful to his idea of Truth, so Ruskin is ever faithful to Nature. When all his errors and paradoxes and contradictions shall have been utterly forgotten, this his great praise will remain: No man since Wordsworth's brightest days ever did half so much to teach his countrymen, and those who speak his language, how to appreciate and honor that silent Nature which "never did betray the heart that loved her."

CHARLES READE.

A FEW days ago I came by chance upon an old number of an illustrated publication which made a rather brilliant start in London four or five years since, but died, I believe, not long after. It sprang up when there was a sudden rage in England for satirical portraits of eminent persons, and it really showed some skill and humor in this not very healthful or dignified department of art. This number of which I speak has a humorous cartoon called "Companions of the Bath," and representing a miscellaneous crowd of the celebrated men and women of the day enjoying a plunge in the waves at Havre, Dieppe, or some other French bathing-place. There are Gladstone and Disraeli; burly Alexandre Dumas and small, fragile Swinburne; Tennyson and Longfellow; Christine Nilsson and Adelina Patti, the two latter looking very pretty in their tunics and *caleçons*. Most of the likenesses are good, and the attitudes are often characteristic and droll. Mr. Spurgeon flounders and puffs wildly in the waves; Gladstone cleaves his way sternly and earnestly; Mario floats with easy grace. One group at present attracts very special attention. It represents a big, heavy, gray-headed man, ungainly of appearance, whom a smaller personage, bald and neat, is pushing off a plank into the water. The smaller man is Dion Boucicault; the larger is Mr. Charles Reade. This was the time when Reade and Boucicault were working together in "Foul Play." The insinuation of the artist evidently was that Boucicault, always ready for any plunge into the waves of sensationalism, had to give a push to his hesitating companion in order to impel him to the decisive "header."

The artist has been evidently unjust to Mr. Reade. Indeed, one can hardly help suspecting that there must have been some little personal grievance which the pencil was employed to pay off, after the fashion threatened more than once by Hogarth. Mr. Reade is not an Adonis, but this attempt at his likeness is cruelly grotesque and extravagant. Charles Reade is a big, heavy, rugged, gray man; a sort of portlier Walt Whitman, but with closer-cut hair and beard; a Walt Whitman, let us say, put into training for the part of a stout British vestryman. He impresses you at once as a man of character, energy, and originality, although he is by no means the sort of person you would pick out as a typical romanceist. But the artist who has delineated him in this cartoon, and who has dealt so fairly, albeit humorously, with Tennyson and Swinburne and Longfellow, must surely have had some spite against the author of "Peg Woffington" when he depicted him as a sort of huge human gorilla. It is in fact for this reason only that I have thought it worth while to introduce an allusion to such a caricature. The caricature is in itself illustrative of my subject. It helps to introduce an inevitable allusion to a weakness of Mr. Charles Reade's which makes for him many enemies and satirists among minor authors, critics, and artists in London. To a wonderful energy and virility of genius and temperament Charles Reade adds a more than feminine susceptibility and impatience when criticism attempts to touch him. With a faith in his own capacity and an admiration for his own works such as never were surpassed in literary history, he can yet be rendered almost beside himself by a disparaging remark from the obscurest critic in the corner of the poorest provincial newspaper. There is no pen so feeble anywhere but it can sting Charles Reade into something like delirium. He replies to every attack, and he discovers a personal enemy in every critic. Therefore he is always in quarrels, always assailing this man and being assailed by that, and to the very utmost of his power trying to prevent the public from appreciating or even recognizing the wealth of genuine manhood, truth, and feeling, which is bestowed everywhere in the rugged ore of his strange and paradoxical character. I am not myself one of Mr. Reade's friends, or even acquaintances; but from those who are, and whom I know, I have always heard the one opinion of the sterling integrity, kindness, and trueheartedness of the man who so often runs counter to all principles of social amenity, and whose bursts of impulsive ill-humor have offended many who would fain have admired.

I said once before in the pages of "The Galaxy," when speaking of another English novelist, that Charles Reade seems to me to rank more highly in America than he does in England. It is only of quite recent years that English criticism of the higher class has treated him with anything like fair consideration. There was a long time of Reade's growing popularity during which such criticism declined altogether to regard him *au sérieux*. Even now he has not justice done to him. But if I cannot help believing that Mr. Reade rates himself far too highly, and announces his opinion far too frankly, neither can I help thinking that English criticism in general fails to do him justice. For a long time he had to struggle hard to obtain a mere recognition. He had during part of his early career the good sense, or the spirit, or the misfortune, according as people choose to view it, to write in one of the popular weekly journals of London which correspond somewhat with the "New York Ledger." I think Charles Dickens described Reade as the one only man with a genuine literary reputation who at that time had ventured upon such a performance. There are indeed men now of undoubted rank in literature who began their career with work like this; but they did not put their names to it, and the world was never the wiser. Reade worked boldly and worked his best, and put his own name to it; and therefore the London press for some time regarded or affected to regard him as an author of that class whose genius supplies weekly instalments of sensation and tremendously high life, to delight the servant girls of Islington and the errand boys of the City. Long after the issue of some of the finest novels Reade has written, the annual publication called "Men of the Time" contained no notice of the author. The odd thing about this is that Reade is an author of the very class which English criticisms of the kind I allude to ought to have delighted to encourage. In the reaction against literary Bohemianism, which of late years has grown up in England, and which the "Saturday Review" may be said to have inaugurated, it became the whim and fashion to believe that only gentlemen with university degrees, only "blood and culture," as the cant phrase was, could write anything which gentlemanly persons could find it worth their while to read. The "Saturday Review" for a long time affected to treat Dickens as a good-humored and vulgar buffoon, with a gift of genius to delight the lower classes. It usually regarded Thackeray as a person made for better things, who had forfeited his position as a gentleman and a university man by descending to literature and to lectures. Now Charles Reade is what in the phraseology of English *caste* would be called a gentleman. He is of good English family; he is a graduate of Magdalen College, Oxford. He is a man of culture and scholarship. His reading, and especially his classical acquirements, I presume to be far wider and deeper than those of Thackeray, who, it need hardly be said, was as Porson or Parr when compared with Dickens. Altogether Reade seems to have been the sort of man whom the "Saturday Review," for example, ought to have taken promptly up and patted on the back and loftily patronized. But nothing of the sort occurred. Reade was treated merely as the clever, audacious concocter of sensational stories. He was hardly dealt with as an artist at all. The reviews only began to come round when they discovered that the public were positively with the new and stirring romancist. What renders this more curious is the fact that the earlier novels were incomparably more highly finished works of art than their successors. "Peg Woffington" and "Christie Johnstone"—the former published so long ago as 1852—seem almost perfect in their symmetry and beauty. "The Cloister and the Hearth" might well-nigh have persuaded a reader that a new Walter Scott was about to arise on the horizon of our literature. All the more recent works seem crude and rough by comparison. They ought to have been the vigorous, uncouth, undisciplined efforts of the author's earlier years. They ought to have led up to the "Cloister and the Hearth" and "Peg Woffington," instead of succeeding them. Yet, if I am not greatly mistaken, it was while he was publishing those earlier and finer products of his fresh intellect that Charles Reade was especially depreciated and even despised by what is called high-class English criticism. He never indeed has had much for which to thank the English critics, and he has never been slow to express his peculiar sense of obligation; but assuredly they treated with greater respect the works which will be soonest forgotten than those on which he may perhaps rest a claim to a more enduring reputation.

The general public, however, soon began to find him out. "Peg Woffington" was a decided success. Its dramatic adaptation is still one of the favorite pieces of the English stage. "It is Never Too Late to Mend" set everybody talking. Reade began to devote himself to exposing this or that social and legal grievance calling for reform, and people came to understand that a new branch of the art of novel-writing was in process of development, the special gift of which was to convert a Parliamentary blue-book into a work of fiction. The treatment of criminals in prisons and in far-off penal settlements, the manner in which patients are dealt with in private lunatic asylums, became the main subject and backbone of the new style of novel, instead of the misunderstandings of lovers, the trials of honest poverty, or the struggles for ascendancy in the fashionable circles of Belgravia. Mr. Reade undoubtedly stands supreme and indeed alone in work of this kind. No man but he can make a blue-book live and yet be a blue-book still. When Dickens undertook some special and practical question, we all knew that we had to look for lavish outpouring of humor, fancy, and eccentricity, for generous pathos, and for a sentimental misapplication or complete elimination of the actual facts. Miss Martineau made dry little stories about political economy; and Disraeli's "Sibyl" is only a fashionable novel and a string of tracts bound up together and called by one name But Reade takes the hard and naked facts as he finds them in some newspaper or in the report of some Parliamentary commission, and he so fuses them into the other material whereof his romance is to be made up that it would require a chemical analysis to separate the fiction from the reality. You are not conscious that you are going through the boiled-down contents of a blue-book. You have no aggrieved sense of being entrapped into the dry details of some harassing social question. The reality reads like romance; the romance carries you along like reality. No author ever indulged in a fairer piece of self-glorification than that contained in the last sentence of "Put Yourself in his Place": "I have taken a few undeniable truths out of many, and have labored to make my readers realize those appalling facts of the day which most men know, but not one in a thousand comprehends, and not one in a hundred thousand realizes, until fiction—which, whatever you may have been told to the contrary, is the highest, widest, noblest, and greatest of all the arts—comes to his aid, studies, penetrates, digests the hard facts of chronicles and blue-books, and makes their dry bones live." To this object, to this kind of work, Reade seems to have deliberately purposed to devote himself. It was evidently in accordance with his natural tastes and sympathies. He is a man of exuberant and irrepressible energy. He must be doing something definite always. He did actually bestir himself in the case of a person whom he believed to be unjustly confined in a lunatic asylum, as energetically as he makes Dr. Sampson do in "Hard Cash," and with equal success. Most of the scenes he describes, in England at least, have thus in some way fallen in to be part of his own experience. Whatever he undertakes to do he does with a tremendous earnestness. His method of workmanship is, I believe, something like that of Mr. Wilkie Collins, but of course the object is totally different. Wilkie Collins collects all the remarkable police cases and other judicial narratives he can find, and makes what Jean Paul Richter called "quarry" of them—a vast accumulation of materials in which to go digging for subjects and illustrations at leisure. Charles Reade does the same with blue-books and the reports of official inquiries. The author of the "Dead Secret" is looking for perplexing little mysteries of human crime; the author of "Hard Cash" for stories of legal or social wrong to be redressed. I need hardly say, perhaps, that I rank Charles Reade high above Wilkie Collins. The latter can string his dry bones on wires with remarkable ingenuity; the former can, as he fairly boasts, make the dry bones live.

Meanwhile, let us follow out the progress of Mr. Charles Reade as a literary influence. He grows to have a distinct place and power in England quite independently of the reviewers, and at last the very storm of controversy which his books awaken compels the reviewers themselves to take him into account. "It is Never Too Late to Mend" raised a clamor among prison disciplinarians. Years after its publication it is brought out as a drama in London, and its first appearance creates a sort of riot in the Princess's Theatre. Hostile critics rise in the stalls and denounce it; supporters and admirers vehemently defend it; speeches are made on either side. Mr. Reade plunges into the arena of controversy a day or two after in the newspapers, assails one of the critics by name, and charges him with having denounced the piece in the theatre, and applauded his own denunciation in the journal for which he wrote.

Some friend of the critic replies by the assertion that one of Mr. Reade's most enthusiastic literary supporters is Mr. Reade's own nephew. All this sort of thing is dreadfully undignified, but it brings an author at all events into public notice, and it did for Mr. Reade what I am convinced he would have disdained to do consciously—it "puffed" his books. An amusing story is told in connection with the production of this drama. An East End manager thought of bringing it out. (The East End, I need hardly say, is the lower and poorer quarter of London.) This manager came and studied the piece as produced at the West End. One of the strong scenes, the sensation scene, was a realistic exhibition of prison discipline. The West End had been duly impressed and thrilled with this scene. But the East End manager shook his head. "It would never do for *me*," he said despondingly to a friend. "Not like the real thing at all. *My* gallery would never stand it. Bless you, my fellows know the real thing too well to put up with *that*."

In this, as in other cases, Mr. Reade's hot temper, immense self-conceit, and eager love of controversy plunged him into discussions from which another man would have shrunk with disgust. He went so far on one occasion as to write to the editor of a London daily paper, threatening that if his books were not more fairly dealt with he would order his publisher to withdraw his advertisements from the offending journal. One can fancy what terror the threat of a loss of a few shillings a month would have had upon the proprietors of a flourishing London paper, and the amount of ridicule to which the bare suggestion of such a thing exposed the irritable novelist. But Reade was, and probably is, incurable. He would keep pelting his peppery little notes at the head of any and everybody against whom he fancied that he had a grievance. I remember one peculiarly whimsical illustration of this weakness, which found its way into print some years ago in London, but which perhaps will be quite new in the United States, and I cannot resist the temptation to reproduce it. Once upon a time, it would seem from the correspondence, Mr. Reade wrote a play called "Gold," which was produced at Drury Lane Theatre. Except from this correspondence I own that I never heard of the play. Subsequently, Mr. Reade presented himself one night at the stage-door of Drury Lane Theatre, and was refused admittance. Mr. Charles Mathews was then performing at the theatre, and Mr. Reade evidently supposed him to have been the manager and responsible for all the arrangements. Therefore he addressed his complaint to the incomparable light comedian, who is as renowned for easy sparkling humor and wit off the stage as for brilliant acting on it. Here is the correspondence; and we shall see how much Mr. Reade took by his motion:

GARRICK CLUB, COVENT GARDEN, November 28.

DEAR SIR: I was stopped the other night at the stage-door of Drury Lane Theatre by people whom I remember to have seen at the Lyceum under your reign.

This is the first time such an affront was ever put upon me in any theatre where I had produced a play, and is without precedent unless when an affront was intended. As I never forgive an affront, I am not hasty to suppose one intended. It is very possible that this was done inadvertently; and the present stage-list may have been made out without the older claims being examined.

Will you be so kind as to let me know at once whether this is so, and if the people who stopped me at the stage-door are yours, will you protect the author of "Gold," etc., from any repetition of such an annoyance?

I am, dear sir, yours faithfully,

CHARLES READE.

To this imperious demand Mr. Reade received next day the following genial answer:

T. R., Drury Lane, November 29.

Dear Sir: If ignorance is bliss on general occasions, on the present it certainly would be folly to be wise. I am therefore happy to be able to inform you that I am ignorant of your having produced a play at this theatre; ignorant that you are the author of "Gold"; ignorant of the merits of that play; ignorant that your name has been erased from the list at the stage-door; ignorant that it had ever been on it; ignorant that you had presented yourself for admittance; ignorant that it had been refused; ignorant that such a refusal was without precedent; ignorant that in the man who stopped you you recognized one of the persons lately with me at the Lyceum; ignorant that the doorkeeper was ever in that theatre; ignorant that you never forgive an affront; ignorant that any had been offered; ignorant of when, how, or by whom the list was made out, and equally so by whom it was altered.

Allow me to add that I am quite incapable of offering any discourtesy to a gentleman I have barely the pleasure of knowing, and moreover have no power whatever to interfere with Mr. Smith's arrangements or disarrangements; and, with this wholesale admission of ignorance, incapacity, and impotence, believe me

Faithfully yours,

C. T. Mathews.

Charles Reade, Esq.

The correspondence got into print somehow, and created, I need hardly say, infinite merriment in the literary clubs and circles of London. Not all disputes with Charles Reade ended so humorously, for the British novelist is as fond of actions at law as Fenimore Cooper used to be. Thus more than one critic has had to dread the terrors of an action for damages when he has ventured in a rash moment to disparage the literary value of Mr. Reade's teaching. Lately, however, in the case of the "Times," and its attack on "A Terrible Temptation," Mr. Reade adopted the unexpected tone of mild and even flattering remonstrance. Whether he thought it hopeless to alarm the "Times" by any threat of action, or feared that if he wrote a savage letter the journal would not even give him the comfort of seeing it in print, I do not know. But he certainly took a meek tone and endeavored to propitiate, and got rather coarsely rebuked for his pains. People in London were amused to find that he could be thus mild and gentle. I do remember, however, that on one occasion he wrote a letter of remonstrance, which was probably intended to be a kind of rugged compliment to the "Saturday Review," a paper which likewise cares nothing about actions for damages. Usually, however, his tone of argument with his critics is perfervid, and his estimate of himself is exquisitely candid. In one of his manifestoes he assured the world that he never allowed a publisher to offer any suggestions with regard to his story, but simply sold the manuscript in bulk—"*c'est à prendre ou à laisser.*" In another instance he spoke of one of his novels as "floating" the serial publication in which it was making its appearance, and which we were therefore given to understand would have sunk to the bottom but for his coöperation. In short, it is well known in London that Mr. Charles Reade's character is disfigured by a self-conceit which amounts to something like mania, and an impatience of criticism which occasionally makes him all but a laughing-stock to the public. Rarely, indeed, in literary history have high and genuine talents been united with such a flatulence of self-conceit.

Probably Reade had reached his highest position just after the publication of "Hard Cash." This remarkable novel, crammed with substance enough to make half a dozen novels, appeared in the first instance in Dickens's "All the Year Round." Dickens himself, if I remember rightly, felt bound to publish a note disclaiming any concurrence in or personal responsibility for the attacks on the private madhouse system, and the whole subject aroused a very lively controversy, wherein, I think, Reade certainly was not worsted. The "Griffith Gaunt" controversy we all remember. I confess that I have no sympathy whatever with the kind of criticism which treats any of Mr. Reade's works as immoral in tendency, and I think the charge was even more absurd when urged against "Griffith Gaunt" than when pressed against the "Terrible Temptation." To me the clear tendency of Reade's novels seems always healthy, purifying, and bracing, like a fresh, strong breeze. I cannot understand how any man or woman could be the worse for reading one of them. They are always novels with a purpose, and I, at least, never could discern any purpose in them which was not honest and sound. I feel inclined to excuse all Reade's vehemence of self-vindication and childish frankness of self-praise when I read some of the attacks against what people try to paint as the immorality of his books. But I need not go into that controversy. Enough to say for my own part that I found "Griffith Gaunt" a grim and dreary book—a tiresome book, in fact; but I saw nothing in it which could with any justice be said to have the slightest tendency to demoralize any reader. I have indeed heard people who are in general fair critics condemn "Adam Bede" as immoral because Hetty is seduced; and I have even heard poor Maggie Tulliver rated as unfit for decent society because she ever allowed even a moment's thought of her cousin's engaged lover to enter her mind. On this principle, doubtless, "Griffith Gaunt" is immoral. There are people in the book who commit sin, and yet are not eaten by lions or bodily carried down below like Don Juan. But if we are to have novels made up only of good people who always do right and the one stock villain who always does wrong, I think the novelist's art cannot too soon be delegated to its only fitting province—the amusement of the nursery. "Griffith Gaunt," however, I regard as a falling off, because it is a sour, unpleasant, and therefore inartistic book. "Foul Play" was a clever *tour de force*, a brilliant thing, made to sell, with hardly more character in it than would suffice for a Bowery melodrama. "Put Yourself in his Place" was a wholesome return to the former style, a marrowy, living blue-book, instinct with power and passion. "A Terrible Temptation" I do not admire. I do not think it immoral, but it hardly calls for any deliberate criticism. Since "Hard Cash" Mr. Reade has, in my opinion, written only one novel which the literary world will care to preserve, and even that one, "Put Yourself in his Place," can hardly be said to add one cubit to his stature.

Mr. Reade has, I believe, rather a passion for dramatic enterprise, and a characteristic faith in his power to turn out a good drama. A season or two back he hired, I am told, a London theatre, in order to have the complete superintendence of the production of one of his novels turned into a drama. I have been assured that the dramatic version was accomplished entirely by himself. If so, I am sure no enemy could have more cruelly damaged the original work. All the character was completely sponged out of it. The one really effective and original personage in the novel did not appear in the play. A number of the most antique and conventional melodramatic situations and surprises were crammed into the piece. All the silly old stage business about mysterious conspiracies carried on under the very ear of the identical personage who never ought to have been allowed to hear them are called in to form an essential feature of the drama. The play, of course, was not successful, although the novel had in it naturally all the elements of a stirring and powerful drama. If Charles Reade really with his own hand converted a vigorous and thrilling story into that limp, languid, and vapid play, it was surely the most awful warning against amateur dramatic enterprise that ever self-conceit could receive undismayed.

Of course we won't rank Mr. Reade as one of the most popular novelists now in England. But his popularity is something very different indeed from that of Dickens, or even from that of Thackeray. In Forster's "Life of Dickens" there is a letter of the great novelist's in which he complains of having been treated (by Bentley, I think) no better than any author who had sold but fifteen hundred copies. I should think the occasions were very rare when Mr. Reade's circulation in England went much beyond fifteen hundred copies. The whole system of publishing is so different in England from that which prevails in America, our fictitious prices and the controlling monopoly of our great libraries so restrict and limit the sale, that a New York reader would perhaps hardly believe how small a number constitute a good circulation for an English novelist. I assume that, speaking roughly, Reade, Wilkie Collins, and Trollope may be said to have about the same kind of circulation—almost immeasurably below Dickens, and below some such abnormal sale as that of "Lothair" or "Lady Audley's Secret," but much above even the best of the younger novelists. I venture to think that not one of these three popular and successful authors may be counted on to reach a circulation of two thousand copies. Probably about eighteen hundred copies would be a decidedly good thing for one of Charles Reade's novels. Of the three, I should say that Wilkie Collins has the most eager readers; that Trollope's novels take the highest place in what is called "society"; and that Reade's rank the best among men of brains. But there is so wide a difference between the popularity of Dickens and that of Reade that it seems almost absurd to employ the same word to describe two things so utterly unlike. It is, indeed, a remarkable proof of Reade's power and success that, setting out as he always does to tell a story which shall convey information and a purpose of some practical kind, he can get any sort of large circulation at all. For one great charm and excellence of our library system is that it creates a huge class of regular, I might almost say professional, novel-readers, who subscribe to Mudie's by the year, want to get all the reading they can out of it, and instinctively shudder at the thought of any novel that is weighted by solid information and overtaxing thought. This is the class for whom and by whom the circulating libraries exist, and Mr. Reade deserves the full credit of having utterly disregarded them, or rather boldly encountered them, and at least to some extent compelled them to read him.

Mr. Reade's position as a novelist may be adjudged now as safely as ever a novelist's place can be fixed by a contemporary generation. He is nearly sixty years old, and he has written about a dozen novels. It is not likely that he will ever write anything which could greatly enhance the estimate the public have already formed of him; and no future failures could affect his past success. I think his career is, therefore, fairly and fully before us. We know how singularly limited his *dramatis personæ* are. He marches them on and off the stage boldly ever so often, and by a change of dresses every now and then he for a while almost succeeds in making us believe that he has a very full company at his command. But we soon get to know every one by sight, and can swear to him or her, no matter by what name or garb disguised. We know the sweet, impulsive, incoherent heroine, who is always contradicting herself and saying what she ought not to say and does not mean to say; who now denounces the hero, and then falls upon his neck and vows that she loves him more than life. This young woman is sometimes Julia and sometimes

Helen and sometimes Grace; she now is exiled for a while on a lonely island, and even she is carried away by a flood; but in every case she is just the same girl rescued by the same hero. That hero is always a being of wonderful mechanical and scientific knowledge of some kind or other, whether as Captain Dodd he makes love to Lucy Fountain, or as Henry Little he captivates Grace Carden, or as the gentleman in "Foul Play" he cures the heroine of consumption and builds island huts better than Robinson Crusoe. Then we have the rough, clever, eccentric personage, Dr. Sampson or Dr. Amboyne, whose business principally is to act a part like that of Herr Mittler in Goethe's novel, and help the characters of the book through every difficulty. Then we have the white-livered sneak, the villain of the book when he is bad enough for such a part; the Coventry of "Put Yourself in his Place"; I forget what his name is in "Foul Play." These are the puppets which principally make up the show. Very vigorously and cleverly do they dance, and capitally do they imitate life; but there are so very few of them that we grow a little tired of seeing them over and over again. Indeed, Charles Reade's array of characters sometimes reminds us of the simple system of Plautus, in which we have for every play the same types of people—the rather stingy father, the embarrassed lover, the clever comic slave, and so forth. It cannot be said that Reade has added a single character to fiction. He understands human nature, or at least such types of it as he habitually selects, very well, and he draws vigorously his figures and groups; but he has discovered nothing fresh, he has rescued no existence from the commonplace and evanescent realistics of life, to be preserved immortal in a work of art. Not one of his characters is cited in ordinary conversation or in the writings of journalists. Nobody quotes from him unless in reference to some one of the stirring social topics which he has illustrated, and even then only as one would quote from a correspondent of the "Times." Every educated man and woman in England is assumed, as a matter of course, to be familiar with the works of George Eliot; but nobody is necessarily assumed to have read Charles Reade. That educated people do read him and do admire him is certain; but it is quite a matter of option with them to read him or let him alone so far as society and public opinion are concerned. There are certain tests and evidences of a novelist's having attained a front-rank place in England which are unmistakable. They are purely social, may be only superficial, and will neither one way nor the other affect the views of foreign critics or of posterity; but they are decisive as far as England is concerned. Among them I shall mention two or three. One is the fact that writers in the press allude to some of his characters without feeling bound to explain in whose novel and what novel the characters appear. Another is the fact that artists voluntarily select from his works subjects for paintings to be sent to the Royal Academy's annual exhibition or elsewhere. A third is the fact that articles about him, not formal reviews of a work just published, appear pretty often in the magazines. Now, whatever may be the genius and merits of an author, I think he cannot be said to have attained the front rank in English public opinion unless he can show these evidences of success; and, so far as I know, Mr. Reade cannot show any of them. For myself, I do not believe that Mr. Reade ever could under any circumstances have become a really great novelist. All the higher gifts of imagination and all the richer veins of humor have been denied to him. Not one gleam of poetic fancy ever seems to have floated across the nervous Saxon of his style. He is a powerful story-teller, who has a manly purpose in every tale he tells, and that is all. That surely is a great deal. No one tells a story more thrillingly. Once you begin to listen, you cannot release yourself from the spell of the *raconteur* until all be done. A strong, healthy air of honest and high purpose breathes through nearly all the stories. An utter absence of cant, affectation, and sham distinguishes them. A surprising variety of descriptive power, at once bold, broad, and realistic, is one of their great merits. Mr. Reade can describe a sea-fight, a storm, the forging of a horseshoe, the ravages of an inundation, the trimming of a lady's dress, the tuning of a piano, with equal accuracy and apparent zest. I once heard an animated discussion in a literary club as to whether the scrap of minute description was artistic and effective or absurd and ludicrous which makes us acquainted with the fact that when Henry Little dragged Grace Carden out of the raging flood, the force of the water washed away the heroine's stockings and garters and left her barefoot. Some irreverent critics would only laugh at the gravity with which the author detailed this important circumstance. Others, however, insisted that this little touch, so homely, and to the profane mind so exceedingly ridiculous, was necessary and artistic; that it heightened the effect of the great word-picture previously shown by the force of its practical and circumstantial reality. However this momentous controversy may settle itself in the estimation of readers, it cannot be denied that some at least of Reade's success is due to the courage and self-reliance which will brave the risk of being ridiculous for the sake of being real and effective. Indeed, Mr. Reade wants no quality which is necessary to make a powerful story-teller, while he is distinguished from all mere story-tellers by the fact that he has some great social object to serve in nearly everything he undertakes to detail. More than this I do not believe he is, nor, despite the evidences of something yet higher which were given in "Christie Johnstone" and "The Cloister and the Hearth," do I think he ever could have been. He is a magnificent specimen of the modern special correspondent, endowed with the additional and unique gift of a faculty for throwing his report into the form of a thrilling story. But it requires something more than this, something higher than this, to make a great novelist whom the world will always remember. Mr. Reade is unsurpassed in the second class of English novelists, but he does not belong to the front rank. His success has been great in its way, but it is for an age and not for time.

THE EXILE-WORLD OF LONDON.

LEICESTER SQUARE and the region that lies around it are conventionally regarded as the exile quarter of London. The name of Leicester square suggests the idea of an exile, as surely and readily, even to the mind of one who has never looked on the mournful and decaying enclosure, as the name of Billingsgate does that of fish-woman, or the name of the Temple that of a law-student. Yet, if a stranger visiting London thinks he is likely to see any exile of celebrity, while pacing the streets which branch off Leicester square, he will be almost as much mistaken as if he were to range Eastcheap in the hope of meeting the wild Prince and Poins.

Many a conspiracy has had its followers and understrappers in the Leicester square region; but the great conspirators do not live there any more. The place is falling, falling; the foreign and distinctive character of the population remains as marked as ever, but the foreigners whom London people would care to see are not to be found there any longer. The exiles who have made part of history, whose names are on record, do not care for Leicester square. They are to be found in Kensington, in Brompton, in Hampstead and Highgate; in the Regent's Park district; a few in Bloomsbury, a few in Mayfair. A marble slab and an inscription now mark the house in King street, St. James's, where Louis Napoleon lodged; and there is a house in Belgrave square dear to all true Legitimists, where the Count de Chambord ("Henri Cinq") received Berryer and his brother pilgrims. Only poor exiles herd together now in London. Only poverty, I suppose, ever causes nationalities to herd together anywhere. The men who group around Leicester square are the exiles without a fame; the subterranean workers in politics; the men who come like shadows, and so depart; the men whose names are writ in water, even though their life-paths may have been marked in blood.

Living in London, I had of late years many opportunities of meeting with the exiles of each class. I know few men more to be pitied than the great majority of those who make up the latter or Leicester square section. On the other hand, I should say that few men, indeed, are more to be envied by any of their fellow-creatures who love to be courted and "lionized," than the political exiles of great name who come to London and do not stay too long there.

Far away as the days of Thaddeus of Warsaw and the conventional and romantic type of exile now seem, there is still a fervent yearning in British society toward the representative of any Continental nationality which happens to be oppressed. No man had ever before received such a welcome in London as Kossuth did; but Kossuth stayed too long, became domesticized and familiarized, and society in London likes its lions to be always new and fresh. Moreover, the late Lord Palmerston, a warm patron of exiles when the patronage went no further than an invitation to a dinner or an evening party, set his face against Kossuth from the first; and polite society soon took the hint.

The man who most completely conquered all society, even the very highest, in London, during my recollection, was the man who probably cared least about it, and who certainly never sought to win the favor of fashion—I mean, of course, Garibaldi. To this day I am perfectly unable to understand the demeanor of the British peerage toward Garibaldi, when he visited London for a few days some years ago. The thing was utterly unprecedented and inexplicable. The Peerage literally rushed at him. He was beset by dukes, mobbed by countesses. He could not by any human possibility have so divided his day as to find time for breakfasting and dining with one-fifth of the noble hosts who fought and scrambled for him. It was a perpetual torture to his secretaries and private friends to decide between the rival claims of a Prime Minister and a Prince of the blood; an Archbishop and a Duchess; the Lord Chancellor and the leader of the Opposition. The Tories positively outdid the Whigs in the struggle for the society of the simple seaman, the gallant guerilla. The oddest thing about the business was, that three out of every four of these noble personages had always previously spoken of Garibaldi—when they did speak of him at all—with contempt and dislike, as a buccaneer and a filibuster.

What did it mean? Was it a little comedy? Was it their fun? Was it a political *coup de théâtre*, to dodge the Radicals and the workingmen out of their favorite hero? Certainly some of Garibaldi's friends suspected something of the kind, and were utterly bewildered and confounded by the unexpected rush of aristocratic admirers, who beset the hero from the moment he touched the shore of England.

It was a strange sight, not easily to be forgotten, to see the manner in which Garibaldi sat among the dukes and marchionesses—simple, sweet, arrayed in the calm, serene dignity of a manly, noble heart. There was something of Oriental stateliness in the unruffled, imperturbable, bland composure, with which he bore himself amid the throng of demonstrative and titled adulators. I do not think he believed in the sincerity of half of it, any more than I did, but he showed no more sign of distrust or impatience than he did of gratified vanity.

The thing ended in a quarrel between the Aristocracy and the Democracy, between Belgravia and Clerkenwell, for the custody of the hero, and Garibaldi escaped somehow back to his island during the squabble. But I think Lady Palmerston let the mask fall for a moment, when, growing angry at the assurance of Garibaldi's humbler friends, and perhaps a little tired of the whole business, she told some gentlemen of my acquaintance, that quite too much work had been made about a person who, after all, was only a respectable brigand. This was said (and it *was* said) at the very meridian of the day of noble homage to the Emancipator of Sicily.

Garibaldi has never since returned to England. Should he ever do so, he will find himself unembarrassed by the attentions of the Windsor uniform and Order of the Garter. The play, however it was got up, or whatever its object, was played out long ago. But the West End is, as a rule, very fond of distinguished exiles, when they come and go quickly; and Lord Palmerston's drawing-room was seldom without a representative of the class. No man ever did less for any great cause than Lord Palmerston did; but he liked brilliant exiles, and, perhaps, more particularly the soldierly than the scholarly class. Such a man as the martial, dashing, adventurous General Türr, for example, was the kind of refugee that Lord and Lady Palmerston especially favored.

Many English peers have, indeed, quite a *spécialité* in the way of patronizing exiles; but, of course, in all such cases the exile must have a name which brings some gratifying distinction to his host. He must be somebody worth pointing out to the other guests. I know that many Continental refugees have chafed at all this, and some have steadily held aloof from it, and declined to be shown off for the admiration of a novelty-hunting crowd. Many, too, have been deceived by it; have mistaken such idle attention for profound and practical sympathy, and have thought that two or three peers and half a dozen aristocratic petticoats could direct the foreign policy of England. They have swelled with hope and confidence; have built their plans and based their organizations on the faith that Park Lane meant the British government, and that the politeness of a Cabinet Minister was as good as the assistance of a British fleet; and have found out what idiots they were in such a belief, and have gone nigh to breaking their hearts accordingly. Indeed, the readiness of all classes in England to rush at any distinguished exile, and become effusive about himself and his cause is very often—or, at least, used to be—a cruel kindness, sure to be misunderstood and to betray—a love that killed.

Nothing could, in its way, have been more unfortunate and calamitous than the outburst of popular enthusiasm in England about the Polish insurrection four years ago. Some of the Polish leaders living in London were completely deceived by it, and finally believed that England was about to take up arms in their cause. An agitation was got up, outside the House of Commons, by an earnest, well-meaning gentleman, who really believed what he said; and inside the House by a bustling, quickwitted, political adventurer, who certainly ought not to have believed what he said. This latter gentleman actually went out to Cracow, in Austrian Poland, and was received there with wild demonstrations of welcome as a representative of the national will of England and the precursor of English intervention. The Polish insurrection went on; and England wrote a diplomatic note, which Russia resented as a piece of impertinence; and there England's sympathy ended. "I think," said a great English Liberal to me, "that every Englishman who helped to encourage these poor Poles and give them hope of English help, has Polish blood on his hands." I think so, too.

I have always thought that Felice Orsini was in some sort a victim to the kind of delusion which English popularity so easily fosters. I met Orsini when he came to England, not very long before the unfortunate and criminal attempt of the Rue Lepelletier; and I was much taken, as most people who met him were, by the simplicity, sweetness, and soldierly frankness of his demeanor. He delivered some lectures in London, Manchester, Liverpool, and other large towns, on his own personal adventures—principally his escape from prison—and though he had but a moderate success as a lecturer, he was surrounded everywhere by well-meaning and sympathizing groups, the extent of whose influence and the practical value of whose sympathy he probably did not at first quite understand. He certainly had, at one time, some vague hopes of obtaining for the cause of Italian independence a substantial assistance from England. A short experience cured him of that dream; and I fancy it was then that he formed the resolution which he afterward attempted so desperately to carry out. I think, from something I heard him say once, that Mazzini had endeavored to enlighten him as to the true state of affairs in England, and the real value of the sort of sympathy which London so readily offers to any interesting exile. But I do not believe Mazzini's advice had much influence over Orsini. Indeed, the latter, at the time I saw him, had but little respect for Mazzini. He spoke with something like contempt of the great conspirator. It would have been well for Orsini if he had, in one thing at least, followed the counsels of Mazzini. People used to say, some years ago, that odious and desperate as Orsini's attempt was, it at least had the merit of frightening Louis Napoleon into active efforts on behalf of Italy. There was so much about Orsini that was worthy and noble that one would be glad to regard him as even in his crime the instrument of good to the country he loved so well. But documentary and other evidence has made it clear since Orsini's death that the negotiations which ended in Solferino and Villafranca were begun before Orsini had ever planned his murderous enterprise. The fact is, that, during the Crimean war, Cavour first tried England on the subject, through easy-going and heedless Lord Clarendon—who hardly took the trouble to listen to the audacious projects of his friend—and then turned to France, where quicker and shrewder ears listened to what he had to say.

I have spoken of Orsini's contempt for Mazzini. Such a feeling toward such a man seems quite inexplicable. Many men detest Mazzini; many men distrust him; many look up to him as a prophet, and adore him as a chief; but I am not able to understand how any one can think of him with mere contempt. For myself, I find it impossible to contemplate without sadness and without reverence that noble, futile career; that majestic, melancholy dream. But it must be owned that an atmosphere of illusion sheds itself around Mazzini wherever he goes. I believe the man himself to be the very soul of truth and honor; and yet I protest I would not take, on any political question, the unsupported testimony of any devotee of Mazzini to any fact whatsoever. Mazzini's own faith is so sublimely transcendental, so utterly independent of realities and of experience, that I sincerely believe the visions of the opium-eater are hardly less to be relied on than the oracles and opinions of the great Italian. And yet the force of his character, the commanding nature of his genius, are such that his followers become more Mazzinian than Mazzini himself. There is something a good deal provoking about the manner of the minor followers of Mazzini. I mean in England. I do not speak of such men as my friend, Mr. Stansfeld, now a Lord of the Treasury, or my friend, Mr. P. A. Taylor, M. P. These are men of ability and men of the world, whose enthusiasm and faith, even at their highest, are under the control of practical experience and the discipline of public life. But I speak of the minor and less responsible admirers, the men and women who accept oracle as fact, aspiration as experience, the dream as the reality. The calm, self-satisfied way in which they deal with contemporary history, with geography, with statistics, with possibilities and impossibilities, in the hope of making you believe what they firmly believe—that Italy could, if only she had proclaimed herself Republican, have driven the Austrians into the sea in 1859, and the French across the Alps in 1860, while at the same time quietly kicking Pope, Bourbon, and Savoy out of throned existence. The confident and imperturbable assurance with which they can do all this—and I have never met with any genuine devotee of Mazzini who could not—is something to make one bewildered rather than merely impatient. For it is true in politics as in literature or in fashion, the admiring imitator reproduces only the defects, the weaknesses, the mannerisms and mistakes of the original. Mazzini himself is, I need hardly say, a singularly modest and retiring man. While he lived in London, he shrank from all public notice, and was seen only by his friends and followers. He sought out nobody. "Sir," said Mr. Gladstone, addressing the Speaker of the House of Commons, one night, when a fierce and factious attack was made on Mr. Stansfeld as a follower of the great exile, "I never saw Signor Mazzini.' Yet Gladstone was by far the most prominent and influential of all the English sympathizers with the cause of Italian liberty. One would have thought it impossible for such a man as Mazzini to live for years in the same city with Gladstone without the two ever chancing to meet. But for the modest seclusion and shrinking way of Mazzini, such a thing would, indeed, have been impossible.

Louis Blanc is, perhaps, the only Revolutionary exile who, in my time, has been everywhere and permanently popular in London society. The fate of a political exile in a place like London usually is to be a lion among one clique and a *bête noir* in another. But Louis Blanc has been accepted and welcomed everywhere, although he has never compromised or concealed one iota of his political opinions. I think one explanation, and, perhaps, *the* explanation of this somewhat remarkable phenomenon, is to be found in the fact that Louis Blanc never for an hour played the part of a conspirator. He seems to have honorably construed his place in English society to be that of one to whom a shelter had been given, and who was bound not to make any use of that shelter which could embarrass his host. In London he ceased to be an active politician. He refused to exhibit himself *en victime*. He appealed to no public pity. He made no parade of defeat and exile. He went to work steadily as a literary man, and he had the courage to be poor. When he appeared in public it was simply as a literary lecturer. He was not very successful in that capacity. At least, he was not what the secretary of a lyceum would call a success. He gave a series of lectures on certain phases of society in Paris before the great Revolution, and they were attended by all the best literary men in London, who were, I think, unanimous in their admiration of the power, the eloquence, the brilliancy which these pictures of a ghastly past displayed. But the general public cared nothing about the *salons* where wit, and levity, and wickedness prepared the way for revolution; and I heard Louis Blanc pour out an *apologia* (I don't mean an apology) for Jean Jacques Rousseau in language of noble eloquence, and with dramatic effect worthy of a great orator, in a small lecture-room, of which three-fourths of the space was empty. Since that time he has delivered lectures occasionally at the request of mechanics' institutions and such societies; but he has not essayed a course of lectures on his own account. Everyone knows him; everyone likes him; everyone admires his manly, modest character and his uncompromising Republicanism. Lately he has lived more in Brighton than in London; but wherever in England he happens to be, he lives always as a simple citizen; has never been raved about like Kossuth, or denounced like Mazzini; and has occupied himself wholly with his historical labors and his letters to a Paris newspaper.

Another exile of distinction who lived for years in London apart from politics and heedless of popular favor was Ferdinand Freiligrath, the German poet. Freiligrath had to leave Prussia because of his political poems and writings. He had undergone one prosecution and escaped conviction, but Prussia was not then (twenty years ago) a country in which to run such risks too often. So Freiligrath went to Amsterdam and thence to London. He lived in London for many years, and acted as manager of a Swiss banking-house. His life was one of entire seclusion from political schemes or agitations. He did not even, like his countryman and friend, Gottfried Kinkel, take any part in public movements among the Germans in London—and he certainly never went about society and the newspapers blowing his own trumpet, and keeping his name always prominent, like the egotistical and inflated Karl Blind. Indeed, so complete was Freiligrath's retirement that many Englishmen living in London, who delighted in some of his poems—his exquisite, fanciful, melodious "Sand Songs" his glowing Desert poems, his dreamy, delightful songs of the sea, and his burning political ballads—were quite amazed to find that the poet himself had been a resident of their own city for nearly half a lifetime. Freiligrath has now at last returned to his own country. His countrymen invited him home, and raised a national tribute to enable him to give up his London engagement and withdraw altogether from a life of mere business. In a letter I lately received from

Freiligrath's daughter (a young lady of great talent and accomplishments, recently married in London), I find it mentioned that Freiligrath expected soon to receive a visit from Longfellow in Germany—the first meeting of these two old friends for a period of some five-and-twenty years.

Alexander Herzen, the famous Russian exile, the wittiest of men, endowed with the sharpest tongue and the best nature, has left us. For many years he lived in London and published his celebrated *Kolokol*—"The Bell," which rang so ominously and jarringly in the ears of Russian autocracy. He has now set up his staff in Geneva, a little London in its attractiveness to exiles; and his arrowy, flashing wit gleams no longer across the foreign world of the English metropolis. I do not know how long Herzen had lived in London, but I fancy the difficulties of the English language must have proved insurmountable to him—a strange phenomenon in the case of a Russian. Certainly he never, so far as I am aware, either spoke or wrote English.

The latest exile of great mark whom we had among us in London was General Prim. When his attempt at revolution in Spain failed some two years ago, Prim went into Belgium. There some pressure was brought to bear upon him by the Ministry, in consequence, no doubt, of certain pressure brought to bear by France, and Prim left Brussels and came to live in London. He lived very quietly, made no show of himself in any way, and was no doubt hard at work all the time making preparation for what has since come to pass. To all appearance he had an easy and careless sort of life, living out among his private friends, going to the races and going to the opera. But he was incessantly planning and preparing; and he told many Englishmen candidly what he was preparing for. There were many men in London who were looking out for the Spanish Revolution months before it came, on the faith of Prim's earnest assurances that it was coming. So much has of late been written about Prim that his personal appearance and manner must be familiar to most readers of newspapers and magazines. I need only say that there is in private much less of the *militaire* about him than one who had not actually met him would be inclined to imagine. He is small, neat, and even elegant in dress, very quiet and perhaps somewhat languid in manner, looking wonderfully young for his years, and without the slightest tinge of the Leicester square foreigner about him. He is rather the foreigner of Regent street and the stalls of the opera house—any one who knows London will at once understand the difference. Prim impressed me with a much greater respect for his intellect, even from a literary man's point of view, than I had had before meeting and conversing with him. I think those who regard him as a mere *sabreur*, the ordinary Spanish leader of a successful military revolution, are mistaken. His animated and epigrammatic conversation seemed to me to be inspired and guided by an intellectual depth and a power of observation and reflection such as I at least was not prepared to find in the dashing soldier of the Moorish campaign.

There is one class of the obscure exiles, different from both the favored and the poorest, whose existence has often puzzled me. A political question of moment begins to disturb the European continent. Immediately there turns up in London, and presents himself at your door (supposing you are a journalist with acknowledged sympathies for this or that side of the question) a mysterious and generally shabby-looking personage, who professes to know all about it, and volunteers to supply you with the most authentic information and the most trustworthy "appreciation" of any events that may transpire. He wants no money; his information is given for the sake of "the cause." You ask for credentials, and he produces recommendations which quite satisfy you that his objects are genuine, although, oddly enough, the persons who recommend him do not seem to have anything whatever to do with the cause he represents. He comes, for example, to talk about the affairs of Roumania, and he brings letters and vouchers from literary friends in Paris. He professes to be an emissary from the Cretans, and his recommendations are from a Manchester cotton-firm. Anyhow, you are satisfied; you ask no explanations; you assume that your Paris or Manchester friends have enlarged the sphere of their sympathies since you saw them last, and you repose confidence in your new acquaintance. You are right. He brings you information, the most rapid, the most surprising, the most accurate. Such a man I knew during the Schleswig-Holstein agitation, which ended in the Danish war of four years since. He was a Prussian—a waif of the Berlin rising of 1848. Was he in the confidence of Von Beust, and Bismarck, and Palmerston, and all the rest of them? I venture to doubt it; yet if he had been, he could hardly have been more quick and accurate in all the information he brought me. Evening after evening he brought a regular minute of the proceedings of the day at the Conference of London, which was sitting with closed doors, and pledged to profoundest secrecy. Perhaps this was only guesswork! Here is one illustration. The Conference was held because some of the European Great Powers, England and France especially, desired to save Denmark from a struggle against the immeasurably superior force of Prussia and Austria. A certain proposal was to be made to the Conference by England and France on the part of Denmark. So much we all knew. One evening my friend came to me, and bade me announce to the world that the proposal had been made that day, and indignantly rejected—by Denmark! The story seemed preposterous, but I relied on my friend. Next day I was laughed at; my news was denounced and repudiated. The day after it was proved to be true—and Denmark went to war.

The last time I saw my friend was in the spring of 1866. He came to tell me that Prussia had resolved—at least that Bismarck had resolved—on war with Austria. "Stick to that statement," he said, "whatever anybody may say to the contrary—unless Bismarck resigns." I took his advice. At this time I am convinced that the English government had not the least idea that a war was really coming. The war came; but I never saw my friend any more.

Another of my mysterious acquaintances was an old, white-haired, grave, placid man who turned up in London during the early part of the French occupation of Mexico. He was a passionate Republican and anti-Bonapartist. He was a friend and apparently a confidant of Juarez, and was thoroughly identified with the interests of the Republicans in Mexico, although himself a Frenchman. I doubt whether I have ever met with a finer specimen of the courtly old gentleman, the class now beginning to disappear even in France, than this mysterious friend of the Mexican Republic. He might have been fresh from the Faubourg St. Germain, such was the grave, dignified, and somewhat melancholy grace of his courtly bearing. Yet he had evidently lived long in Mexico, and he was an ardent Republican of the red tinge; there was something of the old *militaire* about him, too, which lent a certain strength to his bland and placid demeanor. I never quite knew what he was doing in London. He was not what is called an "unofficial representative" of Juarez (at this time diplomatic relations between England and Mexico were of course broken off) for he never seemed to go near any of our ministers or diplomatists, and his only object appeared to be to supply accurate information to one or two Liberal journals which he believed to be honestly inclined toward the right side of every question. His information was always accurate, his estimate of a critical situation was always justified by further knowledge and the progress of events, his predictions always came true. He looked like a poor man, indeed, like a needy man; yet he never seemed to want for money, and he neither sought nor would have any compensation for the constant and valuable information he afforded. His knowledge of European and American politics was profound; and though he spoke not one word of English he seemed to understand all the daily details of our English political life. He was a constant visitor to me (always at night and late) during the progress of the Mexican struggle. When the Mexican Empire was nearly played out he came and told me the end was very, very near, and that in the event of Maximilian's being captured it would be impossible for Juarez to spare his life. He did not tell me that he was at once returning to Mexico, but I presume that he did immediately return, for that was the last I saw or heard of him.

During the quarrels between the Prussian Representative Chamber and Count von Bismarck (before the triumph of Sadowa had condoned for the offences of the great despotic Minister), I had a visit, one night, from a mysterious, seedy, snuffy old German. He came, he said, to develop a grand plan for the extinction of the Junker or Feudal party. Why he came to develop it to me I do not know, as it will presently be seen that I could hardly render it any practical assistance. It was, like all grand schemes, remarkably simple in its nature. Indeed, it was literally and strictly Captain Bobadil's immortal plan; although my German visitor indignantly repudiated the supposition that he had borrowed it, and declared, I believe, with perfect truth, that he had never heard of Captain Bobadil before. The plan was simply that a society should be formed of young and devoted Germans who should occupy themselves in challenging and killing off, one by one, the whole Junker party. My friend made his calculations very calmly, and he did not foolishly or arrogantly assume that the swordsmanship of his party must needs be always superior to that of their adversaries. No; he counted that there would be a certain number of victims among his Liberal heroes, and made, indeed, a large allowance, left a broad margin for such losses. But this, in no wise affected the success of his plan. The Liberals, were many, the Junkers few. It would simply be a matter of time and calculation. Numbers must tell in the end. A day must come when the last Junker would fall to earth—and then Astrea would return. Now the man who talked in this way was no lunatic. He had nothing about him, except his plan, which denoted mental aberration. His scheme apart, he was as steady and prosy an old German as you could meet under the lindens of Berlin or on the Lutherplatz of Königsberg. He was, moreover, as earnest, argumentative, and profoundly wearisome over his project as if he were expounding to an admiring class of students the relations of the Ego and Non-Ego. I need hardly add that one single beam, even the faintest, of a sense of the ridiculous, never shone in upon him during his long and eloquent exposition of the patriotic virtue, the completeness and the mathematical certainty of his ingenious project.

Let me close my random reminiscences with one recollection of a sadder nature. Some three or four years ago there came to London from Naples an Italian of high education and character—a lawyer by profession; a passionate devotee of Italian unity, and filled naturally with a hatred of the expelled Bourbons. This gentleman had discovered in one of the Neapolitan prisons a number of instruments of torture—rusty, hideous old iron chairs, and racks, and screws, and "cages of silence," and such other contrivances. He became the possessor of these, and he obtained from the new government a certificate of the genuineness of his treasure-trove—that is to say, a certificate that the things were actually found in the place where the owner professed to have found them. The Italian authorities, of course, could say nothing as to whether they had or had not been used as instruments of torture in any modern reign. They may have lain rusting there since hideous old days when the Inquisition was a fashionable institution; they may have been used—public opinion and Mr. Gladstone said things as horrible had been done—in the blessed reign of good King Bomba. The Neapolitan lawyer firmly believed that they had been so used; and he became inspired with the idea that to take these instruments, first to London and then to the United States, and exhibit them, and lecture on them, would arouse such a tempest of righteous indignation among all peoples, free or enslaved, as must sweep kingcraft and priestcraft off the earth. This idea became a faith with him. He brought his treasure of rusty iron to London, and proposed to take a great hall and begin the work of his mission. I endeavored to dissuade him (he had brought some introductions to me). I told him frankly that, just at that time, public opinion in London was utterly indifferent to the Bourbons. The fervor of interest about the Neapolitan Revolution had gone by; people were tired of Italy, and wanted something new; the Polish insurrection was going on; the great American Civil War was occupying public attention; London audiences cared no more about the crimes of the Bourbons than about the crimes of the Borgias. He was not to be dissuaded. He really believed at first that he could induce some great English orator, Gladstone or Bright, to deliver lectures on those instruments and the guilt of the system which employed them. Then he became more moderate, and applied to this and that professional lecturer—in vain. No one would have anything to do with a project so obviously doomed to failure—he himself spoke no English. At last he induced a lady who was somewhat ambitious of a public career, to lecture for him; and he took a great hall for a series of nights, and advertised largely, and went to great expense. I believe he staked all he had in money or credit on the success of the enterprise; and the making of money was not his object; he would have cheerfully given all he had to create a flame of public indignation against despotism. Need I say what a failure the enterprise was? The London public never manifested the slightest interest in the exhibition. The lecture-hall was empty. I believe the poor Neapolitan tried again and again. The public would not come, or look, or listen. He spent his money in vain; he got into debt in vain. His instruments of torture must have inflicted on their owner agonies enough to have satisfied Maniscalco or Carafa. At last he could bear it no longer. He wrote a few short letters to some friends (I have still that which I received—a melancholy memorial), simply thanking them for what efforts they had made to assist him in his object, acknowledging that he had been over sanguine, and intimating that he had now given up the enterprise. Nothing more was said or hinted. A day or two after, he locked himself up in his room. Somebody heard an explosion, but took no particular notice. The lady who had endeavored to give voice to my poor friend's scheme came, later in the day, to see him. The door was broken open—and the poor Neapolitan lav dead, a pistol still in his hand, a pistol bullet in his brain.

THE REVEREND CHARLES KINGSLEY.

I WONDER how many of the rising generation in America or in England have read "Alton Locke"? Many years have passed since I read or even saw it. I do not care to read it any more, for I fear that it would not now sustain the effect of the impression it once produced on me, and I do not desire to destroy or even to weaken that impression. I know the book is not a great work of art. I know that three-fourths of its value consists in its blind and earnest feeling; that the story is heavily constructed, that many of the details are extravagant exaggerations, and that the author after all was not in the least a democrat or a believer in human equality. I have not forgotten that even then, when he braved respectable public opinion by taking a tailor for his hero, he took good care that the tailor should have genteel relations. Still I retain the impression which the book once produced, and I do not care to have it disturbed. Therefore I do not read or criticise "Alton Locke" any more; I remember it only as it struck me long ago—as a generous protest against the brutal indifference, literary and political, which left the London artisan so long to toil and suffer and sicken, to run into debt, to drink and fight and pine and die, in the darkness. Is it necessary—perhaps it is—to explain to some of my readers the story of "Alton Locke"? It is the story of a young London tailor-boy who has instincts and aspirations far above his class; who yearns to be a poet and a patriot; who loves and struggles in vain; who is supposed to sum up in his own weakly body all the best emotions, the vainest pinings, the wildest wishes, the most righteous protests of his fellows; who joins with the Chartist movement for lack of a better way to the great end, and sees its failure, and himself utterly broken down goes out to America to seek a new life there, and only beholds the shore of the promised land to die. Here at least was a grand idea. Here was the motive of a prose epic that ought to have been more thrilling to modern ears than the song of Tasso. The effect of the work at the time was strengthened by the fact that the author was a clergyman of the Church of England, who was believed to be a man of aristocratic family and connections. The book was undoubtedly a great success in its day. The strong idea which was in the heart of it carried it along. The Rev. Charles Kingsley became suddenly famous.

"Alton Locke" was published more than twenty years ago. Then Charles Kingsley was to most boys in Great Britain who read books at all a sort of living embodiment of chivalry, liberty, and a revolt against the established order of baseness and class-oppression in so many spheres of our society. The author of "Alton Locke" about the same time delivered a sermon in the country church where he officiated, so full of warm and passionate protest against the wrongs done to the poor by existing systems, that his spiritual chief, the rector or dean or some other dignitary, arose in the church itself—morally and physically arose, as Mrs. Gamp did—and denounced the preacher. Need it be said that the report of so unusual and extraordinary a scene as this excited our youthful enthusiasm into a perfect flame for the minister of the State Church who had braved the public censure of his superior in the cause of human right? For a long time Charles Kingsley was our chosen hero—I am speaking now of young men with the youthful spirit of revolt in them, with dreams of republics and ideas about the equality of man. If I were to be asked to describe Charles Kingsley now, having regard to the tendency of his writings and his public attitude, how should I speak of him? First, as about the most perverse and wrong-headed supporter of every political abuse, the most dogmatic champion of every wrong cause in domestic and foreign politics, that even a State Church has for many years produced. I hardly remember, in my practical observation of politics, a great public question but Charles Kingsley was at the wrong side of it. The vulgar glorification of mere strength and power, such a disgraceful characteristic of modern public opinion, never had a louder-tongued votary than he. The apostle of liberty and equality, as he seemed to me in my early days, has of late only shown himself to my mind as the champion of slave-systems of oppression and the iron reign of mere force. Is this a paradox? Has the man undergone a wonderful change of opinions? It is not a paradox, and I think Charles Kingsley has not changed his views. Perhaps a short sketch of the man and his work may reconcile these seeming antagonisms and make the reality coherent and clear.

I was present at a meeting not long since where Mr. Kingsley was one of the principal speakers. The meeting was held in London, the audience was a peculiarly Cockney audience, and Charles Kingsley is personally little known to the public of the metropolis. Therefore when he began to speak there was quite a little thrill of wonder and something like incredulity through the listening benches. Could that, people near me asked, really be Charles Kingsley, the novelist, the poet, the scholar, the aristocrat, the gentleman, the pulpit-orator, the "soldier-priest," the apostle of muscular Christianity? Yes, that was indeed he. Rather tall, very angular, surprisingly awkward, with thin, staggering legs, a hatchet face adorned with scraggy gray whiskers, a faculty for falling into the most ungainly attitudes, and making the most hideous contortions of visage and frame; with a rough provincial accent and an uncouth way of speaking, which would be set down for absurd caricature on the boards of a comic theatre; such was the appearance which the author of "Glaucus" and "Hypatia" presented to his startled audience. Since Brougham's time nothing so ungainly, odd, and ludicrous had been displayed upon an English platform. Needless to say, Charles Kingsley has not the eloquence of Brougham. But he has a robust and energetic plain-speaking which soon struck home to the heart of the meeting. He conquered his audience. Those who at first could hardly keep from laughing; those who, not knowing the speaker, wondered whether he was not mad or in liquor; those who heartily disliked his general principles and his public attitude, were alike won over, long before he had finished, by his bluff and blunt earnestness and his transparent sincerity. The subject was one which concerned the social suffering of the poor. Mr. Kingsley approached it broadly and boldly, talking with a grand disregard for logic and political economy, sometimes startling the more squeamish of his audience by the Biblical frankness of his descriptions and his language, but, I think, convincing every one that he was sound at heart, and explaining unconsciously to many how it happened that one endowed with sympathies so humane and liberal should so often have distinguished himself as the champion of the stupidest systems and the harshest oppressions. Anybody could see that the strong impelling force of the speaker's character was an emotional one; that sympathy and not reason, feeling rather than logic, instinct rather than observation, would govern his utterances. There are men in whom, no matter how robust and masculine their personal character, a disproportionate amount of the feminine element seems to have somehow found a place. These men will usually see things not as they really are, but as they are reflected through some personal prejudice or emotion. They will generally spring to conclusions, obey sudden impulses and instincts, ignore evidence and be very "thorough" and sweeping in all their judgments. When they are right they are—like the young lady in the song—very, very good; but like her, too, when they happen to be wrong they are "horrid." Of these men the author of "Alton Locke" is a remarkable illustration. It seems odd to describe the expounder of the creed of Muscular Christianity as one endowed with too much of the feminine element. But for all his vigor of speech and his rough voice, Mr. Charles Kingsley is as surely feminine in his way of reasoning, his likes and dislikes, his impulses and his prejudices, as Harriet Martineau is masculine in her intellect and George Sand in her emotions.

Mr. Charles Kingsley is a man of ancient English family, very proud of his descent, and full of the conviction so ostentatiously paraded by many Englishmen, that good blood carries with it a warrant for bravery, justice, and truth. The Kingsleys are a Cheshire family; I believe they date from before the Conquest—it does not much matter. I shall not apply to them John Bright's epigram about families which came over with William the Conqueror and never did anything else; for the Kingsleys seem to have been always an active race. They took an energetic part in the civil war during Charles the First's time, and stood by the Parliament. I am told that the family have still in their possession a commission to raise a troop of horse, given to a Kingsley and signed by Oliver Cromwell. One of the family emigrated to the New World with the Pilgrim Fathers, and I believe the Kingsley line still flourishes there like a bay-tree. Irrepressible energy, so far as I know, seems to have always been a characteristic of the household. Charles Kingsley was born near Dartmouth, in Devonshire; every one who has read his books must know how he revels in descriptions of the lovely scenery of Devon. He was for a while a pupil of the Rev. Derwent Coleridge, son of the poet, and he finally studied at Magdalene College, Cambridge. Mr. Kingsley was originally intended for the legal profession, but he changed his mind and went into the church. He was first curate and soon after rector of the Hampshire parish of Eversley, the name of which has since been so constantly kept in association with his own. I may mention that Mr. Kingsley married one of a trio of sisters—the Misses Grenfell—a second of whom was afterwards married to Mr. Froude, and is since dead, while the third became the wife of one of the foremost English journalists. Passing away from these merely personal facts, barely worth a brief note, we shall find that Kingsley's real existence, if I may use such a phrase, began and developed under the guidance of a remarkable man and under the inspiration of a strange movement. The man to whose leadership and teaching Mr. Kingsley owed so much was the Rev. Frederick Denison Maurice, who died in the first week of last April.

It would not be easy to explain to an American reader the meaning and the extent of the influence which this eminent man exercised over a large field of English society. The life of Mr. Maurice contains nothing worthy of note as to facts and dates; but its spirit infused new soul and sense into a whole generation. He was not a great speaker or a great thinker; he was not a bold reformer; he had not a very subtle intellect; I doubt whether his writings will be much read in coming time. He was simply a great character, a grand influence. He sent a new life into the languid and decaying frame of the State Church of England. He quickened it with a fresh sense of duty. His hope and purpose were to bring that church into affectionate and living brotherhood with modern thought, work, and society. An early friend and companion of John Sterling (the two friends married two sisters), Maurice had all the sweetness and purity of Carlyle's hero, with a far greater intellectual strength. Mr. Maurice set himself to make the English Church a practical influence in modern thought and society. He did not believe in a religion sitting apart on the cold Olympian heights of dogmatic theology, and looking down with dignified disdain upon the common life and the vulgar toils of humanity. He held that a church, if it is good for anything, ought to be able to meet fair and square the challenge of the skeptic and the infidel, and that it ought to concern itself about all that concerns men and women. One of the fruits of his long and valuable labor is the Workingmen's College in Red Lion Square, London, an institution of which he became the principal and to which he devoted much of his time and attention. Only a few weeks before his death he presided at one of the public meetings of this his favorite institution. He was the parent of the scheme of "Christian socialism," which sprang into existence more than twenty years ago and is bearing fruit still—a scheme to set on foot coöperative associations among working men on sound and progressive principles; to help the working men by advances of capital, in order that they might thus be enabled to help themselves. One of Mr. Maurice's earliest and most ardent pupils was Charles Kingsley; another was Thomas Hughes. In helping Mr. Maurice to carry out these schemes Kingsley was brought into frequent intercourse with some of the London Chartists, and especially with the working tailors, who have nearly all a strong radical tendency. Kingsley's impulsive sympathies took fire, and flamed out with the novel "Alton Locke, Tailor and Poet."

That extraordinary Chartist movement, so long in preparation and so suddenly extinguished, how completely a thing of the past it seems to have become! Only twenty-four years have passed since its collapse. Men under forty can recall, as if it were yesterday, all its incidents and its principal figures. People in the United States know that my friend Henry Vincent is still only in his prime; he was one of its earliest and foremost leaders. But it seems as old and dead as a peasant-war of the Middle Ages. It was a strange jumble of politics and social complaints. It was partly the blind, passionate protest of working men who knew that they had no right to starve and suffer in a prosperous country, but who hardly knew where the real grievance lay. It was partly the protest of untaught and eager intelligence against the brutal apathy of government which would do nothing for national education. Its political demands were very modest. Some of them have since been quietly carried into law; some of them have been quietly dismissed into the realm of anachronisms. Chartism was indeed rather a wild cry, a passionate yearning of lonely men for combination, than any definite political enterprise. One looks back now with a positive wonder upon the savage stupidity of the ruling classes which so nearly converted it into a rebellion. Of course it was in some instances seized hold of by selfish and scheming politicians, who played with it for their own purposes. Of course it had its evil counsellors, its false friends, its cowards, and its traitors. But on the whole there was a noble spirit of manly honesty pervading the movement, which to my mind fills it with a romantic interest and ought to secure for it an honorable memory. It found leaders in many cases outside its own classes. There was, for example, "Tom Duncombe," a sort of Alcibiades of English Radicalism; a brilliant talker in Parliament, a gay man of fashion, steeped deep in reckless debt and sparkling dissipation; hand and glove with the fast young noblemen of the West End gambling houses, and the ardent Chartist working men of Shoreditch and Clerkenwell. There was Feargus O'Connor—huge, boistering, fearless—a burlesque Mirabeau with red hair; a splendid mob-speaker, who could fight his way by sheer strength of muscle and fist through a hostile crowd; vain of his half-mythical descent from Irish kings, even when he delighted in being hail fellow well met with tailors and hod-carriers; revelling in the fiercest struggles of politics and the wildest freaks of prolonged debauchery. O'Connor tried to crowd half a dozen lives into one, and the natural result was that he prematurely broke down. For a long time before his death he was a mere lunatic. A strange fact was that as his manners were always eccentric and boisterous, he had become an actual madman for months before those around him were fully aware of the change. In the House of Commons the freaks of the poor lunatic were for a long time supposed to be only more marked eccentricities, or, as some thought, insolent affectations of eccentricity. He would rise while Lord Palmerston was addressing the House, walk up to the great minister, and give him a tremendous slap on the back. One night he actually assaulted a member of the House, and the Speaker ordered his arrest. Feargus sauntered coolly out into the lobbies. The sergeant-at-arms was bidden to go forth and arrest the offender. Lord Charles Russell (brother of Earl Russell), then and now sergeant-at-arms, is a thin, little, feeble man. I have been told by some who witnessed it that the scene in the lobbies became highly amusing. Lord Charles went with reluctant steps about his awful task. By this time everybody was beginning to suspect that O'Connor was really a madman. Anyhow, he was a giant, and at his sanest moments perfectly reckless. Now it is not a pleasant task for a weak and little man to be sent to arrest even a sane giant; but only think of laying hands on a giant who appears to be out of his senses! The dignity of his office, however, had to be upheld, and Lord Charles trotted quietly after his huge quarry. He cast imploring looks at member after member, but it was none of their business to interfere, and they had no inclination to volunteer. Some of them indeed were deeply engrossed in speculations as to what would happen if Feargus were suddenly to turn round. Would the sergeant-at-arms put his dignity in his pocket and actually run? Or, if he stood his ground, what would be the result? Happily, however, just as Feargus and his unwilling pursuer reached Westminster Hall, the eager eye of Lord Charles Russell descried a little knot of policemen; he hailed them; they came up, and the sergeant-at-arms did his duty and the capture was effected. I can well remember seeing O'Connor, somewhere about this time, sauntering through Covent Garden market, with rolling, restless gait; his hair, that once was fiery red, all snowy white; his eye gleaming with the peculiar, quick, shallow, ever-changing glitter of madness. The poor fellow rambled from fruit-stall to fruit-stall, talking all the while to himself, sometimes taking up a fruit as if he meant to buy it, and then putting it down with a vacant laugh and walking on. It was a pitiable spectacle. His light of reason soon flickered out altogether, and death came to his relief.

I must not omit to mention, when speaking of the Chartist leaders, the brave, disinterested, and highly-gifted Ernest Jones, who sacrificed such bright worldly prospects for the cause of the People's Charter. Long after the Charter and its agitation were dead, Jones emerged into public life again, still comparatively a young man, and he seemed about to enter on a career both brilliant and valuable. An immature and unexpected death interposed.

However, I have wandered away from the subject of my paper. Charles Kingsley came to know the principal working men among the Chartists, and his impulsive nature was greatly influenced by their words and their lives. Most of their leaders drawn from other classes, O'Connor especially, he distrusted and disliked. But the rank and file of the movement, the working men, the sufferers, the "prolétaires" as they would be called nowadays, attracted his kindly heart. Chartism had fallen. It collapsed suddenly in 1848; died amid Homeric laughter of the public. It fell mainly because it had come to occupy a false position altogether. Partly by ignorance, partly by the selfish folly of some of its leaders, and partly by the severity of the government measures, the movement had been driven into a dilemma which it never originally contemplated. It must either go into open rebellion or surrender. It was jammed up like MacMahon at Sedan. Chartism had no real wish to rebel, although of course the flame of the recent revolution in Paris had glared over it and made it wild; and it had no means of carrying on a revolt for a single day. So it could only surrender; and the surrender took place under conditions which made it seem utterly ridiculous. Kingsley was seized with the idea of crystallizing all this into a romance. He had as a further stimulant and guide the work which Henry Mayhew was then publishing, 'London Labor and the London Poor," a serial which by its painful and startling revelations was working a profound impression on England. Mayhew's narratives were often inaccurate, for he could not conduct the whole enterprise himself, and had sometimes to call in the aid of careless and untrustworthy associates, who occasionally found it easier to throw off a bit of sentimental or sensational romance than to pursue a patient inquiry. But the general effect of the publication was healthful and practical, and it became the parent of nearly all the efforts that followed to lay bare and ameliorate the condition of the London poor. There can be no doubt that it had a great influence on the impressionable mind of Charles Kingsley. He wrote "Alton Locke," and the book became a great success. The Tailor and Poet was the hero of the hour. "Blackwood" at once christened Alton Locke "Young Remnants;" but Young Remnants survived the joke. The novel is full of nonsense and extravagance; and with all its sympathy for tailors, it has a great deal of Kingsley's characteristic affection for rank and birth. But it had a really great idea at its heart, and struck out one or two new characters—especially that of the old Scotch bookseller—and it made its mark. The peculiarity, however, to which I wish now especially to direct attention is its utter absence of practical thinking-power. Nowhere can you find any proof that the author is able to think about anything. An idea strikes him; he seizes it, and, to use Hawthorne's expression, "wields it like a flail." Then he throws it down and takes up something else, to employ it in the same wild and incoherent fashion. This is Kingsley all out, and always. He is not content with developing his one only gift of any literary value—the capacity to paint big, striking pictures with a strong glare or glow on them. He firmly believes himself a profound philosopher and social reformer, and he will insist on obtruding before the world on all occasions his absolute incapacity for any manner of reasoning on any subject whatsoever. Wild with intellectual egotism, and blind to all teaching from without, Kingsley rushes at great and difficult subjects head downwards like a bull. Thus he tackled Chartism, and society, and competition, and political economy, and what not, in his "Alton Locke"; and thus he has gone on ever since and will to the end of his chapter, always singling out for the display of his powers the very subjects whereof he knows least, and is by the whole constitution of his intellect and temperament least qualified to judge.

I am writing now rather about Kingsley himself than about his books, with which the readers of "The Galaxy" are of course well acquainted. I therefore pass over the many books he produced between "Alton Locke" and "Westward Ho!"—and I dwell upon the latter only because it illustrates the next great idea which got hold of the author after the little fever about Chartism had passed away. I suppose "Westward Ho!" may be regarded as the first appearance of the school of Muscular Christianity. Mr. Kingsley started for our benefit the huge British hero who could do anything in the way of fighting and walking, and propagated the doctrines of the English Church. To read the Bible and to kill the Spaniards was the whole duty of the ideal Briton of Elizabeth's time, according to this authority. The notion was a success. In a moment our literature became flooded with pious athletes who knocked their enemies down with texts from the Scriptures and left-handers from the shoulder. All these heroes were of necessity "gentlemen." One of the principal articles of the new gospel according to Kingsley was that truth, valor, muscle, and theological fervor were only possessed in their fulness by the scions of good old English county families. Other nations seldom had such qualities at all; never had them to perfection; and even favored Britain only saw them properly illustrated in country gentlemen of long descent. Of course this sort of thing, which was for the moment a sincere idea with Kingsley, became a mere affectation among his followers and admirers. The fighting-parson pattern of hero was for a while as great a bore as the rough and ugly hero after Jane Eyre's "Rochester," or the colossal and corrupt guardsman whom "Guy Livingstone" sent abroad on the world. Certainly Kingsley's hero was a better style of man than Guy Livingstone's, for at the worst he was only an egotistical savage, and not a profligate. But I think he did a good deal of harm in his day. He helped to encourage and inflate that feeling of national self-conceit which makes people such nuisances to their neighbors, and he fostered that odious reverence for mere force and power which Carlyle had already made fashionable. Kingsley himself appears to have become "possessed" by his own idea as if by some unmanageable spirit. It banished all his chartism and democracy and liberalism, and the rest of it. Under its influence Kingsley out-Carlyled Carlyle in the worship of strong despotisms and force of any kind. He went out of his way to excuse slavery in the Southern States. He became the fervent panegyrist of Governor Eyre of Jamaica. When two sides were possible to any question of human politics, he was sure to take the wrong one. Nothing for long years, I think, has been more repulsive, and in its way more mischievous, than the cant about "strength" which Kingsley did so much to diffuse and to glorify.

Meanwhile his irrepressible energy was always driving him into new fields of work. It never allowed him time to think. The moment any sort of idea struck him, he rushed at it and crushed it into the shape of a book or an essay. He wrote historical novels, philosophical novels, and theological novels. He wrote poetry—yards of poetry—volumes of poetry. There really is a great deal of the spirit of poetry in him, and he has done better things with the hexameter verse than better poets have done. There was for a long time a fervid school of followers who swore by him, and would have it that he was to be the great English poet of the century. He published essays, tracts, lectures, and sermons without number. He seems to have made up his mind to publish in book form somehow everything that he had spoken or written anywhere. He inundated the leading newspapers with letters on this, that, and the other subject. He was appointed professor of modern history at the University of Cambridge on the death of Sir James Stephen, and he launched at once into a series of lectures, which were almost immediately published in book form. Why he published them it was hard for even vanity itself to explain, because with characteristic bluntness he began his course with the acknowledgment that he really knew nothing in particular about the subjects whereon he had undertaken to instruct the University and the world. He made up in courage, however, for anything he may have lacked in knowledge. He went bravely in for an onslaught on the positive theory of history—on Comte, Mill, Buckle, Darwin, and everybody else. He made it perfectly clear very soon that he did not know even what these authors profess to teach. He flatly denied that there is any such thing as an inexorable law in nature. He proved that even the supposed law of gravitation is not by any means the rigid and universal sort of thing that Newton and such-like persons have supposed. How, it may be asked, did he prove this? In the following words: "If I choose to catch a stone, I can hold it in my hands; it has not fallen to the ground, and will not till I let it. So much for the inevitable action of the laws of gravity." This way of dealing with the question may seem to many readers nothing better than downright buffoonery. But Kingsley was as grave as a church and as earnest as an owl. He fully believed that he was refuting the pedants who believe in the inevitable action of the law of gravitation, when he talked of holding a stone in his hand. That an impulsive, illogical man should on the spur of the moment talk this kind of nonsense, even from a professor's chair, is not perhaps wonderful; but it does seem a little surprising that he should see it in print, revise it, and publish it, without ever becoming aware of its absurdity.

In the same headlong spirit Mr. Kingsley rushed into his famous controversy with Dr. John Henry Newman. I have already, when writing of Dr. Newman, alluded to this controversy, which for a time excited the greatest interest and indeed the greatest amusement in England. I only refer to it now as an illustration of the surprising hotheadedness and lack of thinking power which characterize the author of "Alton Locke." Dr. Newman preached a sermon on "Wisdom and Innocence." Mr. Kingsley went out of his way to discourse and comment on this sermon, and publicly declared that its doctrine was an exhortation to disregard truth. "Dr. Newman informs us that truth need not and on the whole ought not to be a virtue for its own sake." Of course this was as grave a charge as could possibly be made against a great religious teacher. It was doubly odious and offensive to Dr. Newman because it was the revival of an old and familiar charge against the church he had lately entered. It was made by Kingsley in an off-hand, careless sort of way, as if it were something acknowledged and indisputable—as if some one were to say, "Horace Greeley informs us that a protective tariff is often useful," or "Henry Ward Beecher is in favor of early rising." Newman wrote with a cold civility to ask in what passage of his writings any such doctrine was to be found. Of course nothing of the kind was to be found. If it were possible to conceive of any divine in our days holding such a doctrine, we may be perfectly certain that he would never put it into print. Newman was known to all the world as the purest and most austere devotee of what he believed to be the truth. He had sacrificed the most brilliant career in the Church of England for his convictions, and, strange to say, had yet retained the admiration and the affection of those whose religious fellowship he had renounced. Kingsley had but one course in fairness and common sense open to him. He ought to have frankly apologized. He ought to have owned that he had spoken without thinking; that he had blurted out the words without observing the gravity of the charge they contained; and that he was sorry for it. But he did not do this. He published a letter, in which he said that Dr. Newman having denied that his doctrine bore the meaning Mr. Kingsley had put upon it, he (Kingsley) could only express his regret at having mistaken him. This was nearly as bad as the first charge. It distinctly conveyed the idea that but for Dr. Newman's subsequent explanation and denial, certain words of his might fairly have been understood to bear the odious meaning ascribed to them. Dr. Newman returned to the charge, still with a chill urbanity which I cannot help thinking Kingsley mistook for weakness or fear. He pointed out that he had never denied anything; that there was nothing for him to deny; that Mr. Kingsley had charged him with teaching a certain odious doctrine, and he therefore asked Mr. Kingsley to point to the passage containing the doctrine, or frankly own that there was no such passage in existence. Kingsley thereupon took the worst, the most unfair, and as it proved the most foolish course a man could possibly have pursued. He went to work to fasten on Newman by a constructive argument, drawn from the general tendency of his teaching, a belief in the doctrine of which he was unable to find any specific statement. Then opened out that controversy, which was quite an event in its time, and set everybody talking. Newman's was an intellect which must be described as the peer of Stuart Mill's or Herbert Spencer's. He was a perfect master of polemical science. He could write, when he thought fit, with a vitriolic keenness of sarcasm. When he had allowed Kingsley to entangle himself sufficiently, Newman fairly opened fire, and the rest of the debate was like a duel between some blundering, wrong-headed cudgel-player from a village green, and some accomplished professor of the science of the rapier from Paris or Vienna. Not the least amusing thing about the controversy was the manner in which it put Kingsley into open antagonism with his own teaching. He endeavored gratuitously and absurdly to convict Dr. Newman of a disregard for the truth, because Newman believed in the miracles of the saints. For, he argued, a man of Newman's intellect could not believe in such things if he inquired into them. But he did not inquire into them; he taught that they were not to be questioned but accepted as orthodox. Thereby he showed that he preferred orthodoxy to truth—"truth, the capital virtue, the virtue of virtues, without which all others are rotten." Now, that sounds very well, and we all agree in what Kingsley says of the truth. But Kingsley had not long before been assailing Bishop Colenso for his infidelity. Kingsley declared himself shocked at the publication of a work like Dr. Colenso's, which claimed and exercised a license of inquiry that seemed to him "anything but reverent." He distinctly laid it down that the liberty of religious criticism must be "reverent," and "within the limits of orthodoxy!" Now, I am not challenging Mr. Kingsley's doctrine as to the limit of religious inquiry. That forms no part of my purpose. But it is perfectly obvious that if to limit inquiry within the bounds of orthodoxy shows a disregard for truth in John Henry Newman, the same practice must be evidence of a similar disregard in Charles Kingsley. Of course Kingsley never thought of this—never thought about the matter at all. He disliked Colenso's teaching on the one hand and Newman's on the other. He said the first thing that came into his mind against each in turn, and never heeded the fact that the reproach he employed in the former case was utterly inconsistent with that which he uttered in the other. I do not believe, however, that the controversy did Kingsley any harm. Nobody ever expected consistency or rational argument from him. People were amused, and laughed, and perhaps wondered why Dr. Newman should have taken any trouble in the matter at all. But Kingsley remained in popular estimation just the same as before—blundering, hot-headed, boisterous, but full of brilliant imagination, and thoroughly sound at heart.

Thus Charles Kingsley is always at work. Lately he has been describing some of the scenery of the West Indies, and proclaiming the virtues of Australian potted meats. He has thrown his whole soul into the Australian meat question. The papers have run over with letters from him intended to prove to the world how good and cheap it is to eat the mutton and beef brought in tin cans from Australia. I believe Mr. Kingsley acknowledges that all his energy and eloquence have been unequal to the task of persuading his servants to eat the excellent food which he is himself willing to have at his table. He has also been lecturing on temperance, and delivering a philippic against Darwin. He has also written a paper condemning and deprecating the modern critical spirit. There is one rule, he insists, "by which we should judge all human opinions, endeavors, characters." That is, "Are they trying to lessen the sum of human misery, of human ignorance? Are they trying, however clumsily, to cure physical suffering, weakness, deformity, disease, and to make human bodies what God would have them? . . . If so, let us judge them no further. Let them pass out of the pale of our criticism. Let their creed seem to us defective, their opinions fantastic, their means irrational. God must judge of that, not we. They are trying to do good; then they are children of the light." This is not, perhaps, the spirit in which Kingsley himself criticised Newman or Colenso. But if we judge him according to the principle which he recommends, he would assuredly take high rank; for I never heard any one question his sincerity and his honest purpose to do good. Of course he is often terribly provoking. His feminine and almost hysterical impulsiveness, and his antiquated, feudal devotion to rank, are difficult to bear always without strong language. His utter absence of sympathy with political emancipation is a lamentable weakness. His self-conceit and egotism often make him a ludicrous object. Still, he has an honest heart, and he tries to do the work of a man; and he is one of those who would, if they could, make the English State Church still a living, an active, and an all-pervading influence. As a preacher and a pastor he often reminds me of the Rev. Henry Ward Beecher. Of course he is far below Mr. Beecher in all oratorical gifts, as well as in political enlightenment; but he has the same prefervid and illogical nature, the same vigorous, self-sufficient temperament, the same tendency to "slop over," the same generous energy in any cause that seems to him good.

It will be inferred that I do not rate Mr. Kingsley very highly as an author. He can describe glowing scenery admirably, and he can vigorously ring the changes on his one or two ideas—the muscular Englishman, the glory of the Elizabethan discoverers, and so on. He is a scholar, and he has written verses which sometimes one is on the point of mistaking for poetry, so much of the poet's feelings have they about them. He can do a great many things very cleverly. He belongs to a clever family. His brother, Henry Kingsley, is a spirited and dashing novelist, whom the critics sneer at a good deal, but whose books always command a large circulation, and have made a distinctive mark. Perhaps if Charles Kingsley had done less he might have done better. Human capacity is limited. It is not given to mortal to be a great preacher, a great philosopher, a great scholar, a great poet, a great historian, a great novelist, an indefatigable country parson, and a successful man in fashionable society. Mr. Kingsley seems never to have quite made up his mind for which of these callings to go in especially, and being with all his versatility not at all many-sided, but strictly one-sided, and almost one-ideaed, the result of course has been that, touching success at many points, he has absolutely mastered it at none. His place in letters has been settled this long time. Since "Westward Ho!" at the latest, he has never added half a cubit to his stature. The "Chartist Parson" has, on the other hand, been growing more and more aristocratic, illiberal, and even servile in politics. His discourse on the recovery of the Prince of Wales was the very hyperbole of the most old-fashioned loyalty—a discourse worthy of Filmer, and utterly out of place in the present century. Muscular Christianity has shrunk and withered long since. The professorship of modern history was a failure, and has been given up. Darwin is flourishing, and I am not certain about the success of Australian beef. All this acknowledged, however, it must still be owned that, failing in this, that, and the other attempt, and never probably achieving any real and enduring success, Charles Kingsley has been an influence and a name of mark in the Victorian age. I cannot, indeed, well imagine that age without him, although his presence is sometimes only associated with it as that of Malvolio with the court of the fair lady in "Twelfth Night." Men of far greater intellect have made their presence less strongly felt, and imprinted their image much less clearly on the minds of their contemporaries. He is an example of how much may be done by energetic temper, fearless faith in self, an absence of all sense of the ridiculous, a passionate sympathy, and a wealth of half-poetic descriptive power. If ever we have a woman's parliament in England, Charles Kingsley ought to be its chaplain; for I know of no clever man whose mind and temper more aptly illustrate the illogical impulsiveness, the rapid emotional changes, the generous, often wrong-headed vehemence, the copious flow of fervid words, the vivid freshness of description without analysis, and the various other peculiarities which, justly or unjustly, the world has generally agreed to regard as the special characteristics of woman.

MR. JAMES ANTHONY FROUDE.

MR FROUDE, I perceive, is about to visit the United States. *Reddas incolumem!* He is a man of mark—with whatever faults, a great Englishman. It will not take the citizens of New York and Boston long to become quite as familiar with his handsome, thoughtful face as the people of London. Mr. Froude rarely makes his appearance at any public meeting or demonstration of any kind. He delivers a series of lectures now and then to one of the great solemn literary institutions. He is a member of some of our literary and scientific societies. He used at one time occasionally to attend the meetings of the Newspaper Press Fund Committee, where his retiring ways and grave, meditative demeanor reminded me, I cannot tell why, of Nathaniel Hawthorne. He has many friends, and mingles freely in private society, but to the average public he is only a name; to a large proportion of that average public he is not even so much. I presume he might walk the Strand every day and no head turn round to look after him. I presume it would not be difficult to get together a large public meeting of respectable and intelligent London rate-payers of whom not one could tell who Mr. Froude was, or would be aroused to the slightest interest by the mention of his name. Who, indeed, *is* generally known or cared about in London? I do not say universally known, for nobody enjoys that proud distinction, not even the Prince of Wales—nay, not even the Tichborne claimant. But who is ever generally known? Gladstone and Disraeli are; and Bright is. Dickens was, and, to a certain extent, Thackeray. Archbishop Manning and Mr. Spurgeon are, perhaps; and I cannot remember anybody else just now. Palmerston, in his day, was better known than any of these; and the Duke of Wellington was by far the most widely known of all. The Duke of Wellington was the only man who during my time was nearly as well known in London as Mr. Greeley is in New York. "How can you, you know?" as Mr. Pecksniff asks. We have four millions of people crowded into one city. It takes a giant of popularity indeed to be seen and recognized above that crowd. As for your Brownings and Spencers and Froudes and the rest, your mere men of genius—well, they have their literary celebrity and they will doubtless have their fame. But average London knows and cares no more about them than it does about you or me.

Therefore, let not any American reader, when I describe Mr. Froude as a man of mark and a great Englishman, assume that he is a man of mark with the crowd. Let no American visitor to London be astonished if, finding himself in the neighborhood of Mr. Froude's residence, and stepping into half a dozen shops in succession to ask for the exact address of the historian, he should hear that nobody there knew anything about him. Nobody but scholars and literary people knew anything about the late George Grote, one of the few great philosophic historians of the modern world. Compared with the influence of Mr. Grote upon average London, that of Mr. Froude may almost be described as sensational; for Froude has stirred up literary and religious controversy, and has been denounced and has personally defended himself, and in that way must have attracted some attention. At all events, when New York has seen and heard Mr. Froude, she will have seen and heard one of the men of our time in the true sense; one of the men who have toiled out a channel for a fresh current of literature to run in, and whose name can hereafter be omitted from no list of celebrities, however select, which pretends to illustrate the characteristics of the Victorian age in England.

Mr. Froude is a Devonshire man, son of a Protestant archdeacon. He was educated in Westminster School, and afterward at the famous Oriel College, Oxford. He is now some fifty-four or fifty-five years of age, but seems, and I hope is, only in his prime. Froude is a waif of that marvellous Oxford movement which began some forty years ago, and of which the strange, diversely operating influence still radiates through English thought and society. That movement was a peculiar theological *renaissance*, which partly converted itself into a reaction and partly into a revolt. It began with the saintly and earnest Keble; its master spirits were John Henry Newman and Dr. Pusey. It proposed to vindicate for the Protestant Church the true place of spiritual heir to the apostles and universal teacher of the Christian world. Newman, Pusey, and others worked in the production of the celebrated "Tracts for the Times." The results were extraordinary. The impulse of inquiry thus set going seemed to shake all foundations of agreement. It was an explosion which blew people various ways, they could hardly tell why or how. It made one man a ritualist, another an Ultramontane Roman Catholic, a third a skeptic. Like the two women grinding at the mill in the Scripture, two devoted companions, brothers perhaps, were seized by that impulse and flung different ways. Before the wave had subsided it tossed Mr. Froude, then a young man of five or six and twenty, clear out of his intended career as a clergyman of the Church of England. He had taken deacon's orders before the change came on him, which drove him forth as the two Newmans had been driven; but his course was more like that of Francis Newman than of John Henry. He seemed, indeed, at one time likely to pass away altogether into the ranks of the skeptics. Skepticism is in London attended with no small degree of social disadvantage. To be in "society," you must believe as people of good position do. Dissent of any kind is unfashionable. A shrewd friend of mine says a dissenter can never enter London. Dissent never gets any further than Hackney or Clapham, a northern and a southern suburb. Allowance being made for a touch of satirical exaggeration, the saying is very expressive, and even instructive. Probably, however, the odds are more heavily against mere dissent than a bold, intellectual skepticism, which may have a piquant and alluring flavor about it, and make a man a sort of curiosity and lion, so that "society" would tolerate him as it does a poet. There was, however, nothing in exclusion from fashionable society to frighten a man like Froude, who, so far as I know, has never troubled himself about the favor of the West End. His first work of any note (for I pass over "The Shadows of the Clouds," a novel, I believe, which I have never read nor seen) was "The Nemesis of Faith." This work was published in 1848, and is chiefly to be valued now as an illustration of one stage of development through which the intellect of the author and the tolerance of his age were passing. "The Nemesis of Faith" was declared a skeptical and even an infidel book. It was sternly censured and condemned by the authorities of the university to which Mr. Froude had belonged. He had won a fellowship in Exeter College, Oxford; the college authorities punished him for his opinions by depriving him of it. "The Nemesis of Faith" created a sensation, an excitement and alarm, which surely were extravagant even then and would be impossible now. Its doubts and complaints would seem wild enough to-day. Men of any freshness and originality so commonly begin—or about that time did begin—their career with a little outburst of skepticism, that the thing seems almost as natural as it seemed to Major Pendennis for a young peer to start in public life as a professed republican. Besides, we must remember that "The Nemesis of Faith" was published in what the late Lord Derby once called the pre-scientific age. It was the time when skepticism dealt only in the metaphysical or the emotional, and had not congealed into the far more enduring and corroding form of physical science. As well as I can remember, "The Nemesis of Faith"—which I have not seen for years—was full of life and genius, but not particularly dangerous to settled beliefs. However, a storm raged around it, and around the author; and finally Mr. Froude himself seems to have reconsidered his opinions, for he subsequently withdrew the book from circulation. Its literary success, however, must have shown him clearly what his career was to be. He was at this time drifting about the world in search of occupation; for he found himself cut off from the profession of the Church, on which he had intended to enter, and yet he had, if I am not mistaken, passed far enough within its threshold to disqualify him for admission to one of the other professions. He began to write for the "Westminster Review," which at that time was in the zenith of its intellectual celebrity, and for "Fraser's Magazine." His studies led him especially into the history of the Tudor reigns, and most of his early contributions to "Fraser" were explorations in that field. Out of these studies grew the "History of England," on which the fame of the author is destined to rest. Mr. Froude himself tells us that he began his task with a strong inclination toward what may be called the conventional and orthodox opinions of the character of Henry VIII.; but he found as he studied the actual records and state papers that a different sort of character began to grow up under his eyes. I can easily imagine how his emotional and artistic nature gradually bore him away further and further in the direction thus suddenly opened up, until at last he had created an entirely new Henry for himself. Of course the old traditional notion of Henry, the simple idea which set him down as a monster of lust and cruelty, would soon expose its irrationality to a mind like that of Froude. But, like the writers who, in revolt against the picture of Tiberius given by Tacitus, or that of the French Revolution woven by Burke, have painted the Roman Emperor as an archangel, and the Revolution as a stainless triumph of liberty, so Mr. Froude seems to have been driven into a positive affection and veneration for the subject of his study. In 1856 the first and second volumes appeared of the "History of England from the Fall of Wolsey to the Death of Elizabeth." There has hardly been in our time so fierce a literary controversy as that which sprang up around these two volumes. Perhaps the war of words over Buckle's first volume or Darwin's "Origin of Species could alone be compared with it. Mr. Froude became famous in a moment. The "Edinburgh Review" came out with a fierce, almost a savage attack, to which Mr. Froude replied in an article which he published in "Fraser" and to which he affixed his own signature. Mr. Froude, indeed, has during his career fought several battles in this open, personal manner—a thing very uncommon in England. He has had many enemies. The "Saturday Review" has been unswerving in its passionate hostility to him, and has even gone so far as to arraign his personal integrity as a chronicler. Rumor in London ascribes some of the bitterest of the "Saturday Review" articles to the pen of Mr. Edward A. Freeman, author of "The History of Federal Government," "The History of the Norman Conquest of England," and many historical essays—a prolific writer in reviews and journals. Then as the successive volumes of Froude's work began to appear, and the historian brought out his famous portraiture of Elizabeth and Mary, it was but natural that controversy should thicken and deepen around him. The temper of parties in Great Britain is still nearly as hot as ever it was on the characters of Mary and Elizabeth. Not many years ago Thackeray was hissed in Edinburgh, because in one of his lectures he said something which was supposed to be disparaging to the moral character of Mary of Scotland. Then the whole question of Saxon against Celt comes up again in Mr. Froude's account of English rule in Ireland. Everybody knows what a storm of controversy broke around the historian's head. He was accused not merely of setting up his own personal prejudices as law and history, but even of misrepresenting facts and actually misquoting documents in order to suit his purpose. I do not mean to enter into the discussion, for I am not writing a criticism of Mr. Froude's history, but only a chapter about Mr. Froude himself. But I confess I can quite understand why so many readers, not blind partisans of any cause, become impatient with some of the passages of his works. He coolly and deliberately commends as virtue in one person or one race the very qualities, the very deeds which he stigmatizes as the blackest and basest guilt in others. "Show me the man, and I will show you the law," used to be an old English proverb, illustrating the depth which judicial partisanship and corruption had reached. "Show me the person, and I will show you the moral law," might well be the motto of Mr. Froude's history. But I believe Mr. Froude to be utterly incapable of any misrepresentation or distortion of facts, any conscious coloring of the truth. Indeed, I am rather impressed by the extraordinary boldness with which he often gives the naked facts, and still calmly upholds a theory which to ordinary minds would seem absolutely incompatible with their existence. It appears to be enough if he once makes up his mind to dislike a personage or a race. Let the facts be as they may, Mr. Froude will still explain them to the discredit of the object of his antipathy. His mode of dealing with the characters and actions of those he detests, might remind one of the manner in which the discontented subjects of the perplexed prince in "Rabagas" explain every act of their good-natured ruler: "Je donne un bal—luxe effréné! Pas de bal—quelle avarice! Je passe une revue—intimidation militaire! Je n'en passe pas—je crains l'esprit des troupes! Des pétards à ma fête—l'argent du peuple en fumée! Pas de pétards—rien pour les plaisirs du peuple! Je me porte bien—l'oisivite! Je me porte mal—la débauche! Je bâtis– gaspillage! Je ne bâtis pas—et le prolétaire?"

However that may be, it is certain that the "History" placed Mr. Froude in the very front rank of English authors. He had made a path for himself

He refused to accept the thought of what is commonly called a science of history, although his own method of evolving his narrative is very often in faithful conformity with the principles of that science. He nad written about political economy, in the very opening of his first volume, in a manner which, if it did not imply an actual contempt for the doctrines of that science, yet certainly showed an impatience of its rule which aroused the anger of the economists. He claimed a reversal of the universal decision of modern history as to the character of Henry VIII. He assailed one of the English Protestant's articles of faith when he denied the virtue of Anne Boleyn. He made mistakes and confessed them, and went to work again. The opening of the Spanish archives in the castle of Simancas flooded him with new lights and required a reconstruction of much that he had done. The progress of his work became one of the literary phenomena of the age. All eyes were on it. The rich romantic splendor of the style, the singular power and impressiveness of the historical portraits, fascinated everybody. Orthodox Protestants looked on him as a sort of infidel or pagan, despite his admiration for Queen Bess, because, with all his admiration, he exposed her meannesses and her falsehoods with unsparing hand. Catholics insisted on regarding him as a mere bigot of Protestantism, although he condemned Anne Boleyn. Mr. Froude has always shown a remarkable freedom from prejudice and bigotry. Some of his closest friends are Catholics and Irishmen. I remember a little personal instance of liberality on his part which is perhaps worth mentioning. There was an official in the Record or State Paper Office of England who had become a Roman Catholic, and was, like most English Catholics, especially if converts, rather bigoted and zealous. This gentleman, Mr. Turnbull, happened to be employed some years ago in arranging, copying, and calendaring the Elizabethan State papers. The Evangelical Alliance Society got up a cry against him. They insisted that to employ a Roman Catholic in such a task was only to place in his hands the means of falsifying a most important period of English history, and they argued that the temptation would be too strong for any man like Mr. Turnbull to resist. There sprang up one of those painful and ignoble disputations which are even still only too common in England when religious bigotry gets a chance of raising an alarm. I am sorry to say that so influential a journal as the "Athenæum" joined in the clamor for the dismissal of Mr. Turnbull, who was not accused of having done anything wrong, but only of being placed in a position which might perhaps tempt some base creatures to do wrong. Mr. Turnbull was a gentleman of the highest honor, and, unfortunately for himself, an enthusiast in the very work which then occupied him. Mr. Froude was then engaged in studying the period of history which employed Mr. Turnbull's labors. The opinions of the two men were utterly at variance. Mr. Turnbull must have thought Froude's work in the rehabilitation of Henry VIII., and the glorification of Elizabeth positively detestable. But Mr. Froude bore public testimony to the honor and integrity of Mr. Turnbull. "Mr. Turnbull," Froude wrote, "could have felt no sympathy with the work in which I was engaged; but he spared no pains to be of use to me, and in admitting me to a share of his private room enabled me to witness the ability and integrity with which he discharged his own duties." Bigotry prevailed, however. Mr. Turnbull was removed from his place, and died soon after, disappointed and embittered. But Froude the man is not Froude the author. The man is free from dislikes and prejudices; the author can hardly take a pen in his hand without being suffused by prejudices and dislikes. Take for example his way of dealing with Irish questions, not merely in his history, but in his miscellaneous writings. Mr. Froude has some little property in the west of Ireland, and resides there for a short time every year. He has occasionally detailed his experiences, and commented on them, in the pages of "Fraser." I shall not give my own view of his apparent sentiments toward Ireland, because I am obviously not an impartial judge; but I shall take the opinion of the London "Spectator," which is. The "Spectator" declares that "it may be not unfairly said that Mr. Froude simply loathes the Irish people; not consciously perhaps, for he professes the reverse. But a certain bitter grudge breaks out despite his will now and then. It colors all his tropes. It adds a sting to the casual allusions of his language. When he wants a figure of speech to express the relation between the two islands, he compares the Irish to a kennel of fox-hounds, and the English to their master, and declares that what the Irish want is a master who knows that he is a master and means to continue master." In his occasional studies of contemporary Ireland from the window of his shooting lodge in Kerry, Mr. Froude exhibits the same strange mixture of candor as to fact and blind prejudice as to conclusion which so oddly characterizes his history. He recounts deliberately the most detestable projects—he himself calls them "detestable;" the word is his, not mine—avowed to him by the agents of great Irish landlords, and yet his sympathy is wholly with the agents and against the occupiers. He tells in one instance, with perfect delight, of a mean and vulgar exhibition of triumphant malice which he says an agent, a friend of his, paraded for the humiliation of an evicted and contumacious tenant. The "Spectator" asks in wonder whether it can be possible that "Mr. Froude, an English gentleman by birth and education, an Oxford fellow, is not ashamed to relate this act as an heroic feat?" Indeed, Mr. Froude seems to associate in Ireland only with the "agent" class, and to take all his views of things from them. His testimony is therefore about as valuable as that of a foreigner who twelve or fifteen years ago should have taken his opinions as to slavery in the South from the judgment and conversation of the plantation overseers. The "Spectator" observed, with calm severity, that Mr. Froude's unlucky accounts of his Irish experiences were "a comical example of the way in which an acute and profound mind can become dull to the sense of what is manly, just, and generous, by the mere atmosphere of association." Let me say that I am convinced, however, that all this blind and unmanly prejudice is purely literary; that it is taken up and laid aside with the pen. As I have already said, some of Mr. Froude's closest friends are Irishmen—men who are incapable of associating with any one, however eminent, who really felt the coarse and bitter hatred to their country which Mr. Froude in his wilder moments allows his too fluent pen to express. In fact Mr. Froude is nothing of a philosopher. He settles every question easily and off hand by reference to what Stuart Mill well calls the resource of the lazy—the theory of race. Celts are all wrong and Anglo-Saxons are all right, and there is an end of it. If he has any philosophy and science of history, it is this. It explains everything and reconciles all seeming contradictions. Nothing can be at once more comprehensive and more simple. But there is still something to be added to this story of Mr. Froude's Irish experiences; and I mention the whole thing only to illustrate the peculiar character of Mr. Froude's emotional temperament, which so often renders him untrustworthy as a historian. In the particular instance on which the "Spectator" commented, it turned out that Mr. Froude was entirely mistaken. He had misunderstood from beginning to end what his friend the agent told him. The agent, the landlord (a peer of the realm), and others hastened to contradict the historian. There never had been any such eviction or any such offensive display. Mr Froude himself wrote to acknowledge publicly that he had been entirely mistaken. He seemed indeed to have always had some doubt of the story he was publishing; for he sent a proof of the page to the agent "to be corrected in case I had misunderstood him." But the agent's alterations, "unluckily, did not reach me in time;" and as Mr. Froude could not wait for the truth, he published the error. Thus indeed is history written! This was Mr. Froude's published version of a statement made *viva voce* to himself; and his version was wrong in every particular—in fact, in substance, in detail, in purport, in everything! I venture to think that this little incident is eminently characteristic, and throws a strong light on some of the errors of the "History of England."

Mr. Froude has taken little or no active part in English politics. I do not remember his having made any sign of personal sympathy one way or the other with any of the great domestic movements which have stirred England in my time. I presume that he is what would be generally called a Liberal; at least it is simply impossible that he could be a Tory. But I doubt if he could very distinctly "place himself," as the American phrase is, with regard to most of the political contentions of the time. I cannot call Mr. Froude a philosophical Radical; for the idea which that suggests is of a school of thought and a system of training quite different from his, even if his tendencies could possibly be called Radical. It is rather a pity that so much of the best and clearest literary intellect of England should be so entirely withdrawn from the practical study of contemporary politics. No sensible person could ask a man like Mr. Froude to neglect his special work, that for which he has a vocation and genius, for the business of political life. But perhaps a better attempt might be made by him and others of our leading authors to fulfil the conditions of the German proverb which recommends that the one thing shall be done and the other not left undone. Mr. Froude has taken a more marked interest in the quasi-political question lately raised touching the connection between England and her colonies. Of recent years a party has been growing up in England who advocate emphatically the doctrine that the business of this country is to educate her colonies for emancipation. These men believe that as time goes on it will become more and more difficult to retain even a nominal connection between distant colonies and the parent country. The Dominion of Canada and the Australian colonies, both separated by oceans from England, are now practically independent. They have their own parliaments, and make their own laws; but England sends out a governor, and the governor has still a nominal control indeed, which in some rare cases he still exercises. Now what is to be the tendency of the future? Will this practical independence tend to bind the colonial system more strongly up into that of the central empire, as the practical independence of the American or the Swiss States keeps them together? Or is the time inevitable when the slight bond must be severed altogether and the great colonies at last declare their independence? Would it, for example, be possible always to maintain the American Union if several thousand miles of ocean divided California in one direction from Washington, and several thousand miles of another ocean lay between Washington and the South? This is the sort of question political parties in England have lately been asking themselves. One party, mainly under an impulse once given by a chance alliance between the Manchester school and Goldwin Smith, affirm boldly that ultimate separation is inevitable, and that we ought to begin to prepare ourselves and the colonies for it. This party made great way for awhile. They said loudly, they announced as a principle, that which had been growing vaguely up in many minds, and which one or two statesmen had long before put into actual form. More than twelve years ago Mr Gladstone delivered a lecture on our colonial system which plainly pointed to this ultimate severance and bade us prepare for it. Mr. Lowe, the present Chancellor of the Exchequer, himself an old colonist, had talked somewhat cynically in the same way. Mr. Bright was well known to favor the idea; so was Mr. Mill. With the sudden and direct impulse given by Mr. Goldwin Smith, the thought seemed to be catching fire. England had voluntarily given up the Ionian Islands to Greece; there was talk of her restoring Gibraltar to Spain. Mr. Lowe had spoken in the House of Commons with utter contempt of those who thought it would be possible to hold Canada in the event of a war with the United States. Governors of colonies actually began to warn their population that the preparation for independence had better begin. Suddenly a reaction set in. A class of writers and speakers came up to the front who argued that the colonies were part of England's very life system; that they were her friends, and might be her strength; that it was only her fault if she had neglected them; and that the natural tendency was to cohesion rather than dissolution. This party roused at once the sympathy of that large class of people who, knowing and caring nothing about the political and philosophical aspects of the question, thought it somehow a degradation to England, a token of decay, a confession of decrepitude, that there should be any talk of the severance of her colonies. Between the two, the tide of separatist feeling has decidedly been rolled back for the present. The humor of the present day is to devise means—schemes of federation or federative representation for example—whereby the colonies may still be kept in cohesion with England. Now, among the men of intellect who have stimulated and fostered this reactionary movement, if it be so—at all events, this movement toward the retention of the colonies—Mr. Froude has been a leading influence. He has advocated such a policy himself, and he has instilled it into the minds of others. He has formed silently a little school who take their doctrines from him and expand them. The colonial question has become popular and powerful. We have every now and then colonial conferences held in London, at which everybody who has any manner of suggestion to make, or crotchet to air, touching the improvement or development of our colonial system, goes and delivers his speech independently of everybody else. In the House of Commons the party is not yet very strong; but if it had a leader there, it would undoubtedly be powerful. There is even already a visible anxiety on the part of cabinet ministers to drop all allusion to the fact that they once talked of preparing the colonies for independence. We now find that it is regarded as unpatriotic, un-English, ungrateful, and I know not what, to say a word about a possible severance, at any time, between the parent country and her colonies. In one of Mr. Disraeli's novels a political party, hard up for a captivating and popular watchword, is thrown into ecstasies when somebody invents the cry of "Our young Queen and our old Constitution." I think the cry of "Our young colonies and our old Constitution" would be almost as taking now. It is curious, however, to note how both the movement and the reaction came from scholars and literary men—not from politicians or journalists. Many eminent men had talked of gradually preparing the colonies for independence; but the talk never became an impulse and a political movement until it came from Mr. Goldwin Smith. On the other hand, countless vociferous persons had always been bawling out that

England must never part with a rock on which her flag had waved; but all this sort of thing had no effect until Mr. Froude and his school inaugurated the definite movement of reaction. Mr. Goldwin Smith sent the ball flying so far in one direction, that it seemed almost certain to reach the limit of the field. Mr. Froude suddenly caught it and sent it flying back the way it had come, and beyond the hand which had originally driven it forth. It is not often that the ideas of "literary" men have so much of positive influence over practical controversy in England.

For a long time Mr. Froude has been the editor of "Fraser's Magazine," a periodical which I need not say holds a high position, and to which the editor has contributed some of the finest of his shorter writings. He is assisted in the work of editing by Mr. William Allingham, who is best known as a young poet of great promise, and who is probably the closest personal friend of Alfred Tennyson. "Fraser's" is always ready to open its columns to merit of any kind, and is willing to put before the public bold and original views of many political questions which other periodicals would shrink from admitting. As a rule English magazines, even when they acknowledge a dash of the philosophic in them, are very reluctant to give a place to opinions, however honestly entertained, which differ in any marked degree from those of society at large. The "Fortnightly Review" may be almost regarded as unique in its principle of admitting any expression of opinion which has genuineness and value in it, without regard to its accordance with public sentiment, or even to its inherent soundness. "Fraser," of course, makes no pretension to such deliberate boldness. But "Fraser" will now and then venture to put in an article, even from an uninfluential hand, which goes directly in the teeth of accepted and orthodox political opinion. For example, it is not many months since it published an article written by an English working man ("The Journeyman Engineer," a sort of celebrity in his way) to prove that republicanism is becoming the creed of the English artisan. Now, in any English magazine which professes to be respectable, it is almost as hazardous a thing to speak of republicanism in England as to speak of something indecent or blasphemous. "Fraser" also made itself conspicuous some years ago as a bold and persevering advocate of army reform, and ventured to press certain schemes of change which then seemed either revolutionary or impossible, but which since then have been quietly realized.

I think I have given a tolerably accurate estimate of Mr. Froude's public work in England. I have never heard him make a speech or deliver a lecture, and therefore cannot conjecture how far he is likely to impress an audience with the manner of his discourse; but the matter can hardly fail to be suggestive, original, and striking. I can foresee sharp controversy and broad differences of opinion arising out of his lectures in the United States. I cannot imagine their being received with indifference, or failing to hold the attention of the public. Mr. Froude is a great literary man, if not strictly a great historian. Of course every one must rate Froude's intellect very highly. He has imagination; he has that sympathetic and dramatic instinct which enables a man to enter into the emotions and motives, the likings and dislikings of the people of a past age. His style is penetrating and thrilling; his language often rises to the dignity of a poetic eloquence. The figures he conjures up are always the semblances of real men and women. They are never wax-work, or lay figures, or skeletons clothed in words, or purple rags of description stuffed out with straw into an awkward likeness to the human form. The one distinct impression we carry away from Froude's history is that of the living reality of his figures. In Marlowe's "Faustus" the Doctor conjures up for the amusement of the Emperor a procession of stately and beautiful shadows to represent the great ones of the past. When the shadows of Alexander the Great and his favorite pass by, the Emperor can hardly restrain himself from rushing to clasp the hero in his arms, and has to be reminded by the wizard that "these are but shadows not substantial." Even then the Emperor can scarcely get over his impression of their reality, for he cries:

> I have heard it said
> That this fair lady, whilst she lived on earth,
> Had on her neck a little wart or mole;

and lo! there is the mark on the neck of the beautiful form which floats across his field of vision. Mr Froude's shadows are like this: so deceptive, so seemingly vital and real; with the beauty and the blot alike conspicuous; with the pride and passion of the hero, and the heroine's white neck and the wart on it. Mr. Froude's whole soul, in fact, is in the human beings whom he meets as he unfolds his narrative. He is not an historical romancist, as some of his critics have called him. He is a romantic or heroic portrait painter. He has painted pictures on his pages which may almost compare with those of Titian. Their glances follow you and haunt you like the wonderful eyes of Cæsar Borgia or the soul-piercing resignation of Beatrice Cenci. But is Mr. Froude a great historian? Despite this splendid faculty, nay, perhaps because of this, he wants the one great and essential quality of the true historian, accuracy. He wants altogether the cold, patient, stern quality which clings to facts—the scientific faculty. His narrative never stands out in that "dry light" which Bacon so commends, the light of undistorted and clear Truth. The temptations to the man with a gift of heroic portrait-painting are too great for Mr. Froude's resistance. His genius carries him away and becomes his master. When Titian was painting his Cæsar Borgia, is it not conceivable that his imagination may have been positively inflamed by the contrast between the physical beauty and the moral guilt of the man, and have unconsciously heightened the contrast by making the pride and passion lower more darkly, the superb brilliancy of the eyes burn more radiantly than might have been seen in real life? The world would take little account even if it were to know that some of the portraits it admires were thus idealized by the genius of the painter; but the historian who is thus led away is open to a graver charge. It seems to me impossible to doubt that Mr. Froude has more than once been thus ensnared by his own special gift. What is there in literature more powerful, more picturesque, more complete and dramatic than Froude's portrait of Mary Queen of Scots? It stands out and glows and darkens with all the glare and gloom of a living form, that now appears in sun and now in shadow. It is almost as perfect and as impressive as any Titian. But can any reasonable person doubt that the picture on the whole is a dramatic and not an historical study? Without going into any controversy as to disputed facts—nay, admitting for the sake of argument that Mary was as guilty as Mr. Froude would make her—as guilty, I mean, in act and deed—yet it is impossible to contend with any show of reason that the being he has painted for us is the Mary of history and of life. To us his Mary now is a reality. We are distinctly acquainted with her; we see her and can follow her movements. But she is a fable and might be an impossibility for all that. The poets have made many physical impossibilities real for us and familiar to us. The form and being of a mermaid are not one whit less clear and distinct to us than the form and being of a living woman. If any of us were to see a painting of a mermaid with scales upon her neck, or with feet, he would resent it or laugh at it as an inaccuracy, just as if he saw some gross anatomical blunder in a picture of an ordinary man or woman. Mr. Froude has created a Mary Queen of Scots as the poets and painters have created a mermaid. He has made her one of the most imposing figures in our modern literature, to which indeed she is an important addition. So of his Queen Elizabeth; so, to a lesser extent, of his Henry VIII., because, although there he may have gone even further away from history, yet I think he was misled rather by his anxiety to prove a theory than by the fascination of a picture growing under his own hands. Everything becomes for the hour subordinate to this passion for the picturesque in good or evil. Mr. Froude's personal integrity and candor are constantly coming into contradiction with this artistic temptation; but the portrait goes on all the same. He is too honest and candid to conceal or pervert any fact that he knows. He tells everything frankly, but continues his portrait. It may be that the very vices which constitute the gloom and horror of this portrait suddenly prove their existence in the character of the person who was chosen to illustrate the brightness and glory of human nature. Mr. Froude is not abashed. He frankly states the facts; shows how, in this or that instance, Truth did tell shocking lies, Mercy ordered several massacres, and Virtue fell into the ways of Messalina. But the portraits of Truth, Mercy, and Virtue remain as radiant as ever. A lover of art, according to a story in the memoirs of Canova, was so struck with admiration of that sculptor's Venus that he begged to be allowed to see the model. The artist gratified him; but so far from beholding a very goddess of beauty in the flesh, he only saw a well-made, rather coarse-looking woman. The sculptor, seeing his disappointment, explained to him that the hand and eye of the artist, as they work, can gradually and almost imperceptibly change the model from that which it is in the flesh to that which it ought to be in the marble. This is the process which is always going on with Mr. Froude whenever he is at work upon some model in which for love or hate he takes unusual interest. Therefore the historian is constantly involving himself in a welter of inconsistencies and errors which affect the artist in nowise. Henry is a hero on one page, although he does the very thing which somebody else on the next page is a villain for even attempting. Elizabeth remains a prodigy of wisdom and honesty, Mary a marvel of genius, lust, cruelty, and falsehood, although in every other chapter the author frankly accumulates instances which show that now and then the parts seem to have been exchanged; and it often becomes as hard to know, by any tangible evidence, which is truth and which falsehood, which patriotism and which selfishness, as it was to distinguish the true Florimel from the magical counterfeit in Spenser's "Faery Queen."

This is a grave and a great fault; and unhappily it is one with which Mr. Froude seems to have been thoroughly inoculated. It goes far to justify the dull and literal old historians of the school of Dryasdust, who, if they never quickened an event into life, never on the other hand deluded the mind with phantoms. The chroniclers of mere facts and dates, the old almanac-makers, are weary creatures; but one finds it hard to condemn them to mere contempt when he sees how the vivid genius of a man like Froude can lead him astray. Mr. Froude's finest gift is his greatest defect for the special work he undertakes to do. A scholar, a thinker, a man of high imagination, a man likewise of patient labor, he is above all things a romantic portrait painter; and the spell by which his works allure us is therefore the spell of the magician, not the power of the calm and sober teacher.

SCIENCE AND ORTHODOXY IN ENGLAND.

"THE old God is dead above, and the old Devil is dead below!" So sang Heinrich Heine in one of his peculiarly cheerful moods; and I do not know that any words could paint a more complete picture of the utter collapse and ruin of old theologies and time-honored faiths and superstitions. Irreverent and even impious as the words will perhaps appear to most minds, it is probable that not a few of those who would be most likely to shudder at their audacity are beginning to think with horror that the condition ot things described by the cynical poet is being rapidly brought about by the doings of modern science. Many an English country clergyman, many an earnest and pious Dissenter, must have felt that a new and awful era had arrived—that a modern war of Titans against Heaven was going on, when such discourses as Professor Huxley's famous Protoplasm lecture could be delivered by a man of the highest reputation, and could be received by nearly all the world with, at least, a respectful consideration. In fact, the delivery of such discourses does indicate a quite new ordeal for old-fashioned orthodoxy, and an ordeal which seems to me far severer than any through which it has yet passed. It would be impossible to exaggerate the importance of the struggle which is now openly carried on between Science and Orthodox Theology. I need hardly say perhaps that I utterly repudiate the use of any such absurd and unmeaning language as that which speaks of a controversy between science and religion. One might as well talk of a conflict between fact and truth; or between truth and virtue. But orthodox theology in England, whether it be right or wrong, is certainly a very different thing from religion. Were it wholly and eternally true it could still only bear the same relation to religion that geography bears to the earth, astronomy to the sidereal system, the words describing to the thing described. I may therefore hope not to be at once set down as an irreligious person, merely because I venture to describe the war indirectly waged against orthodox theology, by a new school of English scientific men, as the severest trial that system has ever yet had to encounter, and one through which it can hardly by any possibility pass wholly unscathed.

In describing briefly and generally this new school of English science, and some of its leading scholars, I should say that I do so merely from the outside. I am not a scientific man professionally; and, even as an amateur, can only pretend to very slight attainment. But I have been on the scene of controversy, have looked over the field, and studied the bearing of the leading combatants. When Cressida had seen the chiefs of the Trojan army pass before her and had each pointed out to her and described, she could probably have told a stranger something worth his listening to, although she knew nothing of the great art of war. Only on something of the same ground do I venture to ask for any attention from American readers, when I say something about the class of scientific men who have recently sprung up in England, and of whom one of the most distinguished and one of the most aggressive has just been elected President of the British Association for the Advancement of Science.

This school is peculiarly English. So far as I know, it owes nothing directly and distinctly to the intellectual initiative of any other country. Both in metaphysical and in practical science there has been a sudden and powerful awakening, or perhaps I should say *renaissance*, in England lately. Three or four years ago Stuart Mill wrote that the sceptre of psychology had again passed over to England; and it seems to me not too much to say that England now likewise holds the sceptre of natural science. It is evident to every one that the leaders of this new school stand in antagonism which is decided, if not direct, to the teachings of orthodox theology.

The recent election of Professor Huxley as President of the British Association was accepted universally as a triumph over the orthodox party. Professor Owen, who undoubtedly possesses one of the broadest and keenest scientific intellects of the age, has lately been pushed aside and has fallen into something like comparative obscurity because he could not, or would not, see his way into the dangerous fields opened up by his younger and bolder rivals. Professor Owen held on as long as ever he could to orthodoxy. He made heavy intellectual sacrifices at its altar. I do not quite know whether in the end it was he who first gave the cold shoulder to orthodoxy, or orthodoxy which first repudiated him. But it is certain that he no longer stands out conspicuous and ardent as the great opponent of Darwin and Huxley. He has, in fact, receded so much from his old ground that one finds it difficult now to know where to place him; and perhaps it will be better to regard him as out of the controversy altogether. If he had done less for orthodoxy, where his labors were vain, he might have done much more for science, where his toil would always have been fruitful. Undoubtedly, he is one of the greatest naturalists since Cuvier; his contributions toward the facts and data of science have been valuable beyond all estimation; his practical labors in the British Museum would alone earn for him the gratitude of all students. Owen is, or was, to my mind, the very perfection of a scientific lecturer. The easy flow of simple, expressive language, the luminous arrangement and style which made the profoundest exposition intelligible, the captivating variety of illustration, the clear, well-modulated voice, the self-possessed and graceful manner—all these were attributes which made Owen a delightful lecturer, although he put forward no pretensions to rhetorical skill or to eloquence of any very high order. But while there can hardly have been any recent falling off in Owen's intellectual powers, yet it is certain that he was more thought of, that he occupied a higher place in the public esteem, some half dozen years ago than he now does. I think there has been a general impression of late years that in the controversy between theology and science, Owen was not to be relied upon implicitly. People thought that he was trying to sit on the two stools; to run with the theological hare, and hold with the scientific hounds. Indeed, Owen is eminently a respectable, a courtly *savant*. He does not love to run tilt against the prevailing opinion of the influential classes, or to forfeit the confidence and esteem of "society.' He loves—so people say—the company of the titled and the great, and prefers, perhaps, to walk with Sir Duke than with humble Sir Scholar. All things considered, we may regard him as out of the present controversy, and, perhaps, as left behind by it and by the opinions which have created it. The orthodox do not seem much beholden to him. Only two or three years ago an orthodox association for which Owen had delivered a scientific lecture, refused on theological grounds to print the discourse in their regular volume. On the other hand, the younger and more ardent *savans* and scholars sneer at him, and refuse to give him credit for sincerity at the expense of his intelligence. They believe that if he chose to speak out, if he had the courage of his opinions, he would say as they do. He has ceased to be their opponent, but he is not upon their side; he is no longer the champion of pure orthodoxy, but he has never pronounced openly against it.

Flippant people allude to him as an old fogy; let us say more decently that Richard Owen already belongs to the past.

"Free-thinking" has never been in England a very formidable rival of orthodox theology. Perhaps there is something in the practical nature of the average English mind which makes it indifferent and apathetic to mere speculation. The ordinary Englishmen understands being a Churchman or a Dissenter, a Roman Catholic or a no-Popery man ; but he hardly understands how people can be got to concern themselves with mere sceptical speculation. Writings like those of Rousseau, for example, never could have produced in England anything like the effect they wrought in France. Of late years the effects of "free-thinking" (I am using the phrase merely in the vulgar sense) have been poor, feeble and uninfluential—wholly indeed without influence over the educated classes of society. A certain limited and transient influence was once maintained over a small surface of society by the speeches and the writings of George Jacob Holyoake. Holyoake avowed himself an Atheist, conducted a paper called (I think) "The Reasoner," was prosecuted under the terms of a foolish and discreditable act of Parliament, and had for a time something of notoriety and popular power. But Holyoake, a man of pure character and gentle manners, is devoid of anything like commanding ability, has no gleam of oratorical power, and is intellectually unreliable and vacillating. Under no conceivable circumstances could he exercise any strong or permanent control over the mind or the heart of an age: and he has of late somewhat modified his opinions, and has greatly altered his sphere of action, preferring to be a political and social reformer in a small and modest way to the barren task of endeavoring to uproot religious belief by arguments evolved from the depth of the moral consciousness. Holyoake, the Atheist, may therefore be said to have faded away.

His old place has lately been taken by a noisier, more egotistic and robust sort of person, a young man named Bradlaugh, who at one time dubbed himself "Iconoclast," and, bearing that ambitious title, used to harangue knots of working men in the North of England with the most audacious of free-thinking rhetoric. Bradlaugh has a certain kind of brassy, stentorian eloquence and a degree of reckless self conceit which almost amount to a conquering quality. But he has no intellectual capacity sufficient to make a deep mark on the mind of any section of society and he never attempts, so far as I know, any other than the old, time-worn arguments against orthodoxy with which the world has been wearily familiar since the days of Voltaire. Indeed, a man who gravely undertakes to prove by argument that there is no God, places himself at once in so anomalous, paradoxical and ridiculous a position that it is a marvel the absurdity of the situation does not strike his own mind. A man who starts with the reasonable assumption that belief is a matter of evidence and then goes on to argue that a Being does not exist of whose non-existence he can upon his own ground and pleading know absolutely nothing, is not likely to be very formidable to any of his antagonists. Orthodox theologians, therefore, are little concerned about men like Bradlaugh—very often perhaps are ignorant of the existence of any such.

I only mention Holyoake and Bradlaugh at all because they are the only prominent agitators of this kind who have appeared in England during my time. I do not mean to speak disparagingly of either man. Both have considerable abilities ; both are, I am sure, sincere and honest. I have never heard anything to the disparagement of Bradlaugh's character. Holyoake I know personally, and esteem highly. But their influence has been insignificant, and cannot have any long duration. I only speak of it here to show how feeble has been the head made against orthodoxy in England by professed infidelity in our time. There was, indeed, a book written some years ago by a man of higher culture than Holyoake or Bradlaugh, and which made a bubble or two of sensation at the time. I mean "The Creed of Christendom," by William Rathbone Greg, a well-known political and philosophical essayist, who wrote largely for the "Edinburgh Review" and the "Westminster Review" and more lately for the "Pall Mall Gazette," and has now a comfortable place under government. But the "Creed of Christendom," though a clever book in its way, made no abiding mark. It was read and liked by those whose opinions it expressed, but I question if it ever made one single convert or suggested a doubt to a truly orthodox mind. I mention it because it was the only work of what is called a directly infidel character, not pretending to a scientific basis, which was contributed to the literature of English philosophy by a man of high culture and literary reputation during my memory. It will be understood that I am speaking now of works modeled after the old fashion of sceptical controversy, in which the authors make it their avowed and main purpose to assail the logical coherence and reasonableness of the Christian faith by arguments which, sound or unsound, can be brought to no practical test and settled by no possible decision. Such works may be influential among nations which are addicted to or tolerant of mere religious speculation; it is only a calling aloud to solitude to address them to the English public. Even books of a very high intellectual class, such for example as Strauss's "Life of Jesus," are translated into English in vain. They are read and admired by those already prepared to admire and eager to read them—the general public takes no heed of them.

I have ventured into this digression in order to show the more clearly how important must be the influence of that new school of science which has aroused such a commotion among the devotees of English orthodoxy. There is not, so far as I know, among the leading scientific men of the new school one single professed infidel in the old fashioned sense. The fundamental difference between them and the orthodox is that they insist upon regarding all subjects coming within the scope of human knowledge as open to inquiry and to be settled only upon evidence. I suppose a day will come when people will wonder that a scientific man, living in the England of the nineteenth century, could have been denounced from pulpits because he claimed the right and the duty to follow out his scientific investigations whithersoever they should lead him. Yet I am not aware that anything more desperately infidel than this has ever been urged by our modern English *savans.*

Michel Chevalier tells a story of a French iconoclast of our own time who devoted himself to a perpetual war against what he considered the two worst superstitions of the age—belief in God and dislike of spiders. This aggressive sage always carried about with him a golden box filled with the pretty and favorite insects I have mentioned; and whenever he happened to be introduced to any new acquaintance he invariably plunged at once into the questions—"Do you believe in a God, and are you afraid of spiders?"—and without waiting for an answer, he instantly demonstrated his own superiority to at least one conventional weakness by opening his box, taking out a spider, and swallowing it. I think a good deal of the old-fashioned warfare against orthodoxy had something of this spider-bolting aggressiveness about it. It assailed men's dearest beliefs in the coarsest manner, and it had commonly only horror and disgust for its reward. There is nothing of this spirit among the leaders of English scientific philosophy to-day. Not merely are the practically scientific men free from it, but even the men who are called in a sort of a contemptuous tone "philosophers" are not to be accused of it. Mill and Herbert Spencer have as little of it as Huxley and Grove. Indeed the scientific men are nothing more or less than earnest, patient, devoted inquirers, seeking out the truth fearlessly, and resolute to follow wherever she invites. Whenever they have come into open conflict with orthodoxy, it may be safely assumed that orthodoxy threw the first stone. For orthodoxy, with a keen and just instinct, detests these scientific men. The Low Church party, the great mass of the Dissenting body (excluding, of course, Unitarians) have been their uncompromising opponents. The High Church party, which, with all its mediæval weaknesses and its spiritual reaction, does assuredly boast among its leaders some high and noble intellects, and among all its classes earnest, courageous minds, has, on the contrary, given, for the most part, its confidence and its attention to the teachings of the *savans*. We have the testimony of Professor Huxley himself to the fact that the leading minds of the Roman Catholic Church do at least take care that the teachings of the *savans* shall be understood, and that they shall be combated, if at all, on scientific and not on theological grounds.

No man is more disliked and dreaded by the orthodox than Thomas Huxley. Darwin, who is really the *fons et origo* of the present agitation, is hardly more than a name to the outer world. He has written a book, and that is all the public know about him. He never descends into the arena of open controversy; we never read of him in the newspapers. I know of no instance of a book so famous with an author so little known. Even curiosity does not seem to concern itself about the individuality of Darwin, whose book opened up a new era of controversy, spreading all over the world, and was the sensation in England of many successive seasons. Herbert Spencer, indeed, has lived for a long time hardly noticed or known by the average English public. But then none of Spencer's books ever created the slightest sensation among that public, and three out of every four Englishmen never heard of the man or the books. Herbert Spencer is infinitely better known in the United States than he is in England, although I am far from admitting that he is better appreciated even here than by those of his countrymen who are at all acquainted with his masterly, his unsurpassed, contributions to the philosophy of the world. The singular fact about Darwin is that his book was absolutely the rage in England; everybody was bound to read it or at least to talk about it and pretend to have understood it. More excitement was aroused by it than even by Buckle's "History of Civilization;" it fluttered the petticoats in the drawing-room as much as the surplices in the pulpit; it occupied alike the attention of the scholar and the fribble, the divine and the schoolgirl. Yet the author kept himself in complete seclusion, and, for some mysterious reason or other, public curiosity never seemed disposed to persecute him. Therefore the theologians seem to have regarded him as the poet does the cuckoo, rather as a voice in the air than as a living creature; and they have not poured out much of their anger upon him personally. But Huxley comes down into the arena of public controversy and is a familiar and formidable figure there Wherever there is strife there is Huxley. Years ago he came into the field almost unknown like the Disinherited Knight in Scott's immortal romance; and, while the good-natured spectators were urging him to turn the blunt end of the lance against the shield of the least formidable opponent, he dashed with splendid recklessness, and with spearpoint forward, against the buckler of Richard Owen himself, the most renowned of the naturalists of England. Indeed Huxley has the soul and spirit of a gallant controversialist. He has many times warned the orthodox champions that if they play at bowls they must expect rubbers; and once in the fight he never spares. He has a happy gift of shrewd sense and sarcasm combined; and, indeed, I know no man who can exhibit a sophism as a sophism and hold it up to contempt and laughter more clearly and effectively in a single sentence of exhaustive satire.

It would be wrong to regard Huxley merely as a scientific man. He is likewise a literary man, a writer. What he writes would be worth reading for its style and its expression alone, were it of no scientific authority; whereas we all know perfectly well that scientific men generally are read only for the sake of what they teach, and not at all because of their manner of teaching it—rather indeed despite of their manner of teaching it. Huxley is a fascinating writer, and has a happy way of pressing continually into the service of strictly scientific exposition illustrations caught from literature and art—even from popular and light literature. He has a gift in this way which somewhat resembles that possessed by a very different man belonging to a very different class—I mean Robert Lowe, the present English Chancellor of the Exchequer, who owes the greater part of his rhetorical success to the prodigality of varied illustration with which he illumines his speeches, and which catches, at this point or that, the attention of every kind of listener. Huxley seems to understand clearly that you can never make scientific doctrines really powerful while you are content with the ear of strictly scientific men. He cultivates, therefore, sedulously and successfully, the literary art of expression. A London friend of mine, who has had long experience in the editing of high-class periodicals, is in the habit of affirming humorously that the teachers of the public are divided into two classes: those who know something and cannot write, and those who know nothing and can write. Every literary man, especially every editor, will cordially agree with me that at the heart of this humorous extravagance is a solid kernel of truth. Now, scientific men very often belong to the class of those who know something, but cannot write. No one, however, could possibly confound Thomas Huxley with the band of those to whom the gift of expression is denied. He is a vivid, forcible, fascinating writer. His style as a lecturer is one which, for me at least, has a special charm. It is, indeed, devoid of any effort at rhetorical eloquence; but it has all the eloquence which is born of the union of profound thought with simple expression and luminous diction. There is not much of the poetic, certainly, about him; only the occasional dramatic vividness of his illustrations suggests the existence in him of any of the higher imaginative qualities. I think there was something like a gleam of the poetic in the half melancholy half humorous introduction of Balzac's famous "Peau de Chagrin," into the Protoplasm lecture. But Huxley as a rule treads only the firm earth, and deliberately, perhaps scornfully, rejects any attempts and aspirings after the clouds. His mind is in this way far more rigidly practical than that even of Richard Owen. He is never eloquent in the sense in which Humboldt for example was so often eloquent. Being a politician, I may be excused for borrowing an illustration from the political arena, and saying that Huxley's eloquence is like that of Cobden; it is eloquence only because it is so simply and tersely truthful. The whole tone of his mind, the whole tendency of his philosophy, may be observed to have this character of quiet, fearless, and practical truthfulness. No seeker after truth could be more earnest, more patient, more disinterested. "Dry light," as Bacon calls it—light uncolored by prejudice, undimmed by illusion, undistorted by interposing obstacle—is all that Huxley desires to have. He puts no bound to the range of human inquiry. Wherever man may look, there let him look earnestly and without fear. Truth is always naked and not ashamed. The modest, self-denying profession of Lessing that he wanted not the whole truth, and only asked to be allowed the pleasing toil of investigation, must be almost unintelligible to a student like Huxley; and indeed is only to be understood by any active inquirer, on condition that he bears in mind the healthy and racy delight which the mere labor of intellectual research gave to Lessing's vigorous and elastic mind. No subject is sacred to Huxley; because with him truth is more sacred than any sphere of inquiry. I suppose the true and pure knight would have fearlessly penetrated any shrine in his quest of the Holy Grail.

Professor Huxley's nature seems to me to have been cast in a finer mould than that of Professor Tyndall, for example. Decidedly, Tyndall is a man of great ability and earnestness. He has done, perhaps, more practical work in science than Huxley has; he has written more; he sometimes writes more eloquently. But he wants, to my thinking, that pure and colorless impartiality of inquiry and judgment which is Huxley's distinguishing characteristic. There is a certain coarseness of materialism about Tyndall; there is a vehement and almost an arrogant aggressiveness in him which must interfere with the clearness of his views. He assails the orthodox with the temper of a Hot Gospeller. Perhaps his Irish nature is partly accountable for this warm and eager combativeness: perhaps his having sat so devotedly at the feet of his friend, the great apostle of force, Thomas Carlyle, may help to explain the unsparing vigor of his controversial style. However that may be, Tyndall is assuredly one of the most impatient of sages, one of the most intolerant of philosophers. If I have compared Huxley to the pure devoted knight riding patiently in search of the Holy Grail, I may, perhaps, liken Tyndall to the ardent champion who ranges the world, fiercely defying to mortal combat any and every one who will not instantly admit that the warrior's lady-love is the most beautiful and perfect of created beings. His temper does unquestionably tend to weaken Tyndall's authority. You may trust him implicitly where it is only a question of a glacial theory or an atmospheric condition; but you must follow the Carlylean philosopher very cautiously indeed where he undertakes to instruct you on the subject of races. The negro, for example, conquers Tyndall altogether. The philosopher loses his temper and forgets his science the moment he comes to examine poor black Sambo's woolly skull, and remembers that there are sane and educated white people who maintain that the owner of the skull is a man and a brother. In debates which cannot be settled by dry science, Huxley's sympathies almost invariably guide him right: Tyndall's almost invariably set him wrong. During the American Civil war, Huxley, like Sir Charles Lyell and some other eminent scientific men, sympathized with the cause of the North: Tyndall, on the other hand, was an eager partisan of the South. A still more decisive test severed the two men more widely apart. The story of the Jamaica massacre divided all England into two fierce and hostile camps. I am not going to weary my readers with any repetition of this often-told and horrible story. Enough to say that the whole question at issue in England in relation to the Jamaica tragedies was whether the belief that a negro insurrection is impending justifies white residents in flogging and hanging as many negro men and women, unarmed and unresisting, as they can find time to flog and hang, without any ceremony of trial, evidence, or even inquiry. I do not exaggerate or misstate. The ground taken by the advocates of the Jamaica military measures was that although no insurrection was going on yet there was reasonable ground to believe an insurrection impending; and that therefore the white residents were justified in anticipating and crushing the movement by the putting to death of every person, man or woman, who could be supposed likely to have any part in it. Of course I need hardly tell the student of history that this is exactly the ground which was taken up, and with far greater plausibility and better excuse, by the promoters of the massacre of Saint Bartholomew. They said: "We have evidence, and are convinced, that these Huguenots are plotting against us. If we do not put them down, they will put us down. Let us be first at the work and crush them." The Jamaica question then raised a bitter controversy in England. Naturally, John Bright and Stuart Mill and Goldwin Smith took one side of it: Thomas Carlyle and Charles Kingsley and John Ruskin the other. That was to be expected: any one could have told it beforehand. But the occasion brought out men who had never taken part in political controversy before: and then you saw at once what kind of hearts and sympathies these new agitators had. Herbert Spencer emerged for the first time in his life, so far as I know, from the rigid seclusion of a silent student's career, and appeared in public as an active, hard-working member of a political organization. The American Civil War had drawn Mill for the first time into the public arena of politics; the Jamaica massacre made a political agitator of Herbert Spencer. The noble human sympathies of Spencer, his austere and uncompromising love of justice, his instinctive detestation of brute, blind, despotic force, compelled him to come out from his seclusion and join those who protested against the lawless and senseless massacre of the wretched blacks of Jamaica. So, too, with Huxley, who, if he did not take part in a political organization, yet lent the weight of his influence and the vigor of his pen to add to the force of the protest. During the whole of that prolonged season of incessant and active controversy, with the keenest intellects and the sharpest tongues in England employing themselves eagerly on either side, I can recall to mind nothing which, for justice, sound sense, high principle, and exquisite briefness of pungent sarcasm, equaled one of Huxley's letters on the subject to the "Pall Mall Gazette." The mind which was not touched by the force of that incomparable mixture of satire and sense would surely have remained untouched though one rose from the dead. The delicious gravity with which Huxley accepted all the positions of his opponents, assumed the propositions about the high character of the Jamaica governor and the white residents, and the immorality of poor Gordon and the negroes, and then reduced the case of the advocates of the massacre to "the right of all virtuous persons, as such, to put to death all vicious persons, as such," was almost worthy of Swift himself.

On the other hand, Professor Tyndall plunged eagerly into the controversy as a defender of the policy and the people by whose authority the massacre was carried on. I do not suppose he made any inquiry into the facts—nothing of his that I read or heard of led me to suppose that he had; but he went off on his Carlylean theory about governing minds, and superior races, and the right of strong men, and all the rest of the nonsense which Carlyle once made fascinating, and his imitators have lately made vulgar. I think I am not doing Tyndall an injustice when I regard him as a less austere and trustworthy follower of the pure truth than Huxley. In fact Tyndall is a born controversialist. Some orthodox person once extracted from Huxley, or from some of his writings, the admission that "the truth of the miracles was all a question of evidence," and seemed to think he had got hold of a great concession therein. Possibly the admission was made in the spirit of sarcasm, but it none the less expressed a belief and illustrated a temper profoundly characteristic of Thomas Huxley. With him everything is a question of evidence; nothing is to be settled by faith or by preliminary assumption. I am convinced that if you could prove by sufficient evidence the truth of every miracle recorded in Butler's "Lives of the Saints," Professor Huxley would bow resignedly, and accept the truth—wanting only the truth, whatever it might be. But I think Tyndall would rage and chafe a great deal, and I suspect that he would use a good many hard words against his opponents before he submitted to acknowledge aloud the defeat which his inner consciousness already admitted. And yet I think it would be at least as difficult to convince Huxley as it would be to convince Tyndall that Saint Denis walked with his head under his arm, or that Saint Januarius (was it not he?) crossed the sea on his cloak for a raft.

I do not know whether it comes strictly within the scope of this essay to say much about Herbert Spencer, who is rather what people call a philosopher than a professionally scientific man. But assuredly no living thinker has done more to undermine orthodoxy than the author of "First Principles." I have already said that Spencer is much more widely known in this country than in England. During the first few weeks of my sojourn in the United States I heard more inquiries and more talk about Spencer than about almost any other Englishman living. Spencer's whole life, his pure, rigorous, anchorite-like devotion to knowledge, is indeed a wonderful phenomenon in an age like the present. He has labored for the love of labor and for the good it does to the world, almost absolutely without reward. I presume that as paying speculations Herbert Spencer's works would be hopeless failures; and yet they have influenced the thought of the whole thinking world, and will probably grow and grow in power as the years go on. It is, I suppose, no new or unseemly revelation to say that Spencer has lived for the most part a life of poverty as well as of seclusion. He is a sensitive, silent, self-reliant man, endowed with a pure passion for knowledge, and the quickest, keenest love of justice and right. There is something indeed quite Quixotic, in the better sense, about the utterly disinterested and self-forgetting eagerness with which Herbert Spencer will set himself to see right done, even in the most trivial of cases. Little, commonplace, trifling instances of unfairness or injustice, such as most of us may observe every day, and which even the most benevolent of us will think himself warranted in passing by, on his way to his own work, without interference, will summon into activity—into positively unresting eagerness—all the sympathies and energies of Herbert Spencer, nor will the great student of life's ultimate principles return to his own high pursuits until he has obtained for the poor sempstress restitution of the over-fare exacted by the extortionate omnibus-conductor, or seen that the policeman on duty is not too rough in his entreatment of the little captured pickpocket. As one man has an unappeasable passion for pictures, and another for horses, so Herbert Spencer has a passion for justice. All this does not appear on first, or casual, acquaintance; but I have heard many striking, and some very whimsical, illustrations of it given by friends who know Spencer far better than I do. Indeed I should say that there are few men of great intellect and character who reveal themselves so little to the ordinary observer as Herbert Spencer does. His face is, above all things, commonplace. There is nothing whatever remarkable, nothing attractive, nothing repelling, nothing particularly unattractive, about him. Honest, homespun, prosaic respectability seems to be his principal characteristic. In casual and ordinary conversation he does not impress one in the least. Almost all men of well-earned distinction seem to have, above all things, a strongly-marked individuality. You meet a man of this class casually; you have no idea who he is; perhaps you do not even discover, have not an opportunity of discovering, that he is a man of genius or intellect; but you do almost invariably find yourself impressed with a strong individual influence—the man seems to be somebody—he is not just like any other man. To take illustrations familiar to most of us—observe what a strongly-marked individuality Charles Dickens, John Bright, Disraeli, Carlyle, Lord Ellenborough, Lord Salisbury have; what a strongly-marked individuality Nathaniel Hawthorne had, Wendell Phillips, Charles Sumner, William Cullen Bryant, Horace Greeley have. Now, Herbert Spencer is the very opposite of all this. All that Dr. Johnson said of Burke might be conveniently reversed in the case of Spencer. The person sheltering under the hedge, the ostler in the yard, might talk long enough with him and never feel tempted to say when he had gone, "There has been a remarkable man here." A London *litterateur*, who had long been a devotee of Herbert Spencer, was induced some year or two back to go to a large dinner-party by the assurance that Spencer was to be there and was actually to have the chair next to his own at table. Our friend went, was a little late, and found himself disappointed. Next to him on one side was a man whom he knew and did not care about; on the other side, a humdrum, elderly, respectable, commonplace personage. With this latter, for want of a better, he talked. It was dull, commonplace, conventional talk, good for nothing, meaning nothing. The dinner was nearly over when our friend heard some one address his right-hand neighbor as "Spencer." Amazed out of all decorum, he turned to the commonplace, dull-looking individual, and broke out with the words "Why, you don't mean to say that you are Herbert Spencer?" "Oh, yes," the other replied, as quietly as ever, "I am Herbert Spencer."

I have wandered a little from my path; let me return to it. My object is to illustrate the remarkable and fundamental difference between the nature of the antagonism which old-fashioned orthodoxy has to encounter to-day, and that which used to be its principal assailant. The sceptic, the metaphysician, the "infidel" have given way to the professional *savant.* Nobody now-a-days would trouble himself to read Tom Paine; hardly could even the scepticism of Hume or Gibbon attract much public attention. Auguste Comte has been an influence because he endeavored to construct as well as to destroy. I cannot speak of Comte without saying that Professor Huxley seems to me grievously, and almost perversely, to underrate the value of what Comte has done. Huxley has not, I fancy, given much attention to historical study, and is therefore not so well qualified to appreciate Comte as a much inferior man of a different school might be. Moreover, Huxley appears to have a certain professional, and I had almost said pedantic, contempt for anything calling itself science which cannot be rated and registered in the regular and practical way. To me Comte's one grand theory or discovery, call it what you will, seems, whether true or untrue, as strictly a question of science as anything coming under Huxley's own professional cognizance. But I have already intimated that the character of Huxley's intellect seems to me acute and penetrating, rather than broad and comprehensive. Perhaps he is all the better fitted for the work he and his compeers have undertaken to do. They have taken, in this regard, the place of the Rousseaus and Diderots; of the much smaller Paines and Carliles (please don't suppose I am alluding to Thomas Carlyle); of the yet smaller Holyoakes and Bradlaughs. Those only attempted to destroy: these seek to construct. Huxley and his brethren follow the advice which is the moral and the sum of Goethe's "Faust"—they "grasp into the present," and refuse to "send their thoughts wandering over eternities." They honestly and fearlessly seek the pure truth, which surely must be always saving. Let me say something more.

This advance-guard of scientific scholars alone express the common opinion ot the educated and free Englishmen of to-day. The English journals, I wish distinctly to say, do not express it. They do not venture to express it. There is a tacit understanding that although it would be too much to expect an intelligent journalist to write up old-fashioned orthodoxy, yet at least he is never to be allowed to write it down. It is not very long since one of the most popular, successful and influential of London journals sneered at the Parliamentary candidature of my friend, Professor Fawcett, M. P., on the ground that he was a man who, as an advocate of the Darwinian theory, admitted that his great-grandfather was a frog. Yet I know that the journal which indulged in this vapid and vulgar buffoonery is written for by scholars and men of ability. Now, this is indeed an extreme and unusual instance of journalism, well cognizant of better things, condescending to pander to the lowest and stupidest prejudices. But the same kind of thing, although not the same thing, is done by London journals every day. You cannot hope to get at the religious views of cultivated and liberal-minded Englishmen through the London papers. "The right sort of thing to say," is what the journalists commit to print, whatever they may think, or know, or say as individuals and in private. But the scientific men speak out. They, and I might almost say they alone, have the courage of their opinions. What educated people venture to believe, they venture to express. Nor do they keep themselves to audiences of *savans* and professors and the British Association. Huxley delivers lectures to the working men of Southwark; Carpenter undertook Sunday evening discourses in Bloomsbury; Tyndall, with all the pugnacity of his country, is ready for a controversy anywhere. Sometimes the duty and honor of maintaining the right of free speech have been claimed by the journalists alone; sometimes, when even the journals were silent, by the pulpit, by the bar, or by the stage. In England to-day all men say aloud what they think on all great subjects save one—and on that neither pulpit, press, bar nor stage cares to speak the whole truth. The scientific men alone are bold enough to declare it, as they are resolute to seek it. I think history will hereafter contemplate this moral triumph as no less admirable, and no less remarkable, than any of their mere material conquests.

www.ingramcontent.com/pod-product-compliance
Lightning Source LLC
LaVergne TN
LVHW012326100826
845148LV00017B/349

* 9 7 8 1 4 2 5 5 2 1 3 9 4 *